The Secrets of Voyaging

MYSTICAL TREATISES OF
MUHYIDDIN IBN ʿARABI

ALREADY AVAILABLE

The Universal Tree and the Four Birds
al-Ittiḥād al-kawnī

The Four Pillars of Spiritual Transformation
Ḥilyat al-abdāl

FORTHCOMING TITLES

The Secret of the Divine Names
Kashf al-maʿnā

Annihilated in Contemplation
Kitāb al-fanāʾ fiʾl-mushāhada

Technical Terms of Sufism
al-Iṣṭilāḥāt al-Ṣūfīya

Muḥyiddīn Ibn ʿArabī

The Secrets of Voyaging

Kitāb al-Isfār ʿan natāʾij al-asfār

Introduction, Translation and Commentary
ANGELA JAFFRAY

Arabic edition
DENIS GRIL, ABRAR AHMED SHAHI AND ANGELA JAFFRAY

ANQA PUBLISHING • OXFORD

Published by Anqa Publishing
PO Box 1178
Oxford OX2 8YS, UK
www.anqa.co.uk

First published 2015

Cover design: Michael Tiernan and Stephen Hirtenstein
Cover photograph: Stephen Hirtenstein

British Library Cataloguing in Publication Data.
A catalogue record for this book is available from the British Library.

ISBN: 978 1 905937 43 1

Printed and bound in the UK by
TJ International, Padstow, Cornwall

CONTENTS

A Biography of Ibn ʿArabī 1

Introduction 7

The Voyage Pro and Con 8

Style and Language 10

Related Genres: Manuals of *Sulūk*, *Isrāʾ* and *Miʿrāj* Literature, *Tafsīr* and *Qiṣaṣ al-anbiyāʾ* 14

Date of Composition 25

Influence of the *Isfār* 27

Description of the Manuscripts 29

Some Remarks on the Translation 30

TRANSLATION AND EDITION

Contents 34

Prologue 35

The Lordly Voyage from the Cloud to the Sitting on the Throne, Assumed by the Name 'The All-Merciful' 50

The Voyage of Creation and Command, which is the Voyage of Originating 53

The Voyage of the Noble Qurʾan 58

The Voyage of the Vision in the [Outer] Signs and Inner Signification 62

The Voyage of Trial 71

The Voyage of Enoch (Idrīs), which is the Voyage of Glorious Height and Elevation in Position and Rank 80

The Voyage of Salvation, which is the Voyage of Noah 85

The Voyage of Guidance, which is the Voyage of Abraham, the Intimate Friend 91

The Voyage of Approach and No Turning Back, which is the Voyage of Lot towards Abraham, the Intimate Friend 96

The Voyage of Ruse and Trial in the Account of Jacob and Joseph 98
The Voyage of the Divine Appointment of Moses 103
The Voyage of Good Pleasure 108
The Voyage of Anger and Return 111
The Voyage of Striving on Behalf of One's Household 114
The Voyage of Fear 118
The Voyage of Caution 122

COMMENTARY

The Title of the Book: *al-Isfār ʿan natāʾij al-asfār* 135
Reference to the *Isfār* in the *Futūḥāt* 138
The Prologue 139
The Three Voyages 142
The Voyage 'with God' 143
The Modes and Perils of the Voyage 145
Movement 148
Words Relating to Voyaging 157
The Voyagers 175
Knowledge vs. Practice: Towards the Eschaton 176
The Jew and the *Gharqad* Bush 179
The Lordly Voyage from the Cloud to the Sitting on the Throne, Assumed by the Name the All-Merciful 182
The Voyage of Creation and Command 185
The Voyage of the Noble Qurʾan 187
The Voyage of the Vision in the [Outer] Signs and Inner Signification 191
Adam: The Voyage of Trial 208
Enoch/Idrīs: The Voyage of Might and Elevation in Place and Degree 214
Noah: The Voyage of Salvation 219
Abraham: The Voyage of Guidance 235
Lot: The Voyage of Approach and No Turning Back 247
Jacob and Joseph: The Voyage of Ruse and Trial 252
The Six Voyages of Moses 257

Conclusion 293
Bibliography 295
Index of Qur'anic Verses 309
Index of Hadith 317
Index of Quotations from the *Futūḥāt* 319
General Index 323

ACKNOWLEDGEMENTS

This translation and its commentary have been a decade in the making and might never have seen the light of day were it not for the encouragement, support, and wisdom of the following individuals.

I am thankful, first of all, to my inspired editors, Stephen Hirtenstein and Michael Tiernan, whose remarkable insights and painstaking attention to detail are evident on every single page of this book. They saved me from many a pitfall on this road and kept me from abandoning the voyage when I had all but given up.

Many thanks to my scrupulous copyeditor, Hannah Kenner, whose queries helped me clarify – to the best of my ability – a great number of murky and ambiguous passages.

I am indebted to Yusuf Mullick for his expert proofreading, especially of the Arabic text and transliteration.

I am deeply grateful to Denis Gril, whose French translation of the *Isfār* provided essential clarification when the Shaykh's Arabic locutions seemed utterly impenetrable.

James Robinson, my faithful and enthusiastic companion in *devoir*, read and commented on various versions of this text more times than I can count, and kept my spirits up throughout this challenging enterprise. My gratitude to him knows no bounds.

Last, but in no ways least, I would like to thank my thirteen beloved feline friends and Zen Masters – Finjan, Louie, Bilqis, Marjan, Zorby, Kippie, Mimi, Toby, Tiki, Mazi (RIP), Mitzi, Edi and Avi – for their crazy wisdom.

A BIOGRAPHY OF IBN ʿARABĪ[1]

Muḥyīddīn Ibn ʿArabī, known to his admirers as the Shaykh al-Akbar, or greatest shaykh, was born in 1165 in Murcia, Spain. When he was seven his family moved to Seville. There, despite a tendency common at the time among aristocratic youth to combine Qurʾan study with worldly diversions, a strong inclination towards the devotional life began to emerge in the young Ibn ʿArabī. Even as an adolescent he undertook retreats and began to realize the panoply of mystical stations he describes in his various writings.

In his very first retreat he was seized by a kind of divine attraction or ecstasy, rather than proceeding by disciplined stages as most Sufi aspirants were accustomed to do. This completely involuntary illuminative event was followed by a more sober conversion in a rare triple vision of the Prophets Jesus, Moses and Muḥammad, who guided his return to God and kept him ever under their protection. He considered Jesus his first master and, under his influence, pledged himself to an ascetic life. He gave away his possessions to his father and subsequently lived on gifts and alms, trusting in God for all his needs. He was to become successively the disciple of Moses, then all the other prophets, terminating with Muhammad himself, who is said to incorporate the teachings of all previous prophets. In addition, he studied the traditional Islamic sciences, such as Qurʾan interpretation and Prophetic traditions, with some of the foremost scholars of Andalusia.

By around the age of twenty, he had acquired his first Sufi teacher, Abū al-ʿAbbās al-ʿUraybī,[2] an illiterate peasant, whom he met in Seville. Among this shaykh's many virtues was that, according to Ibn

1. I have relied primarily on two excellent biographies of Ibn ʿArabī: *Quest for the Red Sulphur*, by Claude Addas, and *The Unlimited Mercifier*, by Stephen Hirtenstein.

2. Various other spellings of this name – for example, ʿUryānī or ʿUryābī – have appeared in texts perhaps due to the lack of dots under the *yāʾ* and/or *bāʾ* in some MSS.

'Arabī, he had realized the station of perfect servitude, the highest of all stations. This is the station of the People of Blame, the *malāmiyya*, about whom Ibn 'Arabī has much to say in his writings. Al-'Uraybī was not the only shaykh that young Ibn 'Arabī frequented during the thirty years he spent in Andalusia before his departure to the east. In his two compendia devoted to Andalusian saints, he lists and describes some seventy-one Sufi shaykhs, four of them women, from whom he received important spiritual direction.[3]

Ibn 'Arabī's own spiritual state was made clear to him in three successive visions between the years of 1190 and 1202. In them, he saw all of the messengers and prophets as well as 'all the believers – those who have been and those who will be – until the Day of Resurrection.'[4] In one vision, the prophets and messengers assembled to congratulate him at being designated the Seal of the Muhammadan Sainthood – the heir to the Seal of the Prophets, Muhammad. As he explains in his *Futūḥāt*, the Seal of the Muhammadan Sainthood combines all the qualities of all the saints and, since prophets are also saints, it includes all the qualities of all the prophets excluding those pertaining to their legislative roles.

In 1193, Ibn 'Arabī made his first journey beyond the Iberian Peninsula to North Africa. He stayed in Tunis for a year studying with Shaykh al-Mahdawī, a disciple of the famous Algerian saint Abū Madyan.[5] His initial reception was less than cordial, thanks to the alarming claims that he made about himself. In a display that might be classified as unruly speech – something ecstatic Sufis were often criticized for – he recited the following:

3. Many of the Sufi masters with whom Ibn 'Arabī studied are described in his *Rūḥ al-quds* and *al-Durrat al-fākhira*, partially translated by Austin as *Sufis of Andalusia*.

4. *Fut.*III:323, trans. Addas, *Quest*, p.74.

5. Although Abū Madyan was Andalusian by birth, it was in North Africa that he began to follow the Path. Eventually he settled in Bijaya, Algeria and is buried in Tlemcen, where he is considered the town's protector. The grave of 'Sidi Boumediene', as he is called by the Algerians, is a place of pilgrimage. The Rai singer Cheb Khaled's 'Sidi Boumediene' became an international hit in the mid-1980s.

I am the Qurʾan and the seven repeated verses [of the Fātiḥa];
I am the spirit of the spirit, not the spirit of moments ...[6]

And so on. This is quite a claim for a twenty-eight year old, relatively unknown, wayfarer to make!

When Ibn ʿArabī returned to Andalusia, he began to compose the first of his more than 300 works. His primary activity, however, seems to have been spiritual wayfaring in order to study Sufism and hadith. Between the years 1195 and 1200, Ibn ʿArabī made many trips between Spain and North Africa, while concurrently traversing another landscape not visible to the physical eye. To many of these purely spiritual locales he gave evocative names, such as 'God's Vast Earth' where 'spirits are corporealized and bodies spiritualized,'[7] and the 'Abode of Light', where all destinies are known from beginning to end.

But the greatest vision he experienced at this time was no doubt the spiritual ascent he made in imitation of the Prophet Muhammad's corporeal ascent to the seven heavens and to the Divine Presence Itself. To briefly summarize, after being stripped of his corporeal nature, the Shaykh ascended in spirit to the seven heavens where he was welcomed by and conversed with Adam, Jesus and John the Baptist, Joseph, Enoch (Idrīs), Aaron, Moses and finally, in the seventh heaven, Abraham, leaning against the celestial Kaʿba. In each heaven he questioned its ruling prophet about matters that puzzled him.

Beyond the seventh heaven lies the goal of every *miʿrāj*: the Lote Tree of the limit, where the Shaykh became, as he puts it, 'nothing but light'.[8] He realized that, despite the multiplicity of God's Names and Attributes, there is but a single Essence to which they refer, and that 'the journey that [he] made was only inside [him]self, and it was towards [him]self he had been guided.'[9] From that exalted state he returned to earthly consciousness with the task of guiding others to a realization of God.

6. *Fut.*I:9.
7. Corbin, *Creative Imagination*, p.4.
8. *Fut.*III:350, trans. Addas, *Quest*, p.156.
9. Ibid.

The year 1200 marks the beginning of the Shaykh's journey to the east. He was never again to return to Spain. From North Africa, he went first to Cairo then to Hebron – where he visited the tomb of Abraham – then Jerusalem, where he prayed at the al-Aqṣā Mosque. His final goal was Mecca, where he intended to perform the pilgrimage.

Among many visions and meetings with remarkable personages experienced on his voyage and in Mecca itself, was the Shaykh's encounter with the strange figure he calls the *fatā*, a term which is roughly equivalent to knight. One evening, when the Shaykh was performing the ritual circumambulations, a mysterious youth accosted him. After their conversation, recounted in the poetry and rhymed prose of the *Futūḥāt*'s first chapter, a pact between them was concluded. The result of this epiphany is the some 2000 folio pages of the *Futūḥāt*, a mystical masterpiece.

The Shaykh was to stay roughly two years in Mecca, but once he left there he spent nearly twenty years (1204–20) travelling back and forth across Syria, Palestine, Anatolia, Egypt, Iraq and the Hijaz. He acquired many disciples and even became an advisor to the Seljuq sultan Kaykāʾūs. It is difficult to follow the constant peregrinations of the Shaykh during this period – it seems that he was constantly on the move, tirelessly carrying out God's command to counsel His servants.

It was not until the final twenty years of his life that Ibn ʿArabī ceased his peregrinations and in 1221 settled permanently in Damascus. From 1223 until his death in 1240, we do not have any evidence that the Shaykh ever left Syria. Whether addressing jurists or Sufis, rulers or simple folk, the Shaykh made it a point to convey his message, orally and in his many writings, to all the believers he encountered and at the level of their varied understandings. Some of the texts he wrote were short, composed at a single sitting, some ran to hundreds of pages – even thousands of pages, in the case of the *Futūḥāt* – and were the product of years of labour.

At the end of 1229, an event occurred that resulted in the writing of the Shaykh's best-known work, the *Fuṣūṣ al-ḥikam*, or 'Bezels of Wisdom'. In a dream, he saw the Prophet Muhammad holding a book. The Prophet told him: 'This is the book of the *Fuṣūṣ al-ḥikam*. Take and give it to humanity so that they may obtain benefit from it.'[10] The entirety of the book was, according to Ibn 'Arabī, inspired by the Prophet with no personal input on his part whatsoever. Twenty-seven prophets, each incorporating a facet of sainthood, are discussed in turn. The *Fuṣūṣ* has remained to this day his most provocative and most frequently commented-upon work.

The Shaykh died in Damascus in November 1240. Over the centuries, his teachings spread east as far as China, disseminated by devoted students – many of them gifted mystics and poets in their own right. For the past century, the western world has also played a part in this process, as scholars and translators continue the effort to bring the Shaykh's remarkable writings to the attention of the contemporary world.

10. *Fuṣūṣ*, p.47, trans. Austin, *Bezels*, p.45.

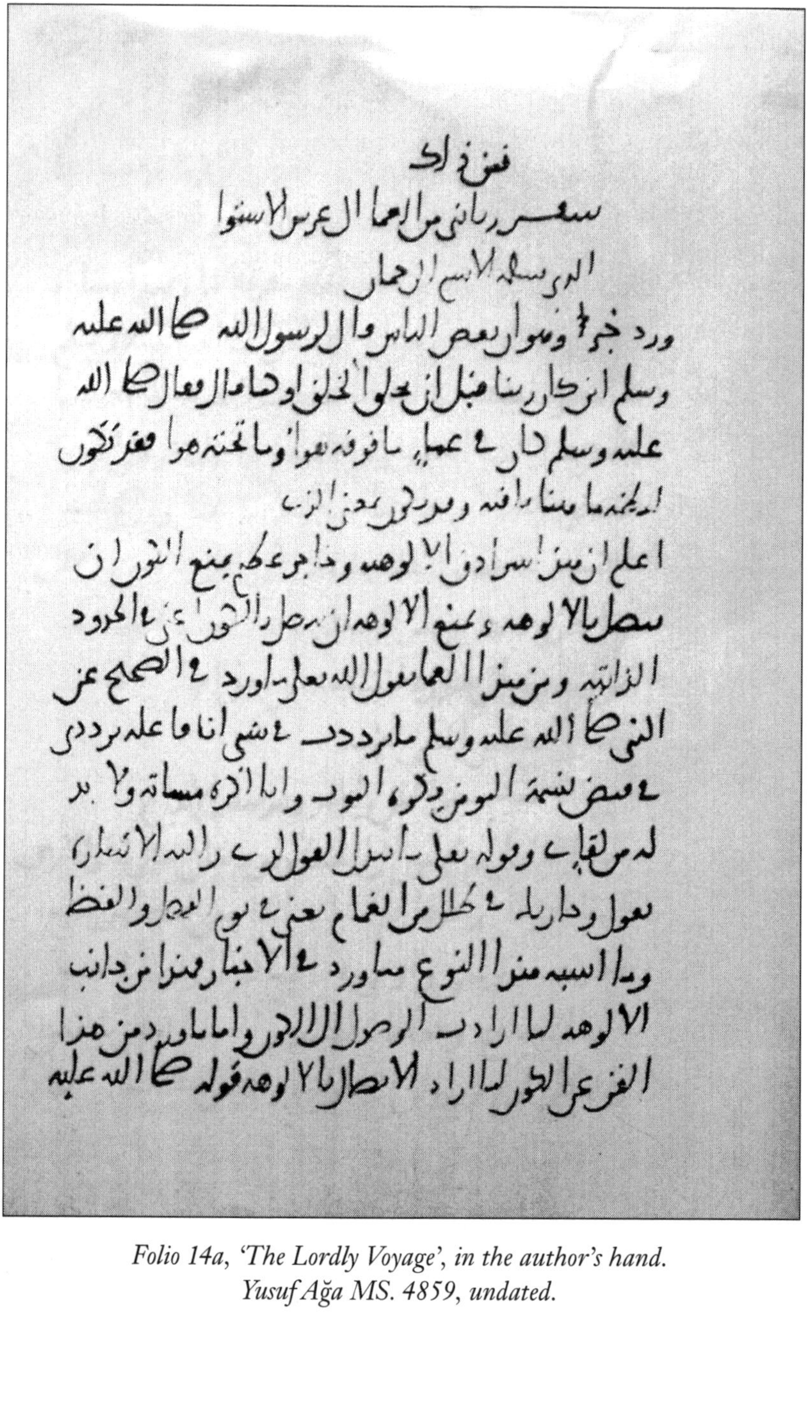

فمن ذلك

سفر ربانى من العماء الى العرش الاستواء

الذى يسلكه الاسم الرحمان

ورد خبر فى سؤال بعض الناس قال لرسول الله صلى الله عليه
وسلم اين كان ربنا قبل ان يخلق الخلق او خلقه فقال صلى الله
عليه وسلم كان فى عماء ما فوقه هواء وما تحته هواء فعرفنا كون
العماء ما بيننا ذاته ومورد ضمير يعنى الرب

اعلم ان من اسرار الالوهة وحجاب عظمة يمنع النور ان
يتصل بالالوهة ويمنع الالوهة ان يتصل [illegible] الحدود
الذاتية ومن هذا العما قول الله تعالى وما ورد فى الصحيح عن
النبى صلى الله عليه وسلم ما ترددت فى شىء انا فاعله ترددى
فى قبض نسمة المؤمن يكره الموت وانا اكره مساءته ولا بد
له من لقائى وقوله تعالى [illegible] الله الا [illegible]
[illegible] فى ظلل من الغمام [illegible]
وما اشبه هذا النوع مما ورد فى الاخبار فهذا من جانب
الالوهة لما ارادت الوصول الى الكون واما ما ورد من هذا
الفن عن الكون لما اراد الاتصال بالالوهة فقوله صلى الله عليه

Folio 14a, 'The Lordly Voyage', in the author's hand.
Yusuf Ağa MS. 4859, undated.

INTRODUCTION

In the *Futūḥāt*'s Chapter 190, on the Voyager, Ibn 'Arabī describes a poignant exchange between God and the gnostic voyager who, through repeated mystical unveilings at numerous spiritual and conceptual waystations, has come to see God in everything. The voyager wants nothing more than to throw down his traveller's staff and find rest in his goal. But God informs him that this is impossible: voyaging has no end, either in this life or the hereafter.

The statement 'life is a journey' is one of the most overused tropes to describe the stages of our sojourn on this earth. It is a measure of the genius of the Shaykh al-Akbar – himself no stranger to wayfaring – that in his numerous works, dedicated either fully or in part to the voyage, he manages to present a dazzling array of original insights that never fail to engage the mind and heart of his reader. Aside from a number of independent spiritual ascent narratives, the Shaykh devotes five chapters of his *magnum opus*, the *Futūḥāt*, merely to explaining characteristics of the voyage. His remarks are not confined to those five chapters alone, for within a great many of the other 554 chapters are passages on voyaging that serve to fascinate, perplex and inspire.

The Secrets of Voyaging (*Kitāb al-isfār 'an natā'ij al-asfār*), which we present here in its first English translation,[1] is a subtle and intriguing text. Not readily classifiable, it blends elements of *qiṣaṣ al-anbiyā'* (tales of the prophets), Sufi initiatic – or *sulūk* (wayfaring) – manuals, heavenly ascent literature and Qur'an commentaries while remaining, as do the majority of his works, completely *sui generis*. On the surface, as the Arabic title indicates, it is dedicated primarily to 'unveiling the results of the voyages', specifically those having

1. The *Isfār* has been translated into French by Denis Gril as *Le Dévoilement des effets du voyage*; into Spanish by Carlos Varona Nervion as *El splendor de los frutos del viaje*; and into Urdu by Abrar Ahmed Shahi as *Ruhani Asfar aur un ke samaraat*.

to do with three metaphysical entities – the Divine Name 'Lord', the Creation and the primordial Qur'an – and seven major Prophets – Adam, Enoch (Idrīs), Noah, Abraham, Lot, Joseph and Moses, with Muhammad's Night Journey and Ascent serving as a kind of paradigmatic fulcrum between the two. The reader is expected to emulate the Prophetic journeys in a suprasensible fashion, much as Ibn ʿArabī himself did, in order to learn to decipher the secrets that these voyages contain. But that is not all. This multifaceted work has as a subtext a discussion of how to read and interpret the Qur'an in general. These two major themes thread through the entirety of the work, each contributing to the other. In short, it is a work designed to indicate to readers the signs on the horizon and in themselves,[2] an undertaking that necessarily precedes any knowledge a person can have of their Lord.

The Voyage Pro and Con

Ibn ʿArabī's incessant peregrinations in roughly the first part of his life can be assigned to a horizontal or geocentric axis, but concurrently he was voyaging along a vertical, spiritual axis.[3] Thus he resolved in himself the dispute, often found in Sufi manuals, between the supporters and detractors of wayfaring, since not all Sufis found the actual practice of taking to the road in search of esoteric knowledge either salutary or necessary. This latter view is charmingly presented by the Ṣufi expositor of states and stations, al-Qushayrī, in the following anecdotes:

> I heard the master Abū ʿAlī al-Daqqāq – may God have mercy on him – say: 'In a village called "Farakhk" near [the city of] Nishapur there lived a Sufi master, who had written a number of books on Sufi science. Someone once asked him: "Shaykh, have you ever traveled?" He, in turn, asked: "[Are you asking about] travel in the

2. Q.41:53: 'We shall show them Our signs on the horizons and within themselves.'

3. Morris has described the interaction of these two axes in 'He Moves You', pp.62–3, and *Reflective Heart*, pp.36–7. See also Hirtenstein, *Unlimited Mercifier*, pp.117–18.

> earth or travel in the heavens? As for the former, the answer is no; as for latter, yes."' I also heard him [al-Daqqāq] – may God have mercy on him – say: 'One day, when I resided in Merv, a Sufi came to me, saying: "I have traveled a long way in order to meet you!" I told him: "Had you parted ways with your lower soul, one step would have sufficed for you."'[4]

Travel for egoistic purposes was definitely shunned – one can only imagine what Ibn ʿArabī's opinion would be of today's tourists photographing each other at holy sites. Travel for commerce was a necessary evil and could scarcely be criticized when Islam's Prophet was, in his early life, a merchant deeply involved in the caravan economy of Mecca.[5] Pilgrimage to Mecca for the *ḥajj* was a religious obligation for those physically and financially able. But the wayfaring of the mystically inclined received a mixed vote. It was reportedly eschewed by such great early Sufis as Abū Qāsim al-Junayd (d. 910), Sahl b. ʿAbdallāh al-Tustarī (d. 896), and Abū Yazīd al-Bisṭāmī (d. 874 or 877), while others such as Ibrāhīm b. Adham (d. *c.* 777/8) favoured it. Many, for example Abū ʿUthmān al-Ḥīrī (d. 910) and Abū Bakr al-Shiblī (d. 945), followed the pattern of spending their early life on the road then later settling down to direct their attention inwards.[6] Thus the first part of their life's journey was dedicated to seeing God's signs and examples (*ʿibar*)[7] in the world, to seeking wisdom at the foot of great masters and even to escaping from the society of humankind altogether, while the latter part focused on the internal journey of the heart exclusively. This was the pattern followed by Ibn ʿArabī.

The fruits of his experiences – his unveiling resultant from his own travels, both inward and outward, are found in numerous

4. Al-Qushayrī, *al-Risāla*, trans. Knysh as *al-Qushayrī's Epistle on Sufism*, pp. 297–8.

5. Ibn ʿArabī himself puts an occasional favourable spin on the merchant's voyage by saying that even if the merchant believes he is travelling for his own gain, his labours benefit an entire community.

6. Al-Qushayrī, *al-Risāla*, trans. Knysh, *Epistle on Sufism*, p. 297.

7. See Commentary p. 169 for a discussion of this central term.

passages, chapters and entire treatises devoted to the voyage. As the *Isfār* makes clear, the only travel Ibn ʿArabī unqualifiedly approved of was that in which the voyager did not take a single step by himself but was 'carried' by the Real, whether spiritually, physically or both together. It is a voyage that beautifully typifies the Shaykh's love of paradox: a voyage in which the voyager stays perfectly still.

Style and Language

The first thing that must be pointed out regarding the *Isfār* is that it is an esoteric book among esoteric books. What I mean by that is that in the Shaykh's own list of his works, the *Fihris al-muʾallafāt*, the *Isfār* is listed as one of the books that is not yet ready to be publicly distributed.[8] Its name is ninth in a section listing sixteen books under the heading marked with the Arabic letter *bāʾ* (= two in numerological calculation) and designated with an additional letter that may well have some sort of esoteric meaning. The *Isfār* is thus called *rāʾ bāʾ*.[9] It was most likely intended to be read privately by advanced students under the guidance of the Shaykh himself. The compactness of the exposition demands expansion and supplementation, and its obscurity of language and meaning calls for repeated readings. The background knowledge Ibn ʿArabī assumes in his reader is prodigious: total recall of Qurʾanic verses and Prophetic traditions; biographies and mystical teachings of the Sufis; *belles-lettres*; the entire philosophic curriculum, including – in the case of the *Isfār* – psychology, astronomy and optics; theology (*kalām*) and Law; and last, but certainly never least, the hermetic sciences of alchemy, astrology and language mysticism. Moreover, readers of Ibn ʿArabī's works who are quite comfortable with the traditional notions and terminology of the aforementioned subjects will suddenly find the ground shifting under their feet as the Shaykh

8. *Fihris al-muʾallafāt*. See Yahia, *Histoire et classification*, pp. 39–42.
9. Is one to make anything of the fact that the two letters spell *rabb*, Lord?

brings to light novel and sometimes subversive meanings based on his own 'unveiling'.

In addition, as James Morris has remarked with reference to the *Futūḥāt*, the treatment of these subjects proceeds in an apparently disorderly fashion with many a shift in perspective; connections between titles given to chapters and their content are frequently obscure and the verses that grace some of the prose sections sometimes seem to serve more to bewilder the reader than to clarify the discussion.[10] That this difficult style is intentional and not the result of disordered thinking does not make it any easier for the reader.

It may be helpful to offer a partial explanation of the Shaykh's distinctive way of presenting his teachings by saying that his primary model was the Qur'an, which also scatters its kaleidoscopically shifting themes and fragmented narratives among its 114 chapters. As in the Holy Writ, it is up to the reader of Ibn 'Arabī's works to ferret out the keys that are seldom to be found where expected, to connect the dots, as it were, and to struggle to integrate the teaching. This more often than not ends in an impasse, and bewilderment – if not annoyance – sets in. Intuition, more than intellectual acuity, is a *sine qua non* to deciphering the text, but it comes as a gift, a flash of understanding. It is not something that can come from casual reading or even prolonged reflection with one's intellect upon the meaning of the Shaykh's words.

Like many of his earlier short mystical treatises, such as *al-Isrā'*,[11] *Mashāhid al-asrār al-qudsiyya*,[12] *al-Ittiḥād al-kawnī*[13] and *'Anqā' mughrib*,[14] the *Isfār* is especially notable for its ingenious word play and subtle allusions. We find constant reference to words and their meanings in the *Isfār* as we do in other Akbarian works. The Shaykh often traces a word back to its real or imagined root in order to give

10. Morris, 'Ibn 'Arabī's "Esotericism"', pp.40–1.

11. Ed. S. al-Hakim.

12. Ed. and trans. into Spanish by S. al-Hakim and P. Beneito as *Las Contemplaciones de los Misterios* and into English by C. Twinch and P. Beneito as *Contemplation of the Holy Mysteries*.

13. Ed. and trans. into French by D. Gril as *Le Livre de l'Arbre et des Quatre Ouiseaux* and into English by A. Jaffray as *The Universal Tree and the Four Birds*.

14. Trans. into English by G. Elmore as *Islamic Sainthood in the Fullness of Time*.

it an added dimension, such as his derivation of *munāfiq*, hypocrite, from the word meaning 'burrow' (*nāfiqā'*),[15] and he examines the presumed etymology of personal nouns as well. For example, Lot, he claims, derives from *lūṭ*,[16] attachment; Isḥāq (Isaac) is connected with 'crushing';[17] the name of the town Yaqīn near Hebron comes from *yaqīn*, certainty; and Noah's water-belching furnace, the *tannūr*, is really composed of two separate elements: the particle *ta-* and the word for light, *nūr*.[18]

Many of the chapters of the *Isfār*, in particular the last ones, include short snippets of verse of the Shaykh's composition. There are seventeen poems in total by the author himself, most only one or two lines and none exceeding five lines. There is also an occasional outpouring of rhymed prose, which adds a touch of eloquence and an oracular quality to this treatise. But for the most part, the style of this treatise is sober, prosaic and direct, its language deceptively clear.[19] It soon becomes apparent to the reader that each carefully chosen word that the Shaykh employs – a care that extends to the simplest of particles, in the case of Arabic this sometimes consists of a single letter – is a plant with the deepest of roots. Beneath the surface of the text as written there flourishes a network of interwoven meanings that gives to the individual themes and images a rich and complex coherence.

Edward F. Edinger, a student of C. G. Jung, has called this kind of methodology 'network thinking'.

> Network thinking is neither linear nor meandering and associational. It's purposeful, but it is also concerned with elaborating a network of expanded meanings derived from a central image. It is

15. *Isfār*, Para. 67.
16. Ibid. Para. 44.
17. Ibid. Para. 43.
18. In other texts by the Shaykh, Mūsā (Moses) is said to be derived from the Coptic *mū* meaning 'water' and *sā* meaning 'tree' (*Fuṣus*, trans. Austin, *Bezels*, p. 254), and Nūh (Noah) is connected with lament (*nawḥ*); see *Fut.*III:49 (Chap. 313).
19. Because of its compactness and tendency to present the material without much explanation, it is best read in conjunction with relevant passages in the *Futūḥāt*, as we have done in composing our Commentary.

thinking that is oriented around a center, and moves radically to and from that center, circumambulating it. It goes back and forth, returning to the central image again and again, building up a rich associative cluster of interconnecting images – something like a spider web.[20]

Thus we find certain themes reappearing, migrating across chapters in the *Isfār* – and not halting at the boundaries of the *Isfār* itself but crossing over into the Shaykh's other texts, especially his massive *Futūḥāt*. C.-A. Gilis has astutely remarked that in reading Ibn ʿArabī, one needs to always 'bring together what is dispersed'[21] in numerous short treatises in the form of supplementary teachings.[22] Sometimes the themes are quite apparent, such as the dominant metaphors of voyage, unveiling and revelation; some perhaps glide by nearly unnoticed, such as haste, generosity, jealousy, wariness, guidance and ruse. To these must be added the apocalyptic 'signs on the horizon' that are simultaneously concealed and revealed within the narratives of the text. Beneath it all lies an interlocking weave of Qur'anic verses and motifs to which the reader returns again and again.

If the central theme can be summed up with the Qur'anic injunction: 'Travel through the earth and see what was the end of those before [you]' (Q.30:42), readers of all kinds will find that the *Isfār* itself is a kind of voyage where much will be revealed and even more will remain tantalizingly concealed. At the same time, it is a vehicle, conveyance, riding beast from which they will descend at intervals to take note of the 'signs on the horizons and in themselves' and to consider the voyages of others who preceded them, human or otherwise – learning, if they are wise, from their examples.

20. Edinger, *Mysterium Lectures*, p. 20.

21. In method, the Shaykh quite consciously follows the model of the Qur'an as both an assembling (*qur'ān*) and dispersing (*furqān*) text. See our Commentary on Paras. 18–21.

22. See *Le Livre du Mīm*, p. 11. Gilis refers the reader to his *René Guenon*, Chap. 7. See also Morris's highly instructive article, 'Ibn 'Arabī's Rhetoric of Realisation', Parts I and II; see especially p. 104 of Part II, where he calls this method '"scattering" (*tabdīd*): the puzzle effect'.

Related Genres: Manuals of Sulūk, Isrā' and Mi'rāj Literature, Tafsīr and Qiṣaṣ al-anbiyā'

Although a detailed history of the various types of literature suggestive of the *Isfār* is beyond the scope of this study, a brief overview of these forms may serve to point out Ibn 'Arabī's distinct contribution to, and surpassing of, these genres.

Guides to Spiritual Wayfaring (*sulūk*)[23]

Quite early on in Sufism, the stages of a life dedicated to approaching, if not achieving 'union' with God were likened to the stages on a journey. The esoteric trajectory was termed '*ṭarīqa*', mystical path, in harmony with its exoteric counterpart '*sharī'a*' or Law – also originally a path to water. In addition to advising on the etiquette of actual physical travel, books on *sulūk*, wayfaring,[24] or chapters on *sulūk* within the increasingly popular Sufi manuals, such as Abū Ismā'īl 'Abdallāh al-Ansārī al-Harawī's (d. 1088) *Manāzil al-sā'irīn* (Waystations of the Travellers),[25] tended to elevate the idea of wayfaring to the spiritual plane, even if they included chapters on actual travel. Ibn 'Arabī's predecessors, such as al-Qushayrī in his *Risāla*, al-Sarrāj in *Kitāb al-Luma'* and al-Makkī in *Qūt al-qulūb*, stress moral edification and proper conduct[26] with the added idea of progress from station to station (*maqām*) along the Sufi path; each stage consists of an ethical character trait or virtue the dervish must assume before

23. The root from which *sulūk* derives appears twelve times in the Qur'an: 15:12; 16:69; 20:53; 23:27; 26:200; 28:32; 39:20; 69:32; 71:20; 72:17, 27; 74:42.

24. See Commentary for further discussion of this term.

25. Abū Ismā'īl 'Abd Allāh al-Ansārī al-Harawī (d. 1088) was a renowned mystic of Herat. Ibn 'Arabī's disciple al-Kāshānī wrote a commentary on this work. Ibn 'Arabī mentions al-Harawī in the *Futūḥāt*. See *Fut.*II.280 (Chap. 167).

26. One type of *sulūk* literature had specifically to do with the proper behaviour of subjects with kings, and included advice for viziers, judges, soldiers, etc. In the Sufi adaptation of this genre, the King was taken to be God. See, for example, the fifth part of Najm al-Dīn Rāzī's *Mirṣād al-i'bād min al-mabdā' ilā al-ma'ād*, trans. Algar.

moving to the next stage. It is not uncommon for the author to begin with 'Repentance' and in the section of the *Futūḥāt* that follows this model[27] that is precisely where Ibn 'Arabī begins.

But with Ibn 'Arabī, the idea of *sulūk* was expanded to include an entire constellation of interrelated terms, based on the Arabic root *n-z-l*, linking together the procession of lunar phases through the moon's 'mansions', cosmic cycles, revelation of Qur'anic verses (*tanzīl*), the wayfarer's 'dismounting' spots along the path and places of divine/human interaction (*manāzil/munāzalāt*).[28] These latter two are best explained by the Shaykh himself:

> A 'waystation' is a station in which God descends (*nuzūl*) to you, or within which you alight (*nuzūl*) upon Him. Notice the difference between descend 'to' (*ilā*) and alight 'upon' (*'alā*). A 'mutual waystation' is that He desires to descend to you and places within your heart a seeking to alight upon Him. Your resolve undergoes a subtle, spiritual movement in order to alight upon Him and you come together with Him between these two *nuzūl*s: your alighting upon Him, before you reach the waystation, and His descent to you – that is, the attentiveness of a divine name – before He reaches the waystation. The occurrence of this coming together outside of the two waystations is called a 'mutual waystation.'[29]

When there is a vision of the Real, it never occurs except in a mutual waystation (*munāzala*) between an ascent and a descent. The

27. Section II, *Mu'āmalāt*, or mutual interactions, comprises 115 chapters.

28. Section IV of the *Futūḥāt* is devoted to waystations (*manāzil*) and Section V to mutual waystations (*munāzalāt*).

29. *Fut.*II.577–8 (Chap. 271), trans. Chittick, *SPK*, p.279. In *SDG* (p.114), Chittick remarks that perhaps 'mutual waystation' is not the best translation of this term: '… though it suggests what he has in mind and can be employed without a great deal of explanation. Literally, the term means "mutual descent". It derives from the root *n-z-l*, from which we have *nuzūl* and *tanazzul*, both of which are usually translated as "descent". *Nuzūl* may also mean getting down from one's mount, and this implies stopping at a dwelling to rest. Hence the term *manzil* or "waystation" is the place where one descends from one's mount to rest during a journey. In a "mutual waystation", both God and the servant "descend" in order to meet each other, as travellers might descend from their horses in order to meet in a camp. The descent of the servants to God, then, is connected to the idea that when they rise up to Him through a *mi'rāj*, they travel on their own Burāq – the steed that took Muhammad on his *mi'rāj* – and then "descend" from their Burāq to meet with God.'

ascent is from us and the descent is from Him. Ours is the 'drawing near' and His is the 'coming down', since 'coming down' must be from what is higher. Ours is the ascending and His is the receiving of those who arrive at Him.[30]

The mutual waystations described by Ibn 'Arabī number seventy-eight, the same number of times that the fourteen isolated letters found at the beginning of some Qur'anic suras appear.[31] All but one of these mutual waystations are headed by God's enigmatic addresses to the Shaykh. As in the preceding section on waystations, the order is in reverse, from the *nūn* of Sura 68 to the *alif* of Sura 2.[32] Hence, we see that the idea of voyaging through the waystations and mutual waystations is intimately entwined with the Qur'anic 'descents' upon its reciters.

Ibn 'Arabī's *Isfār* cannot be called a manual of *sulūk* in the common sense since there is little or no concern for an easily followed hierarchical and orderly description of stages along the Sufi way, such that one could use it as a kind of 'how to' manual. It is much more subtle than that. Nevertheless, there are certain features that it shares with the more common paradigm. First of all, it uses the trope of travel to present a series of exemplary tales that are said to produce 'results' – the *natā'ij* of the Arabic title.[33] To take but one example, the results of Adam's voyage are: (1) he learns and contemplates the Names of his Lord and their results, in particular His Name 'the Forgiver', which only becomes possible because of his disobedience; (2) he gains: response, repentance, seeking forgiveness, pardon, fear and the safety that comes after fear; and (3) he gains: knowledge of composition, development and dissolution.[34] Presumably, the

30. *Fut.*III.117 (Chap. 331). See also the poem in *Fut.*I.237 that opens Chap. 41, on the People of the Night.

31. *alif, lām, mīm, nūn, kāf, ḥā', sīn, 'ayn, ṣād, yā', tā', hā', kāf, rā'*.

32. See Gilis, *Études complémentaires*, p.134. See also *Fut.*I.173ff. (Chap. 22) where the group of twenty-nine suras that begin with the isolated letters is discussed under the rubric 'Station of Symbols'.

33. See Commentary for further analysis of this term.

34. See *Isfār*, Paras. 30 and 31. One of the more obscure questions is the connection of the various enumerated 'results' with the narrative of the prophet in question.

aspirant who sets out on the Adamic voyage has the possibility of gaining the same knowledge.

Isrāʾ and *Miʿrāj* Literature[35]

The account of the Prophet Muhammad's Night Journey (*isrāʾ*) and Ascent to the Heavens (*miʿrāj*), based on the enigmatic Qurʾanic references found in Suras 17 and 53, Prophetic hadiths and early biographical literature, eventually became subject to mystical imitation. Although the Night Journey and Ascent tend to become conflated under the designation *miʿrāj*, they actually involve two separate stages. The Night Journey, as it generally came to be interpreted in later tradition, consisted of the Prophet Muhammad being carried through the air on the fantastic steed Burāq from his home in Mecca to the Noble Sanctuary in Jerusalem.[36] Hence it was a horizontal voyage. The second stage was vertical, as Muhammad ascended through the heavens to greet a series of prophets in their particular heavens, generally listed as Adam (Moon), Jesus (Mercury), Joseph (Venus), Enoch/Idrīs (Sun), Aaron (Mars), Moses (Jupiter) and Abraham (Saturn), before proceeding on to his encounter with the Divine.

Ibn Arabī wrote a number of works based on prophetic and/or personal *isrāʾ* and *miʿrāj* themes, including *K. al-Isrāʾ*,[37] two very different renditions in the *Futūḥāt*,[38] *K. al-Ittiḥād al-kawnī* and *K. al-Anwār*.[39] But strictly speaking, the *Isfār* does not fall under this

35. For general background see Amir-Moezzi, *Le Voyage initiatique*; Colby, *Subtleties of the Ascension* and respective bibliographies; Sells, *Early Islamic Mysticism*.

36. The earliest interpretations did not specify Jerusalem as the final point in this voyage. Indeed some took the 'furthest mosque' to mean heaven. Some modern scholars have conjectured that the mention of Jerusalem was an Umayyad ploy to focus attention on this city rather than on Mecca, which was then under the control of the hostile forces of ʿAbd Allāh b. al-Zubayr. See Schrieke and Horovitz, 'Miʿrādj', p. 97.

37. Ed. al-Hakim.

38. Chaps. 167 and 367.

39. Trans. into English by Harris as *Journey to the Lord of Power*. For background on Ibn ʿArabī's treatment of this theme, see Morris, 'The Spiritual Ascension', Parts I and II. See also Gril's 'Journey through the Circles of Inner Being'.

genre. Although certain episodes are linguistically connected to the notion of *isrāʾ* – notably the voyage of Lot and certain voyages of Moses – not all the episodes described in the *Isfār* are Night Journeys and/or ascents, and the treatment of Muhammad's *isrāʾ* and *miʿrāj* is confined to one chapter. In that one chapter, however, Ibn ʿArabī manages to bring out a number of intriguing interpretations, based on a close reading of the Qurʾanic text, such that it could be considered as drawing from this genre.

Tafsīr[40]

Qurʾan commentary has a long and somewhat disputed history, since its beginnings are unclear and development not clearly definable. Whether the Prophet Muhammad encouraged speculation on the meaning of verses is not known, but A. Rippin mentions the second Caliph ʿUmar's reluctance to interpret the Qurʾan, or at least its ambiguous verses.[41] The earliest period lacks complete manuscripts, and one has to rely on fragmentary evidence and often mere titles of no longer extant texts. The formative and classical periods are better known, and it was at this time that *tafsīr*s began to show a clear tendency to interpret the text according to the aims and interests of their expounders, be they grammarians, legists, theologians, Shiʿis or mystics. *Jāmiʿ al-bayān ʿan taʾwīl āy al-Qurʾān* by Abū Jaʿfar al-Ṭabarī (d. 923), a vast and useful exegesis, attentive primarily to Prophetic traditions and grammatical investigation, is considered by most scholars to be the beginning of the classical age of Qurʾan commentary.

In its mature phase, *tafsīr* composition burgeoned. It was during this period that Ibn ʿArabī is said to have written a commentary of the Qurʾan which no longer survives; the work that goes under his name is actually by his student ʿAbd al-Razzāq al-Kashānī (d. 1330), although it is a thoroughly Akbarian interpretation.[42] Although

40. For a historical overview and excellent enumeration of sources, consult Rippin, 'Tafsīr'.

41. Ibid.

42. See Lory, *Les commentaires ésotériques*.

the loss of the Shaykh's original work is lamentable, the presence of Qur'anic commentary is not lacking in his many treatises that survive. In fact, it probably would not be an exaggeration to say that Ibn ʿArabī's entire *oeuvre* is a commentary on the Qur'an, enhanced and supported by his extensive personal mystical revelations. The Shaykh was thoroughly steeped in the Qur'an, quoting from it on virtually every page of every work, with seemingly perfect recall of its words and themes, able to bring together statements found scattered throughout the Holy Book, following the trail of a single word. Nearly every significant word sheds light on a different facet of the text, evoking different Qur'anic resonances with each renewed encounter. In some cases, the effect is to put the sacred text in dialogue with itself and its reader/reciter in astounding ways.

One should point out the *Futūḥāt*'s remarkable 114-chapter section[43] which takes the reader in reverse order through the suras of the Qur'an, treating various themes suggested by the text and by his own inner guidance, culminating in a list of 'knowledges' one receives at this particular station; and the *Fuṣūṣ*, where each chapter is dedicated to a prophet and replete with Qur'anic prooftexts.

The *Isfār* has as one of its major themes the voyage/unveiling one undergoes when one sets out to interpret (from root *ʿ-b-r*) or more literally to 'cross over' (from the outward form to the inner meaning of) the Qur'an.[44] Like the voyage over land or sea, or the unveiling of what is customarily veiled, textual interpretation can be fraught with danger, even if one never leaves home. Ibn ʿArabī's caution against the type of interpretation known as *ta'wīl* is oft-repeated.[45] Since

43. Chaps. 270–383.

44. See Commentary, pp. 250–1.

45. *Ta'wīl* derives from the second form of the Arabic root *'-w-l*, whose basic meaning is 'to return' or 'go back to'. As Lane explains in his lexicon (cited in Khan, 'Nothing but Animals', p. 27): 'Although it may often be rendered by interpretation, [...] it more properly signifies (1) the rendering in a manner not according to the letter or overt sense [...], (2) reducing a thing to its ultimate intent [...], or (3) reducing one of two senses or interpretations, which an expression bears [...] to that which suits the apparent meaning.' Khan has perceptively noted that it is perhaps this 'reductive interpretation' that Ibn ʿArabī objects to: 'Instead of choosing between literal and non-literal meanings, any reading of a Qur'anic verse must work through its literal meanings, affirming them to the end. This is far from

ta'wīl is the expression one usually associates with Sufi commentary, as opposed to the more 'orthodox' *tafsīr*, this dislike of *ta'wīl* seems at first inexplicable. Is not what Ibn 'Arabī does *ta'wīl*? It seems that the Shaykh is going back to the Qur'anic caveat against *ta'wīl*, as found in Sura 3:7: 'But those in whose hearts is deviation follow the part [of the Qur'an] that is ambiguous, seeking discord, and desiring to interpret (*ta'wīl*) [what is ambiguous]; but no one knows its interpretation except Allah.' As he states in the *Futūḥāt*: 'If we interpret what He has brought, we will be taking it back to rational speculation. Hence we will have worshipped our own intellects and based His Being upon our [own] existence.'[46] He is particularly harsh with the 'exoteric scholars' who, while ignorant themselves, criticize the People of God for their lack of formal learning when it is they to whom God unveils the meanings of what is ambiguous in the Noble Book.[47]

Interpretation as rooted in the word *'abara* means passing over, moving, travelling from the obvious to the less obvious, from the limited to the infinite.[48] With Ibn 'Arabī, interpretation is never fixed. Hence we find in his many works – and often in the same work – any number of different facets and insights relating to the same Qur'anic verses. This multifarious approach resembles his remarks on Qur'an recitation when it is performed properly. The reciter who recites from the heart, whether silently or aloud, receives the revelation anew every time he recites, while the recitation of those who do not, who become fixated on the text itself in its written or heard form, never leaves their throat.[49] As Ibn 'Arabī writes:

---

saying that Ibn 'Arabi's literalism is equivalent to a belief that Qur'anic expressions have single meanings. Ibn 'Arabi draws the listener's attention to the polysemy of Qur'anic expressions by dint of his expositions of their etymologies and amphibologies. The reader must not abandon any one of the multiple literally grounded meanings of an expression, even if they contradict one another. The faculty that wrongfully enforces the logic of noncontradiction is the intellect.'

46. *Fut.*IV.197 (Chap. 558).

47. See *Fut.*I.279ff. (Chap. 54).

48. See Commentary for further discussion of this term.

49. See *Fut.*III.414 (Chap. 370), IV.482 (Chap. 560). See also *Fut* III.128 (Chap. 334): 'As the Messenger of God – peace and blessings upon him – said in the case of some people

> The Qur'an is forever renewed when it descends upon the hearts of those who recite it. Whoever recites it does so only from the renewal of the descent from God, the Wise, the Praiseworthy. The hearts of the reciters upon whom it descends are a Throne upon which it sits.[50]

Two notable modern figures – one Jewish, one Christian – have written similar thoughts on this subject that are worthy of citation. The first is Martin Buber who, in a lecture on the Bible, urged his audience to encounter the Bible

> as though it were something entirely unfamiliar, as though it had not been set before you ready-made. ... Let whatever may happen occur between yourself and it. You do not know which of its sayings and images will overwhelm and mold you ... But hold yourself open. Do not believe anything a priori; do not disbelieve anything a priori. Read aloud the words written in front of you; hear the word you utter and let it reach you.[51]

The second is Thomas Merton, also known as the Trappist Father Louis, who remarks that people think of the Scriptures as old, very old, in contrast with, say, the news, which is new every day. But in reality it is quite the opposite:

---

among those who memorized the letters of the Qur'an: 'They recite the Qur'an [but] it does not pass beyond their throats', in other words, it descends from the imagination, which is in the anterior part of the brain, to the tongue which translates it; but it does not pass beyond their throats to the heart in their chests. So nothing of it arrives at their hearts. [The Prophet] said about them: "They penetrate the religion as the arrow penetrates the game in which you do not see a trace of the blood of the game."' Hadith found numerous times in the canonical collections, for example, al-Bukhārī, *Ṣaḥīh*, *aḥādīth al-anbiyā'* 4.55.558, *manāqib* 4.56.807 and 808, *maghāzī* 5.59.638, *faḍa'il al-Qur'ān* 6.61.578, *adab* 8.73.184, *murtaddīn* 9.84.64–8; *tawḥīd* 9.93.527, 651; Muslim, *Ṣaḥīḥ*, *zakāt* 5.44, 45; Mālik, *Muwaṭṭā*, *Qur'an* 15.10.

50. *Fut.*III.127–8 (Chap. 334), which corresponds to Sūrat Qāf, named for one of the enigmatic letters that begin certain suras and the initial letter of 'Qur'an'. The Throne, which has been linked symbolically to the Jewish Merkabah as described by the Prophet Ezekiel (see Beneito 'Ark of Creation', pp. 20ff.), is the Seat of the All-Merciful. See *Isfār*, The Lordly Voyage, pp. 50–2.

51. From a 1926 speech. In Polish: *Talking about God*, pp. 53–4; cited from Fox, *Five Books of Moses*.

> The Gospel is handed down from generation to generation *but it must reach each one of us brand new, or not at all.* If it is merely 'tradition' and not news, it has not been preached or not heard – it is not Gospel.
>
> But our ideas of news, the newspapers' idea of news, might lead us to believe that any word *except* what came from God was news. As if what was said by God had to be so fixed, so determined, so rigid in its set form that it could never be anything new, never unpredictable, never astonishing, never frightening. If there is no risk in revelation, if there is no fear in it, if there is no challenge in it, if it is not a word which creates whole new worlds, and new beings, if it does not call into existence a new creature, our new self, then religion is dead and God is dead. Those for whom the Gospel is old, and old *only*, have killed it for the rest of men. The life of the Gospel is its newness.[52]

In a cosmos that is constantly created afresh with each breath, it is only the ignorant who regard the recitation of a sacred text as unchanging and its interpretation as fixed. The person who has allowed the text to penetrate his heart – such as Abū Yazīd al-Bisṭāmī, who did not die until he had memorized the entire Qur'an – or made it manifest in every aspect of his demeanour, not only continually finds new meanings in the text, but also seeks to embody in his or her actions what the verses demand, as the Prophet Muhammad is said to have done:

> When the Messenger of God – peace and blessings upon him – in his recitation of the Qur'an came across a verse of grace … he would ask God for His favour. And when he encountered a verse of punishment and threat … he would seek God's protection. If he encountered a verse magnifying God … he would glorify Him in the way that that verse gave him to laud God. If he encountered a verse relating to narrative stories and the divine judgment that occurred in the centuries before him … he would interpret it. If he encountered a verse having to do with legal determination … he decided in himself to whom that legal determination would be

52. *Conjectures of a Guilty Bystander*, p.127. Author's italics.

> directed ... This is the very essence of meditating upon the verses of the Qur'an and understanding it.[53]

Ibn ʿArabī tends to favour interpretation that is both privileged by unveiling and firmly rooted in the Arabic language as opposed to *ta'wīl*, which in his view is an intellectual exercise that falls short of its aim and leads its practitioner astray. As a recent scholar of Sufi Qur'an commentaries puts it:

> It is this close attention to the etymological and grammatical possibilities of the text which distinguishes Ibn ʿArabī's approach to Qur'ānic interpretation, an approach based on the assumption that all the possible meanings which the Arabic language allows for any given word or group of words in the Qur'ān are valid. To reject any one of these meanings is to limit God's knowledge, to imply He was unaware of the various ways in which His Book could be interpreted.[54]

Tales of the Prophets (*qiṣaṣ al-anbiyā'*)[55]

The genre known as *qiṣaṣ al-anbiyā'*, or tales of the prophets, evolved from oral narratives circulating in the Arabian peninsula disseminated by individuals whose knowledge of the prophets derived chiefly from their interactions with People of the Book; in fact, some may have been Jewish converts to the Muslim faith. Although fragments of 8th- and 9th-century collections exist, it is really around the 10th century that the genre evolved to supplement the sometimes sketchy narrations given in the Qur'an. Drawing on Qur'an, *tafsīr*s, hadith, histories, Jewish and Christian midrash and oral legends, the stories of the prophets were popular compendia of moral exempla (*ʿibar*) appealing to the imagination because of their rhetorical power and engaging folk elements. Stories of the prophets often served as warnings of the fate of those who disobeyed Allah and were brought

53. *Fut.*III.128 (Chap. 334).

54. Sands, *Sufi Commentaries*, p.41.

55. For background, see *History of al-Ṭabarī*, trans. Brinner; al-Thaʿlabī, *ʿArā'is al-majālis fī qiṣaṣ al-anbiyā'*, trans. Brinner; al-Kisā'ī, *Tales of the Prophets*, trans. Thackston, Jr; Ibn Kathīr, *Qiṣaṣ al-anbiyā'*, trans. as *Stories of the Prophets* by Geme'ah; Tottoli, *Biblical Prophets*.

to ruin. In this they confirmed the Qur'an's oft-repeated injunction: 'Travel through the earth, and see what was the end of those who rejected Truth' (Q.3:137).

The most prominent writers of *qiṣaṣ al-anbiyā'* were Abū Jaʿfar Muḥammad al-Ṭabarī, author of the multi-volumed *Tā'rīkh al-rusul wa-l mulūk* (*History of the Messengers and Kings*)[56] and who also penned a notable *tafsīr*; Abū Isḥāq al-Thaʿlabī (d. 1036), who wrote the well-known *ʿArā'is al-majālis*; Muḥammad b. ʿAbd Allāh al-Kisā'ī (date uncertain), whose *Qiṣāṣ* contains a wealth of fantastical stories not found elsewhere; and ʿImād al-Dīn Ismāʿīl Ibn Kathīr (d. 1373).[57] Their works contain a host of Biblical and Qur'anic characters as well as legendary figures outside the Scriptures, many more than appear in the *Isfār* or the *Fuṣūṣ*.

Although of all the genres mentioned above, the *qiṣaṣ al-anbiyā'* literature seems the most akin to the *Isfār*'s subject matter and style, Ibn ʿArabī states that in this book he will not recount the well-known stories of the various prophets.[58] For the most part this is an accurate statement, although he draws heavily from both the Qur'an and popular tales that were well known to his audience. But it is clear that Ibn ʿArabī does not want to give a reading that would in effect close off the Book, which must descend upon its reader anew in every reading. 'The one for whom meaning is repeated in his recitation [of the Qur'an] has not recited it as it should be recited. This is an indication of his ignorance.'[59] For this reason, although there is a substantial pool of themes relating to the prophets to draw from, only certain ones are singled out for emphasis in the *Isfār*: Adam's 'fall', for example, as opposed to his being given the totality of Names or being created upon the form of the Real; Joseph's separation from his father rather than the usual emphasis on his skill as a dream interpreter. Hence the reader who is more familiar with the

56. *The History of al-Ṭabarī* runs to forty volumes in translation, only four of which belong to the *qiṣaṣ al-anbiyā'* genre.

57. For bibliography, see n. 55.

58. *Isfār*, Para. 45.

59. *Fut.*IV.367 (Chap. 559).

Shaykh's *Fuṣūṣ* or *Futūḥāt* will be surprised to see different facets in the stories of the prophets than they have previously encountered.

Date of Composition

The precise dating of the *Isfār* remains controversial. Although Gril[60] and Morris[61] write that it is an early work pertaining to the Shaykh's Maghribī period, I believe, in light of a number of factors which will be discussed below, that it is more likely a product of his 'middle' period, after he had left the West but had not yet settled in Damascus, which took place in 1223.

The holograph copy of the *Isfār* found in Konya, Yusuf Ağa 4859, upon which this translation is for the most part based,[62] displays a script more in keeping with the Shaykh's later holograph manuscripts, such as the second recension of the *Futūḥāt* – begun in 1234 and completed in 1238 – and the *Diwān*, completed in 1237.[63] In addition, it has been asserted by individuals experienced in handwriting analysis that the script is that of an elderly and perhaps infirm author.[64] But this does not mean that the *Isfār* itself belongs to the late period. We know that the Shaykh mentions the title of the *Isfār* in the *Futūḥāt*'s Chapters 82[65] and 309,[66] and refers to the notions of *isfār/asfār* in Chapters 191 and 337 of that work. But we find it mentioned also in the Shaykh's own list of his writings, the *Fihris al-mu'allafāt*,[67] composed in 1230, which provides us with a tentative *terminus ad quem*. As for the *terminus a quo*, the *Isfār*'s mention of the

60. See Gril, Introduction to *Dévoilement*, pp. xi–xii.

61. Review of Gril's edn. and trans. of the *Isfār*.

62. The initial pages are not extant. The holograph copy begins with The Lordly Voyage, Para. 10.

63. My thanks to Stephen Hirtenstein for pointing this out to me in correspondence.

64. Again, thanks are due to Stephen Hirtenstein for these observations.

65. *Fut.*II.155.

66. *Fut.*III.37.

67. *Fihris al-mu'allafāt*, ed. Affifi, 'The Works of Ibn 'Arabī', pp. 109–17 and 193–207.

town Yaqīn, situated near Hebron, which the Shaykh visited in 1206, and where he composed a treatise on certainty (*yaqīn*),[68] seems to be a good indication that this visit preceded the *Isfār*'s composition.

Although this is sheer speculation on our part, it appears that we might be able to pinpoint more exactly when and what occasioned the *Isfār*'s composition based on internal evidence found in the text. What we have called the Shaykh's 'middle' period, dating from 1201, when he left on Pilgrimage to Mecca never to return to his native land, and 1223 when he at last settled down in Damascus where he lived until his death in 1240, was a period he devoted to extensive wayfaring in the eastern Islamic world, crisscrossing Anatolia, Palestine and Iraq, with additional visits to Mecca and Egypt. In 1212 he found himself in Baghdad where he had a terrifying vision of the divine hidden deception that figures so strongly in the *Isfār*'s text. He describes this event in the *Futūḥāt*'s Chapter 231, On Deception (*makr*):

> When I was in Baghdad in the year 608 [1212], I saw in a visionary event that the doors of heaven had been opened and the storehouses of Divine Deception were descending like an omnipresent rain. I heard an angel saying, 'What deception has descended tonight!' and I awoke terrified. I considered the way to safety from that, and I could not find it except in knowledge of the Scale set up by the Law. So if anyone desires that God give him good and preserve him from the calamities of deception, let him never let the Scale of the Law drop from his hand.[69]

We will discuss the notion of the divine hidden deception in the Commentary. Suffice it to say here that not only is one of the journeys in the *Isfār* given the title 'The Voyage of Deception and Trial' but the final two journeys, Moses' 'Voyage of Fear' and his 'Voyage of Caution', are largely concerned with this subject. In addition, the text is full of admonition, caution and wariness. Thus it does not seem out of the question that the *Isfār*'s composition was inspired by both his peregrinations through the Islamic east, including

68. *K. al-Yaqīn*, ed. al-Fattāḥ.

69. *Fut.*II.530–1 (Chap. 231), trans. Chittick, *SPK*, pp.267–8, slightly modified. See also *Fut.*III.155 (Chap. 340).

Palestine, traditional home of the Old Testament/Hebrew Bible figures that people his text, and his terrifying vision of Deception which occurred in Baghdad.

Influence of the Isfār

Ibn 'Arabī's views on spiritual travel had direct influence on his followers, primarily in the eastern Islamic lands. Ḥaydar Āmulī (14th century), who considered himself a disciple of Ibn 'Arabī, also described the 100 stations and 1000 substations of mystical journeys[70] in his *Risālat al-Jadāwil* (Treatise of the Diagrams), also known as *Madārij al-sālikīn fī marātib al-'arifīn* (Routes of the Wayfarers in the Levels of the Gnostics).[71]

But the most important work to be influenced by Ibn 'Arabī's enumeration of initiatic voyages was the great Iranian philosopher Mullā Ṣadrā's (d. 1640) *Kitāb al-ḥikma al-muta'āliya fī al-asfār al-'aqliyya al-arba'a (The Transcendent Wisdom Concerning the Four Voyages of the Intellect).*[72] Mullā Ṣadrā may have drawn his inspiration from the *Futūḥāt* rather than from the *Isfār*, however, in that the *Isfār* limits the voyages to three: the voyage from God, the voyage to Him, and the voyage in Him. Mullā Ṣadrā's four voyages, each one a section of his *magnum opus*, are: (1) the voyage from creation/creature (this world) (*khalq*) to the Real (*Ḥaqq*), which introduces the seeker to basic philosophical questions with respect to definitions and ontology. 'In this journey, the seeker moves away from multiplicity and phenomenal deception towards unity and an awareness of the underlying nature of reality';[73] (2) the voyage in the Real with the Real, deals with God's nature and His Attributes, and includes a discussion of the natural sciences: on an initiatic level '[it] is the

70. See Corbin, *The Voyage and the Messenger*, p. 83; see also pp. 138–9.

71. See Āmulī, *Jami' al-asrār wa-manba'al-anwār*, trans. Yate as *Inner Secrets of the Path*. From the Introduction.

72. Lutfi *et al.*, *Shirkat Dār al-Ma'ārif al-Islāmiyyah*, *c.* 1958–69.

73. Rizvi, 'Mulla Sadra'.

stage of the mystic's absorption in the divine essence and his effacement of the self';[74] (3) the voyage from the Real to creation with the Real, deals with issues of theodicy: 'For the mystic, this is the return to sobriety and a realization of the duties of moral agency in this world';[75] and (4) the voyage with the Real in creation, deals with 'the development of the human soul, its origin, becoming and end';[76] '[t]his is the final stage of the mystic's journey, a recognition that everything as a unified whole reflects the ontological unity of the divine ...'.[77]

The influence of Ibn 'Arabī can be seen in the practical and initiatic counterpart to Mullā Ṣadrā's theoretical theosophy as the seeker journeys from the phenomenal world of sense and ego to the stages of ego-annihilation (*fanā'*) and subsistence in God (*baqā'*), followed in its highest expression by a 'return' to 'the world' as God's steward.

In recent years, thanks to Denis Gril's admirable bilingual French and Arabic edition, the *Isfār* has reached a modern audience, not all of them primarily attracted to the esoteric intricacies of the Shaykh's thought but rather to his thoughts that are applicable to the actual process of travel. In a Paris bookstore, the noted travel writer Cees Nooteboom, intrigued by the word 'voyage' in the title and charmed by the Arabic script, picked up a copy of the *Isfār* and, after perusing its contents, purchased it. At the very beginning of his *Nomad's Hotel: Travels in Time and Space*, he speaks about Ibn 'Arabī's reflection on the ubiquitousness of voyaging with respect to everything in existence, and concurs with the Shaykh on how voyaging unveils people's characters (or one's own, he notes, if travelling solo).

74. Ibid.

75. Ibid.

76. n.a. 'Ṣadr al-Dīn Muḥammad Shirazī (or known as: Mullā Ṣadrā)' www.iranchamber.com/personalities/msadra/mulla_sadra.php., accessed May 2014.

77. Rizvi, 'Mulla Sadra'.

Description of the Manuscripts[78]

(Y) Yusuf Ağa 4859 [fols. 12a–48b]. Holograph, undated. Conserved in Konya. Lacking the first several pages. The text begins with 'The Lordly Voyage from the Cloud to the Throne'. Forms the base of the present edition.

(K) Koprülü 713 fols. 30–44. Copied in Konya at the end of Jumādā I 663 H (and not in 633, as stated by O. Yahia) – that is, 25 years after the death of the Shaykh – from his holograph conserved without doubt in the library of Ṣadr al-Dīn Qūnawī. This text, written in an ordinary *naskhī*, is very legible and in great part vocalized.

(B) Beyazit 3785 fols. 94a–131b. Copied in Rabīʿ I 716 H in Kayseri in a beautiful *thuluth*, it resembles K, from which it diverges only rarely in any notable sense. The diacritic points are often missing, but the text is sometimes vocalized. It belonged to the library of Shams al-Dīn Fanārī, according to O. Yahia. There is no evidence that it was copied from the original as the latter claims. Whatever the truth of its provenance, it is said to have been collated.

(S) Shehit Ali 1340 fols. 153b–180b. Copied in 789 H in an ordinary and careless *naskhī*, the text is often faulty. However, copying errors are not enough to account for certain variants. This manuscript must derive from an original that is different from the two preceding ones. This is often the case with Ibn ʿArabī, who is known to have disseminated different redactions of the same work.

(L) British Library OR 8348 14 fols. Copied in ordinary and cramped *naskhī*, the diacritic points are often omitted. It resembles the printed text, which leads one to suppose an Indian

78. With the exception of Y and F, the following description has been mostly taken from D. Gril's French edition, pp.xxxii–iii. Since Gril used K as his base, we have modified the translation to reflect this change.

origin, especially since certain errors betray the non-Arab origin of the copyist (For example, *bi-anwār al-ilāhiyya* instead of *bi-l-anwār* or *bi-smi al-ilāhī* instead of *bi-l-ismi*).

(Z) Zāhiriyya 9205 fols. 134b–151b.

(Zh) Zāhiriyya 9655 27 fols. Copied in 1318 H. This very recent copy (1900) derives from the previous one, which is itself hardly any older. They both resemble manuscripts L and Z, into which they introduce new errors. Compare with M. Riyād al-Mālih, *Fihris makhṭūṭāt Dār al-kutub al-Ẓāhiriyya, taṣawwuf*, Damascus 1978, I 79–80, no. 102 and 103.

(F) Fakhr al-Dīn al-Khurāsānī pp. 587–600. Copied in 814 H. From the circle of Sharaf al-Dīn al-Jabartī, the teacher of ʿAbd al-Karīm al-Jīlī.

Some Remarks on the Translation

To say that the writings of Ibn ʿArabī are difficult is a great understatement. The reader who plunges into this vast and shoreless sea expecting smooth waters will be disconcerted to find him or herself buffeted about by increasing waves of disorientatation and bewilderment. In short, the reader should anticipate a voyage in which the intellect will prove an inadequate compass but in which the heart alone can serve as rudder.

It is a commonplace to announce *traduttore traditore* – the translator is a traitor – by frustrated practitioners of the craft, but this seems particularly true in the case of attempting to translate the Shaykh al-Akbar, for whom the Arabic language reveals the reverberations of divine creation itself. Words and meanings are inextricably bound, sound and sense joined in intimate union. And behind it all extends a universe of infinite mystery, radiating from a centre of unknowable fullness, requiring the reader to stretch beyond his or her initial limitations to attempt to understand.

The translation that follows can only hint at the richness of the original. Much of the subtlety and nuance, the graceful turns of phrase and linguistic magic, will be lost in transferring the *Isfār* to its English setting. Notes have been appended to provide assistance to the non-Arabic reader, while references to clarifying passages in the shaykh's voluminous writings – much of which remains untranslated – are intended for further perusal by those able to enjoy the shaykh in his own language. Notes to the translation are primarily sources, cross-references and explanation of terms and concepts that may be obscure; a full commentary comes at the end of the translation.

I have retained the paragraph numbering found in Denis Gril's French translation of the *Isfār* both in the Arabic text and the English translation. Translation of Qur'anic quotations, which are italicized in my translation of the text, are eclectic and often altered to render more adequately Ibn ʿArabī's expressions and meanings. In general, I use the translations of Muhammad Marmeduke Pickthall and Yusuf Ali. I have purposely chosen to leave Qur'anic quotations in an archaic form rather than to give them a more contemporary ring, since I think that maintaining the different linguistic registers is warranted. Bracketed words, for purposes of explanation or clarification, have been kept to a minimum in order to facilitate reading.

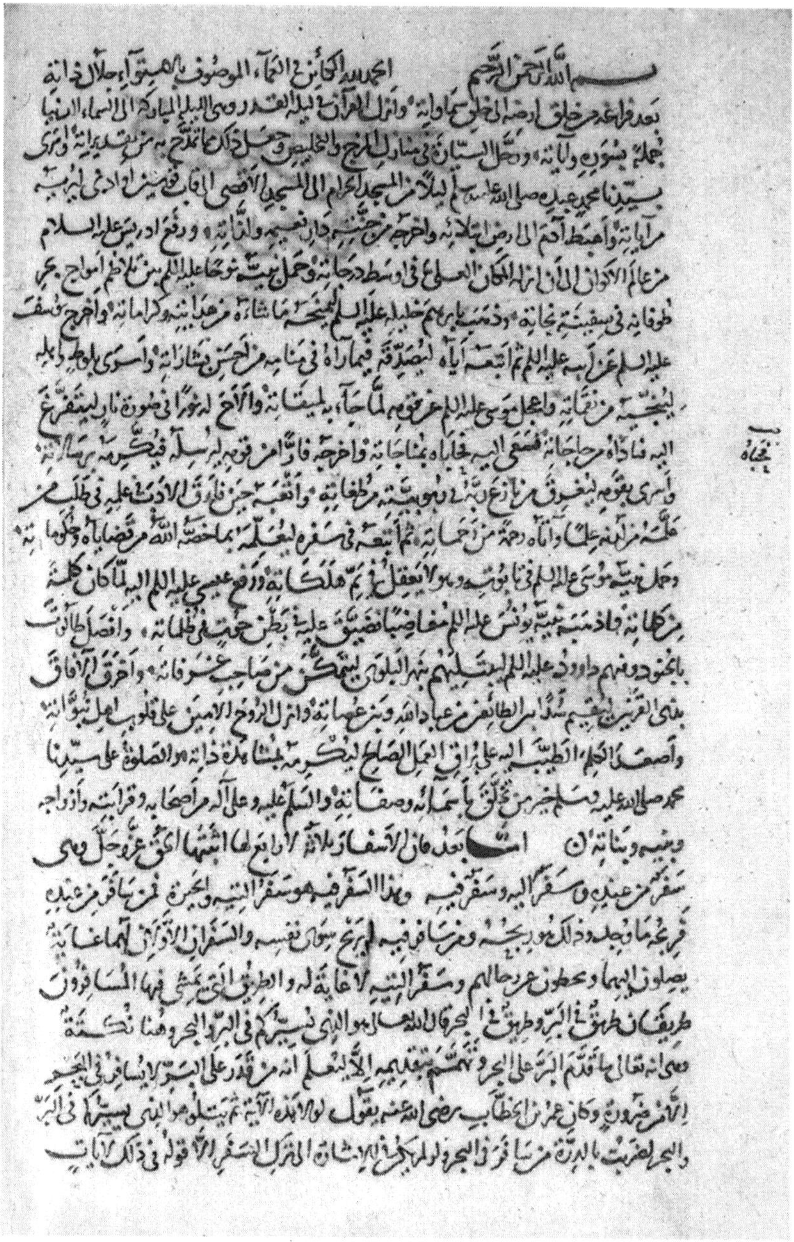

بسم الله الرحمن الرحيم الحمد لله الكائن في العماء الموصوف بالاستواء وإحلال خزائنه
بعد فراغه من خلق أرضه إلى خلق سماواته وأنزل القرآن في ليلة القدر وهي الليلة المباركة إلى السماء الدنيا
جملة بسوره وآياته وفصل السيارة في منازل البروج والتحليل ... وجعل ذلك مما تمدح به من تقدير آياته وأسرى
بسيدنا محمد عبده صلى الله عليه وسلم ليلاً من المسجد الحرام إلى المسجد الأقصى إلى قاب قوسين أو أدنى ليريه
من آياته وأهبط آدم إلى الأرض لابتلائه وأخرجه من جنته دار نعيمه ولذاته ورفع إدريس عليه السلام
من عالم الأكوان إلى ... المكان العلي في أوسط درجاته وحمل نبيه نوحاً عليه السلام بين تلاطم أمواج بحر
طوفانه في سفينة نجاته وذهب بإبراهيم خليله عليه السلام ... ما شاء من ... بنيه وكراماته وأخرج يوسف
عليه السلام عن أبيه عليه السلام ثم أتبعه إياه ليصدق فيما رآه في منامه من حسن بشاراته وأسرى بلوط بأهله
لينجيه من نقماته وأعجل موسى عليه السلام عن قومه لما جاء به لميقاته وآنس له نوراً في صورة نار ليستفرغ
إليه ما أداه من حاجاته فسعى إليه فناداه بمناجاته وأخرجه فاراً من قومه ليرسله فيكرمه برسالاته
وأسرى بقومه ليغرق من نازعه في ربوبيته من طغاته وأتعبه حين ... الأدب عليه في طلب من
علمه من لدنه علماً وآتاه رحمة من رحماته ثم أتبعه في سفره ليعلمه بما خصه الله من قضاياه وحكوماته
وحمل نبيه موسى عليه السلام في تابوته وهو لا يعقل في يم ملكاته ورفع عيسى عليه السلام إليه لما كان كلمة
من كلماته وأذهب نبيه يونس عليه السلام مغاضباً فضيق عليه في بطن حوته في ظلماته وأفصل طالوت
بالجنود وفيهم داود عليه السلام ليبتليهم بنهر البلوى ليميز من صاحب غرفاته وأخرق الآفاق
بذي القرنين ليقيم سد ... الطائفين من عباد الله ومن عصاته وأنزل الروح الأمين على قلوب أهل نبواته
وأصعد الكلم الطيب إليه على براق العمل الصالح ليكرمه بمشاهدة ذاته والصلاة على سيدنا
محمد صلى الله عليه وسلم خير من تحقق بأسمائه وصفاته والسلام عليه وعلى آله من أصحابه وقرابته وأزواجه
وبنيه وبناته أما بعد فإن الأسفار ثلاثة لا رابع لها أثبتها الحق عز وجل وهي
سفر من عنده وسفر إليه وسفر فيه وهذا السفر فيه هو سفر التيه والحيرة فمن سافر من عنده
فربحه ما يجده وذلك ... ومن سافر فيه لم يربح سوى نفسه والسفران الأولان لهما غاية
يصلون إليها ويحطون عن رحالهم وسفر التيه لا غاية له والطريق التي يمشي فيها المسافرون
طريقان طريق في البر وطريق في البحر قال الله تعالى هو الذي يسيركم في البر والبحر وهنا نكتة
وهي أنه تعالى ما قدم البر على البحر ... بتقديمه إلا ليعلم أنه من قدر على البر لا يسافر في البحر
إلا من ضرورة وكان عمر بن الخطاب رضي الله عنه يقول لولا هذه الآية ... يسيركم في البر
والبحر لضربت بالدرة من سافر في البحر ولو ... الإشارة إلى ترك السفر الأول قوله في ذلك آيات

نجاته(?)

Folio 30b, the first page of the text from Koprülü MS. 713, dated 663 H.

THE SECRETS OF VOYAGING

كتاب الاسفار عن نتائج الأسفار

Kitāb al-Isfār ʿan natāʾij al-asfār

By
Muḥyī al-dīn Muḥammad
b. ʿAlī Ibn al-ʿArabī

Translation and Edition

Arabic text edited by Denis Gril,
Abrar Ahmad Shahi and Angela Jaffray

فهرس الموضوعات

(الأرقام تشير إلى الفقرات)

خطبة الكتاب	١
الكلام في السفر	٢–٩
سفر رباني من العماء إلى عرش الاستواء	١٠–١٢
سفر الخلق والأمر وهو سفر الابداع	١٣–١٧
سفر القرآن العزيز	١٨–٢١
سفر الرؤية في الآيات والاعتبار	٢٢–٢٥
سفر الابتلاء وهو سفر الهبوط	٢٦–٣١
سفر إدريس وهو سفر العز والرفعة	٣٢–٣٦
سفر النجاة وهو سفر نوح	٣٧–٤٠
سفر الهداية وهو سفر إبراهيم	٤١–٤٣
سفر الاقبال وعدم الالتفات	٤٤–٤٥
سفر المكر والابتلاء في ذكر يعقوب ويوسف	٤٦–٤٩
سفر الميقات الالهي لموسى	٥٠–٥٤
سفر الرضى	٥٥–٥٧
سفر الغضب والرجوع	٥٨–٦٠
سفر السعي على العائلة	٦١–٦٣
سفر الخوف	٦٤–٦٧
سفر الحذر	٦٨–٧٠

Contents

(The numbers correspond to the paragraphs in the text)

Prologue	1
On Voyaging	2–9
The Lordly Voyage from the Cloud to Sitting on the Throne	10–12
The Voyage of Creation and Command	13–17
The Voyage of the Noble Qur'an	18–21
The Voyage of the Vision in the Signs and Inner Signification	22–25
The Voyage of Trial (Adam)	26–31
The Voyage of Height and Elevation (Enoch)	32–36
The Voyage of Salvation (Noah)	37–40
The Voyage of Guidance (Abraham)	41–43
The Voyage of Approach and No Turning Back (Lot)	44–45
The Voyage of Ruse and Trial (Jacob and Joseph)	46–49
The Voyage of Divine Appointment (Moses)	50–54
The Voyage of Good Pleasure (Moses)	55–57
The Voyage of Anger and Return (Moses)	58–60
The Voyage of Striving on Behalf of One's Household (Moses)	61–63
The Voyage of Fear (Moses)	64–67
The Voyage of Caution (Moses)	68–70

كتاب الاسفار عن نتائج الأسفار

بسم الله الرحمن الرحيم
وصلى الله على سيدنا محمد وعلى آله وسلم

خطبة

١ الحمد لله الكائن في العماء، الموصوف بالاستواء، جلال[1] ذاته، بعد فراغه من خلق أرضه إلى خلق سماواته * وأنزل القرآن في ليلة القدر وهي الليلة المباركة إلى السماء الدنيا جملة بسوره وآياته *

١ ل: جلا

THE SECRETS OF VOYAGING

In the Name of God the All-Merciful, the All-Compassionate.

God's blessings upon our Master Muhammad and his people.

Prologue

§1 Praise be to God, who was in the Cloud,[1] who is described as sitting [on the Throne][2] – the glory of His Essence – after completing the creation from His earth to His heavens.

He sent down the Qur'an on the Night of Power[3] – the *Blessed Night*[4] – to the nearest heaven, with all of its suras and verses.

1. According to a hadith (found in *Al-Jāmi' al-ṣaḥīḥ, wa-huwa sunan al-Tirmidhī, Tafsīr*, Sura 11:1; Ibn Māja, al-Sunan, Muqaddima 13; Aḥmad IV 11, 12), the Prophet Muhammad was asked: 'Where was (*kāna*) our Lord before He created the creatures?' He answered: 'He was in a Cloud, above and below which was no air.' Although no temporal or spatial terms apply to God in His unknowable Essence, human beings must grapple with the limits of language, which inevitably assigns a time to actions. The Arabic *kāna* is sometimes used to denote an atemporal existence rather than a simple past tense. Ibn 'Arabī points this out in *Fut.* II.692 (Chap. 299): 'The word *kāna* derives from *kawn* (being), which is the same as *wujūd* (existence). So the Prophet may as well have said: "God is existent, and nothing is with Him in His Being."' For an alternative translation of *kā'in* as 'coming to be', in which the evolving relationship of the Divine to creation from the point of view of creation can be traced, see Chittick, *SPK*, p. 125. See also *Fut.*II.310 (Chap. 177), where the Shaykh outlines five *kaynūnāt* – relationships of God's being: (1) being in the Cloud; (2) being on the Throne; (3) being in the heavens; (4) being in the earth; and (5) the all-encompassing being with all existent things.

The word 'Cloud' (*'amā'*) in similar fashion strives to indicate a nebulous condition of pure potentiality preceding creation. In the *Futūḥāt*, this Cloud is equated with the absolute nondelimited Imagination in which all forms are revealed or are 'opened up' (*f-t-ḥ*). The Shaykh also claims that the Cloud is the Real, since it is the unmanifest Breath within the Breather that becomes manifest in all things (*Fut.*II.310, Chap. 177).

2. See Q.20:5: 'The All-Merciful, who sits on the Throne.' This decidedly anthropomorphic description was dealt with by interpreters in a number of ways; the theological school of al-Ash'arī, for example, claimed that God does indeed sit but not in the same way that sitting can be attributed to human beings.

3. Arabic: *laylat al-qadr*. See Q.97:1–5.

4. See Q.44:3: 'We sent it down in a Blessed Night, for We wish to warn.' According to Ibn 'Arabī, the Night of Power can be any night of the year; it is not limited to a certain night within the month of Ramadan. He claimed to have seen it occur several times outside the month of Fasting. See *Fut.*I.658 (Chap. 71); IV.486 (Chap. 560), hence it is best to treat every

ورحّل السيارة في منازل المزج والتخليص، وجعل ذلك مما تمدّح[٢] به من تقديراتِه * وأسرى بسيّدنا محمد عبده، صلى الله عليه وسلم، ﴿لَيْلاً مِنَ الْمَسْجِدِ الْحَرَامِ إِلَى الْمَسْجِدِ الْأَقْصَى﴾ إلى ﴿قَابَ قَوْسَيْنِ أَوْ أَدْنَى﴾ ليريه من آياتِه * وأهبط آدم إلى أرض ابتلائه، وأخرجه من جنّته دار نعيمه[٣] ولذّاته * ورفع إدريس، عليه السلام، من عالم الأكوان إلى أن أنزله المكان العلي في أوسط درجاته *

٢ ش، ل: يمدح
٣ ل: نعمه

He caused the planets[5] to travel[6] in the waystations of mingling and purification,[7] and made that one of the decrees[8] in which He glories.

He made our Master Muhammad, His servant – God's blessing and peace be upon him – journey *by night from the Masjid al-Ḥarām*[9] *to the Masjid al-Aqṣā*[10] (Q.17:1) to *the distance of two bows' length or nearer* (Q.53:9) in order that He *might show him some of* His *signs* (Q.17:1).

He sent Adam down to the earth in order to try him, removing him from His Garden, the abode of His favour and delights.[11]

He raised Enoch (Idrīs) – peace be upon him – from the world of generated beings, then made him descend at the high place in the centre of His [cosmic] degrees.[12]

---

night's voluntary supplications as if they have the weight of those occurring on the Night of Power, since the Blessed Night moves around the year. See Beneito and Hirtenstein, 'Ibn 'Arabī's Treatise'.

5. Arabic: *sayyāra*. From the root *s-y-r*, which carries the connotations of moving, setting out, travelling. See Commentary for a discussion of this term.

6. Arabic: *raḥḥala*. See Commentary for a discussion of this term associated with voyaging.

7. Arabic: *al-mazj wa-al-takhlīṣ*. This may have to do with the conjunctions (mingling) and disjunctions (purification) of the planets, which play a role in the processes of generation and corruption in the cosmos. See also *Fut.*II.435 (Chap. 198, section 16) where these two terms are also conjoined to describe the work of God's shaping the cosmos with His Name 'the Wise' (*al-Ḥakīm*): 'The cosmos belongs to mingling and the afterlife belongs to purification.' In this case, the two terms seem to suggest alchemical processes, in that this world is a place of multiplicity and mixtures (various corruptions of gold) while the afterlife returns the soul to the pure gold of its essence. There is also a connection between the planets and alchemy in that each of the planets is associated with one of the baser metals.

8. Arabic: *taqdīrāt*. From the same root as *qadr* (see above, n.4, *laylat al-qadr*), *q-d-r*, in its second form, has to do with exercising careful thought when arranging or determining some affair. When the subject is God, the verb often has to do with His decreeing, determining, and predestining. It is also found in the Qur'an with the sense of God's making or placing, as in: 'He made for [the moon] its mansions' (Q.10:5) and 'He made therein its foods in due proportion' (Q.41:9). See Lane, *Lexicon*, vol. 7, p.2495.

9. Literally: the Inviolable Place of Worship, Mecca.

10. Respectively translated as the Inviolable Mosque (literally 'place of prostration'), namely Mecca, and the Far Distant Mosque, commonly interpreted to mean Jerusalem. Neither of these geographical sites is named in the Qur'an, hence early commentators differed in their assignation of these mosques to actual locales. See Commentary, pp.200–2.

11. For Adam's 'Fall', see Q.2:35–8; 7:19–25.

12. See Q.19:56–7: 'And make mention in the Book of Enoch/Idrīs. Lo! He was most veracious and a prophet; and We raised him to a high positon.' God raised Enoch to the sun,

وحمل نبيّه نوحاً، عليه السلام، بين تلاطم أمواج بحر طوفانه في سفينة نجاته * وذهب بإبراهيم خليله، عليه السلام، ليمنحه ما شاء من هدايته وكراماته * وأخرج يوسف، عليه السلام، عن أبيه،عليه السلام، ثم أتبعه أباه ليصدقه فيما رآه في منامه من أحسن بشاراته * وأسرى بلوط وأهله ليُنجيه من نقماته * وأعجل موسى، عليه السلام، عن قومه لما جاء ربه لميقاته * وألاح له نوراً في صورة نار ليتفرَّغ إليه فناداه من حاجاته * فسعى إليه فحاباه بمناجاته * وأخرجه فاراً من قومه ليرسله بتكرمته برسالاته * وأسرى بقومه

He bore His prophet Noah – peace be upon him – among the crashing waves of the sea of His flood, within the Ark[13] of His salvation.[14]

He travelled with His intimate friend Abraham – peace be upon him – in order to bestow upon him His abundant guidance and grace.[15]

He made Joseph – peace be upon him – leave his father – peace be upon him – and then made his father follow him in order to confirm the finest of tidings he had seen in his dreams.[16]

He made Lot and his family journey by night[17] in order to save him from His vengeance.[18]

He made Moses – peace be upon him – hasten from his people when his Lord came to the appointed meeting.[19] He made a light shine for him in the form of a fire so that he would concern himself solely with Him, and He called to him from the source of his needs.[20] He hastened to Him, and He favoured him with His intimate conversation.[21] He caused him to set out, fleeing from his people,[22] in order that He might send him as a prophet, by graciously bestowing upon him His message. And He made his people journey by night

---

which is in the fourth – or middle – heaven. With respect to the degrees of existence, this degree is the centre, the place of the spiritual Pole (*quṭb*) around whom all of existence turns.

13. Arabic: *safīna*, literally 'ship'. See Commentary for a discussion of the various terms for Ark.

14. Noah's story is found in: Q.7:59–64; 10:71–4; 11:25–49; 23:23–31; 26:105–22; 54:9–17; and 71:1–25.

15. Arabic: *karāmāt*. May also be translated as 'charismatic gifts'.

16. Joseph's story is found chiefly in Q.12:1–111.

17. See Q.11:81: 'So travel with thy people in a part of the night, and let not one of you turn round – [all] save thy wife. Lo! That which smiteth them will smite her [also]. Lo! Their tryst is [for] the morning. Is not the morning nigh?'

18. Note that the mention of Lot is out of order here, both chronologically according to the Bible, and in the chapter sequence of the *Isfār*, where Lot follows Abraham and comes before Joseph. In the *Fuṣūṣ* as well, the chapter on Lot is displaced chronologically. It comes eight chapters after the chapter on Abraham and four after the chapter on Joseph.

19. See Q.7:143.

20. The story of Moses and the Fire (the biblical Burning Bush) is found in Q.20:9–16; 27:7–9; 28:29–30.

21. Arabic: *munājāt*. See *Fut.*II.571ff. (Chap. 270).

22. 'His people' here meaning Pharaoh's family. Moses fled after having killed an Egyptian who was mistreating a Hebrew slave. See Q.28:15; 26:21.

ليغرَق من نازع ربَّه في ربوبيته من طُغاته * وأتبعه حين فارق الأدب في علمه في طلب من علَّمه من لَدُنْه علماً، وآتاه رحمة من رحماته * ثم أتبعه في سفره ليعلِّمه بما خصه الله[4] من قضاياه وحكوماته (1) * وحمل نبيَّه موسى، عليه السلام، في تابوته وهو لا يعقل في يمّ هلكاته * ورفع عيسى، عليه السلام، إليه لما كان كلمة من كلماته *

٤ ب، ش، ل: + به

in order to drown one of His tyrants[23] who vied with his Lord over His Lordship.[24] When he departed from courtesy with respect to his knowledge,[25] He made him go in search of the one to who[m He] *taught knowledge from* His *Presence* (Q.18:65) and gave mercy from His mercy.[26] Then He made him continue on in his voyage in order to teach him those decrees and judgements of His for which God had singled him out. And He carried His prophet Moses – peace be upon him – in His ark[27] upon the waters which would have destroyed him before he had reached the age of reason.

He elevated Jesus – upon him be peace – to Him, since he was one of His Words.[28]

23. The reference is, of course, to Pharaoh.

24. See Q.79:24: 'And proclaimed: "I [Pharaoh] am your Lord the Highest."'

25. See also *Fut.*I.203 (Chap. 31). As Gril tells us in the notes to his translation (p. 2, n. 4), there is a prophetic tradition that attests to Moses' lack of courtesy: 'Moses was preaching among the Children of Israel. Someone asked him: "Who is the wisest of men?" He answered: "I am." God took him to task because he had not referred his knowledge back to Him. He revealed to him: I have a servant where the two rivers meet who is wiser than you.' See al-Bukhārī, *Ṣaḥīḥ*, *tafsīr* Surat al-Kahf, VI:110. That person was, of course, al-Khiḍr, whose story is told in Sura 18, al-Kahf. Another example of lack of courtesy on Moses' part was his asking his Lord to show Himself: 'And when Moses came to Our appointment and his Lord had spoken unto him, he said: "My Lord! Show me [Thy Self], that I may gaze upon Thee (Q.7:143)."' 'Moses was prevented from the vision only because he asked for it without a divine command being revealed to him.' *Fut.*III.116 (Chap. 331). The *Isfār* gives two related instances of this danger and temptation, once in connection with Abraham who asks for a righteous son and consequently is tested with the near-sacrifice of Ishmael [see Para. 41], and once in connection with Joseph, who manages to resist the possibility of acquiring sciences from the Universal Soul because no command has come regarding it [Para. 48]. All of these examples are associated with God's 'jealousy', which we discuss in the Commentary.

26. This passage refers to Moses' encounter with al-Khiḍr.

27. Here the Arabic is *tābūt*, which also means 'chest, coffer, coffin' and is the word used for the Ark of the Covenant (see Q.2:248). Moses was placed in this 'ark' when he was an infant in order to save him from Pharaoh's decree. See Q.20:39. This story is not part of the Moses cycle of six voyages described in the *Isfār*.

28. 'Behold! The angels said: "O Mary! Allah giveth thee glad tidings of a Word from Him"' (Q.3:45); 'Christ Jesus the son of Mary was an apostle of Allah, and His Word, which He bestowed on Mary, and a spirit proceeding from Him' (Q.4:171). With respect to God's raising him, see Q.3:55: 'Behold! Allah said: "O Jesus! I will take thee and raise thee to Myself and clear thee [of the falsehoods] of those who blaspheme"', and in response to the dispute over whether Jesus died on the Cross or not, the Qur'an replies: 'Nay, Allah raised him up unto Himself; and Allah is Exalted in Power, Wise' (Q.4:158). There is no further mention of Jesus in the *Isfār*.

وأذهب نبيَّه يونس، عليه السلام، مغاضِباً فضيق عليه في بطن حوتٍ في ظلماته * وأفصل طالوتَ بالجنود وفيهم داود، عليه السلام، ليبْتَلِيَهم بنهر البلوى ليتمكن مَن صاحب غرفاته (2) * وأخرق الآفاق بذي القرنين ليقيمْ سداً بين الطائعين من عباد الله وبين عُصاته (3) * وأنزل الروح الأمين على قلوب أهل نُبُوّاته (4) * وأصعد الكلِم الطيّب إليه على بُراق العمل الصالح ليُكْرِمه بمشاهدة ذاته (5)

ه ل: فيقيم

He made His prophet Jonah – upon him be peace – set forth full of anger, and confined him in His dark places in the belly of the whale.[29]

He made Saul *set out with* his *army*, among whom was David – peace be upon him – to test them with the river of tribulation,[30] in order to give power to the one who cupped his hands.[31]

He split the horizons with the Possessor of the Two Horns[32] in order to make a barrier between those of God's servants who obey Him and those who disobey.

He sent the Trustworthy Spirit[33] upon the hearts of those worthy of His prophecy.[34]

He made the good words ascend to Him upon the Burāq[35] of the *righteous deed*[36] in order to honour [Muhammad] with contemplation of His Essence.[37]

29. See Q.37:139ff. There is no further mention of Jonah in the *Isfār*.

30. See Q.2:249: 'And when Saul set out with the army, he said: "Lo! Allah will try you by [the ordeal] of a river. Whosoever therefore drinketh thereof he is not of me, and whosoever tasteth it not is of me, save him who taketh [thereof] in the cup of his hand." But they drank thereof, all save a few of them. And after he had crossed [the river], he and those who believed with him, they said: "We have no power on this day against Goliath and his hosts." But those who knew that they would meet their Lord exclaimed: "How many a little company hath overcome a mighty host by Allah's leave! Allah is with the steadfast."' The story recounts the Israelites' campaign against Goliath, when Saul put his army to the test to see who would follow him into battle. Those who tarried at a certain river to drink were the unfaithful, while those who followed him to victory were his loyal supporters.

31. There is no further mention of this figure in the *Isfār.*

32. Arabic: Dhū al-Qarnayn. He is often considered to be Alexander the Great. See Q.18:83–98. The story of the barrier against Gog and Magog is found in Q.18:94 and in various hadith. Gog and Magog were interpreted by some to be two evil Turkic tribes, who were restrained from harming people by a great wall that Dhū al-Qarnayn and the people built. In the final days, the wall will collapse and Gog and Magog will be unleashed on the world to wreak destruction. For the latest scholarship on the Alexander legend, including the story of Gog and Magog, see Doufikar-Aerts, *Alexander Magnus Arabicus*. There is no further mention of this figure in the *Isfār*.

33. The angel Gabriel.

34. See Q.26:192–4: 'And lo! It is a revelation of the Lord of the Worlds, which the Faithful Spirit hath brought down upon thy heart, that thou mayest be [one] of the warners.' *Ahl nubuwwātihi* can also mean 'the people of his [Muhammad's] prophecy', which would make sense of the plural 'hearts'.

35. The fabulous steed upon which Muhammad rode during his celestial ascent.

36. See Q.35:10: 'To Him ascends the good word. He exalts every righteous deed.'

37. According to a hadith found in numerous sources, Muhammad claimed that he was 'sent with the totality of words' (*jawāmiʿ al-kalim*), signifying the synthetic nature of the

* والصلاة على سيّدنا محمد، صلى الله عليه وسلم، خير من تخلّق بأسمائه وصفاته * والسلام عليه وعلى آله من أصحابه وقراباته وأزواجه وبنيه وبناتِه *

٢ أما بعد: فإن الأسفار ثلاثة، لا رابع لها أثبتها الحق – عز وجل – وهي سفر من عنده وسفر إليه وسفر فيه. وهذا السفر فيه هو سفر التِيه والحيْرة، فمن سافر من عنده فربِحه ما وُجِدَ[٦] وذلك هو ربحه. ومن سافر فيه[٧] لم يربح سوى نفسه. والسفران الأوّلان لهما غاية يصلون إليها ويحطّون

٦ شُكل في ك: وُجِدَ ؛ وفي ب: وَجَدَ

٧ ب، ش: إليه

Blessings upon our Master Muhammad – God's blessing and peace be upon him – the best of those who have assumed the attributes of His Names and Attributes.[38] Peace be upon him and his people among his companions, his intimates, his wives, his sons and his daughters.[39]

[The Three Voyages and the Two Routes]

§2 There are three kinds of voyage – not four. The Real – may He be magnified and glorified – has affirmed them. They are: the voyage *from* Him,[40] the voyage *to* Him and the voyage *in* Him. The voyage *in* Him is the voyage of wandering[41] and bewilderment. Whoever voyages *from* Him, his gain is what he finds[42] – that is his gain – while whoever voyages *to* Him,[43] gains nothing but Him. The first

Muhammadian revelation. Here these good words are personified as Muhammad himself riding Burāq, the personification of the righteous deed, on the night of his *mi'rāj*.

38. Assuming the Names and Attributes of God is a Sufi technical term. The seeker divests himself of his own egoic traits and clothes himself in the traits of the Divinity.

39. S. Hirtenstein in private correspondence has alluded to a subtle point in this otherwise formulaic phrase. By the insertion of the preposition *min* ('from among'), Ibn 'Arabī suggests that not all members of the mentioned groups are to be considered the Prophet's people. See a similar discussion regarding the People of the House and the People of the Qur'an, pp.275–7.

40. Arabic: *al-safar min 'indahu*. This could also be translated as 'the voyage [beginning] at Him'.

41. Arabic: *tīh*. It may also be translated as desert, trackless wilderness or labyrinth, as well as haughtiness and pride. The verb *tāha* can also mean to wander in one's mind, to become insane.

42. The root *w-j-d* can mean both 'be' and 'find'. In one manuscript (K) it is vocalized as passive: *wujida* – 'to be found', or 'to exist'; another (B) vocalizes it as active: *wajada* 'to find.' The phrase is thus ambiguous. But since Ibn 'Arabī in Para. 28 names Adam, Eve and Satan as examples of those who voyage '*min 'inda-llāh*' – from God's Presence – and gives what they have found (*wajada*), I am inclined to vocalize the word as '*wajada*'. The 'gain' for Adam and Eve is toil leading to felicity while the 'gain' for Satan is ease that leads to wretchedness.

43. MS. K has *fī* (= in), while MSS. B and S have *ilā* (= to). *Ilā* seems to make more sense in terms of balance since the other two voyages have already been described. We cannot determine what the author's intention was here, since the holograph manuscript is missing its preliminary paragraphs, including this one. If one prefers *fī* to *ilā* here, the translation could be read as 'He who voyages in Him gains only his own soul', a reading that is certainly possible. Note also that the pronoun 'H/him' is ambiguous in any case, and may refer to the Real or the voyager himself. For further description of the three voyages, see Para. 7.

عن رِحالهم. وسفر التيه لا غايةَ له. والطريق التي يمشي فيها المسافرون طريقان: طريق في البرّ وطريق في البحر. قال الله – عز وجل: ﴿هُوَ الَّذِي يُسَيِّرُكُمْ فِي الْبَرِّ وَالْبَحْرِ﴾ (يونس ٢٢) وهنا نكتة وهي أنه – تعالى – ما قدَّم البر على البحر وتهمَّم بتقديمه إلا ليُعلم أنه من قدر على البر لا يسافر في البحر إلا من ضرورة. (6) وكان عمر بن الخطاب، رضى الله عنه، يقول: لو لا هذه الآية – ثم يتلو ﴿هُوَ الَّذِي يُسَيِّرُكُمْ فِي الْبَرِّ وَالْبَحْرِ﴾ – لَضربتُ بالدِّرَة من سافر في البحر. ولو لم يكن في الاشارة إلى ترك السفر[٨] إلا قوله في ذلك: ﴿إِنَّ فِي ذَلِكَ لَآيَاتٍ لِكُلِّ صَبَّارٍ شَكُورٍ﴾ (لقمان ٣١ والشورى ٣٣) لكانت هذه الآية كافية. (7)

ثم نقول: وما منها سفر من هذه الثلاثة الأسفار إلا وصاحبه فيه على خطر إلا إن يكون محمولاً كالاسراء. فكل من سُوفِرَ به نجا، وكل من سافر من غير أن يُسافَر به فهو على خطر.[٩]

٨ ش: + في البحر

٩ ش: + عظيم

two voyages have a goal where they arrive and dismount from their journey, while the voyage of wandering has no goal.

The route the voyagers follow consists of two routes: a land route and a sea route. God the Most High said: *He it is who maketh you to go on the land and the sea* (Q.10:22). There is a subtle point here. The Most High placed *land* before *sea* and stressed its importance by placing it first[44] only to let one know that whoever is able to travel by land should not travel by sea except out of necessity. ʿUmar b. al-Khaṭṭāb[45] – may God be pleased with him – used to say: 'Were it not for this verse' – and he recited: *He it is who maketh you to go on the land and the sea* – 'I would have whipped whoever travels by sea.'[46] If the only indication to abandon the sea voyage were His words: *In that are signs for every steadfast, grateful [heart]* (Q.31:31; 42:33),[47] these verses would suffice.

Then we say that among these three voyages there is not one that does not expose its companion to danger unless he is carried as if on a Night Journey. Everyone who is made to voyage on such a journey is saved, while everyone who voyages without being taken on that journey is in danger.

44. The Qur'an always puts 'land' before 'sea' in this expression. See Q.6:59, 63, 97; 17:70; 30:40.

45. The second caliph.

46. I am unable to find the source of this tradition. It is known, however, that Caliph ʿUmar forbade sea travel for a time. See Khalilieh, *Islamic Maritime Law*, pp. 3–4.

47. Sura 31:31: 'Hast thou not seen how the ships glide on the sea by Allah's grace, that He may show you of His signs? Lo! Therein indeed are signs for every steadfast, grateful [heart].' Sura 42:32–3: 'And of His signs are the ships like banners on the sea. If He will He calmeth the wind so that they keep still upon its surface – Lo! Herein verily are signs for every steadfast, grateful [heart].' Gril (*Dévoilement*, p. 4, n. 14) points out that there are two additional Qur'anic verses, ending with the same phrase that mention or hint at the perils of the sea: God's address to Moses: '"Bring out thy people from the depths of darkness into light, and teach them to remember the Days of Allah." Verily in this there are signs for such as are firmly patient and constant, grateful and appreciative' (Q.14:5); and referring to the people of Saba': 'But they said: "Our Lord! Place longer distances between our journey-stages": but they wronged themselves. At length We made them as a tale, and We dispersed them all in scattered fragments. Lo! Herein verily are signs for every steadfast, grateful heart' (Q.34:19).

٣ ثم إنه لما كان الوجود مبدأه على الحركة لم يتمكَّن أن يكون فيه سكون لأنه لو سكن لعاد إلى أصله وهو العدم. فلا يزال السفر أبداً في العالم العُلْويّ والسُفْليّ. والحقائق الالهية كذلك لا تزال في سفر غاديةً[١٠] ورائحة. وقد جاء النزول الرَّبَاني إلى السماء الدُّنيا (8) وقد جاء الاستواء إلى السماء على ما يعطيه التنزيه[١١] ونفْي المماثلة والتشبيه. وأما العالم العلوي فلا تزال الأفلاك دائرة بمن فيها لا تسكن، ولو سكنتْ بطُل الكون، وتمّ[١٢] نظام العالم وانتهى. وسِباحة[١٣] الكواكب في الأفلاك سفرٌ لها ﴿وَالْقَمَرَ قَدَّرْنَاهُ مَنَازِلَ﴾ (يس ٣٩) وحركات الأركان الأربعة، وحركات المولدات في كل دقيقة بالتغير[١٤] والاسْتِحالات[١٥] في كل نفَس، وسفر الأفكار في محمود ومذموم، وسفر الأنفاس من المتنفَّس،[١٦] وسفر الأبصار في المبصَرات يقظةً ونوماً وعبورها من عالم إلى عالم بالاعتبار. وهذا كله سفر بلا شك عند كل عاقل. وقد ذهب بعضهم إلى أن عالم

١٠ ل: عادية
١١ ط: التنزيل
١٢ ش: - تم
١٣ ب، ل، ط: سياحة
١٤ ب: والتغيير؛ ش: بالتعيين
١٥ ف: والاستحالة
١٦ ش: المتنفسين

§ 3 Since the principle of existence is movement there can be no stillness in existence because, were it to be still, it would return to its root, which is nonexistence. So the voyage in both the higher and lower world never ceases, and the divine realities also do not cease voyaging back and forth. The Lordly descent comes down to the nearest heaven[48] while the sitting on the Throne[49] ascends to the heavens in accordance with what transcendence and the denial of likeness or similarity bestow. As for the supernal world, the spheres do not cease revolving along with those within them, never still. Were they to become still, existence would come to an end and the order of the world would come to a completion and an end. The swimming[50] of the planets in their spheres is a voyage for them: *And for the moon We have appointed mansions* (Q.36:39), as is the movement of the four elements; the movement of generated beings in every minute; the changes and transmutations in every breath;[51] the voyage of the thoughts within the praiseworthy and blameworthy;[52] the voyage of the breaths in the process of breathing; the voyage of the eyes among the visible objects, while awake or asleep, and their passage[53] from one world to another through 'crossing over':[54] all of this is undoubtedly a voyage for every intelligent human being. Some hold the opinion that, since

48. Reference to the sound hadith, found in the canonical collections: 'Our Lord descends every night to the nearest heaven in the last third of the night and says: "Who will invoke Me so I can answer Him; who will ask Me so I may give to him, who will ask for My pardon so that I may forgive him?"' al-Bukhārī, *Ṣaḥīḥ*, *tahajjud* 14; Muslim, *Ṣaḥīḥ*, *musāfirīn* 172; Aḥmad b. Ḥanbal, *al-Musnad*, II 433; III, 34.

49. See Q.7:54; 10:3; 20:5; 57:4. See also Q.2:29; 41:11, where *istawā* is translated in a number of different ways, including 'turned to' (Pickthall), 'directed Himself' (Shakīr), or 'set His mind to' (Sale); see Online Qur'an Project, www.al-Quran.info, accessed May 2014.

50. Arabic: *sibāḥa*. The root also means 'to glorify'.

51. May also be read as *nafs* and translated as 'soul'.

52. See *Fut*.II.563 (Chap. 264), On Thoughts. In this chapter, Ibn ʿArabī calls thoughts 'ambassadors' (*sufarāʾ*) to the heart and says that they travel along the five paths of the qualification of acts by the Law (*sharīʿa*): obligatory, recommended, disliked, forbidden and permissible. *Sufarāʾ* derives from the same root as 'voyage' (*safar*).

53. Arabic: *ʿubūr*. The root of this word *ʿ-b-r* is one of the most important in Ibn ʿArabī's lexicon. We have discussed this root on p.20 of the Introduction and in the Commentary.

54. Arabic: *iʿtibār*. Again, this is from the root *ʿ-b-r*. It can also be translated as 'consideration', 'interpretation'. See Introduction and Commentary.

الأجسام من وقت خلَقَه الله لم يزل بجملته نازلاً، ولا يزال في الخلاء (9) الذي لا نهاية له. وعلى الحقيقة فلا نزال[١٧] في سفر أبداً من وقت نشأتنا ونشأة أصولنا إلى ما لا نهاية له. وإذا لاح لك منزل تقول[١٨] فيه: هذا هو الغاية، انفتح عليك منه طريق[١٩] آخر، تزوّدت منه وانصرفت. فما من منزل تُشْرِف[٢٠] عليه إلا ويمكن أن تقول: هو غايتي. ثم إنك إذا وصلتَ إليه، لم تلبثْ أن تخرج عنه راحلاً.

٤ وكم سافرتَ في أطوار المخلوقات إلى أن تكونْتَ دماً في أبيك وأُمّك. ثم اجتمعا من أَجْلك عن قصْد لظهورك أو غير قصد فانتقلتَ مَنِيًّا، ثم انتقلت من تلك الصورة علَقةً إلى مُضْغة إلي عظْم، ثم كُسِيَ العظم لحماً، ثم أُنْشِئْتَ[٢١] نشأةً أُخرى، ثم أُخرجتَ إلى الدنيا، فانتقلتَ إلى الطفولة، ومن الطفولة إلى الصِبا، ومن الصبا إلى الشباب، ومن الشباب إلى الفتوّة، ومن الفتوة إلى الكهولة، ومن الكهولة إلى الشيْخوخة، ومن الشيخوخة إلى الهَرَم وهو أرْذَل العُمر، (10) ومنه إلى البرزخ. فسافرتَ في البرزخ إلى الحشْر، ثم من الحشر أحدثْتَ سفراً إلى الصراط، إمّا إلى جنّة وإمّا إلى نار[٢٢] إن كنت من أهلها، وإن لم تكن من أهلها سافرت من النار إلى الجنة، ومن الجنة إلى كثيب الرؤية (11) فلا تزال تتردَّد[٢٣] بين الجنة

١٧ ك: تزال؛ ل: يزال

١٨ ط: نقول

١٩ ط: طرائق

٢٠ ل: يشرف

٢١ ل: انتشات

٢٢ ب، ش: الجنة ... النار

٢٣ ط: تردد

the time when God created it, the world of bodies does not cease in its totality to descend; it continues to be in the void, which is infinite. In reality, we never cease voyaging from the moment we and our roots are originated, *ad infinitum*. Whenever a waystation appears to you, and you say that it is the goal, another road opens up before you. You supply yourself with provisions for the road and take off. Whatever waystation you come upon, you may say: 'This is my goal.' But when you reach it, it is not long before you set out once more travelling.[55]

§4 How far did you voyage through the stages of created beings until you were generated as blood in your father and mother! Then they came together for your sake, either with or without the intention of bringing you into manifestation. You passed from being sperm; then you passed from that form to a blood clot, then to a tiny piece of flesh and then to bone. Then the bone was clothed with flesh. Then you were originated in another way and pushed out into this world. You passed to infancy, and from infancy to childhood, from childhood to adolescence, from adolescence to adulthood, from adulthood to middle age, and from middle age to old age, which is the worst part of life. From here, you will voyage to the *barzakh*[56] and voyage in the *barzakh* to the Gathering.[57] Then from the Gathering, you undertake a new voyage to the Bridge,[58] either to the Garden or to the Fire, if you are one of its people. If you are not one of its people, you will voyage to the Garden and from the Garden to the

55. The word used here is *rāḥil*, a rather unusual occurrence of this word in the *Isfār*.

56. *Barzakh*: the barrier; the liminal, intermediate world. See Bashier, *Ibn al-ʿArabi's Barzakh*.

57. Arabic: *al-ḥashr*. On the Day of Gathering – that is, Resurrection (*yawm al-ḥashr*) – humankind and animals will be gathered together and the souls of the dead will be reunited with their bodies. For a discussion of the various stages of Resurrection in classical Islam, see Smith and Haddad, *Islamic Understanding of Death and Resurrection*. See also *Fut.*I (Chap. 64) and III.438ff. (Chap. 371).

58. This Bridge, the *Ṣirāṭ*, passes through the Fire and leads to the Garden. For the blessed, its width will increase, easing their passage to Paradise, while for the wretched, it will become as narrow as a hair, resulting in their plunge into the fires of Hell.

والكثيب دائماً أبداً. وفي النار لا يزالون مسافرين من صعود إلى هبوط، ومن هبوط إلى صعود، مثل قِطَع اللحم في القِدرْ على النار ﴿كُلَّمَا نَضِجَتْ جُلُودُهُمْ بَدَّلْنَاهُمْ جُلُوداً غَيْرَهَا لِيَذُوقُوا الْعَذَابَ﴾ (النساء ٥٦).

٥ فما ثَمَّ سكونٌ أصلاً بل الحركة دائمة في الدنيا. ليلٌ ونهارٌ[٢٤] يتعاقبان،[٢٥] فتتعاقب[٢٦] الأفكار والحالات والهيئات بِتعاقُبهما[٢٧] وتعاقبِ الحقائق الالهية عليها،[٢٨] فتارةً تنزل[٢٩] على الاسم الالهي الرحيم، وتارةً على الاسم التوّاب، وتارة على الغفّار، وتارة على الرزّاق وعلى الوهّاب وعلى المُنْتقِم وكلِّ اسمٍ للحضرة الالهية، وهي أيضاً تنزل[٣٠] عليك بما عندها من الوهب والرزق والانتقام والتوبة والمغفرة والرحمة فنزولٌ[٣١] منك عليها بالطلب ونزول منها عليك بالعطاء.

٦ فإذا كان الأمر على هذا فيرجع العبد بفكره ينظر[٣٢] في الفرقان بين السفر الذي كلِّف أن يستعِدّ له وفيه سعادته أعني في الاستعداد وهو السفر إليه والسفر فيه والسفر من عنده، وهذه الأسفار كلها مشروعة له وبين السفر الذي ما كُلِّف أن يستعدّ له كالمشْي في الأرض في المُباح والسفر في

٢٤ ط: ليلاً و نهاراً
٢٥ ش: يتعاقبون
٢٦ ط: فيتعاقب
٢٧ ش: بتعاقبها
٢٨ ب، ل، ط: عليهما
٢٩ ل: ينزل
٣٠ ل: ينزل
٣١ ك: نزول
٣٢ ط: تفكره ينظر

Dune of Vision.[59] You will continue to go back and forth between the Garden and the Dune always and forever. In the Fire, its people will continue to voyage, ascending and descending, descending and ascending, like a piece of meat in the pot set to boil upon the fire. *As often as their skins are consumed We shall exchange them for fresh skins that they may taste the torment* (Q.4:56).

§5 There is no stillness whatsoever, rather continuous movement in this world. Night and day alternate, as do thoughts, states and conditions along with them, and the Divine Realities alternate upon them. Sometimes they descend upon the Divine Name 'All-Merciful'; sometimes the Name 'Ever-turning in Repentance'; sometimes 'All-Forgiving'; sometimes 'All-Provider'; sometimes 'All-Bestower' and 'Avenger' and every Name that belongs to the Divine Presence. They also descend upon you with what they possess of bestowal, provision, vengeance, repentance, forgiveness and mercy. Then there is a descent from you upon these realities through your asking and a descent from them to you through their giving.

§6 Since the matter is like this, the servant reflects again with his thought and looks into the distinction between the voyage that is imposed upon him by Law and the voyage that is not imposed upon him by Law. He looks into the first in order to prepare himself for that. In this – I mean in his preparedness – lies his felicity. This is the voyage to Him, the voyage in Him and the voyage from Him – all of these voyages have been lawfully prescribed for him. And he looks into the voyage that is not imposed upon him by Law in order to prepare himself for that. This is like his going about the earth for

59. See Q.73:14. According to tradition, the Dune of Vision, made of white musk, is situated in the Garden of Eden, the most elevated of the Gardens. It is here that the inhabitants of the Garden will meet to contemplate God. See *Fut.*I.320; III.442. 'If people take their waystations in the Garden, the Real summons them to the vision of Him, and they hurry according to the capacity of their mounts. Their going here is in obedience to their Lord. They include the slow, the quick and the in-between. They assemble at the Dune. Every individual knows his level necessarily. He runs to it and descends only in it, as the infant runs to the breast and iron to the magnet' (*Fut.*III.442).

تجارة الدنيا لتثمير[٣٣] المال وأمثال ذلك، وكسفر نفَسه بالدخول والخروج فإنه من وجهٍ غيرُ مكلَّف به ولا مشروع وإنما تقتضيه[٣٤] النشأة. نسأل الله جميل العاقبة والعافية.

٧ ثم إن المسافرين من عنده على ثلاثة أقسام: مسافرٌ مطرود كإبليس، لعنه الله،[٣٥] وكلِ مشرك، ومسافرٌ غير مطرود لكنه[٣٦] سفرُ خجَلٍ كسفر العُصاة لأنهم لا يقدرون على الاقامة في الحضرة مع المخالفة للحياء الذي غلب عليهم، وسفرُ اجتباءٍ واصطفاء كسفر المرسلين من عنده إلى خلقه ورجوعِ الوارثين العارفين من المشاهدة إلى عالم النفوس بالملك والتدبير والناموس والسياسة.

ثم المسافرون إليه أيضاً ثلاثة: مسافرٌ أشرك به وجسّمه وشبّهه ومثّله ونسب إليه ما يستحيل عليه إذ قال عن نفسه: ﴿لَيْسَ كَمِثْلِهِ شَيْءٌ﴾ (الشورى ١١) فهذا المسافر يصل إلى الحجاب لا يراه أبداً طريداً عن الرحمة. ومسافرٌ نزّهه عن كل ما لا يليق به بل يستحيل عليه مما جاء في المتشابهِ في كتابه، ثم يقول في آخر تنزيهه: والله أعلم بما قاله في

٣٣ ش: ليتميز

٣٤ ب، ش: يقتضيه؛ ط: نقتضيه

٣٥ ل، ط، ظ: - لعنه الله

٣٦ ش: وكذلك

permitted ends, voyaging for the sake of the commerce of this world in order to gain wealth and things like that, and like the voyage of his breath in its inhalation and exhalation, for in a certain way breathing is not prescribed or legally imposed upon him: it is only his constitution that demands it.

We ask God for a beautiful outcome and well-being.

[The Voyagers]

§7 Those who voyage *from* Him are of three kinds: the first is the voyager who is rejected, such as Iblīs – may God curse him – and everyone who associates partners with God.[60]

Another kind of voyager is not rejected but his voyage is one of shame, like the voyage of the sinners; they are not able to stand in the Presence of God because of the shame that overcomes them due to their disobedience.

Then there is the voyage of distinction and selection, such as the voyage of those who are sent from Him to His creatures, and the return of the gnostic heirs from their contemplation to the world of the souls through their exercise of kingship, governance, law and rulership.

The voyagers *to* Him are also three: a voyager who associates partners with Him, gives Him a body, a resemblance and a likeness, or attributes to Him what is impossible, since He said about Himself: *Nothing is as His likeness* (Q.42:11). This voyager, who is rejected by Mercy, will never see Him.

cast out
casts himself out

Then there is a voyager who declares Him free from everything unbefitting Him – indeed impossible for Him – with respect to those ambiguous statements that come in His Book.[61] Then he says in concluding his declaration of God's transcendence: 'God knows

60. In truth, 'To Him all affairs shall be returned (Q.11:123) and 'He is upon a straight path' (Q.11:55). Thus even those who are voyaging from Him will arrive at Him in the end.

61. See also Q.3:7: 'He it is Who has sent down to thee the Book: In it are verses basic or fundamental (of established meaning); they are the foundation of the Book: others are allegorical.'

كتابه. ثم لم يزلْ فيما عدا الشرك والتشبيه خائضاً[37] في المخالفات. فهذا إذا وصل وصل إلى العِتاب لا إلى الحجاب ولا إلى عذاب مؤبَّد،[38] فهذا يتلقّاه الشافعون، ينتظرونه على الباب فيُنْزِلونه عليه خيرَ مُنْزَل لكنه يُعْتَب في عدم الاحترام. ومسافرٌ معصوم و[39]محفوظ قد بسطهما الأُنس والدلال، يخاف الناس ولا يخافون، ويحزن الناس ولا يحزنون لأنهم من الخوف والحزن انتقلوا، ومن انتقل من شيء من المحال أن يَحُطَّ فيه ﴿لَا يَحْزُنُهُمُ الْفَزَعُ الْأَكْبَرُ وَتَتَلَقَّاهُمُ الْمَلَائِكَةُ هَذَا يَوْمُكُمُ الَّذِي كُنْتُمْ تُوعَدُونَ﴾ (الأنبياء ١٠٣) وهي البُشرى التي لهم في الآخرة، فهؤلاء هم المسافرون إليه.

وأما المسافرون فيه فطائفتان: طائفةٌ سافرتْ فيه بأفكارها وعقولها، فضلّتْ عن الطريق ولا بدّ، فإنهم ما لهم دليل في زعْمِهم يدُلّ بهم سوى فكرِهم، وهم الفلاسفة ومن نحا نحْوَهم. وطائفةٌ سُوفِرَ بها[40] فيه، وهم الرسل والأنبياء والمصطفون من الأولياء كالمحقِّقين من رجال

٣٧ ش: خائفاً؛ ط: خالصاً

٣٨ ط: موبدا

٣٩ ش: + مسافر

٤٠ ب، ش: بهم

best what He said in His Book.' Then, besides his denial of association of God with partners and anthropomorphism, he continues to plunge into things that are contravened. If this voyager arrives, he arrives at censure, not at the Veil[62] or at eternal punishment.[63] The intercessors[64] will meet him, waiting at the door. They will welcome him in the best way possible, but he will be censured for his lack of reverence.

Then there is the voyager who is safeguarded and preserved. Familiarity and intimacy have provided him with these two qualities. Other people fear, but he does not fear; other people grieve, but he does not grieve because he has moved beyond fear and grief, and whoever moves beyond something cannot stop there: *The supreme terror will not grieve them, and the angels will welcome them, [saying]: This is your Day which ye were promised* (Q.21:103). This is the good news that they will have in the Hereafter, for they are the voyagers *to* Him.

As for those who voyage *in* Him, they consist of two groups. One group voyages in Him through their reflections and their intellects, so they inevitably stray from the path. They have no guide other than their thoughts to lead them in their conjectures. These are the philosophers and those who follow their way.

The other group is made to voyage *by* Him *in* Him. They are the Messengers, the Prophets and the chosen ones from among the Friends of God – the Verifiers among the Sufi Men such as

62. Hell (Gehenna) has seven doors that are open and one door that is closed, called the door of the Veil; it prevents the vision of God. See *Fut.*I.299 (Chap. 61).

63. In Arabic, these three rhyme: *iʿtāb*, *ḥijāb* and *ʿadhāb*.

64. Intercession is carried out by angels, messengers, prophets and believers. When they have finished interceding 'no one who had faith in a law' or 'did a work laid down by a Law' will remain in the Fire (*Fut.*I.314). See also the *ḥadīth qudsī*: 'There shall come out of Hell-fire he who has said: "There is no god but Allah" and who has in his heart goodness weighing a barley-corn; then there shall come out of Hell-fire he who has said: "There is no god but Allah" and who has in his heart goodness weighing a grain of wheat; then there shall come out of Hell-fire he who has said: "There is no god but Allah" and who has in his heart goodness weighing an atom.' (Found in al-Bukhārī, Muslim, al-Tirmidhī and Ibn Māja.)

الصوفية مثل سَهْل بن عبد الله [التُسْتري] وأبي يزيد [البِسْطامي] وفَرْقَد السَّبْخي (12) والجنيد بن محمد والحسن البصري ومن شُهِرَ منهم ممن يعرفه الناس إلى زماننا هذا.

٨ غير أن الزمان اليوم ليس هو كالزمان الماضي، وسبب ذلك قُرْبه من الدار الآخرة، فكثُرَ الكشفُ في أهله اليوم وصارت لوائحُ الأرواح تبدو وتظهر، فأهل زماننا اليوم أسْرَعُ كشفاً وأكثر شهوداً وأغزر[٤١] معرفةً وأتمّ في الحقائق وأقلّ عملاً من الزمان المتقدَّم فإنهم كانوا أكثر عملاً وأقلُ فتحاً وكشفاً منّا اليوم، وذلك لأنهم أبْعَدُ إلّا زمانَ[٤٢] الصحابة لشهود النبي، صلى الله عليه وسلم، ونزولِ الأرواح عليه فيما بينهم مع الأنفاس كان المنوَّرون منهم عندهم هذا وكانوا قليلين جداً مثل أبي بكر الصديق وعمر بن الخطاب وعلي بن أبي طالب، رضي الله عنهم، وأمثالهم. فالعمل فيما

٤١ ش: أعرب

٤٢ في بقية النسخ: الأزمان (كأنها كلمة واحدة)

Sahl b. ʿAbd Allāh [al-Tustarī],[65] Abū Yazīd [al-Bisṭāmī],[66] Farqad al-Sabakhī,[67] al-Junayd b. Muḥammad,[68] al-Ḥasan al-Baṣrī[69] and others among them who are renowned up to our day.

§8 Nevertheless, times now are not like times past.[70] The reason for this is the proximity of our time to the abode of the Hereafter.[71] Unveiling occurs more often in people today, and flashes of light have appeared and become manifest. The people of our time experience more rapid unveiling and more frequent contemplation, more abundant knowledge and more complete realization of the realities, but they engage in fewer practices than in previous times.[72] The people of former times engaged in more practices but had fewer spiritual openings and unveilings than we have today because they were more distant from the Hereafter. This does not apply, however, to those who lived at the time of the Companions, because they witnessed the Prophet – God's blessing and peace be upon him – and the descent of the Spirits upon him in their midst with every breath. Some among the enlightened experienced these spiritual openings and unveilings, but they were very few, such as Abū Bakr al-Ṣiddīq,[73] ʿUmar b. al-Khaṭṭāb[74] and ʿAlī b. Abī Ṭālib[75] – may God be pleased with

65. Sahl al-Tustarī: d.896.

66. Abū Yazīd al-Bisṭāmī: d.848 or 874.

67. Farqad al-Sabakhī: d.748. Gril (*Dévoilement*, p.9, n.31) refers the reader to Abū Nuʿaym, *Hilyat al-awliyā'* III 44–50 and Ibn Hajar, *Tahdhīb al-tahdhīb* VIII 262–4.

68. al-Junayd: d.910.

69. al-Ḥasan al-Baṣrī: d.728. See Mourad, *Early Islam between Myth and History*.

70. 'This community knows the science of those who preceded [it, as well as] being singled out for sciences that the predecessors did not have – [alluded to] by [the Prophet's] saying: "I learned the knowledge of the first ones" – who are those who preceded him. Then he said: "and the last ones" – and this is the knowledge of what the predecessors did not have. It is what his community after him knows until the Day of Resurrection.' *Fut.*I.144 (Chap. 12).

71. See Commentary.

72. Presumably he means more supererogatory practices above and beyond the obligatory rituals incumbent upon all Muslims.

73. Abū Bakr al-Ṣiddīq: first caliph.

74. ʿUmar b. al-Khaṭṭāb: second caliph.

75. ʿAlī b. Abī Ṭālib: fourth caliph and first Shiʿite imam. It is noteworthy that the third caliph, ʿUthmān, is not mentioned, perhaps because his piety was a subject of dispute.

مضى كان أغلب، والعلم في وقتنا هذا أغلب، والأمر في مزيد إلى نزول عيسى، عليه السلام، فإنه يَكْثُر والركعة اليوم منا كعبادة شخص ممن تقدم عمرَه كلَّه كما قال – صلى الله عليه وسلم: ”للعامل منهم أجرُ خمسين رجلاً يعملون مثل عملكم“. (13) وما أَحْسَنَها من عبارة وألطفَها من إشارة.

وهذا مما ذكرناه لاقتراب[٤٣] الزمان وظهور حكم البرزخ. ألا ترى إلى قوله، صلى الله عليه وسلم: ”لا تقوم الساعة حتى يكلِّم الرجلَ فخذُه بما فعل أهله عَذَبة سوطه“ (14) و”تقول الشجرة: هذا يهودي خلفي اقْتُلْه“. (15) وهذا في الدنيا، فهل هذا إلا من ظهور موطن[٤٤] الآخرة التي هي الدار الحيوان.

فالعلم واحد منتشر يستدعي حَمَلةً. فمهْما كثُر حاملوه بما هم فيه من الصلاح لأنه علم الصالحين قُسِم عليهم، ولهذا قلَّ فيمن تقدم ومن كان عنده منه شيءٌ لم يظهر عليه لأنه غالب عليه. ومهما قلّ حاملوه بما

٤٣ ل: لاقتران؛ ط: من الاقتراب لاقتراب

٤٤ ش: مؤمن؛ ل، ط: أمر

them – and others like them. In the past, practices were more prevalent while in our time knowledge is more prevalent. It will continue to increase until the descent of Jesus[76] – upon him be peace – when a single *rakʿa*[77] of today will be like the lifelong worship of an individual who came before us, just as the Prophet – God's blessing and peace be upon him – said: 'He among them who performs works will receive the wage of fifty men who perform works like your works.'[78] How fine is this expression and how subtle is its allusion!

This, as we have mentioned, is because of the proximity of the time of the eschaton and the manifestation of the authority of the *barzakh*.[79] Do you not see that the Prophet – God's blessing and peace be upon him – said: 'The Hour will not arise until a man's thigh speaks to him of what his wife and the lash of his whip have done.'[80] And: 'The tree will say: there is a Jew behind me. Kill him.'[81] This pertains to this world; what is this if not derived from the manifestation of the homeland of the Hereafter, which is the Abode of Animate Things?[82]

Knowledge is both unique and diffused. It calls for people to bear it. Whenever its bearers become numerous – as long as they are righteous, for it is knowledge belonging to the righteous – it is divided among them. For that reason it was scarce among those who preceded us. Whoever had any of it whatsoever did not manifest it because he was able to dominate it. And whenever its bearers become

76. One of the signs of the Apocalypse is the second coming of Jesus. See Cook, *Studies in Muslim Apocalyptic*.

77. *Rakʿa* – unit of prayer.

78. A hadith found in al-Tirmidhī, *Jāmiʿ*, *tafsīr* 5:11, *Tuhfat al-Ahwadhī* IV 99–100; Abū Dāwūd, *Sunan*, *malāhim* 17; Ibn Māja, *Sunan*, *fitan* 21. The Prophet is addressing his contemporaries, comparing them to those who will come in the final days of this world.

79. The intermediate world of Imagination between pure spirit and dense matter. Within it, as in dreams, spirits take material forms and material forms are spiritualized.

80. A hadith found in al-Tirmidhī, *Jāmiʿ*, *fitan* 19, *Tuhfat al-Ahwadhī* III 213.

81. A hadith found in al-Bukhārī, *Ṣaḥīḥ*, *manāqib* 25 IV 239. Ibn ʿArabī gives the same example in *ʿUqlat al-mustawfiz*. See *Rasāʾil*, p. 123. See Commentary for a discussion of this hadith.

82. In the imaginal world, all things are seen to be animate, not only human beings and animals but vegetation and minerals as well. In the case of some exceptional human beings, the properties of the imaginal world are experienced in this world.

هم[٤٥] فيه العامة من الفساد حصل للصالح منهم موفوراً لأنّ[٤٦] عنده نصيبَ كل مُفسِد فإنه وارِثُه، فلهذا كثر العلم والفتح والكشف في المتأخر، ومن كان عنده منه شيء ظهر عليه لأن علمه غالب عليه لكثرته. فسبحان واهبِ الكل، ولكن مع هذا كله فالآخِر في ميزان الأول ولا بد إذا كان تابعاً له مقتدياً به ولكن من حيث الوزن وهو العمل لا من حيث العلم بالله، فإن العلم بالله لا بد فيه من الميزان و﴿ذَلِكَ فَضْلُ اللهِ يُؤْتِيهِ مَنْ يَشَاءُ وَاللهُ ذُو الْفَضْلِ الْعَظِيمِ﴾ (الحديد ٢١؛ الجمعة ٤).

٩ ونحن إن شاء الله نذكر في هذه العجالة من الأسفار التي وقفنا عليها علماً وعيناً[٤٧] وهي التي وقعت للأنبياء، عليهم السلام، والأسفار الالهية وسفر المعاني في معرض التنبيه على ما يُبغى[٤٨] من الأسفار، فإن الله قد ذكر في القرآن العزيز[٤٩] أسفاراً كثيرة عن[٥٠] أصناف من المخلوقات، فاقتصرنا على هذا القدر.

٤٥ ب: همَّ

٤٦ ش: إلا أنّ

٤٧ ش: غيبا

٤٨ ك، ب: يبغى؛ ط: يبقى؛ ف: بدون النقط.

٤٩ ل: العربي

٥٠ ش: على

few because of the corruption of most of humankind, the righteous person among them attains it abundantly because he comes to have the portion of every corrupt individual; thus he is its heir. Thus knowledge, spiritual opening and unveiling have become more plentiful among the later people, and whoever has any of it manifests it, since his knowledge is able to dominate him because of its abundance. Glorified be the One who bestows to all! Despite all of this, the last is weighed necessarily in the Scale of the first if he follows and emulates him as far as weight – which is practice, not knowledge of God – is concerned, for knowledge of God must have its own Scale.[83] *Such is the bounty of Allah, which He bestoweth upon whom He will, and Allah is of infinite bounty* (Q.57:21; 62:4).

§9 God willing, we shall mention in this vade mecum[84] some of the voyages that we have learned about through knowledge and eyewitnessing. These are the ones undertaken by the Prophets – peace be upon them – divine voyages, voyages of the suprasensible, in order to alert you to what one should seek to obtain[85] from voyages. Although God has mentioned in the Noble Qur'an many voyages undertaken by various sorts of creatures, we have limited ourselves to the following number of voyages.

83. See *Fut.*III.6ff. (Chap. 301) for a discussion of the Scales. See also Commentary.

84. Arabic: *ʿujāla*. His use of this word, based on the root *ʿ-j-l*, meaning haste, fits nicely with the many examples of hastening presented in this treatise. It also serves to continue the metaphor of the voyage, since the *ʿujāla* was a provision of food, such as dates and parched barley, that a rider could eat hastily and without any preparation on a journey. See Lane, *Lexicon*, vol. 5, p.1965. Although to translate *ʿujāla* as 'vade-mecum' loses the sense of the comestible – to translate it as 'snack pack' might be more accurate although anachronistic – it does manage to convey the idea of something handy one might stow in one's backpack for instant use, like a guidebook.

85. Two variants exist: *yubghā* and *yabqā*. If one uses the latter, the translation would be 'what one should seek to obtain from the remaining voyages'.

١٠ فمن ذلك سفر رباني من العماء إلى عرش الاستواء الذي تَسَلَّمه الاسم الرحمن

ورد خبر وهو أن بعض الناس قال لرسول الله، صلى الله عليه وسلم: "أين كان ربنا قبل أن يخلق الخلق" أو كما قال، فقال، صلى الله عليه وسلم: "كان[٥١] في عماءٍ[٥٢] ما فوقه هواء وما تحته هواء" فقد تكون[٥٣] لفظة "ما" هنا نافية وقد تكون بمعنى الذي.

اعلم أن هذا، سُرادِق الألوهية وحاجز عظيم، يمنع الكونَ أن يتَّصِل بالأُلوهة[٥٤] وتمنع الألوهة[٥٥] أن تتصل بالكون، أعني في الحدود الذاتية. ومن هذا العماء يقول الله – تعالى – ما ورد في الصحيح عن النبي، صلى الله عليه وسلم: "ما ترددتُ في[٥٦] شيء أنا فاعلُه تردُّدي في قبض نسمة المؤمن يكره الموت وأنا أكره مُسائَتَه ولا بد له من لقائي". (16) وقوله – تعالى: ﴿مايُبدَّلُ القولُ لديَّ﴾ (ق ٢٩) وإليه الاشارة بقول:[٥٧] ﴿وَجَاءَ رَبُّكَ وَ [الْمَلَكُ صَفًّا صَفًّا﴾ (الفجر٢٢) و﴿هَلْ يَنْظُرُونَ إِلَّا أَنْ يَأْتِيَهُمُ اللهُ][٥٨] فِي ظُلَلٍ مِنَ الْغَمَامِ﴾ (البقرة ٢١٠) يعني في يوم الفصل والقضاء،

٥١ سقط من سائر النسخ إلا نسخة ي

٥٢ ب، ل: عما؛ ش: عمى وكذلك: هوى

٥٣ ب، ل: يكون

٥٤ كذا في ك و ظ وفي سائر النسخ: بالألوهية

٥٥ ل، ط، ظه: الألوهية

٥٦ ك، ب، ش، ل، ظ، ظه، ط: عن

٥٧ سائر النسخ ما عدا ي: بقوله

٥٨ ما بين [..] ناقص في كل النسخ الا في طبعة حيدرآباد دكن، ولعله تكميل من الناشر.

§10 The Lordly Voyage from the Cloud to the Sitting on the Throne,[86] Assumed by the Name 'The All-Merciful'

A report has come that someone asked the Messenger of God – God's blessing and peace be upon him: 'Where was our Lord before He created the creation?' He responded: 'In the Cloud; above which was no air and no air was below it.'[87] The particle *mā* here is negative but it can have the meaning 'which'.[88]

Know that this is the Divine Canopy[89] and the tremendous obstacle that prevents creation from joining the Divinity and prevents the Divinity from joining creation – I mean, with respect to the essential limits.[90] From this Cloud, God the Most High says – and this has come in the *Ṣaḥīḥ* from the Prophet – God's blessing and peace be upon him: 'There is nothing that I hesitate doing as much as I hesitate in seizing the soul of the believer who hates death, and I hate to harm him. But he must meet Me.'[91] The Most High said: *The word that cometh from Me cannot be changed* (Q.50:29). There is an allusion to that in His saying: *And the Lord shall come [with angels, rank on rank]* (Q.89:22) and *[Wait they for naught else than that Allah should come unto them] in the shadows of the clouds [with the angels]?* (Q.2:210), meaning on the Day of Separation and Judgement.[92] Other similar

86. See also *Fut.*III.429 (Chap. 371, section I).

87. Hadith found in al-Tirmidhī, *Jāmiʿ*, *Tafsīr* Sura 11:1; Ibn Māja, *Muqaddima* 13; Ibn Ḥanbal, *Musnad* IV 11, 12.

88. In this case, the phrase would read: 'Which was above the air and below the air.' See previous footnote for reference to this hadith.

89. Arabic (of probable Persian derivation): *surādiq*. It has the original sense of an enclosure around a tent, with its main aim being to conceal its entrance. Gril (*Dévoilement*, p. 12, n. 38) stresses its circular form of protection. See Q.18:29: 'We have prepared for disbelievers Fire. Its Canopy encloseth them.' It should be noted that the Arabic root *s-w-r* (*sūr*) has to do with enclosure.

90. The essential limits or definitions (*ḥudūd dhātiyya*) are attributes that distinguish one thing from another.

91. Hadith found in al-Bukhārī, *Ṣaḥīḥ*, *riqāq* 38, VIII 131; Ibn Ḥanbal, *Musnad* VI 256.

92. Referred to in Q.37:21: 'This is the Day of Separation, which ye used to deny.'

وما أشبه هذا النوع مما ورد في الأخبار، فهذا من جانب الألوهة[٥٩] لما أرادت الوصول إلى الكون.

وأما ما ورد من[٦٠] هذا الفن عن الكون لما أراد الاتصال بالألوهة[٦١] قوله، صلى الله عليه وسلم: "لا أُحْصي ثناءً عليك" (17) وقوله: "أو استأثرتَ به في علم غيبك" (18) وقول أبي بكر الصديق: "العجز عن درك[٦٢] الادراك إدراك." (19)

١١ فلما أوجد دائرة الكون المحيطة المعبَّر عنها بالعرش الذي هو السرير الأقدس فلا بد من ملِك لهذا السرير وهو يريد الايجاد والايجاد ثمرة[٦٣] جود الوجود الالهي ولا بد، فلا بد من الرحمانية أن تكون الحاكمة في هذا الفصل. فاستوى عليه الاسم الرحمان في سرادق العماء الذي يليق بالرحمانية الالهية وهو نوع من العماء الرباني. وكان سفر الرحمانية[٦٤] من العماء الرباني إلى[٦٥] الاستواء العزيز[٦٦] موجودا[٦٧] عن الجود، وما دون العرش موجود عن المستوِي[٦٨] على العرش، وهو الاسم الرحمان الذي وسعت رحمته كل شيء وجوباً ومِنّة.[٦٩] ولما سافر هذا الاسم الرحمان سافرت معه جميع الأسماء المتعلِّقة بالكون فإنها وَزَعتُه وسَدَنته وأُمراؤه كالرازق[٧٠]

٥٩ ب، ل، ظه: الألوهية

٦٠ سائر النسخ ما عدا ي: في

٦١ ب، ل: الألوهية

٦٢ ط: إدراك

٦٣ ط: يمده

٦٤ ش: - الالهية ... الرحمانية

٦٥ ش: - إلى

٦٦ ش: العرش على العرش؛ ل: العرش؛ ط، ظ: العرشي

٦٧ يفهم من مخطوط الأصلي: "موجود" والحاشية غير واضحة. ك، ب، ش، ل، ظ، ظه، ط: موجوداً

٦٨ ش: - موجوداً ... المستوي

٦٩ ش، ل: منه

٧٠ ط: كالرزاق

things have come in the Prophetic reports, for this is from the side of the Divinity when It wants to reach the creatures.

As for what has come like this from the side of the creatures, when they wanted to connect with the Divinity, it is the Prophet's – God's blessing and peace be upon him – saying: 'I count not Your praises before You',[93] his saying: '... that You have kept to Yourself in the knowledge of Your Unseen',[94] and Abū Bakr al-Ṣiddīq's saying: 'Inability to perceive is itself perception.'[95]

§ 11 When the encompassing Circle of Creation[96] was brought into existence, which is interpreted[97] as being the Throne, the Most Holy Dais, it was necessary for there to be a King for it. God wanted to bring things into existence, and existence is the fruit of the generosity of Divine Being, necessarily.[98] All-Mercy had to be the Judge with respect to this separation. So the Name All-Merciful sat upon the Throne in the Canopy of the Cloud, as befitted the Divine All-Mercy, which is an attribute of the Lordly Cloud. All-Mercy's voyage from the Lordly Cloud to the sitting upon the Throne exists out of Generosity. Everything below the Throne comes into existence from the One sitting on the Throne. This is the Name 'All-Merciful', whose mercy embraces everything with existence and favour. When this Name 'All-Merciful' voyaged, all the Names connected to the creatures voyaged with It – Its officers, servants and commanders, such as the Names 'Provider', 'Succourer', 'Giver of Life', 'Giver of

93. Muslim, *Ṣaḥīḥ ṣalāt* 222.II 51. This statement concludes the hadith in which the Prophet seeks refuge in God from God. See also *Isfār*, Para. 64.

94. Part of a Prophetic invocation: 'I ask You with every Name by which You have named Yourself, that You have taught to any one of Your creatures, that You have revealed in Your Book, or that You have kept to Yourself in the knowledge of Your Unseen ...'. Ibn Ḥanbal, *Musnad* I.391, 452.

95. This saying is quoted numerous times in the *Futūḥāt*.

96. Arabic: *dā'irat al-kawn al-muḥīṭa*. See Commentary.

97. Arabic: *mu'abbar*. See Commentary for a discussion of the root *'-b-r*.

98. The words for existence (*wujūd*) and generosity (*jūd*), though derived from different roots, are often associated in Islamic thought. See also *Isfār*, Para. 38.

والاسم المغيث والاسم المحيي والاسم المميت والاسم الضار والاسم النافع وجميع أسماء الأفعال خاصة، فإن كل اسم لا يُعْرَف إلا من فعل فهو من أسماء الأفعال، وهو ممن سافر مع الاسم الرحمان. وكل اسم لا يعرف من فعل فليس له في هذا السفر مدخلٌ البتة.

١٢ فإذا أردتَ[٧١] أن تسافر إلى[٧٢] معرفة ما عدا أسماء الأفعال بأفكارها[٧٣] خرجتْ[٧٤] عن كرة العرش خروجاً غير مبائِن ولا منفصِل وأرادت[٧٥] التعلُّق بالجانب الأقدس الالهي، فوقعتْ[٧٦] في الحِمى وهو سرادق العمَى[٧٧] فتخبَّطت فيه لكن لا بد للواصل أن يلوح له من بوارق الألوهة[٧٨] ما يحصل[٧٩] له به معرفةٌ ما ولهذا سمّاه الصديق بالادراك، وسمّاه الصادق، صلى الله عليه وسلم: "لا أحصي ثناءً عليك." وذلك لما عاين ما لا يقبل ثناءً معيَّناً لكن يقبل الثناء المجهول وهو "لا أحصي ثناء عليك" فإن الحيرة تقتضي ذلك ولا بد، فأصحاب الفكر في عماء وأصحاب الكشف في عماء والكل في عماء لأن الكل في عَمَى،[٨٠] والكل على صورة الكل. وهذا السفر روحُه ومعناه السفر من التنزيه إلى سِدْرة التشبيه من أجل أفهام المخاطبين وهذا أيضاً من العمَى[٨١] عينِهِ.

٧١ ف، ط، ظه: أرادت
٧٢ ط: في
٧٣ ش: بأفعالها
٧٤ ب: خرجتَ
٧٥ ب: أراده
٧٦ ب: فوقعتَ
٧٧ و في سائر النسخ ما عدا ي: العماء
٧٨ ب، ظه: الألوهية
٧٩ ك، ب، ظ، ظه، ط: تحصل
٨٠ في سائر النسخ ما عدا ي: عما
٨١ ل: العماء؛ ط: العما

Death', 'Harmer', 'Benefiter' and all the Names of Acts in particular. Every one of the Names of Acts is known only from an Act that voyaged with the Name 'All-Merciful'. Every Name that is not known from an Act has no way whatsoever to make this voyage.[99]

§ 12 If you desire to voyage to the spiritual knowledge beyond the Names of the Acts by reflecting upon them, [know that these thoughts] leave the sphere of the Throne without being separated or detached [from it], desiring to be attached to the Most Holy Side. So they fall into the sacred precinct, which is the Canopy of the Cloud, and descend in it. However, it is inevitable that some of the divine lightning will flash for the one who arrives, by which he obtains a certain kind of knowledge. For that reason, [Abū Bakr] the Ṣiddīq has called it 'perception' and similarly as [Muhammad] the Ṣādiq[100] – God's blessing and peace be upon him – said: 'I count not Thy praises before Thee.' That is because what he saw could not receive any determinate praise; however, it could receive indeterminate praise, which was: 'I count not Thy praises before Thee.' This is what perplexity inevitably demands. The possessors of reflection are in the Cloud and the possessors of unveiling are in the Cloud. Everything is in the Cloud. All of them are in the Blindness,[101] and all are in the Form of the All. The spirit and meaning of this voyage is the voyage from transcendence to the Lote Tree[102] of Similarity so that those addressed would understand. And this also is from the Blindness itself.

99. The Names of Acts are those which the Divinity and the creatures share.

100. The root *ṣ-d-q* is associated with veracity and sincerity.

101. Arabic: *ʿamā*. Blindness (*ʿamā*) and Cloud (*ʿamāʾ*) often have the same orthography in manuscripts, hence Ibn ʿArabī has availed himself of a kind of play on words here. Blindness is often equated in Ibn ʿArabī with perplexity or bewilderment (*ḥayra*).

102. See Q.53:14, traditionally said to describe Muhammad's second vision during his *miʿrāj*. In this verse, the Lote Tree is called 'the Lote Tree of the Limit'. The reason why it is here called 'Lote Tree of Similarity' is addressed in *Fut.*I.290 (Chap. 58). As Gril (*Dévoilement*, p. 15, n. 46) explains, the first vision transcended the creatures while the second is a return to them. This dual movement of arrival at the Divine Presence followed by a return to the creatures is the subject of *Fut.*I.250ff. (Chap. 45). It is also only at the ontological level of the Lote Tree that creation becomes bifurcated and religious obligation (*taklīf*) comes into play.

١٣ سفر الخلق والأمر وهو سفر الابداع

يقول الله[٨٢] – تعالى: ﴿ثُمَّ اسْتَوَى إِلَى السَّمَاءِ وَهِيَ دُخَانٌ فَقَالَ لَهَا وَلِلْأَرْضِ ائْتِيَا طَوْعاً أَوْ كَرْهاً قَالَتَا أَتَيْنَا طَائِعِينَ فَقَضَاهُنَّ سَبْعَ سَمَاوَاتٍ فِي يَوْمَيْنِ وَأَوْحَى فِي كُلِّ سَمَاءٍ أَمْرَهَا وَزَيَّنَّا السَّمَاءَ الدُّنْيَا بِمَصَابِيحَ وَحِفْظاً ذَلِكَ تَقْدِيرُ الْعَزِيزِ الْعَلِيمِ﴾ (فصلت ١١–١٢) بالفَتْق والفَطْر[٨٣] أوَ لمْ يروا ﴿أَنَّ السَّمَاوَاتِ وَالْأَرْضَ كَانَتَا رَتْقاً فَفَتَقْنَاهُمَا﴾ (الأنبياء ٣٠) وجاء بكلمة ﴿ثُمَّ﴾ بعد خلق الأرض (20) يُؤذِن[٨٤] غالباً بأن الثاني بعد الأول بمَهْلة وهو زمان خلق الأرض وتقدير أقواتها في أربعة أيام من أيام الشأن. يومان لشأنها في عينها[٨٥] وذاتها يومٌ[٨٦] لظهورها وشهادتها ويومٌ لبطونها وغيْبتها ويومان لما أودع فيها من الأقوات الغيْبية والشهادية في يومين.

ثم كان الاستواء الأقدس الذي هو القصود[٨٧] والتوجُّه إلى فَتْق السموات وفَطْرها. فلما قضاهن سبع سموات في يومين من أيام الشأن أوحى في كل سماء أمرها فأودع فيها جميع ما تحتاج إليه المولَّدات

٨٢ زائد في سائر النسخ ما عدا ي، ك: تبارك

٨٣ ط: الرتق

٨٤ ط: تؤذن

٨٥ ك: غيبها

٨٦ ط: ويوم

٨٧ هكذا في الاصل، ك؛ ف، ط: المقصود

§ 13 The Voyage of Creation and Command, which is the Voyage of Originating

God the Most High said: *Then He sat upon the heaven when it was smoke, and said unto it and unto the earth: Come both of you, willingly or loth. They said: We come, obedient! Then He ordained them seven heavens in two Days and inspired in each heaven its command; and We adorned the nearest heaven with lamps, and rendered it inviolable – that is the measuring of the Mighty, the Knower* (Q.41:11–12), by cleaving and splitting: *Have not those who disbelieve known that the heavens and the earth were of one piece, then We cleaved them?* (Q.21:30). He mentioned the word *then* – a grammatical particle which most often informs us that the second action comes after the first because of some delay – after mentioning the creation of the earth. This is the time of the earth's creation and the *measuring* of its kinds of sustenance during the four 'Days of the Divine Task':[103] two days for the task pertaining to their entities and essences, [consisting of] one day for their manifest and visible dimension and one day for their inner and unseen dimension; and two days when He deposited in the earth the unseen and seen kinds of sustenance.

Then there took place the most holy sitting on the Throne – which was the most proper course – and God's attention to cleaving and splitting the heavens. After *He ordained them seven heavens in two days*[104] of the Divine Task, *He inspired in each heaven its command* (Q.41:12) and placed in it everything the generated beings required

103. Arabic: *ayyām al-sha'n*. See Q.55:29: 'Whosoever is in the heavens and the earth is in request of Him. Every day (*yawm*, pl. *ayyām*) He is upon some affair/task (*sha'n*).' Ibn 'Arabī composed a short treatise on the days of creation under the title *Ayyām al-sha'n*. See also Beneito and Hirtenstein, *Seven Days of the Heart*, and the discussion of the *ayyām al-sha'n* in Yousef, *Time and Cosmology*.

104. See Q.41:9–10: 'Say: Is it that ye deny Him Who created the earth in two Days? And do ye join equals with Him? He is the Lord of the Worlds. He set on [the earth], mountains standing firm, high above it, and bestowed blessings on the earth. He measured in it its kinds of sustenance in due proportion, in four Days, in accordance with those who seek.'

من الأمور في تركيبها وتحليلها وتبديلها وتغييرها وانتقالها من حال إلى حال بالأدوار والأطوار وهذا من الأمر الالهي المودَّع في السموات في قوله: ﴿وَأَوْحَى فِي كُلِّ سَمَاءٍ أَمْرَهَا﴾ (فصلت ١٢) من الروحانيات العلية[٨٨] فبرز[٨٩] بالتحريكات الفلكية ليَظْهَر التكوينُ في الأركان بحسب الأمر الذي يكون[٩٠] في تلك الحركة وفي ذلك الفلك.

١٤ فلما فتقها من رتقها ودارت وكانت شفّافة في ذاتها وجِرْمها حتى لا تكون[٩١] ستراً لما وراءها أدركتِ الأبصارُ[٩٢] ما في الفلك الثامن من مصابيح النجوم فيتخيَّل[٩٣] أنها في السماء الدُّنيا والله يقول: ﴿وَزَيَّنَّا السَّمَاءَ الدُّنْيَا بِمَصَابِيحَ﴾ (فصلت ١٢) ولا يلزم من زينة الشيء أن تكون[٩٤] فيه.

وأما قوله ﴿وحفظاً﴾ فهي الرجوم التي تحدُث في كرة الأثير لاحراق الذين يَسْتَرِقون السمع من الشياطين فجعل الله لذلك ﴿شِهَاباً رَصَداً﴾ (الجن ٩) وهي الكواكب ذوات الأذناب ويخترق البصرُ الجوَّ حتى يصل إلى السماء الدنيا، فلا يرى من فطور فينفُذ فيه فينقلب ﴿خَاسِئاً وَهُوَ حَسِيرٌ﴾(الملك ٤) أي قد أعْيا.

٨٨ ك: العقلية
٨٩ ظه: فبرزت
٩٠ ب: تكون
٩١ ش، ل: يكون
٩٢ ط: أدركنا بالأبصار
٩٣ ك، ش، ب: فتتخيل
٩٤ ي: بدون النقط؛ ل، ط، ظ، ظه: يكون.

for their composition, dissolution, transformation, change and passage from one state to another through cycles and phases. This is from the Divine Command, placed in the heavens through His saying: *And He inspired in each heaven its command* (Q.41:12) among the supernal spiritual beings.[105] This command set the spheres in motion so that generative activity would become manifest in the elements, in accordance with the command that was in that movement and in that sphere.

§ 14 After He had cleaved them apart from their cohesive state,[106] they began to revolve. They were transparent in their essences and bodies so that they would not screen[107] what was behind them. Vision perceived the lamps of the stars in the eighth sphere and imagined that they were in the nearest heaven. God said: *We adorned the nearest heaven with lamps* (Q.41:12; 67:5), but it does not follow necessarily from the adornment of the stars that they be in the nearest heaven.

As for His saying *inviolable* (Q.41:12), this has to do with the 'missiles'[108] that arise in the sphere of the ether in order to burn the satans who eavesdrop.[109] God has made for them *a flame in wait* (Q.72:9). These are the comets. Vision pierces the atmosphere until it reaches the nearest heaven and does not see *any flaw*. It penetrates it and *turns back … weakened and made dim* (Q.67:3–4), that is, it becomes *exhausted*.[110]

105. An angel is assigned to every heaven according to Prophetic tradition.

106. Arabic: *ratq*. It makes a nice pairing with *fatq*, 'rending' or 'cleaving'. See also Prayer for Sunday Morning, Beneito and Hirtenstein, *Seven Days of the Heart*, p.40.

107. Arabic: *sitr*. Perhaps an allusion to those mentioned in the same sura who do not heed the message of the revelation: '… between Us and thee is a screen (*sitr*)' (Q.41:5).

108. Arabic: *rujūm*. See Q.67:5: 'And verily We have adorned the nearest heaven with lamps, and We have made them missiles for the devils and for them We have prepared the doom of the flame.' According to a prophetic tradition on the authority of Ibn 'Abbās, the 'satans' here referred to the astrologers and soothsayers. See Pickthall, *Glorious Qur'an*, p.639, n.1.

109. See Q.72:1: 'Say [O Muhammad]: It is revealed unto me that a company of the jinn gave ear, and they said: Lo! We have heard a marvellous Qur'an' and the jinn remark (Q.72:9): 'And we used to sit on places [high] therein to listen.'

110. See n.158 regarding Arabic theories of vision.

وجعل في كل سماء من هذه السبعة كوكباً سابحاً وهو قوله تعالى: ﴿كُلٌّ فِي فَلَكٍ يَسْبَحُونَ﴾ (الأنبياء ٣٣ ويس ٤٠) فتَحْدُث الأفلاكُ بحركات الكواكب لا السمواتِ فتَشْهَدُ الحركاتُ من السبعة السيّارة أن المصابيح في الفلك الثامن.

وزيَّن[٩٥] السماء الدنيا لأن البصر لا يدركها إلا فيها، فوقع الخطاب بحسب ما تعطيه[٩٦] الرؤية، لهذا قال: ﴿زَيَّنَّا السَّمَاءَ الدُّنْيَا بِمَصَابِيحَ﴾ ولم يقل: خلقناها فيها. وليس من شرط الزينة أن تكون[٩٧] في ذات المزيَّن بها ولا بد، فإن الرَّجْل[٩٨] والخَوَل[٩٩] من زينة السلطان وما هم قائمون[١٠٠] بذاته.

١٥ ولما كملت[١٠١] البِنية الانسانية وصحَّتِ التسوية، وكان التوجُّه الالهي بالنفخ العُلْوي في حركة الفلك الرابع من السبعة، وقَبِلَ هذا المسمى الذي هو الانسان لكمال تسويته السرَّ الالهي الذي لم يقبله غيره وبهذا صح له المقامان:[١٠٢] مقام الصورة ومقام الخلافة.

فلما كملت الأرض البدنية ﴿وَقَدَّرَ فِيهَا أَقْوَاتَهَا﴾ (فصلت ١٠) وحصَل فيها قواها الخاصة بها من كونها حيواناً نباتاً كالقوة الجاذبة والهاضمة والماسكة والدافعة والنامية المغذية، وفتقت طبقاتها السبعة من جلد ولحم وشحم وعرق وعصب وعضَل وعظم. استوى السر الالهي الساري فيه مع[١٠٣]

٩٥ ط: زينا
٩٦ ب، ل، ظه: يعطيه؛ ط النقط
٩٧ ش، ل: يكون
٩٨ ب: الرجال؛ ظه: الرحل
٩٩ ش، ط: الخيل
١٠٠ ط: قائمان
١٠١ ب: كمل
١٠٢ ش، ل، ط، ظه: المقامات
١٠٣ ط: منفخ

He placed in each of these seven heavens a floating planet.[111] This is the Most High's saying: *They float, each in an orbit* (Q.21:33; 36:40). The spheres come into existence through the movement of the planets, not the heavens. The movements of the seven floating planets bear witness to the fact that the *lamps* are in the eighth sphere.[112]

He *adorned the nearest heaven* (Q.41:12) because vision perceives only this heaven. Divine discourse confirms vision's experience; for this reason, He says: *We adorned the nearest heaven with lamps* (Q.41:12) and does not say: 'We created in them' for it is not necessarily one of adornment's conditions that it constitute the essence of the adorned object. Men and chattel are some of the adornments of the sultan, but they do not constitute his essence.

§15 When the physical constitution of the human being had been perfected and brought into balance, the Divine Attention produced the supernal exhalation in the movement of the fourth of the seven spheres.[113] This sphere – called 'The Human Being' because of its perfect balance – received the divine secret that nothing else received. For that reason, two stations were made possible for him: the station of the Form and the station of the Vicegerency.[114]

When the earth of his body[115] had been perfected, *He measured in it its kinds of sustenance* (Q.41:10), and He caused it to acquire its specific faculties: those resulting from it being an animal and plant, such as the faculties of attraction, digestion, retention, repulsion, growth and taking nutrition; and its seven layers were cleaved into: skin, flesh, fat, veins, nerves, muscles and bones. The divine secret, flowing in the Human Being with the spiritual exhalation from the

111. These are the seven planets.

112. This is the heaven of the fixed stars.

113. The fourth of the seven spheres is heaven of the sun. The spiritually perfected Human Being is the axis of the universe; all of creation revolves around him or her and derives light from his or her presence. In archetypal terms, this individual is Idrīs/Enoch. See Commentary.

114. The spiritually perfected Human Being who is created in the Form of God and is worthy to be considered His Vicegerent on earth.

115. A clear reference to Human Being as microcosm. The analogy between the macrocosm and microcosm, based on the number seven, continues in the lines that follow.

النفخ الروحي إلى العالم العلوي من البدن وهو بُخارات تصعد كالدخان ففتق فيها سبع سموات: السماء الدنيا وهي الحس[١٠٤] وزينها بالنجوم والمصابيح مثل العينين، وسماء الخيال وسماء الفكر وسماء العقل وسماء الذكر وسماء الحفظ وسماء الوهم.

١٦ ﴿وَأَوْحَى فِي كُلِّ سَمَاءٍ أَمْرَهَا﴾ (فصلت ١٢) وهو ما أودع في الحس من إدراك المحسوسات ولا نتعرَّض[١٠٥] إلى الكيفية[١٠٦] في ذلك للخلاف الواقع فيها وإن كنا نعلم ذلك، فإن علمنا لا يرفع الخلاف من العالَم.

وفي الخيال من المتخيَّلات[١٠٧] وفي العقل من المعقولات، وهكذا في كل سماء ما يشاكلها من جنسها، فإن أهل كل سماء مخلوقون منها وأهل كل أرض مخلوقون منها[١٠٨] فهم بحسب مزاج أماكنهم. وخلق في كل سماء من هذه السبعة كوكباً سابحاً في مقابلة الكواكب السيارة تُسمَّى صفاتٍ، وهي الحياة والسمع والبصر والقدرة والارادة والعلم والكلام

﴿كُلٌّ يَجْرِي إِلَى أَجَلٍ مُسَمًّى﴾ (الرعد ٢ إلخ ...) فلا تدرك[١٠٩] قوة إلا ما خُلِقَتْ له خاصة، فالبصر لا يرى سوى المحسوسات المبصَرات والحسّ ﴿فينقلب ... خاسئاً﴾ (الملك ٤) لأنه[١١٠] لا يجد فَطْراً[١١١] ينفُذ فيه.

١٠٤ ط: الخنس

١٠٥ ل: يتعرض؛ ظ: تتعرض

١٠٦ ش، ل، ظ: للكيفية

١٠٧ ش: التخيلات + ب، ظه، ط: المستحيلات

١٠٨ ل، ط: - وأهل كل أرض مخلوقون منها

١٠٩ ش: ندرك

١١٠ ط: فإنه

١١١ ط: قطرا

body, *sat upon* (Q.41:11) the supernal world, which is like vapours rising like *smoke* (Q.41:11). He *cleaved* in it seven heavens: the nearest heaven, which is sense perception, which He adorned with *stars* and *lamps*, like two eyes; the heaven of the imagination;[116] the heaven of reflective thought; the heaven of the intellect; the heaven of recollection; the heaven of memory; and the heaven of conjecture.[117]

§16 *He inspired in every heaven its command* (Q.41:12). This is the perception of sensible objects that He placed in the senses. We will not go into how that takes place because of the disputes regarding it, even if we know it, for our knowledge of it will not remove the disputes from the world.

As for the imagination, He has placed within it the objects of imagination; and in the intellect He has placed the intelligibles. Similarly, He has placed in every heaven what is like it in its genus, for the inhabitants of every heaven and earth are created from it in accordance with the temperament of their place. He created in each of the seven heavens a 'floating' planet called an 'attribute' that corresponds to the 'floating' planet in the heavens. These are: Life, Hearing, Seeing, Power, Will, Knowledge and Speech, *each runneth unto an appointed term* (Q.13:2, and so on). Every faculty perceives only that for which it was created. The eye sees only sensible and visible things, then the sense comes back '*weakened*' (Q.67:4) because it finds no fissure to penetrate.

116. Arabic: *khayāl*. For Ibn 'Arabī, imagination is not only a faculty of the human being, it also possesses an ontological reality. Ibn 'Arabī calls this latter imagination 'imagination from the outside, like Gabriel in the form of Diḥya. It is an independent, ontological and sound Presence, possessing corporeal forms that are worn by meanings and spirits' (*Fut.* II.296, Chap. 176).

117. Arabic: *wahm*. Although Islamic philosophers such as Avicenna made of *wahm* a faculty of the soul akin to instinct in animals, Ibn 'Arabī uses the more traditional understanding of this word as a kind of supposition, conjecture, imaginal construct or fancy. The order given by Ibn 'Arabī is quite unusual and does not seem to be based on any kind of hierarchy of value, since it seems unlikely that *wahm* should be the highest of the internal senses.

والعقل يثبت هذا كله تشهد[112] بذلك الحركات الفلكية التي في الانسان وذلك بتقدير العزيز العليم.

١٧ فهذا سفرٌ أسْفَر عن مُحَيّاه ودل على تنزيه مولاه ونَتَجَ ظهورَ العالم العلوي، فإن السفر إنما سمّي سفراً لأنه يُسْفِر عن أخلاق الرجال، معناه أنه يظهر ما ينطوي عليه كل إنسان من الأخلاق المذمومة والمحمودة. يقال: سفرت المرأة عن وجهها إذا أزالت بُرْقُعها الذي يستر وجهها فبان للبصر ما هي عليه الصور[113] من الحُسْن والقُبْح. قال الله – تعالى – يخاطب العرب: ﴿والصُبْحِ إذَا أسْفَرَ﴾ (المدثر ٣٤) معناه أظهر إلى الأبصار مبصَراتِها. قال الشاعر:

[وكنت إذا ما جئت ليلى تبرقعت][114] فقد رابني منها الغداة سفورها

فإن العرب جرت عادتهم أن المرأة إذا أرادت أن تُعْلِم أن وراءها شراً سفرت عن وجهها. وكأن[115] هذا القائل قد أعمل الحيلة في الوصول إلى محبوبته، فشعر قومها به وعرفت المرأة بشعورهم، فعندما بصرت به سفرت عن وجهها فعلم أن وراءها الشر، فخاف عليها وانصرف وهو ينشد: "فقد رابني منها الغداة سفورها".

ومن[116] مثل هذا السفر ينزل ربنا وأشباهه. وقد أغنت الاشارة عن البسط ﴿وَاللهُ يَقُولُ الْحَقَّ وَهُوَ يَهْدِي السَّبِيلَ﴾ (الأحزاب ٤).

١١٢ ل، ط: يشهد

١١٣ ك: الصورة

١١٤ الشطر الأول للبيت غير مذكور في: ي، ك، ب، ش، ظه

١١٥ ش، ل، ط، ظ: كان

١١٦ ط: ما

The intellect affirms all of this and bears witness to those movements of the spheres that are within the human being. This is with the *measuring of the All-Mighty, the All-Knowing* (Q.41:12).

§17 This is a voyage that unveils its face, points to the transcendence of its Master and brings about the appearance of the supernal world. 'This voyage is only called "voyage" (*safar*) because it unveils (*yusfiru*) the character traits of the Men'[118] meaning that it brings to light what every human being contains of blameworthy and praiseworthy character traits. One says: 'The woman unveiled her face' when she removes the veil that is covering her face and the forms of her beauty or ugliness appear to the eye. God the Most High said, addressing the Arabs: *And the dawn when it shineth forth* (*asfara*) (Q.74:34), meaning it becomes visible to the eyes that see it. The poet[119] says:

> [When I came to Layla, she veiled her face.][120]
> This morning her unveiling disquieted me.

It was customary among the Arabs that when a woman wanted to let someone know that there was some evil behind her, she would unveil her face. This speaker had availed himself of a ruse to join his beloved, but her tribe was aware of it and the woman knew they were aware. So, when she saw him, she unveiled her face. He knew that behind her lay evil and he was afraid for her and went away, reciting this verse: 'This morning her unveiling disquieted me.'

It is in such a voyage, or one like it, that our Lord descends. This allusion makes further exposition unnecessary. *And Allah speaks the truth and He guides on the Path* (Q.33:4).[121]

118. See al-Sarrāj's *K. al-Luma'* and al-Qushayrī's *Risāla* for this well-known Sufi quotation.

119. Tawba b. al-Ḥumayr (d.*c.* 704 CE). See Commentary for background on this poem.

120. The first part is missing in the holograph manuscript, Y.

121. Ibn 'Arabī frequently ends his chapters with this verse from the Qur'an. In the *Futūḥāt* nearly every chapter ends this way, although in the *Fuṣūṣ* only the chapters on Abraham, Ṣāliḥ and Muhammad do. In the *Isfār*, only five chapters contain this formula at their conclusion: the chapter on creation, the chapter on the *mi'raj*, the chapter on Lot, the chapter on Moses' anger and return, and the last chapter. There is no doubt a reason why only these chapters are singled out, but one that I have yet to discover.

١٨ سفر القرآن العزيز

قال الله – عز وجل: ﴿إِنَّا أَنْزَلْنَاهُ فِي لَيْلَةِ الْقَدْرِ﴾ (القدر ١) السورة بكمالها وهو قوله – تعالى:[١١٧] ﴿إنّا أنزلْناه في ليلةٍ مُباركةٍ﴾ (الدخان ٣) هذا إنزال إنذار.[١١٨] قوله – تعالى: ﴿إنا أنزلناه﴾ يعني القرآن العزيز ﴿في ليلة القدر﴾. قال أهل التفسير نقلاً: نزل جُملةً واحدة إلى السماء الدنيا ثم نزل منها على قلب محمد، صلى الله عليه وسلم، نُجوماً. وهذا سفر لا يزال أبداً ما دام مَتْلُواً بالألسنة سراً وعلانيةً. وليلة القدر الباقية على الحقيقة في حق العبد هي نفسُه إذا صَفَتْ وزَكَتْ، ولهذا قال ﴿فيها يُفْرَقُ كلُّ أمْرٍ حَكِيْمٍ﴾ (الدخان ٤). وكذلك النفس خُلِقَ فيها كلُّ أمرٍ حكيم ﴿فألْهمها فُجورَها﴾ على المعنيين ﴿وتَقْواها﴾ (الشمس ٨) كذلك. وقلبه

١١٧ ش، ط: - تعالى

١١٨ ش، ط: (بالهامش): أنوار

§18 # The Voyage of the Noble Qur'an

God – may He be magnified and glorified – said: *We have sent it down on the Night of Power* (Q.97:1); and the entire *sūra*: *We have sent it down in a Blessed Night* (Q.44:3). This is a descent in order to warn.[122] The Most High's saying: *We have sent it down* means the Noble Qur'an, *on the Night of Power.* The commentators say, according to transmitted tradition, that it was sent down at one time to the nearest heaven.[123] Then it descended from there to the heart of Muhammad – God's blessing and peace be upon him – in fragmented form.[124] This voyage never ceases as long as tongues recite it, whether inwardly or aloud. The Night of Power that really abides in the case of the servant consists of his soul when it is purified and made stainless.[125] For this reason, He said: *In it is distinguished every wise command* (Q.44:3). Similarly, in the soul *every wise command* is created. *He inspired its immorality* – according to its two senses[126] – *and its godwariness* (Q.91:8) likewise. According to the

122. The remainder of the verse reads: 'for We are warners'.

123. Although Ibn 'Arabī does not mention any specific commentators, the sending down of the Qur'an either all at once or piecemeal was a topic of dispute, since the Qur'an itself seems to give contradictory information. On the one hand, Sura 97 implies that it was revealed on one night, the Night of Power. On the other, Sura 17:105–6 states: '(It is) a Qur'an which We have divided (into parts from time to time), in order that thou mightest recite it to men at intervals: We have revealed it by stages.' al-Suyūṭī (*al-Itqān fī 'ulūm al-Qur'ān*, Vol. I pp.39–40) gives three reports from Ibn 'Abbās, in al-Ḥākim, Baihaqī and Nasa'ī, claiming the Qur'an was revealed in two stages: (1) From the Preserved Tablet to the lowest heaven of the world, in a single 'sending down' on the Night of Power. (2) From the heavens to earth upon the heart of Muhammad in stages, the first instance being on the Night of Power during Ramadan, by means of the Angel Gabriel.

124. Arabic: *nujūman*. This is from the same root as *najm*, star, 'as the stars reflect the fragmentary light of the sun' (Gril, *Dévoilement*, p.20, n.53). See Q.25:32: 'Those who reject Faith say: Why is not the Qur'an revealed to him all at once? Thus [is it revealed] that We may strengthen thy heart thereby, and We have rehearsed it to thee in slow, well-arranged stages, gradually.'

125. See Commentary for a discussion of the Night of Power.

126. Arabic: *fujūr*. The sense is that the act may be attributed either to God or to the individual soul, but in cases where the opprobrium might fall on God, it is best to attribute such acts to oneself. See *Fut.*III.211 (Chap. 350). Another sense is that the soul is inspired to know the bad in order to avoid it, in which case the verse has been translated as 'He inspired it as to its wrong and its right.' See *Fut.*III.239 (Chap. 353). Yet a third way to interpret the

في الاعتبار السماء الدنيا التي نزل إليها القرآن مجموعاً، فعاد فُرقاناً بحسب المخاطَبين، فليس حظُّ البصر منه حظَّ السمع. وإنما قلنا نزل إلى قلبك دفعة واحدة، فلسنا نعني إنك حفِظْتَه ووَعَيْتَه فإن كلامنا إنما هو روحاني معْنوي، وإنما أعني أنه عندك ولا تعلم، فإنه ليس من شرط[119] السماء لما نزل إليها القرآن أن يُحْفَظَ[120] نصُّه، ثم إنه ينزل عليك نجوماً منك بكشف غِطائك عنك. وقد رأيتُ ذلك من نفسي في بدْء أمري، ورأيت هذا لشيخي أبي العباس العُرْيَبي[121] (21) من غرب الأندلس من أهل العُلْيا، وسمعت ذلك عن جماعة من أهل طريقنا أنهم يحفظون القرآن أو آيات منه من غير تعليم معلِّم بالتعلُّم المعتاد ولكن يجده في قلبه ينطق بلغته العربية المكتوبة في المصاحف وإن كان أعجمياً. روينا عن أبي يزيد البسطامي، رحمه الله، قال عنه أبو موسى الدَبيلي[122] أنه ما مات حتى استظهر القرآن من غير تلقين ملقِّن معتاد. (22)

١٩ فأما كونه لا يزال ينزل على قلوب العباد لما قام الدليل على استحالة إقامة العرض زمانين وقام الدليل على استحالة انتقاله من محل إلى محل وإنَّ حِفْظ زيد لا ينتقل إلى عمرو، فعندما تسمع الأُذن الملقِّن يُلقي الآية

١١٩ ل: هبوط

١٢٠ ط، ظ: تحفظ

١٢١ ط: العريني، وهذه النسبة غير منقوطة في أكثر النسخ لكنها منقوطة في الأصل

١٢٢ ك: الدُنبلي؛ هذه النسبة غير منقوطة في النسخة الأصلية

inner interpretation, the servant's heart is the nearest heaven to which the Qur'an descends in totality then becomes a Criterion[127] in order to conform to those who are addressed. Thus the portion that the eye receives is not the portion that belongs to the ear. When we say that it descends upon your heart all at once, we do not mean that you have memorized it and know it completely, for our discourse is spiritual and suprasensory only. I mean that it is with you without your being aware of it. Similarly, it is not a condition that, when the Qur'an descends to the nearest heaven, its text is retained. It descends upon you in fragmentary form from yourself, by removing your veil from you. I saw this in my own case when I first entered the Path. I saw it also with my shaykh Abū al-ʿAbbās al-ʿUraybī[128] from the west of al-Andalus, who was one of the people of ʿUlyā. And I heard that someone belonging to our Path memorized the Qur'an or some of its verses without the instruction of a teacher, as is the customary way of teaching. This person found it in his heart and pronounced it in Arabic just as it is written in the copies of the Book even though he was a foreigner. Abū Mūsā al-Dabīlī[129] informed us that Abū Yazīd al-Bisṭāmī – may God be pleased with him – did not die until he had memorized the Qur'an by heart without anyone having taught him in the usual way.[130]

§19 As for the Qur'an's continual descent upon the servants' hearts, it has been proved that it is impossible for an accident to subsist for two consecutive moments or to pass from one place to another. Zayd's memorization cannot pass to ʿAmr. When someone casts a verse into a person's ear, God makes the verse descend upon his heart and he

verse is as Ibn ʿArabī does in *Fut.*I.287 (Chap. 57): Inspiration leading to immorality is from a satan; inspiration leading to godwariness is from an angel.

127. Arabic: *furqān*. See Q.25:1: 'Blessed is He who sent down the criterion to His servant, that it may be an admonition to all creatures.'

128. See Austin, *Sufis*, pp.63–9; Addas, *Quest*, pp.49–51, 61–4, 68–9.

129. Although there is some dispute as to the vowelling of this name, it seems likely that Abū Mūsā hailed from Dabīl, better known as Dvin, the ancient (4th century to 1225 CE) capital of Armenia. It was called Dabīl by the Arabs and is perhaps best known in Islamic history as the birthplace of Saladin's father.

130. See *Fut.*I.607 (Chap. 71), II.20 (Chap. 73), 194 (Chap. 110), III.94 (Chap. 325), 414 (Chap. 370), IV.78 (Chap. 463).

عليها أنزلها الله على قلبه فوعاها، فإن كان القلب في شغل، عاد الملقن فعاد الانزال، فالقرآن لا يزال مُنْزَلاً أبداً. فلو قال إنسان: أنزل الله عليَّ القرآن، لم يكذب، فإن القرآن لا يزال يسافر إلى قلوب الحافظين له.

٢٠ وأما[١٢٣] كون النبي، صلى الله عليه وسلم، إذا جاءه جبريل، عليه السلام، بالقرآن، بادر بقراءته قبل أن يُقْضى إليه وحْيُه. وذلك لقوة كشفه فإنه كان يكشف على ما جاء به جبريل، عليه السلام، فيتلوه ويعجل[١٢٤] به لسانُه قبل أن يقضى إليه وحيه كما يكشف[١٢٥] المكاشف عندنا[١٢٦] ما يخطر لك في قلبك ويتكلم على خاطرك. وهذا غير منكور عند أكثر الناس، فذاك[١٢٧] المحل به ألْيَق لكن أدّبه ربه فأحسن أدبه (23) فقال: ﴿وَلَا تَعْجَلْ بِالْقُرْآنِ مِنْ قَبْلِ أَنْ يُقْضَى إِلَيْكَ وَحْيُهُ﴾ (طه ١١٤) فأمره أن يتأدب مع جبريل، عليه السلام، إذ هو معلِّمه في[١٢٨] الكَلِم الطيب بالعمل الصالح. (24)

٢١ فصل

الانسان الكلي[١٢٩] على الحقيقة هو القرآن العزيز نزل من حضرة نفسه إلى حضرة موجِده[١٣٠] وهي الليلة المباركة لكونها غيباً. والسماء الدنيا

١٢٣ ط: وما
١٢٤ ط: تعجل
١٢٥ ك، ظه: يكشفه
١٢٦ ش، ط: عند
١٢٧ ش: فذلك
١٢٨ ط: - في
١٢٩ ك، ل، ظ: الكل
١٣٠ ط: موحده

retains it. If his heart is distracted, the teacher repeats the verse and the descent is repeated. So the Qur'an never ceases descending. If a person says: 'God makes the Qur'an descend upon me' he has not lied, for the Qur'an continually voyages to the hearts of those who retain it.

§20 When Gabriel – peace be upon him – came to the Prophet – God's blessing and peace be upon him – with the Qur'an, he was surprised that Muhammad could recite it even before his revelation had been concluded. That is because of the power of the Prophet's unveiling, for he had already intuited what Gabriel – peace be upon him – brought. So he recited it, and his tongue hastened to recite it even before his revelation had been concluded, just as one of us who has received unveiling can unveil the thoughts that have come to your heart and can speak about them – most people do not deny this – and that locus, namely the Prophet, is even more able to do so. But his Lord had given him courtesy, and how beautiful was his courtesy![131] He said to him: *And hasten not with the Qur'an ere its revelation hath been completed unto thee* (Q.20:114).[132] Thus He commanded him to observe courtesy with Gabriel – upon him be peace – since he was his teacher with respect to *the Good Word* with the *righteous deed.*[133]

§21

Section

The Universal[134] Human Being is in reality the Incomparable Qur'an[135] that has descended from the Presence of itself to the Presence of the One who brought it into existence. This is the *Blessed Night* because it is hidden. The nearest heaven is the Veil

131. The reference is to a hadith of the Prophet: 'God has taught me courtesy. How beautiful is my courtesy!'

132. See *Fut.*I.83 (Chap. 2) and Gril, '*Adab* and Revelation', p.251.

133. See Q.35:10: 'To Him ascends the Good Word. He exalts every righteous deed.'

134. The holograph manuscript Y reads *al-insān al-kull*, but it seems to me that the sense requires *al-kullī*.

135. Q.15:87: 'We have given you [Muhammad] the seven oft-repeated verses and the Tremendous Qur'ān.'

حجاب العزة الأحْمى الأدنى إليه، ثم جُعِل هناك فرقاناً فنزل[١٣١] نُجوماً بحسب الحقائق الالهية، فإنها تُعطَى أحكاماً[١٣٢] مختلفة، فتفرّق[١٣٣] الانسان لذلك. فلا يزال ينزل[١٣٤] على قلبه من ربه نُجوماً حتى يجتمع هناك ويترك الحجاب وراءه، فيزول عن الأين والكون ويغيب عن الغيب فالقرآن المنزَل حقٌّ كما سماه الله حقاً و "لكل حق حقيقة" (25) وحقيقة القرآن الانساني[١٣٥] كما سُئِلتْ عائشة – رضي الله عنها – عن خُلق النبي، صلى الله عليه وسلم، فقالت: "كان خلقه القرآن." (26) قال العلماء: أرادت قوله – تعالى – فيه: ﴿وَإِنَّكَ لَعَلَى خُلُقٍ عَظِيمٍ﴾ (القلم ٤). فحقِّقْ هذا السفر تَحْمَد عاقبته إن شاء الله تعالى.

١٣١ ط: - ينزل

١٣٢ ط: أحكامها

١٣٣ ط: فيعرف

١٣٤ ط: - ينزل

١٣٥ ك، ب: الانسان

of Incomparability, most inviolable and closest to it.[136] Here the Qur'an was made a Criterion[137] and descended in a fragmentary form in accordance with the Divine Realities, for they give different determinations, and the Human Being is divided because of that. It continues to descend upon his heart from his Lord in a fragmentary form until it is gathered together there. It leaves the Veil behind it and passes away from 'where' and creation, and becomes absent from absence. Thus the Qur'an that has descended is the Truth, as God has called it, and 'every truth has a reality'.[138] The reality of the Human Qur'an[139] is like when 'Ā'isha – may God be pleased with her – was asked about the character of the Prophet – God's blessing and peace be upon him. She answered: 'His character was the Qur'an.'[140] The religious scholars said that what she meant was the Most High's saying about him: *Lo! Thou art of a tremendous character* (Q.68:4).

Realize this voyage and you will praise its outcome, God the Most High willing.

136. Arabic: *ḥijāb al-ʿizza al-aḥmā al-adnā*. Ibn 'Arabī defines this in *Fut*.II.129 as 'blindness and perplexity'. See also *Fut*.I.4; III.93 (Chap. 325). Gril writes that here it signifies the Universal Human Being, one side of whose face is hidden and turned towards God, 'corresponding to the limit between the *qur'ān* and the *furqān*' (*Dévoilement*, p.22, n.62). As *qur'ān* both text and Universal Human Being are gathered together and united, as *furqān* they are differentiated and dispersed.

137. Arabic: *furqān*. See pp.187–90.

138. This was the response of the Prophet to a companion who said to him: 'This morning I find myself truly (*ḥaqqan*) a believer.' Gril (*Dévoilement*, p.23, n.65) has found this source in Nūr al-Dīn al-Haythamī, *Majmaʿ al-zawā'id*, Beirut, 1967, I, 57–8. A similar hadith can be found in the hadith collection of the Shiʿite Muhammad b. Yaʿqūb al-Kulaynī, *Kitāb al-Kāfī*: 'Over every truth there is a reality and above every valid issue there is light. Whatever agrees with the holy Qur'an you must follow and whatever does not agree disregard it' (Chap. 22, hadith 1)

139. The holograph gives '*al-insānī*' and other MSS. give '*al-insān*'. In the latter case it would mean: 'The reality of the Qur'an is the Human Being. This is like when ... .'

140. Hadith found in al-Bukhārī. When 'Ā'isha, the Prophet's wife, was asked about his character, she replied: 'His character was the Qur'an'. The Universal Human Being is a synthesis of all the noble character traits: 'She said that because he was unique in character, and that unique character had to bring together the noble character traits (*makārim al-akhlāq*). God described that character as being 'tremendous' (*'aẓīm*), just as He described the Qur'an in His words 'the tremendous (*'aẓīm*) Qur'an' (Q.15:87). *Fut*.IV.60, trans. Chittick, *SPK*, p.241.

٢٢ سفر الرؤية في الآيات والاعتبار[١٣٦]

وقول الله – تعالى: ﴿سُبْحَانَ الَّذِي أَسْرَى بِعَبْدِهِ لَيْلاً مِنَ الْمَسْجِدِ الْحَرَامِ إِلَى الْمَسْجِدِ الأَقْصَى [الَّذِي بَارَكْنَا حَوْلَهُ] [١٣٧] لِنُرِيَهُ مِنْ آيَاتِنَا﴾ (الاسراء ١)

سبحان من أسرى إليه بعبده ليرى الذي أخفاه من آياتِهِ
كحضوره[١٣٨] في غيْبةٍ[١٣٩] وكسكره في صحوةٍ[١٤٠] والمحو في إثباته

١٣٦ ط: سفر الروية (خرم في الأصل) الله تعالى والاعتبار

١٣٧ سقط من ي، ك

١٣٨ ل: بحضوره

١٣٩ ش، ب، ظ، ظه، ط: غيبه

١٤٠ ط: صحوه؛ ي: بدون النقط

§22 The Voyage of the Vision in the [Outer] Signs and Inner Signification[141]

Glory be to Him, who carried His servant by night from the Inviolable Place of Prostration[142] *to the Farthest Place of Prostration, [the neighbourhood whereof We have blessed,]*[143] *that We might show him of Our signs!* (Q.17:1).

Glory be to Him,[144] who made His servant journey to Him by
night
So that he might see those signs of His that He has hidden –
Such as his presence[145] in absence,[146]
His intoxication[147] in sobriety[148]
And his obliteration[149] in establishment.[150]

141. Arabic: *iʿtibār*. See Commentary for a discussion of this term.

142. In many English translations, *masjid* is translated as 'place of worship'. Here, however, we wish to preserve the basic root meaning of *sajada*, to prostrate oneself, as Ibn 'Arabī will stress in what follows.

143. Missing in the holograph MS. Y.

144. The reader should be aware that Arabic has no capitalization, thus all pronouns in this poem are ambiguous. In certain instances, it seems appropriate to capitalize the pronoun 'He' as referring to the Divinity, but in other cases the pronoun could refer to either servant or Lord.

145. Arabic: *ḥuḍūr*. See *Fut.*II.543 (Chap. 245), which is devoted to this concept. The following sets of terms may best be described as 'a garment of contraries' (*Fut.*II.320, Chap. 178), the warp and woof of love between God and His servant.

146. Arabic: *ghayba*. See *Fut.*II.543 (Chap. 244), devoted to this notion, as well as the following chapter, On Presence. Ibn 'Arabī outlines the various degrees of the servant's absence: with the Real from the Real, with the Real from creation, with creatures from creatures. When the servant is absent from himself, the Real is present with him.

147. Arabic: *sukr*. See *Fut.*II. 544 (Chap. 246), which concerns itself with intoxication. There are degrees of intoxication: natural, rational and divine.

148. Arabic: *ṣaḥw*. See *Fut.*II.546 (Chap. 247), which concerns itself with sobriety. The word is unpointed in the holograph MS. Y, thus it could also be read 'his sobriety'. The degrees of sobriety correspond to the degrees of intoxication.

149. Arabic: *maḥw*. See *Fut.*II.552 (Chap. 252), a chapter devoted to obliteration.

150. Arabic: *ithbāt*. See *Fut.*II.553 (Chap. 253), a chapter devoted to establishment or confirmation. See also *Fut.*II.355 (Chap. 178) for an explanation of these paired terms in relation to love, the lover and the beloved.

ويرى الذي عنه تكوَّن سرُّه — في منعه إن شاءه وهِباته
ويزيل ما أبدى له من جوده — بوجوده والفقر[١٤١] من هيئاته
سبحانه من سيِّدٍ ومُهَيْمِن — في ذاته وسِماته وصفاته

قرن – سبحانه – التسبيح بهذا السفر الذي هو الاسراء لينفي[١٤٢] بذلك عن قلب صاحب الوهم ومن يحكم[١٤٣] عليه خيالُه من أهل التشبيه[١٤٤] والتجسيم ما يتخيَّله في حق الحق من الجهة والحد والمكان. لهذا قال ﴿لِنُرِيَهُ مِنْ آيَاتِنَا﴾ فجعله مسافراً به، صلى الله عليه وسلم، يُعْلِم أن الأمر من عنده – عز وجل – هِبةً إلهية وعناية سبقت له مما لم يخطر بسره ولا اختلج في ضميره.

وجعله ليلاً تمكيناً لاختصاصه بمقام المحبة لأنه اتّخذه خليلاً وحبيباً. وأكده بقوله ﴿لَيْلاً﴾ مع أن الاسراء لا يكون في اللسان إلا ليلاً لا نهاراً لرفع الاشكال حتى لا يتخيل أنه أُسْرِيَ

١٤١ ط، ظ: الفقد؛ ش: الفقه
١٤٢ ط: ينفي
١٤٣ ط: تحكم
١٤٤ ط: الشبه

He sees the One from whom his innermost heart[151]
was generated,
In His withholding, if He wills, and in His giving.
He removes by his existence[152]
The generosity He had shown him,[153]
Poverty being one of his conditions.
Glory be to Him, Master and Protector[154]
In His Essence, Qualities and Attributes.

God – may He be glorified – conjoined glorification with this voyage, which is the Night Journey, in order thereby to expel from the heart of the supposer and the one who associates others with God and corporealizes Him, what he imagines concerning the Real: that direction, limit and place are applicable to Him. Therefore, He said: *In order to show him some of Our signs.* Thus He made the Prophet – God's blessing and peace be upon him – a voyager, informing him that the affair came from Him[155] – may He be magnified and glorified – as a divine gift and prior solicitude, not something that had occurred to his innermost heart or pervaded his innermost mind.

He made this voyage take place by night in order to confirm the Prophet in his election to the station of love, because He took him as an intimate friend and beloved. He assured him with His saying: *by night*, even though the *isrā'*, according to the Arabic language, can only take place at night, not by day. This was in order to remove any

151. Arabic: *sirr*. See n.183 for the various words referring to the heart and their specific meanings.

152. Bestowing existence (*wujūd*) is God's generosity (*jūd*) to all creatures.

153. See *Fut.*II.672 for the eminence of nonexistence and its connection with God's incomparability (*tanzīh*) and glorification. Note that the pronouns are ambiguous here.

154. Arabic: *muhaymin*. This is one of God's Divine Names. See *Fut.*IV.205–6 (Chap. 558). For Ibn 'Arabī, this Name is associated with witnessing, with mutual claims and with the descent of a specific Book, the Qur'an, to a specific community, the community of Muhammad.

155. Arabic: *al-amr min 'inda-hu*. See *Fut.*III.371 (Chap. 369): 'He was made a pure servant and He stripped him of everything, even of the Night Journey. He made him be taken on a night journey and did not attribute the Night Journey to him. If He had wanted to say: Glorified be He who called His servant to journey by night to Him, or to the vision of His signs, so he journeyed by night, He could have said so. But the station prohibited this. So He compelled him, and there was no share of lordship in any of his acts.'

بروحه، ويزيل بذلك من خاطر من يعتقد من الناس أن الاسراء ربما يكون نهاراً، فإن القرآن وإن كان نزل بلسان العرب فإنه خاطب به[١٤٥] الناس أجمعين أصحاب اللسان وغيرَهم.

والليل أحب زمان للمحبّين لجمعهما فيه والخلوة بالحبيب متحقِّقة[١٤٦] بالليل ولتكون[١٤٧] رؤية الآيات بأنوار إلهية[١٤٨] خارجة عن العادة عند العرب مما[١٤٩] لم تكن تعرفها، فإن البصر لا يدرك شيئاً من المرئيات بنوره[١٥٠] خاصة إلا الظلمة. والنور الذي به[١٥١] يكشف الأشياء إذا كان بحيث لا يغلب[١٥٢] قوةَ نور البصر، فإذا غلب كان[١٥٣] حكمه مع نور البصر حكم الظلمة لا يرى سواه إذ كان البصر لا يدرك في الظلمة الشديدة سوى الظلمة. فالبصر يرى بالنور المعتدل النور وما يُظهِر له النور من الأشياء المُدْرَكة. ولا فائدة عند السامع لو كان العروج به نهاراً في رؤية

١٤٥ سقط من: ك

١٤٦ ش: متفقة

١٤٧ ك، ل: ليكون

١٤٨ ل: بأنوار الالهية؛ ط: بالأنوار الالهية

١٤٩ ط: بما

١٥٠ ب: المركبات بنور

١٥١ ب: - به

١٥٢ ط: تغلب

١٥٣ ط: - كان

doubt, lest someone imagine that he was made to journey in spirit only.[156] With that emphasis, He removes the notion from the mind of anyone who believes it that the Night Journey takes place sometimes by day; for the Qur'an – even if it came down in the language of the Arabs – is addressed to all people, both masters of the Arabic language and others.

Night is the time that is dearest to lovers because this is when they meet, and being alone with the beloved takes place at night. It was also so that he would have a vision of the signs, accompanied by the divine lights,[157] which was something extraordinary for the Arabs, something that they had not known before. For the eye does not perceive any visible objects with its own particular light except through the darkness and light by which things are unveiled, as long as the power of the light does not overpower the eye because of its intensity. If light overpowers the eye, then light for it will be the same as darkness. It cannot see anything but light, just as in intense darkness it cannot perceive anything but darkness. Thus it is through moderated light that the eye sees both light and the objects of perception that light makes manifest.[158] The vision and the signs

156. According to the early Muslim proponents of the idea of the Prophet's fully conscious and corporeal ascent, such as al-Ṭabarī (*Tafsīr* xv, 13), there were several proofs for this position: (1) It was a miracle, a unique and unrepeatable sign of his divine prophetic mission, and those who accused him of lying about it were branded as unbelievers; (2) The Qur'an stated that God caused His servant to voyage, not that He caused His servant's spirit to voyage; (3) If the voyage were spiritual, Burāq's services would not have been required. See Schrieke, 'Mi'rādj', p.97.

157. Although Ibn 'Arabī does not say what these 'divine lights' are, it is possible that what he is referring to are the lights of the Divine Names, lights that stem from the non-manifest, suprasensory domain. 'Light' (*nūr*) is one of the Names of God.

158. The theory of vision prevalent in the early Islamic period involved the emanation of light from both luminous objects and the eye itself. Visual rays emitted from the eye were said to take the form of a cone whose vertex was the centre of the eye and whose base extended along the surface of the viewed object. The Qur'an echoes this theory in a verse which describes the weakness of human eyesight when it tries to penetrate the layered seven heavens: 'Again turn thy vision a second time: [thy] vision turns back to thee weakened and made dim, that is exhausted' (Q.67:4). For Ibn 'Arabī, there are individuals – notably the three hundred who are 'upon the foot of Adam', whose visual rays are so acute that they extend to the sphere of fixed stars: 'At the time he opens his eye, its rays connect with the bodies of these stars. Contemplate this distance and contemplate this rapidity!' (*Fut.*II.9, Chap. 73).

الآيات فإنه معلوم له، فلهذا كان ليلاً.

وأتى[١٥٤] أيضاً بقوله ﴿ليلاً﴾ ليحقّق أن الاسراء كان بجسده[١٥٥]، صلى الله عليه وسلم، فإن قوله ﴿أسرى﴾ يغني عن ذكر الليل، فـ ﴿ليلاً﴾ في موضع الحال من عبده كما قال:

يا راحلين إلى المختار من مضر   زرتم جسوماً وزرنا نحن أرواحا

٢٣ وأُدْخِل الباء في قوله ﴿بعبده﴾ لأمرين في نظر المحققين من أهل الله: الأمر الواحد، من أجل المناسبة بين العبودية التي هي الذلة وبين حرف الخفض والكسر، فإن كل ذليل منكسر. وأضافه إلى الهو ولم يكن هنا[١٥٦] اسم ظاهر للحق[١٥٧] إلا من الأسماء النواقص التي لا تتم إلا بصلة وعائد

١٥٤ ك: واما؛ ل: اتا؛ ي: وأتا

١٥٥ ش، ل، ط، ظ: + الشريف

١٥٦ ل: هناك؛ ط: منها

١٥٧ ك، ب: - للحق

would make no sense to the hearer of the report if the ascent had taken place by day, for this is something well known to him. For this reason, it was at night.

He also mentioned *by night* to confirm that the Night Journey was undertaken by the Prophet – God's blessing and peace be upon him – in his noble[159] body. For His saying *He made him journey by night* dispenses with the need to mention 'by night', for 'by night' is in the grammatical place of circumstance[160] referring to 'His servant', as the poet says:

> O you who set out for the chosen one of Muḍar,[161]
> You have visited him corporeally,
> While we have visited him spiritually.[162]

§23 The preposition *bi-* in His saying *His servant* (*bi-ʿabdihi*) is inserted for two reasons, in the opinion of the Verifiers among the people of God. One reason is because of the correspondence between servanthood, which is humility,[163] and the letter of 'lowering'[164] or 'breakage',[165] for every humble person is broken. And He connected *servant* to the *He* – there was no manifest Name here for the Real except for one of the semi-verbal names [*Subḥāna*],[166] which are only completed with a

159. This qualifying adjective is not found in the holograph MS. but is in K. and B.

160. Arabic: *ḥāl*. As Ibn ʿArabī sees it, 'by night' does not have to do with temporal considerations, because for that purpose it is not necessary; time is already inferred in the verb. What it does have to do with is describing the circumstance of the servant's voyage, that is, in his body, which is metaphorically perceived as 'night'.

161. A pre-Islamic tribal confederation. The famous poet Imru'l-Qays was one of its leaders and the Prophet's tribe, Quraysh, was said to be derived from this bloc of tribes. Legend connects the Muḍar with the Meccan sanctuary. See Kindermann, 'Rabīʿa and Muḍar'.

162. This is an excerpt from a poem by Ibn al-ʿArīf.

163. Arabic: *dhilla*, which can also be translated as 'lowness'.

164. Arabic: *khafḍ*. This word means both 'lowering' and pronouncing the last consonant with 'i' (pronounced 'ee').

165. In Arabic, the *kasra* marks the genitive case. It means literally 'break'.

166. Arabic: *asmāʾ nawāqiṣ*. Literally: 'defective names'. In this case it applies to *subḥāna*, which is an indeclinable name, always placed in the accusative case. It is also sometimes said to express wonder. It can be used as a kind of shorthand for such expressions as: 'I declare [or celebrate or extol] the remoteness, or freedom, of God [from every imperfection or impurity, or from anything derogatory from His glory ... or from the imputation of there being any

ف﴿أسرى بعبده﴾ صلته والعائد عليه[158] المُضْمَر، والمضمر غيب بلا شك. وهو هنا مضمر فهو غيب في غيب، فكأنه هو الهو كما تقول:[159] غيب الغيب، فأنبأ بشرف الاسراء.

وكذلك ذِكْر المسجدين، الحرام والأقصى، وهذا يناسب ما ذكرناه من باب العبد وحرف الخفض وهي الباء والمسجد مَفْعِلٌ، موضع سجود الرجل. والسجود عبودية، والحرام يقتضي المنع والحَجْر[160] فهو يطلب العبودية. والأقصى يقتضي البُعد، والعبودية في غاية البُعد من صفات الربوبية. فاختار – سبحانه – لنبيه الشرف الكامل بهذين الأمرين بأعلى ما يكون من صفات الخلق وليس إلا العبودية وما يشاكلها[161] من حروف الخفض، والمساجد والحرام، والأقصى.

وكذلك مما شرفه به في مقابلة هذه العبودية الكلية التي تعطي المعرفة التامة بأنه ما جعل له من أسمائه ما يقيّده به لأن هذه العبودية

١٥٨ ك، ب: اليه

١٥٩ ي: بدون نقط؛ ط: يقول؛ ظ: يقال

١٦٠ ل: الحجب

١٦١ ك، ب، ظه: شاكلها

relative clause [*alladhī asrā bi-ʿabdi*] and resumptive pronoun [*-hi*].[167] Thus the relative clause is *made His servant journey by night* and the resumptive pronoun refers to the 'concealed' pronoun [within *Subḥāna*],[168] and the 'concealed' pronoun is the 'hidden' third-person pronoun[169] without any doubt. *He* is the 'concealed' pronoun here, and *H/he* is 'hidden within hidden',[170] as if h/He were He/he.[171] As you say, the 'unseen of the unseen'. Hence He informs us about the nobility of the Night Journey.

Similarly, the mention of the two places of prostration – the *inviolable* one and the *furthest* one – corresponds to what we have mentioned above concerning the servant and the particle of lowering, which is the *bāʾ*. *Masjid* is a name of place, the place where the man prostrates himself (*sujūd*) – and prostration is servanthood. *Inviolable* requires prevention and prohibition; thus it demands servanthood. *Furthest* requires distance, and servanthood is extremely distant from the attributes of Lordship. Thus He – glorified be He – chose perfect nobility for His Prophet through these two matters: the highest possible attribute of creatures, which is nothing but servanthood and other letters of abasement, and the places of prostration: the *inviolable* one and the *furthest* one.[172]

Also one of the things with which He honoured him, in exchange for this universal servanthood that gives complete knowledge, was by not giving him any of His Names that would restrict him, because

---

equal to Him, or any companion, or anything like unto Him, or anything contrary to Him; or from everything that should not be imputed to Him]' (Lane, *Lexicon*, vol. 4, p. 1290). See Commentary for further discussion of this term.

167. Arabic demands in this case that the preposition *bi-* accompanying the verb be followed by a pronoun, called the *ʿāʾid*.

168. Arabic: *muḍmar*. The word means both 'concealed' and 'personal pronoun'.

169. Arabic: *ghāʾib*. The word means both 'hidden' or 'absent' and 'third-person pronoun'.

170. Arabic: *huwa ghayb fī ghayb*. The pronoun *huwa* is ambiguous and can mean here either He or he.

171. Arabic: *kaʾannahu huwa al-huwa*. The pronouns here are also ambiguous and can mean either He, he, or it. It is possible, therefore, that in the course of the *isrāʾ* and *miʿrāj* the 'he' is concealed in the 'He' and vice versa, as the following paragraph will disclose.

172. See also *Fut*.I.744 (Chap. 72), where the meaning of these designations is discussed in conjunction with a Prophetic hadith.

المذكورة ههنا لا تقتضي تقييداً[١٦٢] باسم إلهي من أسماء التأثير. ولكن تطلب[١٦٣] من الألوهة[١٦٤] ما يشاكلها في الرفعة والتنزيه، فإن العبد إذا رُفِعَ من جميع الوجوه[١٦٥] وأكْرِم، نُزِّهت عبوديتُه عن الصفات السِيادية الربانية الالهية فهو تنزيهها. وإذا وُصِفت بأوصاف الربوبية شُبِّهت، وفي التشبيه هلاكها. قال تعالى: ﴿ذُقْ إِنَّكَ أَنْتَ الْعَزِيزُ الْكَرِيمُ﴾ (الدخان ٤٩) وقال: ﴿كَذَٰلِكَ يَطْبَعُ اللهُ عَلَىٰ كُلِّ قَلْبِ مُتَكَبِّرٍ جَبَّارٍ﴾ (غافر ٣٥) (27) فكذلك الألوهة[١٦٦] إذا كُنِيَ عنها في حق العبد بالأسماء التي تطلب وجود الخلق، فليس ذلك بعُلوّ ولا رفعة في حق العبد المخاطب بتلك الأسماء، فإن فيها ضرباً مشابهاً بما تقتضيه[١٦٧] العبودية من الافتقار إلى الأثر. فكما وفّى[١٦٨] العبودية في هذا الاسراء حقها من جميع الوجوه كذلك وفّى الألوهة حق ما يقتضي[١٦٩] هذا الوفاء المنسوب إلى العبد. فأتى بالهو وبهو الهو الذي هو غيب الغيب.

١٦٢ ك، ب: تغييرا

١٦٣ ط: يطلب

١٦٤ ل: الألوهية

١٦٥ ط، ظ: الوجود

١٦٦ ل: الألوهية

١٦٧ ب: يقتضيه

١٦٨ ط: فى

١٦٩ ي: بدون نقط؛ ب: تقتضي

this aforementioned servanthood does not demand any restriction here by any Divine Name from among the Names that have an effect [on the servant]. Rather, servanthood demands from Divinity what resembles It with respect to elevation and incomparability. For when the servant is elevated in all aspects and honoured, his servanthood is made free of masterly, lordly and divine attributes. This is servanthood's incomparability.[173] If the servant is attributed with lordship, he is made similar; and being made similar is his perdition. God the Most High said: *Taste! Lo! Thou wast forsooth the mighty, the noble* (Q.44:49),[174] and He said: *Thus doth Allah seal over every self-aggrandizing, tyrannical heart* (Q.40:35).[175] Similarly, in the case of the servant, if Divinity is called by Names that demand the existence of the creatures, this is not elevation or height on the part of the servant who is addressed by those Names, for in these Names there is an example similar to the dependence on the effect that servanthood[176] demands.[177] So just as he fully gave servanthood its right in all aspects in this Night Journey, so too did he fully give Divinity the right that this fulfilment attributed to the servant demands. Thus He mentioned the 'He' and the 'he of the He', which is the 'unseen of the unseen.'[178]

173. The verb 'to make free' (*nazzaha*) and the noun 'incomparability' (*tanzīh*) are both represented in Arabic by the root *n-z-h*.

174. The context is the sinner in the Fire who, when alive, falsely claimed for himself might and nobility (or generosity).

175. The entirety of the latter verse reads: 'Those who dispute concerning the signs of Allah without an authority having come to them, great is hatred [of them] in the sight of Allah and in the sight of those who have believed. Thus does Allah seal over every heart [belonging to] any self-aggrandizing tyrant' or 'every self-aggrandizing, tyrannical heart' (*mutakabbir jabbār*) – according to *Tafsīr al-Jalālayn*, 'heart' can be read either as indefinite (*qalbin*) or as the first word in an *iḍāfa* (*qalbi*) (www.quran.com//40, accessed May 2014). The Names al-Mutakabbir and al-Jabbār are God's exclusively, in which case they are perhaps better translated as 'excelling in great actions' and 'compelling', or even in al-Jabbār's other meaning, 'restoring'. See *Fut.*I.421 (Chap. 69), II.153 (Chap. 80), II.166 (Chap. 88), IV.209 (Chap. 558). '[The servant] detaches himself from Divine Names such as these because of the blame that is in them for someone who calls himself by them and manifests with their property in the world' (*Fut.*II.153, Chap. 80).

176. The holograph MS. gives *'ubūdiyya*. Other MSS. have *rubūbiyya* ('lordship').

177. Divine Names such as 'Merciful', 'Forgiver' and so forth cannot exist independently of a corresponding object that will be the recipient of mercy and forgiveness.

178. Here the interpenetration of the 'He' and the 'he' is made clear.

فلما نزل، صلى الله عليه وسلم، من عبوديته إلى ما ذكرناه، أُسْرِيَ به إلى غيب الغيب الذي ذكرناه. فمن هناك شاهد حبيبه[170] الحق أحداً فرداً، فإن المحبة تقتضي الغَيْرة فلا يبقى للعبد أثرٌ، فإن العبد قادرٌ وما عليه تحجير، فما ظهر هنالك أصلاً اسم سوى هذا الهو. ولما كان الوحي كان مسامرة لكونه ليلاً، وأعلى مجالس[171] الحديث المسامرة لأنها خلوة في خلوة، وموضع إدلال وتقريب مصطفى.

٢٤ وأما الآيات التي رآها فمنها في الآفاق ومنها في نفسه. قال – عز وجل– ﴿سَنُرِيهِمْ آيَاتِنَا فِي الْآفَاقِ وَفِي أَنْفُسِهِمْ﴾ (فصلت ٥٣) وقال: ﴿وَفِي أَنْفُسِكُمْ أَفَلَا تُبْصِرُونَ﴾ (الذاريات ٢١) و ﴿قَابَ قَوْسَيْنِ﴾ (النجم ٩) من آيات الآفاق، حقق به مقام العبد من سيده. ﴿أَوْ أَدْنَى﴾ مقام المحبة والاختصاص بالهو. ﴿فَأَوْحَى إِلَى عَبْدِهِ مَا أَوْحَى﴾ (النجم ١٠) مقام المسامرة، وهو هو الهو غيب الغيب، وأيّده ﴿مَا كَذَبَ الْفُؤَادُ

١٧٠ ط: حيثية

١٧١ ل: محاسن

When the Prophet – God's blessing and peace be upon him – descended from his servanthood to what we have mentioned, he was made to journey by night to the 'unseen of the unseen', which we have also mentioned. From there he contemplated his Beloved, the Real, as One, Singular. For love demands jealousy, so there remains no trace of the servant. Thus the servant is powerful and there is no restriction upon him. No Name appears here at all, save this 'He'. The Revelation was an intimate conversation, because it was at night. The highest of the gatherings where conversation takes place is the intimate night-conversation, because it is a 'solitude within a solitude',[179] the place of familiarity and exclusive closeness.

§24 As for the signs that the Prophet saw, some were on the horizons and some were in himself. God – may He be magnified and glorified – said: *We shall show them Our signs on the horizons and in themselves* (Q.41:53), and He said: *And in yourselves. Can ye then not see?* (Q.51:21). And the *distance of two bows' lengths* (Q.53:9) from his Lord is one of the *'signs on the horizon'* (Q.41:53) by which the Prophet realized the station of servant. *Or closer* (Q.53:9) is the station of love and election by the 'He'.[180] *And He revealed to His servant what He revealed* (Q.53:10) is the station of intimate conversation, and it is the 'he of the He',[181] the unseen of the Unseen.[182] He confirmed it with: *The inner heart*[183]

179. Arabic: *khalwa fī khalwa*. The root *kh-l-w* is also related to emptiness and void.

180. 'And if you ask: What is the He? We answer: The essential Unseen (*ghayb*), which one cannot witness. For He is not manifest or a locus of manifestation' (*Fut.*II.128, Chap. 73).

181. Arabic: *huwa huwa al-huwa*.

182. Arabic: *ghayb al-ghayb*. This expression possibly originated with al-Tustarī, who defines it as 'the spiritual self (*nafs al-rūḥ*), the understanding of the intellect (*fahm al-ʿaql*), and the discernment of meaning by the heart (*fiṭnat al-murād bi l-qalb*)'. See *Tafsīr al-Tustarī*, p.182.

183. Arabic: *fuʾād*. The various names for heart (*qalb*) became for the Sufis an entire spiritual physiology, progressing from the external breast, *ṣadr*, the seat of the externals of faith, to the innermost heart, *sirr* (secret), passing through progressively more intimate and subtle levels of *fuʾād* (inner heart) and *lubb* (kernel). *Qalb* itself comes from a root that means 'to change, fluctuate'. See al-Tirmidhī, *Bayān al-farq bayn al-ṣadr wa l-fuʾād wa l-lubb*, trans. Heer, 'A Sufi Psychological Treatise'; Heer and Honerkamp, *Three Early Sufi Texts*. For some early Arab grammarians, *fuʾād* took its name from *fāda*, meaning to put in motion. It is sometimes equated with the pericardium, the heart's (*qalb*) interior. This is the word used in one of the

مَا رَأَى﴾ (النجم ١١) والفؤاد قلب القلب. وللقلب رؤية وللفؤاد رؤية، فرؤية القلب يدركها العمى إذا صدرت عن الحق بإيثار غيره بعد تقريبه إياها ﴿وَلَكِنْ تَعْمَى الْقُلُوبُ الَّتِي فِي الصُّدُورِ﴾ (الحج ٤٦) والفؤاد لا يعمى لأنه لا يعرف الكون وما له تعلُّق إلا بسيده، ولا يتعلق من سيده إلا بغيب الغيب. وهو "هو الهو" لمناسبة المقامات والمراتب. ولهذا قال: ﴿مَا كَذَبَ الْفُؤَادُ مَا رَأَى﴾ فإنه قد يغلط البصر كثيراً وإن كان هذا عين الجهل من قائله، فإنه لا يغلط إلا الحاكم لا ما يدركه الحواسّ، فالذي يقول: "يغلط[172] البصر" لكونه يرى الأمر على خلاف ما هو عليه، فيُكذِّبُه صاحبُه فنفى عنه هذه الصفة لأن الكذب إنما يقع في عالم التشبيه والكثرة، وهنا ليس ثَمَّ تشبيه أصلاً فإن العبد هنا عبد من جميع الوجوه مُنَزَّهٌ مطلق التنزيه في العبودية، وكذلك "غيب الغيب" الذي هو "هو الهو."

١٧٢ كلمة يغلط بدون النقط في أكثر النسخ

lied not in what it saw (Q.53:11). The *inner heart* is the heart of the heart.[184] The heart has one vision and the inner heart has another vision. Blindness can overtake the heart's vision if it departs from the Real by preferring what is other than Him after having come close to Him.[185] [*For indeed it is not the eyes that grow blind,*] *but it is the hearts, which are within the breasts* (Q.22:46). But the inner heart does not become blind, because it does not know creation. It is attached to its Master alone, and its Master is attached only to the 'unseen of the unseen' and to the 'he of the He', because of the correspondence of the stations and the levels.[186] For this reason He said: *The inner heart lied not in what it saw* (Q.53:11). The eye frequently may err, even if this is sheer ignorance on the part of someone who says it. For what errs is only what judges, not what the senses perceive. Whoever claims that it is the eye that errs, since it sees something other than as it really is, will be called a liar by his companion.[187] God denied this attribute of the Prophet because lying occurs only in the world of similarity and multiplicity. Here there is no similarity at all, for the servant here is a servant in every respect, absolutely incomparable with respect to servanthood, and similarly he is the 'unseen of the Unseen', which is the 'he of the He'.[188]

Qur'anic passages describing Muhammad's *mi'rāj*: 'The inner heart (*fu'ād*) lied not in what it saw' (Q.53:11).

184. Arabic: *qalb al-qalb*.

185. An example of this might be found in Abraham's plea for a righteous son, which distracts him from his single-hearted devotion to God. See Para. 41.

186. This passage suggests through the intertwining of the personal pronoun 'H/he' (which in Arabic is not distinguished by a capital letter) the extraordinary intimacy between the innermost part of the servant and his Lord.

187. Ibn 'Arabī is most likely referring here to himself.

188. Arabic: *huwa al-huwa*. See Commentary for a discussion of this central point.

٢٥ والآيات التي رآها في نفسه مشاكلته لهو الهو بعبودة[١٧٣] العبودة في غيب الغيب بعين[١٧٤] قلب القلب الذي هو الفؤاد وما كل[١٧٥] أحد يراها. وآيات الآفاق ما ذكره، عليه السلام، مما رأى في النجوم والسموات والمعارج العُلى والرفرف الأدنى وصريف الأقلام والمستوى وما غشى الله به سدرة المنتهى. وهذا كله مما[١٧٦] حول هذا المقام المختص[١٧٧] بالعبد الذي أُقيم فيه في غيب الغيب. وقد نبّه على هذا بقوله: ﴿الَّذِي بَارَكْنَا حَوْلَهُ﴾ ولم يذكر بركة المقام لأنه فوق الذكر لعدم التشبيه، وهو مقام يُتخطَّف الناسُ منه لعِزّته، فالمسجد[١٧٨] الحرام للمسجد الأقصى كالجنة مع النار "حُفَّت الجنةُ بالمكارِه" (28) ﴿أَوَ لم يروْا أنّا جعلْنا حَرَماً آمِناً ويُتَخَطَّفُ الناسُ من حوْلِهِ﴾ (العنكبوت ٦٧) "وحُفَّت النارُ بالشهوات" ﴿إِلَى الْمَسْجِدِ

١٧٣ ك: لعبودة

١٧٤ ل، ط، ظ: لعين

١٧٥ ل، ط: كان

١٧٦ ط: - مما

١٧٧ ط: المخصص

١٧٨ ل، ط: والمسجد

§25 The signs that the Prophet saw in himself are his resemblance to the 'h/He of the H/he' belonging to the 'servitude of the servitude'[189] in the 'unseen of the unseen', with the eye of the heart's heart, which is the inner heart. Not everyone sees them. The *signs on the horizon* are those which the Prophet – God's blessing and peace be upon him – mentioned. Among the things that he saw were: the stars, the heavens, the supernal stairs, the lowest *rafraf*,[190] the scratching of the Pens,[191] the sitting on the Throne and that with which God covered the Lote Tree of the Limit. All of this is found around the station specific to the servant, which is established in him in the 'unseen of the unseen'. He has notified us of that by His saying: *the environs whereof We have blessed* (Q.17:1). He did not mention the blessing of the station since it is beyond mentioning because of its lack of similarity. It is the station that people are wrenched from because of its inaccessibility. The *Inviolable Place of Prostration* to the *Farthest Place of Prostration* is like the Garden to the Fire.[192] 'The Garden is surrounded by hardships' – *Have they not seen that We have appointed a sanctuary immune while humankind are ravaged all around them?* (Q.29:67) – 'and the Fire is surrounded by desires'.[193] *To the Farthest*

189. Arabic: *ʿubūdat al-ʿubūda*. For the difference between two closely related terms, *ʿubūda* (servitude) and *ʿubūdiyya* (servanthood), see *Fut.*II.128 (Chap. 73) and II.213ff. (Chap. 130). *ʿUbūda* describes an essential and pure quality. It is the lowest of the low. It is, for example, said of the earth that it is so low that even the lowly walk upon it (*Fut.*II.214). 'Servitude is the servant's being ascribed to his Lord. Then, after that, there is 'servanthood' which is his being ascribed to the divine locus without any opposition' (*Fut.*II.88, Chap. 73). Servitude offers no resistance to God's command. When an entity is called into existence, it exists. With servanthood, choice to obey or disobey enters the picture. Muhammad's servitude is given expression in his prostration without being commanded to do so, a result of prostration itself being called into existence in the locus of Muhammad. 'In this world, the knowers of God worship their Lord through servitude, since they have no relationship except to Him. But everyone other than them is ascribed to servanthood' (ibid.).

190. The exact meaning of this word is uncertain, whether Muhammad's conveyance was a kind of litter or a cushion of some sort, but words from this root also have the sense of gleaming, fluttering, verdant.

191. Arabic: *ṣarīf al-aqlām*. The scratching of the Pens refers to the writing of the destiny of all creatures on the heavenly tablet. The sound was heard by the Prophet during his heavenly ascension.

192. In other words, the two could not be further apart.

193. See Muslim, *Ṣaḥīḥ*, *janna*, I 8 142: 'Anas b. Malik reported: Paradise is surrounded by hardships and the Hell-fire is surrounded by temptations.'

﴿الْأَقْصَى الَّذِي بَارَكْنَا حَوْلَهُ﴾ فبطنٌ لِظهرٍ وظهرٌ لِبطن. (29) ونتج[١٧٩] هذا السفرُ مشاهدةَ ما ذكرناه من غيب الغيب. والكلام في هذا المقام يطول فلْنَقْبِض العِنان. ويكفي هذا القدر من الاشارة التي أوردناها فيه ﴿وَاللهُ يَقُولُ الْحَقَّ وَهُوَ يَهْدِي السَّبِيلَ﴾ (الأحزاب ٤).

٢٦ سفر الابتلاء

وهو سفر الهبوط من علو إلى سفل ومن قرب إلى بعد فيما يظهروكأنه مناقض للسفر الذي تقدّمه وقته وقته[١٨٠] وإن لم يَقْوَ قوَّتَه

قال الله – عز وجل – يخاطب آدم وحواء ومن نزل معهما فقال ﴿قُلْنَا اهْبِطُوا مِنْهَا جَمِيعاً﴾ (البقرة ٣٨). وقد تكلمنا على سفر الأب الأول في الروحانيات وهو أبو آدم وأبو العالم وهو حقيقة محمد، صلى الله عليه وسلم، وروحه. فلنتكلم على سفر الأب الأول[١٨١] الجسمي وهو أبو محمد، صلى الله عليه وسلم، وأبو بني آدم كلهم خاصة، فكل واحد منهما أبٌ وابنٌ لصاحبه من هذا الوجه.

١٧٩ ش: انتج؛ ط: ينتج

١٨٠ ش، ل، ط، ظ: وفيه ما فيه

١٨١ سقط من جميع النسخ ما عدا: ي

Place of Prostration whose environs We have blessed – an inner dimension corresponding to an outer dimension and an outer dimension corresponding to an inner dimension.[194]

This voyage results in contemplating what we have mentioned regarding the 'unseen of the unseen'. The discussion about this station is lengthy, so let us pull back on the reins. This much of the allusion that we have presented suffices. *And Allah speaks the truth and He guides on the Path* (Q.33:4).

§26 The Voyage of Trial

This is the voyage of the fall from high to low and from proximity to distance, in appearance.[195] It is as if it were the contrary of the voyage that immediately preceded it, although it does not have the same force.

God – may He be magnified and glorified – said, addressing Adam and Eve and the one[196] who descended with them: *We said: Go down, all of you, from hence* (Q.2:38). We have already spoken about the voyage of the First Father among the spiritual beings, namely the Father of Adam and the Father of the universe.[197] This is the Reality and Spirit of Muhammad – God's blessing and peace be upon him. So let us speak specifically about the voyage of the first corporeal father, who is the father of Muhammad – God's blessing and peace be upon him – and the father of the sons of Adam, all of them. Each of the two is both father and son of the other from this viewpoint.

194. See also Q.57:13: '… a wall will be put up betwixt them, with a gate therein. Within it will be Mercy throughout, and without it, all alongside, will be Punishment!' See also *Fut.*I.745 (Chap. 72).

195. Arabic: *fīmā yaẓhar*. As S. Hirtenstein has pointed out to me, this expression may also mean 'in manifestation', hence it is a voyage that extends from the highest level of creation to the lowest.

196. Namely Satan.

197. The first father in the spiritual dimension is the Muhammadan Reality while in the material dimension it is Adam. Hence, from one point of view Muhammad is the father of Adam, even if his corporeal existence occurred much later. From the point of view of corporeal existence, Adam is the father of Muhammad and all human beings. See al-Hakim, *Mu'jam*, pp.38ff.

فاعلم – وفّقنا اللهُ وإياك – أن الله – تعالى – إذا أراد أن يحدث أمراً أشار إليه بعلامات لمن فهمها يتقدم على وجود الشيء تسمَّى مقدمات الكون يشعر بها أهل الشعور. وكثيراً ما يطرأ هذا في الوجود في عالم الشهادة ولا سيما إذا ظهر في موضع ما لا يليق بذلك الموضع، فإنه يخاف من ظهور ما يناسب ما ظهر. وهذه الطِيرَة عند العرب والفأل، فما كان مما تحمده النفس كان فألاً وما كان مما يكرهونه كان عندهم طيرة. ولهذا أحب الشارع، صلى الله عليه وسلم، الفأل وهو الكلمة الحسنة وكره الطيرة، أي كره أن يتطيّر بشيء. والفأل عند العرب خير والطيرة شر ﴿وَنَبْلُوكُمْ بِالشَّرِّ وَالْخَيْرِ فِتْنَةً﴾ (الأنبياء ٣٥) ولا فاعلَ إلا الله. وهو، صلى الله عليه وسلم، يكره أن يُتطيَّر بما يُجريه اللهُ من المقدور، فإن في[١٨٢] كراهة ذلك عدم احترام الألوهة، والأولى أن يَتلقَّى ما لا يوافق الغرضَ منهما بالحمد والتسليم والرضا والانقياد ورؤية ما دفع الله مما هو أعظم من الذي نزل. كان عمر بن الخطاب، رضي الله عنه، يقول في مثل هذا: "ما أصابني الله بمصيبة إلا رأيت أن لله عليّ فيها ثلاثَ نِعَم: إحدى، ذلك كونها لم تكن في ديني.

١٨٢ ش، ل، ط، ظ: - في

Know – may God give us and you success – that when God the Most High wants to originate something, He indicates to those who understand them signs that precede the existence of the thing, called the premises of creation, that people of discernment are aware of. In existence this often happens in the world of witnessing,[198] especially when something appears in a place that does not suit that place. Then one fears that something corresponding to what has appeared will become manifest. This is called by the Arabs an evil omen (*ṭīra*)[199] or a good omen (*fa'l*).[200] What the soul praises is a good omen and what it dislikes is a bad omen. For this reason, the Lawgiver – God's blessing and peace be upon him – loved the good omen – which is the 'goodly word' – and he disliked the bad omen; that is, he disliked it if anyone gave a bad omen about anything.[201] The *fa'l*, according to the Arabs, is good and the *ṭīra* is bad. *We try you with evil and with good, as an ordeal* (Q.21:35). There is no agent save God and the Prophet – God's blessing and peace be upon him – disliked it, if anyone gave a bad omen about a decree that God had carried out, for in that is a lack of respect for the Divinity. It is best to receive what does not agree with one's aim with praise, acceptance, contentment and compliance, and to see that God has warded off what would have been greater than what occurred. 'Umar b. al-Khaṭṭāb – may God be pleased with him – used to say concerning something like this: 'God the Most High never caused any misfortune to reach me but that I saw three favours in it: the first was that it did not involve my religion; the second was that it

198. The world of sense perception.

199. Arabic: *ṭīra*. This comes from the same root as *ṭayr*, 'bird', whose cries and flight were often viewed as bad omens.

200. According to one tradition (quoted by Lane, *Lexicon*, vol. 6, p.109), 'he (the Prophet) used to love the *fa'l* and dislike the *ṭīra*'.

201. In a hadith related in al-Bukhārī's *Ṣaḥīḥ*: 'It is narrated on the authority of Abu Hurairah that the Messenger of God said: "There is no *ṭīra*, and the best omen is the *fa'l*." They asked, "What is the *fa'l*?" He said, "A good word that one of you hears."' See *Fut.*II.149 (Chap. 77), where this hadith is associated with the incident mentioned in the Qur'an when the Prophet 'frowned and turned away when the blind man came to him' (Q.80:1–2). '[The Messenger of God] sought [the good omen] by supplicating the Real, and the appearance of signs is only manifested to someone who is described as "seeing"' (*Fut.*II.149).

الثانية، كونها كانت ولم يكن ما هو أعظم منها. الثالثة، ما لي فيها من الأجر وحط الخطايا". فانظر إلى حضوره وحسن نظره فيما يبتليه الله به، رضي الله عنه.

٢٧ ولما كان الأمر هكذا جارياً عرفناه بحكم العادة والتجربة، ولم تتقدم[١٨٣] لآدم، عليه السلام، عادة ولا تجربة لهذا الفن، فلم يتفطَّن آدم، عليه السلام، لتحْجير الله عليه الأكل من الشجرة. وموطن الجنة لا يقتضي التحجير فإنه يأكل منها من فيها ما شاء[١٨٤] ويتبوَّأ منها حيث يشاء. فلما وقع التحجير في موطن لا يقتضي ذلك عرفنا أنه لا بد أن تظهر حقيقة ذلك الأمر[١٨٥] وأنه يُستنْزَل من عالم السعة والراحة إلى عالم الضيق والتكليف. ولو عرفها آدم ما تهنَّأ زمان مُقامه في الجنة. ومن جملة ما نسب آدم إلى نفسه من الظلم في قوله: ﴿رَبَّنَا ظَلَمْنَا أَنْفُسَنَا﴾ (الأعراف ٢٣) حيث لم نتفطَّن[١٨٦] لاشارتك بالتحجير والمنع في موطن التسريح والاباحة، ولهذا نُهِيَ ولم يُؤمَر أمرَ إيجاب. وكان حاملاً للمخالف من ولده في ظهره والطائع، فأوقع المخالفة عن حركة المخالِف، فلما رماه من صُلْبه ما بلغنا أن آدم [عليه السلام] عصى ربه بعد ذلك أبداً. وأُفْرِدَ بالمعصية دون أهله في قوله ﴿وَعَصَى آدَمُ رَبَّهُ﴾ (طه ١٢١) والنهي

١٨٣ ك: تقدّم

١٨٤ ط: يشاء

١٨٥ ك، ط: الأثر

١٨٦ ش: تتفطن؛ ط، ظ: يتفطن، وفي النسخة الاصلية بدون النقط

had not been greater; and the third was the recompense and the reduction of sin that it contained for me.'[202] So regard his presence and the fine way he viewed what God had imposed upon him – may God be pleased with him – as a trial.

§27 Since this is how the matter usually occurs, we know it through its property of being habitual and part of experience. But Adam had no prior habit or experience of this kind. Adam – upon him be peace – did not comprehend God's forbidding him to eat from the tree. The place of the Garden did not require interdiction, so he ate in it whatever he wanted and went wherever he wanted. When interdiction occurs in a place where it is not required, we know that inevitably the reality of that matter will become manifest, and that it will descend from the world of vastness and leniency to the world of narrowness and obligation.[203] Had Adam known this, he would not have felt pleasure during the time of his stay in the Garden. Among all the injustices that Adam ascribed to himself in his saying: *Our Lord, we have wronged ourselves* (Q.7:23) was not comprehending God's interdiction and prohibition in a place where things are permitted and allowed. For that reason, he was given a negative and not a positive command.

Among his children, he bore in his loins those who would be disobedient and those who would be obedient to God's Law. Disobedience stemmed from the movement of the first disobedient one.[204] We have not heard that Adam – peace be upon him – ever disobeyed his Lord after he cast his posterity from his loins. He, and not his wife, was singled out as disobedient in His saying: *And Adam disobeyed his Lord* (Q.20:121), even though the prohibition fell upon both of them,

202. See also *Fut.*I.746 (Chap. 72), III.15 (Chap. 303), IV.460–1 (Chap. 560).

203. Arabic: *taklīf*. The word suggests an imposition of a task or duty, often onerous. It is frequently associated with the obligation to observe the various positive and negative commands of God's Law. This world is the arena of *taklīf*; in the hereafter one is no longer commanded to carry out these obligations.

204. 'Adam denied so his children denied, Adam forgot so his children forgot, Adam made mistakes so his children made mistakes.' al-Tirmidhī, *Jāmiʿ*, *Tafsīr* Sura 7:3: 'Little it is ye remember of admonition.'

وقع عليهما، والفعل وقع منهما[١٨٧] لأنها جزءٌ منه فكأنه[١٨٨] ما ثَمَّ إلا هو ولأنه أقرب إلى الذكرى من حواء ﴿فنسي﴾ (طه ١١٥) والمرأة أَنْسى من الرجل، ولهذا قامت المرأتان في الشهادة مقام الرجل الواحد لأن الله - [تعالى] - يقول: ﴿فَإِنْ لَمْ يَكُونَا رَجُلَيْنِ فَرَجُلٌ وَامْرَأَتَانِ مِمَّنْ تَرْضَوْنَ مِنَ الشُّهَدَاءِ أَنْ تَضِلَّ إِحْدَاهُمَا فَتُذَكِّرَ إِحْدَاهُمَا الْأُخْرَى﴾ (البقرة ٢٨٢)، وذلك لأن[١٨٩] المرأة شِقٌ من الرجل، فامرأتان شقان، وشقان نشأة كاملة، فامرأتان رجل واحد، فهي ناقصة الخلق مُعْوجّة في النشء لأنها ضِلَع فانْحَدَرتْ[١٩٠] من اللفظ (30) ولم تذكر. وذكر آدم، عليه السلام، لنقيض ما ذكرناه في حواء. ونسيان آدم، عليه السلام، إنما كان لما أخبره الله به من عداوة إبليس. وما تخيَّل آدم، عليه السلام، أن أحداً يُقْسِم بالله كاذباً، فلما أقسم بالله إنه ناصِحٌ لهما فيما ذكره لهما تناولا من الشجرة المنهي عنها. وفي هذا تنبيه في أن الاجتهاد لا يسوغ مع وجود النص في المسألة. وفي عداوة إبليس لحواء بُشْرى لها بالسعادة لأنها لو كانت من حزب الشيطان ما كان عدواً لها.

١٨٧ و في سائر النسخ ما عدا ي: عنهما

١٨٨ ط: فكأنها

١٨٩ ك، ب، ظه: أن

١٩٠ ش، ل، ط، ظ: فاهدرت

and the act was attributed to both of them, because she is a part of him – so it is as if there were only him – and because he was more likely to remember than Eve, but *he forgot* (Q.20:115).[205] Woman is more forgetful than man. For that reason, two women take the place of one man in the case of testimony, because God said: *And if two men be not at hand, then a man and two women, of such as ye approve as witnesses, so that if the one erreth [through forgetfulness] the other will remember* (Q.2:282). That is because woman is a part of man, so two women are two parts, a complete constitution. Two women then are equivalent to one man. Woman is incomplete with respect to her creation, curved in constitution, because she is a rib,[206] which derives from the word 'curved'. She did not remember, but Adam – peace be upon him – remembered, in contradistinction to what we have mentioned regarding Eve. The forgetfulness of Adam – peace be upon him – is because of what God has informed us about: the enmity of Iblīs. Adam – peace be upon him – did not imagine that anyone would swear a lying oath by God. When Iblīs swore by God that he was giving them advice concerning what he mentioned to them, they took from the prohibited tree. In this there is a warning: any attempt to engage in independent reasoning concerning a question is not permitted when there is a text.[207] In Iblīs's enmity towards Eve there are good tidings to her of felicity, for had she belonged to the party of Satan, he would not have been her enemy.

* Correction - 'remembered due to being the opposite of what we have said about Eve.'
† 'is because of what God informed him about: the enmity of Iblis

205. See Q.20:115: 'And verily We made a covenant of old with Adam, but he forgot.'

206. The word *ḍilʿ* (rib) derives from *ḍaliʿa*, which means to be curved or crooked.

207. Ibn 'Arabī does not favour legal rulings based on personal opinion (*ra'y*) or analogical reasoning (*qiyās*); for him, these, along with interpretation (*ta'wīl*), overstep God's limits. See *Fut.*I.242 (Chap. 42): 'He who halts at the limits of his Master, obeys His regulations, and does not oppose Him in anything He has brought, according to the limit that He ordained for him, without any addition by means of analogical reasoning (*qiyās*) or independent opinion (*ra'y*), or subtraction by means of interpretation (*ta'wīl*), treats his genus among human beings as he has been commanded to treat them, whether believer, unbeliever, disobedient, friend, or hypocrite.'

والذم تعلق بصورة الكسب لا بالفاعل المكتسب، ولو تعلق الذمّ بالمكتسب لبَغَضْنا العُصاة، ونحن إنما نكره منهم المعصية، ولا تزال المعصية مكروهة أعني معصية الله. وكذلك أيضاً لا تقع الكراهة منا على السبب المعصي به، فإنه قد يُنْسَخ تحريمُه ويرجع حلالاً فتزول الكراهة. فلو تعلق الذمّ به لعينه لم يزل مذموماً. فتعلُّق الذم إنما هو بأمر دقيق خفي إضافي يكاد لا يثبت وكذلك الحمد، فافهم. وتفطّنت المعتزلة لسِرٍّ في هذه المسألة ما تنبَّهت[191] له الأشاعرة، وهو سرٌّ دقيق حسن، فحقِّق النظر فيه تجد الذي عثرت عليه المعتزلة.

٢٨ ثم نرجع ونقول: فلما وقع ما وقع من آدم وحواء أُهْبِطا إلى الأرض. فهذا سفرٌ في الظاهر من عنده وكذلك سفر إبليس من عنده. فوجد إبليس في سفره الملك والراحة التي يؤول بها إلى الشقاء الدائم، ووجد آدم المشقة والتعب والتكليف الذي يؤول به إلى السعادة. وكان من علوّ سفره هذا، أنه سافر من شهوة نفسه إلى معرفة عبوديته، فإن الجنة لمجرَّد الشهوات، لهذا قال: ﴿لَكُمْ فِيهَا مَا تَشْتَهِي أَنْفُسُكُمْ﴾ (فصلت ٣١).

١٩١ ط: فاتبهت

Blame is connected with the form of the acquired act,[208] not with the acquiring agent. If blame were connected with the acquirer, we would hate the disobedient person, but we dislike only the act of disobedience. Disobedience – I mean, disobedience to God – is always disliked. Similarly, it does not occur to us to dislike the cause of disobedience, for the interdiction could be abrogated and the act would become permitted again. Then dislike would cease. If blame were connected with the cause itself, it would always be blamed. Attaching blame is only because of a subtle, hidden, relative affair that is quite unstable, and the same is true of praise. So understand. The Muʿtazilites have understood a secret regarding this question that the Ashʿarites are not aware of. It is a subtle and fine secret. Thoroughly reflect upon it and you will find what the Muʿtazilites discovered.[209]

§28 Now let us return to our subject. We say: When what happened to Adam and Eve took place, they descended to the earth. This voyage appeared to be a voyage *from* Him; similarly, the voyage of Iblīs was *from* Him. Iblīs found in his voyage dominion and ease that would lead him in the end to eternal wretchedness. Adam found trouble, toil and obligation that would lead him in the end to felicity. The elevation of this voyage of his was to voyage from his soul's desire to knowledge of his servanthood, for the Garden belongs exclusively to desires. For that reason He said: *There ye will have [all] that your souls desire* (Q.41:31).[210]

208. Arabic: *kasb*. There was extensive debate in Islamic theological circles about precisely this notion in connection with human free will vs. God's determination of all acts. For background, consult Cahen, 'Kasb', and its bibliography; Abrahamov, 'Acquisition'; see also the studies by Frank, 'Moral Obligation', and 'Structure of Created Causality'; Gardet and Anawati, *Introduction*; Schwartz, '"Acquisition" (*kasb*)'; and Wolfson, *Philosophy of the Kalam*, pp.663–719.

209. See *Fut.*I.299 (Chap. 61). Things in themselves, without reference to the Law, are neither praiseworthy nor blameworthy. A lie (considered bad in itself) told in order to save a life is praiseworthy; a truth (considered good in itself) told in order to harm someone is blameworthy.

210. See also the Prophetic hadith: 'None among the people of the Garden says to a thing "Be" but that it is.'

وأكمل له هنا لباسه، فإنه كان في الجنة صاحب لباس واحد وهو الريش، ولم يعرف طَعْماً للِباس التقوى (31) لأن الجنة ليست بمحل للتقوى لأنها نعيم كلها، والتقوى يطلب ما يتقى منه، فإذن فلا يكون في الجنة. ولما لم يكن عنده، عليه السلام، لباس التقوى ووقع النهي لم يكن له [علم][١٩٢] بما يتّقيه إذ التقوى من صفات هذا الدار وما عدا الجنة. فلما نزل من الجنة أُنْزِل عليه لباسُ سَتْر[١٩٣] النشأة ولباسُ التقوى، ثم نُهِيَ وأُمِرَ وكُلِّف. فلم تُتَصوّر[١٩٤] منه بعد ذلك مخالفةٌ لحماية[١٩٥] هذا اللباس. فصار نزوله إلى هذه الدار من تمام نشأته ومرتبته، ثم رحلته إلى الجنة من كمال مرتبته ونفسه. والدنيا دارُ تمامٍ والآخرة دارُ كمال، وليس بعد

١٩٢ في سائر النسخ ما عدا ي، ك

١٩٣ ط: سر

١٩٤ في سائر النسخ ما عدا ي: يتصور

١٩٥ ط: حماية

God finished clothing him here, for in the Garden he had only one garment: feathers.[211] He had no taste of the *raiment of godfearing*[212] because the Garden is not a place of godfearing; all of it is bliss. Godfearing demands something to be wary of, thus it does not exist in the Garden. Since Adam had no *raiment of godfearing*, when the negative command came, he had no knowledge[213] of what would protect him, since godfearing is one of the attributes of this abode, not of the Garden. When he descended from the Garden, the clothing that would cover his configuration and the clothing of godfearing were revealed to him. Then he was addressed with the negative command, the positive command and the obligation.[214] Disobedience was not conceivable from him after that because of the protection of this clothing. His descent to this abode resulted in the completion of his configuration and his level. Then his [subsequent] journey[215] to the Garden was because of the perfection of his level and his soul. This world is the abode of completion while the next world is the abode of perfection.[216] There is nothing

211. See Q.7:26: 'O Children of Adam! We have revealed unto you raiment to conceal your shame, and splendid vesture/feathers (*rīsh*), but the raiment of godfearing (*taqwā*), that is best. This is of the revelations of Allah, that they may remember!'

212. Arabic: *taqwā*. See above note. For Ibn 'Arabī's notion of the raiment of *taqwā*, see *Fut.*IV.163 (Chap. 521), which stems from the Qur'anic verse: 'So make provision for yourselves; for the best provision is godfearing (*taqwā*)' (Q.2:197). See also Ibn 'Arabī, 'Ibn al-'Arabī's Testament', trans. Elmore, pp.6–7, 25.

213. Missing in the holograph MS.

214. The Qur'an uses the Arabic root *n-h-y* to prohibit: usury (Q.4:161); declaring that God is three as the Christians do (Q.4:171); worshipping gods other than Allah (Q.6:56); disobeying the Messenger of God (Q.58:8); taking as guardians those who combat Muslims over religion, drive them out of their homelands, or support those who drive them out (Q.60:9). Muslims are forbidden in general to commit grave sins (Q.16:90).

As for positive commands, using the Arabic root *a-m-r*, the Qur'an commands: rendering trusts to whom they are due (Q.4:58); judging and behaving justly (Q.4:58; 7:29; 16:90); giving due attention to God by turning to Him in the mosques and calling upon Him; being sincere to Him in religion (Q.7:29; 39:11; 98:5); worshipping only Allah (Q.5:117; 9:31; 12:40; 13:36; 39:11; 98:5); believing and submitting (Q.6:14; 6:71; 10:104; 27:91; 40:66); remaining on the right course (Q.11:112; 42:15); giving to relatives (16:90); inclining to truth (Q.98:5); establishing prayer (Q.98:5); and giving *zakāt* (charity) (Q.98:5).

215. Arabic: *riḥla*. See Commentary.

216. The Arabic terms *tamām* (completeness) and *kamāl* (perfection), which are sometimes viewed as synonymous, are here given as distinct attributes. As Lane points out in his *Lexicon*, Vol. 1, p.315, *tamām* has a sense of lacking nothing, being free from defect, whole

الكمال مطلب، فما بعد الدار من دار أصلاً.

٢٩ فأقام آدم، عليه السلام، في سفره هذا يقْتني المعارف الكسبية من جهة التكليف التي لم تكن تحصل[١٩٦] له دون التكليف. وهذا أن الدنيا دار تمام للعبد واقتناء المعارف الفكرية التي لا يعطيها[١٩٧] إلا الدنيا، فإن نشأة الجنة كشفٌ كلُّها. وأخذ[١٩٨] يقتني معارف التدبير والتفصيل والحُسن والأحسن والأَوْلى والأحرى ومعرفة الترتيب ابتداءً، وهذا لا يكون إلا في الدنيا من أجل كثافة النشأة والبخارات المانعة من الكشف، فيحتاج إلى قوة لا تكون[١٩٩] له إلا بوجود هذه الموانع، ولولاها لم تعطه فهذا من تمامه. ولهذا قال سهل بن عبد الله ليس للعقل فائدة في الانسان إلا ليدفع به الانسان سلطان شهوته خاصة، وإذا غلبت الشهوة، بقي العقل لا حكم له.

ومما يؤيد ما ذكره سهل ما أطلعَنا اللهُ – تعالى – عليه عند كشف الأسرار فأرانا في أسرارنا بإلهامه الأنزه أن الملائكة في المعارف خُلِقَتْ وكذلك الجمادات والنبات.[٢٠٠] والحيوان خُلِق في المعارف والشهوة،

١٩٦ ب، ط: يكن يحصل
١٩٧ ط، ظه: تعطيها؛ ي: بدون النقط
١٩٨ ط: واحد؛ ي: بدون النقط
١٩٩ ب، ط، ظ: يكون
٢٠٠ في سائر النسخ ما عدا ي: النباتات، لكن أسلوب الشيخ في الفتوحات وكما هنا: "النبات."

further to seek after perfection, and there is no abode after that abode whatsoever.

§29 Adam – peace be upon him – undertook on this voyage of his to gather the knowledge that is acquired by means of obligation and cannot be acquired without it. This is because this world, for the servant, is the abode of completion and gathering deliberative knowledge that only this world provides, while the configuration of the Garden is all unveiling. He began to gather knowledge of governance, of discernment of the good, the better, and the most appropriate, and the knowledge of ordering from the beginning. This can only take place in this world because of the density of the constitution and the vapours that prevent unveiling. He required a faculty that he did not have until these obstacles existed. Were it not for them, he would not have been given it. This is part of his completion. Therefore, Sahl b. ʿAbd Allāh [al-Tustarī] said: 'The intellect is of no use in the human being unless the human specifically uses it to repulse the authority of his desire.[217] If desire overcomes him, the intellect remains without any authority.'

Confirming what Sahl has mentioned is what God the Most High informed us about when unveiling the secrets. He made us see in our innermost souls[218] by means of His most transcendent inspiration that the angels are created in gnosis,[219] just as the inanimates, the plants and the animals are created in gnosis and desire. For

---

and complete, while *kamāl* indicates all this plus the idea of excellence and virtue. *Tamām* implies a former lack or deficiency that has been corrected, whereas *kamāl* does not necessarily imply any prior defect.

217. Arabic: *shahwa*. Also sometimes translated as 'appetite'. For Ibn ʿArabī, *shahwa* is 'an instrument of the soul' (*Fut*.II.189, Chap. 108) in its seeking pleasure, whether that pleasure be 'high' or 'low'. Thus desire may be for sensory pleasures, such as food and sexual intercourse, or for more intangible pleasures, such as power and reputation. 'It is necessary for every believer … to set aside every affair that leads to the heart's occupation with anything but God, for it is a temptation in his case. It is necessary that his intellect overcome his desire (*shahwa*)' (ibid.). According to Ibn ʿArabī, *shahwa* is always associated with the natural world, and its location is the animal soul. See *Fut*.II.192–3 (Chap. 109), which specifically discusses the difference between *shahwa* and *irāda*, the desire associated with the rational soul.

218. Arabic: *asrār*, literally 'secrets'.

219. Arabic: *maʿārif*. Note that in Arabic the noun is plural.

ولهذا هو مع معرفته وشفقته من الساعة لا يرجع عن شهوته، وشفقتُهُ من أجل ما تصير إليه مع ما يراه[٢٠١] من المخالفة منّا. رأى بعضهم رجلاً يضرب رأس حمار له. فنهاه عن ذلك، فقال له الحمار: دَعْه، فإنه على رأسه يضرب. (32) والانسان خُلِقَ في المعارف الضرورية والشهوة والعقل، فبعقله يرد شهوته.

٣٠ ومما اقتناه آدم، عليه السلام، في معصيته وسفره من أسماء ربه ومن آثارها ومشاهدتها الذي لم يكن[٢٠٢] قبل ذلك يعرفه. وهو الغافر والمغفرة، وإن كان الغفور فمن أجل أن معصيته شديدة بالنسبة إلى مقامه تقتضي[٢٠٣] ما تقتضيه مائة ألف معصية من غيره مثلاً، وهو – سبحانه – في حق هذا الغير غفور، فقد يكون غفوراً في حق آدم من هذا الوجه، وغافراً من كونها مخالفةً واحدةً. وربما وقعت بتأويل منه، ولو نسي النهي ما عوقب أصلاً، وإنما نسي ما ذكرناه.

٢٠١ ط: نراه
٢٠٢ ط: التي لم تكن
٢٠٣ ش، ط، ظ: يقتضي

that reason, despite his gnosis and his apprehension concerning the Hour, the human being does not renounce his desire. His apprehension concerns what will happen to him because of his disobedience. One of the Men of God saw a man beating the head of his donkey and tried to prevent him from doing that. The donkey said to him, 'Let him. It is his own head he is beating.'[220] The human being was created in necessary gnosis, desire and intellect. Through his intellect he repels his desire.

§30 Among the things that Adam – peace be upon him – gained as a result of his disobedience and his voyage were some of the Names of his Lord, their effects and their contemplation, which he did not know prior to that. They are: the Forgiver and forgiveness, even if God is the Oft-Forgiving;[221] for Adam's grave disobedience with respect to his station demanded, for example, what a thousand acts of disobedience from someone else would demand. He – glorified be He – in the case of this other person is also the Repeatedly Oft-Forgiving, but in the case of Adam He is Oft-Forgiving in this respect but also [simply] Forgiving because his disobedience happened only once. Disobedience may have occurred because of an interpretation[222] he made. Had he forgotten the interdiction, he would not have been punished at all. He forgot only what we have mentioned.

220. Gril (*Dévoilement*, p.35, n.81) notes that the same story is recounted in al-Sarrāj (Nicholson, *K. al-Luma'*, p.316). It is also repeated in the *Futūḥāt*: see II.678; III.261; III.489. Ibn 'Arabī's source appears to be al-Qushayrī, where it appears as such: 'I heard Abu Hatim al-Sijistani say: I heard Abu Nasr al-Sarraj say: I heard al-Husayn b. Ahmad al-Razi say: I heard Abu Sulayman al-Khawwas say: "One day I was riding a donkey. It was pestered by flies and kept shaking its head. As I was beating its head with a stick that I held in my hand, the donkey raised his head and uttered: "Keep beating! You yourself will be beaten on your head!"' Al-Husayn [b. Ahmad al-Razi] asked Abu Sulayman: 'Did it indeed happen to you?' He answered: 'Yes, it did, [exactly] as you have heard!' (Trans. Knysh, *Epistle on Sufism*, p.369.)

221. *Al-Ghāfir* as opposed to *al-Ghafūr*. See *Fut.*IV.214–15 (Chap. 558) where the degrees of God's 'covering' or 'concealing' sins are, in order of greater encompassment: *Ghāfir*, *Ghaffār*, *Ghafūr*. The latter two are intensive forms, meaning 'forgiving much or repeatedly'.

222. Arabic: *ta'wīl*. Here we have an example of Ibn 'Arabī's disapproval of this form of interpretation. See Commentary.

وكذلك اقتنى[٢٠٤] الاجتباء والتوبة والاستغفار والعفو والخوف والأمن الوارد عقيب الخوف، فإنه أشد لذة من الاستصحاب.

٣١ وكذلك نتج له هذا السفر معرفة التركيب والانشاء والتحليل. فعرف من ذلك نشأة بِنْيته بتعاقب الأدوار شيئاً بعد شيء بخلاف تكوين الجنة، فإنه دفعةٌ في حق الناظر. وإن الهمّ مصروفٌ في الجنة لمجرد اللذة والنعيم، والهم في الدنيا مصروف إلى الزيادة من العلم والبحث عنه، فلهذا يعرف[٢٠٥] من هنا ما لا يعرفه من هناك. فينتج له سفره من مثل هذا كثيراً والأسفار كثيرة، وأخاف من التطويل. وهذا السفر الآدمي يحوي على كثير يحتاج أن يُفْرَد له ديوانٌ، وكذلك كل سفر ذكرناه ونذكره في هذا الكتاب، فألْحِقْ ما سكتْنا عنه بما تكلمنا عليه على[٢٠٦] ما يناسب، تُرْشَدْ إن شاء الله – عز وجل.

٢٠٤ ش، ط، ظ: اقتناء

٢٠٥ ك: يعرفه

٢٠٦ ط: - على

Similarly, he obtained election, repentance, seeking forgiveness, pardon, fear and the safety that comes after fear, for it is more pleasant than if he had had it all along.[223]

§31 Another result of this voyage is knowledge of composition, development and dissolution. Adam learned from it how his corporeal make-up was constituted according to the succession of cycles, one thing after another, in contradistinction to how things are generated in the Garden, for generation in the Garden takes place all at once for the observer. He also knew that in the Garden one's concern is directed to sheer pleasure and bliss, while one's concern in this world is directed to increasing knowledge and searching for it. For this reason, he knows here what he does not know there. His voyage results in many things like this.

The voyages are many, but I fear being overlong in my discussion. This Adamic voyage contains so many sciences that one could devote an entire compendium to it, as is the case with every voyage we have mentioned in this book. So put together whatever we have + been silent about ~~with what you~~ can ~~complete of it~~ insofar as it is compatible, and you will be rightly directed, God – may He be magnified and glorified – willing!

+ with what we have spoken of

223. Ibn ʿArabī is fond of this *faraj baʿd al-shidda* (relief following distress) motif of enjoying safety and security much more when one has suffered than if it is part of one's everyday experience. See, for example, *Fut.*I.256: 'When safety (*amān*) comes upon him, following strong fear, he finds a sweetness and pleasure from the safety that he had never known.' See also *Fut.*II.437, where Ibn ʿArabī states that qualities are known only by their opposites, hence safety is truly appreciated only by someone who has feared for his life.

٣٢ سفر إدريس، عليه السلام، وهو سفر العز والرفعة مكاناً ومكانةً

قال الله تعالى: ﴿وَاذْكُرْ فِي الْكِتَابِ إِدْرِيسَ إِنَّهُ كَانَ صِدِّيقاً نَبِيًّا وَرَفَعْنَاهُ مَكَاناً عَلِيًّا﴾ (مريم ٥٦–٥٧) ويقال إنه أول من كتب بالقلم من بني آدم، فأول إمداد القلم الأعلى له – عليه السلام. كان قد أُسْرِيَ به إلى أن بلغ السماء السابعة فصارت السماوات كلها في حوْزته.

٣٣ واعلموا[٢٠٧] أن السموات كلها قد جعلها الله محل العلوم[٢٠٨] الغيبية المتعلقة بما يُحْدِث الله في العالم من الكائنات: جوهرها وعَرَضها، صغيرها وكبيرها، وأحوالها وانتقالاتها. وما من سماء إلا وفيه علمٌ مودع بيد أمينها، وأودع الله نزول ذلك الأمر إلى الأرض في حركات أفلاكها وحلول كواكبها في منازل الفلك الثامن. وجعل لكواكب هذه السموات السبع اجتماعات وافتراقات وصعوداً وهبوطاً. وجعل آثارها مختلفة، وجعل منها ما يكون بينه وبين كواكب أُخَر مناسبةً،

٢٠٧ ك: واعلم (في الحاشية: في نسخ اعلموا)

٢٠٨ ط: محلا لعلوم

§32 *The Voyage of Enoch (Idrīs), peace be upon him, which is the Voyage of Glorious Height and Elevation in Position and Rank*[224]

God the Most High said: *And make mention in the Book of Idrīs. Lo! He was most veracious and a prophet; and We raised him to a high position* (Q.19:56–7). He is said to have been the first among the sons of Adam to write with a pen.[225] The first spiritual efflux[226] of the Supernal Pen was his – peace be upon him. He was made to voyage until he reached the seventh heaven,[227] so all of the heavens were in his compass.

§33 Know that God made all the heavens places for the hidden sciences associated with the beings God originated in the cosmos: substance and accident; small and large; their states and their movements. There is no heaven but that there is a science deposited in it in the hand of its guardian.[228] God has deposited in the mansions of the eighth sphere[229] the descent of that command towards the earth in the movements of their spheres and in the passage of their planets. He made for the planets of these seven heavens conjunctions and disjunctions, ascendant and descendant, and He made their influences different.[230] He made an affinity between some planets and

224. Arabic: *makān/makāna*. *Makān* has to do with position or place; *makāna* has to do with rank. See *Fuṣūṣ*, chapter on Idrīs, for a discussion of these two words, based on a single Arabic root. *Makāna* may also be translated as 'degree'.

225. See *Fut.*I.327 (Chap. 67), where Ibn 'Arabī attests to the Prophet Muhammad's claim that Idrīs was sent with the knowledge of writing. See Commentary for the association of this figure with the Egyptian Thoth and the Greek Hermes.

226. Arabic: *imdād*. The word for ink (*midād*) is also from this root.

227. The heaven of Saturn.

228. Every heaven has an angel guardian.

229. The sphere of fixed stars.

230. The combinations of cold, hot, wet and dry give four qualities: cold and dry, cold and wet, hot and dry, hot and wet. Three zodiacal signs are assigned to each combination. Cold and dry are the earth signs: Capricorn, Taurus and Virgo; cold and wet are the water signs: Cancer, Scorpio and Pisces; hot and dry are the fire signs: Aries, Leo and Sagittarius; hot and wet are the air signs: Aquarius, Libra and Gemini.

وجعل منها ما يكون بينه وبين كواكب أخر منافرةً كلية. وذلك أنه إذا أودع عند الواحد ضد ما أودعه عند الآخر كانت المنافرة، لا أنهم أعداءٌ. وإنما ذلك لحقائق خلقهم الله تعالى عليها تقضي[٢٠٩] بذلك. وشغلهم[٢١٠] بطاعة ربهم وتسبيحهِ ﴿لَا يَعْصُونَ اللهَ مَا أَمَرَهُمْ﴾ (التحريم ٦) كما جاء في خِلْقة مالِك خازن النار أنه ما ضحك قط بخلاف رِضْوان الذي خُلِق من فرح وسرور.[٢١١] وكلاهما عبدان صالحان مطيعان ليس بينهما عداوة ولا شحْناء، غير أن الآثار هنا في العالم الأسفل تنبعث عن تلك الحقائق وعندنا أغراضنا قائمة، فيقع[٢١٢] بيننا التحاسُد والعداوة، والأصل من ذلك.

وأمّا عدم المنافرة بين المتناسِبَيْن منها، فهو أن أوجد الواحد على خلاف ما أوجد الآخر، لا على ضدّه، فكل ضد خلاف وما كل خلاف ضدٌّ، فإن وكيل السماء السابعة يُضادّ وكيل السماء السادسة حتى أن ما يعلمه صاحب السماء السادسة إذا صار وقت الحكم فيه للمَلك الموكَّل به[٢١٣] في السماء السابعة أفسد ما أصلحه صاحب السماء السادسة كما يفعل أيضاً صاحب السادسة إذا أصلح ما يفسده صاحب السابعة. وكل مَلَك ما عنده أنه يفسد، وإنّما نقول[٢١٤] في فعله إنه أصلح من حيث أنه امتثل فيه أمرَ ربّه وأدّى ما أُمِّنَ عليه، وهو الأمر الذي ذكر الله أنه أوحى به السموات فقال – عزّ من قائل: ﴿وَأَوْحَى فِي كُلِّ سَمَاءٍ أَمْرَهَا﴾ (فصلت ١٢).

٢٠٩ ط: يقضي

٢١٠ ط: يشغلهم

٢١١ ط: سرور وفرح

٢١٢ ب، ط: فتقع

٢١٣ في سائر النسخ ما عدا ي: فيه

٢١٤ ي: بدون النقط؛ ش، ل، ط، ظ: وإنما يقول

He made a total aversion between others. That is because when He deposited in one the contrary of what He deposited in the other, there was an aversion, not that they are essentially enemies. This is only because the realities, upon which God the Most High created them, demand this. They, *who resist not Allah in that which He commandeth them* (Q.66:6), occupy themselves with obedience to their Lord and with praising Him. It has come regarding the disposition of the angel Mālik – the guardian of the Fire – that he never laughs, in contradistinction to the angel Riḍwān,[231] who is created happy and joyful. Both of them are righteous and obedient servants; there is no enmity or rancour between them. However, the influences here in the lower world stem from these realities, and with us they stem from our own personal interests. Thus there occurs between us envy and enmity, but the root is from that.

As for the lack of aversion between two mutually corresponding things, it is because one has been brought into existence in a different way than the other, but is not its contrary. Every contrary is different, but not every different is contrary. The trustee of the seventh heaven is the contrary of the trustee of the sixth heaven, so that the angel-trustee of the sixth heaven does not know when it has become time for authority to pass to the angel who is its trustee in the seventh heaven. This latter corrupts[232] what the angel-trustee of the sixth heaven has set right, just as the angel-trustee of the sixth heaven sets right what the angel-trustee of the seventh heaven has corrupted. It is not that every angel corrupts, but we say only concerning his activity that he sets right, in that he obeys the order of his Lord and executes what has been entrusted to him. This is the order that God the Most High has mentioned that He reveals to the heavens, as He – may He be magnified and glorified – says Himself: *He revealed in each heaven its command* (Q.41:12).[233]

231. Riḍwān is the angelic guardian of the Garden.

232. Corrupts in the sense of disordering or changing from one form to another, not in the sense of causing some moral evil. See, for example, *Fut.*III.459 (Chap. 373): 'In place of "corruption", we were saying only "the manifestation of one form and the elimination of another".'

233. See *Fut.*I.324 (Chap. 66) in which Idrīs imparts knowledge to the people, supporting

٣٤ فإذا أَنِسْتَ بهذا القدر وعلمتَ أنه لا يطعن في العقد، وإلا فأيّة فائدة كانت في قول الله تعالى: ﴿وَالنُّجُومُ مُسَخَّرَاتٌ بِأَمْرِهِ﴾ (النحل ١٢) فبماذا سخّرها في هذا يا أخي[٢١٥] وأشباهِهِ؟ أليس الله قد سخر العالم[٢١٦] بعضه لبعض؟ فقال: ورفع بعضَكم فوقَ بعضٍ درجاتٍ لِيتّخذَ بعضُكم بعضاً سُخْرياً[٢١٧] وقال: ﴿وَسَخَّرَ لَكُمْ مَا فِي السَّمَاوَاتِ وَمَا فِي الْأَرْضِ﴾ (الجاثية ١٣) فذكر أن في السماء أُموراً مسخَّرة لنا مثل الأرض، فلا يقدح في عقيدة مسلم كونُه يعلم ما أُوحِيَ في السماء من أمرها، وفيماذا سخر[٢١٨] عالَمها. ولو كان ذلك لاطَّرَدَ في الأرض و[٢١٩] السماء. ونحن في كل زمان نهرب إلى الأسباب التي نصبها الله لنا وعرّفنا بها على جهة أنها مسخَّرة، لا على أنها فاعلة نعوذ بالله ﴿لَا أُشْرِكُ بِهِ أَحَداً﴾ (الجن ٢٠). وإنما كفَّر الشارع من اعتقد أن الفعل للكواكب لا لله أو[٢٢٠] أن الله يفعل الأشياء بها، هذا هو الكفر والشرك. وأمَّا من يراها مسخرة وأن الله أجراها حكمةً فلا، بل من جهل[٢٢١] ما أودع الله فيها وما أوحى الله فيها من الأمور ورتّب فيها من الحِكَم فقد فاته خيرٌ كثير وعلمٌ كبير و ﴿فَمَاذَا بَعْدَ الْحَقِّ إِلَّا الضَّلَالُ﴾ (يونس ٣٢).

٢١٥ في سائر النسخ ما عدا ي: سخرها يا أخي في هذا وأشباهه

٢١٦ ك (في الحاشية): ليس في خطه العالم؛ ب: العالم، مكتوب في الحاشية

٢١٧ إشارة إلي الآية المباركة: ﴿وَرَفَعْنَا بَعْضَهُمْ فَوْقَ بَعْضٍ دَرَجَاتٍ لِيَتَّخِذَ بَعْضُهُمْ بَعْضاً سُخْرِيًّا﴾ (الزخرف ٣٢)

٢١٨ ط: سخرها

٢١٩ ط: + في

٢٢٠ ب، ش، ط، ظ: و

٢٢١ ط: جهة

§34 If you recognize that decree, you know that it does not refute the pact – for if this were not the case, what use would there be in God the Most High's saying: *And the stars are made subservient by His command* (Q.16:12)? Why has He made them subservient with respect to this and similar things, my brother? Has God not made some things in the cosmos subservient to others? He said: 'And He raised some of you above others in degree, so that some of you might take service from others';[234] and He said: *And He hath subjected unto you whatsoever is in the heavens and whatsoever is in the earth* (Q.45:13). He has mentioned that in the heavens there are things that are subjected to us, just as there are in the earth, and so a Muslim's belief is not diminished if he knows what has been revealed in the heaven of their command[235] and by what their world has been subjected. If that were not the case, he would be in complete agreement with [whatever is in] the earth and the heavens. At every time, we flee to the secondary causes[236] that God has set up for us; He has made us know that they are subjected to a divine command and are not themselves agents. We seek refuge in God. *I ascribe unto Him no partner* (Q.72:20). The Lawgiver[237] has declared that whoever believes that the act belongs to the stars and not to God, or that God made things through them, is an unbeliever. This is unbelief and association of others with God. As for one who sees that the stars are subjected to God's command and that God has set their course with wisdom, this is not the case. Indeed, much good and great knowledge has escaped someone who is ignorant of what God has deposited in the stars and those commands that God has revealed in them and set in order from His wisdom. *After the truth what is there save error?* (Q.10:32).

---

it with proofs that were not gained by reflective thought and which were confirmed by the heavenly signs.

234. An allusion to: 'And *We* raised some of them above others in degree that some of them may take service from others' (Q.43:32; italics mine).

235. God's command to the stars.

236. Arabic: *asbāb*. God creates these secondary causes as intermediaries but He remains the First Cause of all. It is noteworthy that Ibn 'Arabī uses the verb 'flee' in connection with secondary causes. See Commentary.

237. Muhammad.

٣٥ واعلم أن إدريس، عليه السلام، لما علم أن الله – تعالى– بالعلم الذي أوحاه إليه قد ربط العالم بعضَه ببعضه، وسخر بعضَه لبعضه، ورأى أن عالم الأركان مخصوص بالمُولَّدات، رأى اجتماعات الكواكب وافتراقها في المنازل واختلاف الكائنات واختلاف الحركات الفلكية، ورأى السريعة والبطيئة، وعرف أنه مهما جعل سيره وسفره مع البطيء أن السريع يدخل تحت حُكْمه، فإن الحركة دورية لا خطّية، فلا بد أن يرجع عليه دور الصغير السريع، فيعلم من مجاورة المتثبِّط[٢٢٢] فائدة المُسْرع (33). فلم ير ذلك إلا في السماء السابعة، فأقام عندها ثلاثين سنة يدور معها في قطع[٢٢٣] فلك البروج في مركز تدوير وكيلها، وفي الفلك الحامل لفلك التدوير، والفلك الحامل لأفلاك التداِوير، وهو الذي يدور به فلك البروج.

فلما عاين ما أوحى الله في السماء، وعاين أن الكواكب قريبة الاجتماع من برج السرطان، فعلم أنه لا بد أن يكون اللهُ يُنزل ماءً عظيماً وطوفاناً عاماً لِما تحققه من العلم ومشى في دقائق الفلك، فعلم الجُملَ والتفصيل.

٣٦ ثم نزل فاختصَ من أبناء دينه وشرعه ممن عرف أنّ فيه ذكاءً وفِطنة، فعَلَّمهم ما شاهد وما أودع الله من الأسرار في هذا العالم[٢٢٤] العُلوي، وأنه من جملة ما أوحى الله في هذه السموات أنه يكون طوفانٌ عظيم ويهلك الناس ويُنْسى العلم. وأراد بقاء هذا العلم على من يأتي بعدهم، فأمر بنقشها في الصخور والأحجار. ثم رفعه الله المكان العلي فنزل

٢٢٢ ش: المتبطي؛ ط: الهبط

٢٢٣ ط: نطع

٢٢٤ ط: العلم

§35 Know that Enoch – upon him be peace – knew, through knowledge that He revealed within him, that God the Most High had joined some parts of the cosmos to others and had subjected some parts to others. He saw that the world of the elements is specific to generated beings. He saw the conjunctions and disjunctions of the stars in the heavenly mansions, and the difference between the generated beings and the difference between the movements of the spheres. He saw swiftness and slowness, and knew that, whenever he made his passage and voyage slow, swiftness entered under his authority; for movement is circular, not along a straight line, and the cycle of the small rapid sphere must return to that of the slower one. He learned from being near to the slow one what the utility of the rapid one was.[238] He saw that only in the seventh heaven, so he stayed there for thirty years,[239] circling with it as he traversed the zodiacal sphere in the sphere of rotation of its guardian, as well as in the sphere bearing the sphere of rotation and the sphere bearing the spheres of rotations, which is the one which makes the zodiacal sphere rotate.

When he saw what God had revealed in heaven and had seen that planets were nearly in conjunction in the zodiacal sign of Cancer, he knew from the knowledge he had verified and from going about in the degrees of the sphere that God would inevitably send down a great amount of water and a universal flood.

§36 So he descended and selected from among the sons of his religion and his law those he knew possessed sharpness of mind and perspicacity. He taught them what he had contemplated and the secrets that God had deposited in this supernal world. Among the things that God had revealed in these heavens was the news that there would be a great flood that would destroy the people, and that knowledge would be forgotten. He wanted to preserve this knowledge for those who would come after them, so he ordered it to be inscribed upon stones

238. See *Fut.*III.417 (Chap. 371). These are all observations known to the astronomers, which, for the believer, increase his belief in God but for the unbeliever lead him to false reliance on secondary causes.

239. The planet Saturn has an orbit of approximately thirty years.

بفلك الشمس وهو الفلك الرابع وسط الأفلاك السماوية وهو القلب لأن فوقه خمسَ كُوَر وتحته مثل ذلك. فأعطاه الله في هذا السفر الذي رفعه به و[225] إليه مقام القُطبية والثبات، وجعل الأمر يدور عليه وعنده يجتمع الصاعد والنازل.

ونتج له هذا السفر علم الزمان والدهر وما يكون فيه وعلم الزمان من أسنى المعارف الموهوبة، ونتج له روحانية الليل والنهار وما سكن فيهما.

فمن سافر إلى عالم قلبه كما سافر إدريس عاين الملكوت الأفخم، وتجلّى له الجبروت الأعظم، وعاين سرّ الحياة الذي هو روحها والساري بها في جميع الحيوانات. وفرق بين الروح الكثير والروح القليل، وأعطى كلَّ ذي حقّ حقَّه، وعرف مراتبَ نفوسِه[226] السُفْلية ومراتب أرواحه العُلْوية، وانبعاث الفروع من الأصول وانعطاف الفروع على

٢٢٥ في سائر النسخ: - و

٢٢٦ ط: من كتب نقوشه

and rocks. Then God elevated him to the high place, then made him descend to the sphere of the sun, which is the fourth sphere, the middle sphere of the heavens. It is the heart, because above it are five spheres and similarly five below it.[240] In this voyage, in which God elevated him towards Himself, He gave him the station of the Pole and constancy. He made the command revolve around him. What ascends and what descends meet at him.

He gained from this voyage knowledge of time and the Aeon and what will come to be. Knowledge of time is one of the most sublime bestowed sciences. He gained knowledge of the spiritual beings of the nighttime and the daytime and what rests in them.[241]

Whoever voyages to the world of his heart[242] – the voyage of Enoch – sees the most splendid *malakūt*,[243] and the most magnificent *jabarūt*[244] discloses itself to him. He sees the secret of life, which is its spirit that courses through all animate beings.[245] He distinguishes between the spirit of many and the spirit of few. He gives each thing that has a due its due. He knows the levels of the inferior souls and the levels of the superior souls; the rising[246] of the branches from the roots; the bending of the branches towards the

240. This enumeration of the spheres, totalling eleven with the sun at the centre, differs from the one presented in the Enoch/Idrīs chapter of the *Fuṣūṣ*. There the total number of spheres is given as seven above and seven below. The enumeration of five spheres above and five below suggests a diagram similar to the Kabbalistic Tree of Life where *Tiferet* represents the sun with five *sefirot* above and five below.

241. See Q.10:6: 'Verily, in the alternation of the night and the day, and in all that Allah hath created, in the heavens and the earth, are signs for those who fear Him' and Q.24:44: 'Allah alternates the night and the day. Indeed in that is a lesson (*'ibra*) for those who have vision.'

242. The heart is the centre of the human configuration just as Idrīs in the sun is at the centre of the heavens.

243. The realm of angelic beings. The word *malakūt* – a loan word from Aramaic – appears four times in the Qur'an, twice as the 'kingdom of the heavens and the earth' (Q.6:75; 7:185), and twice as the 'sovereignty of all things' (Q.23:88; 36:83).

244. The realm of spiritual realities and pure intelligences. The word – which is a loan word from Aramaic – does not appear in the Qur'an but it is found in hadith together with *malakūt* to describe God's sovereignty.

245. For this reason, he along with Khiḍr and the angel Gabriel are said to engender life everywhere they step.

246. Arabic: *inbi'āth*. This root is also associated with sending forth and resurrection.

الأصول،[٢٢٧] وصورة الكون وحكمة الدور وما أشبه هذه المعارف. ويكفي هذا القدر من سفر إدريس – عليه السلام.

٣٧ سفر النجاة وهو سفر نوح، عليه السلام

لما عرف نوح، عليه السلام، أن القِران[٢٢٨] الذي قدره الله وأجراه[٢٢٩] حكمةً[٢٣٠] قد قرب وقتُه، ورأى أن ذلك يكون في برج السرطان وهو مائي،[٢٣١] وهو البرج الذي خلق الله الدنيا به، وهو منقلب غير ثابت. ولما كان البرج بهذه الصفة وكان[٢٣٢] طالِع الدنيا به شاء الحق بفنائها وانقلابها إلى الدار الآخرة مثل طالعها وهو الأسد، برجٌ ثابتٌ، وهذه حكمةُ عليمٍ. فأخذ نوح، عليه السلام، يُنشئ السفينة ولم تكن[٢٣٣] آيتُه، صلى الله عليه وسلم، في القِران ولا في الطوفان. فإنه ربما أدرك علم ذلك بعضُ أصحابه من العلماء فشورِكَ فيه، فجُعِل آيتُه التنور. ولو قال بالقِران لكان علماً لا علامة ولا آية. ولهذا سَخِرَ به، قومُه

٢٢٧ ط: الوصول
٢٢٨ ط: القرآن
٢٢٩ ب: أجرى
٢٣٠ ب، ط: حكمه
٢٣١ ي، ك، ب، ش، ل، ظ: ماؤي
٢٣٢ في كل النسخ ما عدا ي: فكان
٢٣٣ ي: غير منقوطة؛ ط: يكن

roots; the form of the cycles;[247] the wisdom of the rotation and other sciences like these.

This much suffices regarding the voyage of Enoch – peace be upon him.

§37 The Voyage of Salvation, which is the Voyage of Noah, peace be upon him

Noah – peace be upon him – found out that the time of the celestial conjunction, which God in His wisdom had decreed and set in motion, was approaching. He saw that it would be in the zodiacal sign of Cancer, which is an aqueous sign. It is the sign with which God created this world;[248] it is mobile, not fixed. Since the sign had this attribute, and the ascendant of this world was in it, the Real wanted to annihilate it[249] and transfer it to the next world, like its ascendant, Leo – a fixed sign.[250] This is the wisdom of an All-Knowing One.

Noah – peace be upon him – began to build the Ark.[251] His sign[252] had nothing to do with the conjunction or the Flood,[253] for then one of his companions who were gnostics might have grasped knowledge of this and shared it with him. So his sign was made the Furnace.[254] If he had announced the conjunction, it would have been knowledge rather than a marker or a sign. Because of this, his people mocked him; some of the astrologers among the people of his generation

247. The word is difficult to make out in the holograph MS. MS. K. reads it as *kawn*, creation.

248. The zodiacal sign of Cancer is a mobile aqueous sign. 'Its angels hold the key to creation of the world.' Burckhardt, *Mystical Astrology*, p.23. Mobile signs 'are related to the development of the states of this world'.

249. Arabic: *fanā'*. See *Fut.*II (Chaps. 220 and 221).

250. The zodiacal sign of Leo is a fixed igneous sign. 'Its angels hold the key to the creation of the world to come.' Burckhardt, *Mystical Astrology*, p.23. Fixed signs 'regulate the relatively superior world'.

251. Arabic: *safīna*. See Commentary.

252. Arabic: *āya*. This is not the sign of the zodiac here but a sign from God of Noah's prophecy.

253. The words conjunction (*qirān*) and flood (*ṭūfān*) rhyme.

254. Arabic: *tannūr*. See Commentary.

وربما سخر به أصحابُ علمِ التعاليم من أهل عصره حتى كان من أمره ما كان. وخلف ابنُه لكونه عملاً غير صالح ﴿فَكَانَ مِنَ الْمُغْرَقِينَ﴾ (هود ٤٣).

٣٨ وسافر نوح بأصحابه وجعل في السفينة ﴿مِنْ كُلٍّ زَوْجَيْنِ اثْنَيْنِ﴾ (هود ٤٠) وقال: ﴿ارْكَبُوا فِيهَا بِسْمِ اللهِ مَجْرَاهَا وَمُرْسَاهَا إِنَّ رَبِّي لَغَفُورٌ رَحِيمٌ﴾ (هود ٤١) بعد ما فار التَّنورُ وألْقَتِ الحاملاتُ حمْلَها، فجُمِعَ له في الاهلاك بين المائين: ماء الأرض وماء السماء. ولم تزل تجري بهم السفينة ﴿فِي مَوْجٍ كَالْجِبَالِ﴾ ونوح، عليه السلام، ينادي: ﴿يَا بُنَيَّ ارْكَبْ مَعَنَا﴾ (هود ٤٢) والابن ينادي: ﴿سَآوِي إِلَى جَبَلٍ يَعْصِمُنِي مِنَ الْمَاءِ﴾ ونوح، عليه السلام، يقول: ﴿لَا عَاصِمَ الْيَوْمَ مِنْ أَمْرِ اللهِ إِلَّا مَنْ رَحِمَ﴾ (هود ٤٣) وهم أهل السفينة. فإن دعاءه: ﴿لَا تَذَرْ عَلَى الْأَرْضِ مِنَ الْكَافِرِينَ دَيَّاراً﴾ (نوح ٢٦) سبقتْ وأُجيبَتْ. فغرِقَ من آوى إلى الجبل وكل من لم يكن في السفينة. ثم جاء النداء من الغيب من الهو،[٢٣٤] فإنه لم يذكر المنادي نفسه فيه، وجاء بالقول دون النداء للقرب، (34) فبلعت

٢٣٤ ب، ط: الهواء؛ ش: الهوى؛ ل: الهوا

also mocked him, until what took place took place. His son was left behind because of an unrighteous deed, *and he was among those who drowned* (Q.11:43).

§38 Noah voyaged with his companions and placed in the Ark *two of every kind* (Q.11:40), and said: *Embark therein! In the name of Allah be its course and its mooring. Lo! My Lord is All-Forgiving, All-Merciful* (Q.11:41).[255]

When the Furnace began to boil[256] and the clouds heavy with rain threw down their burden,[257] the two waters – that of the earth and that of the heaven – were joined together in the destruction. The Ark continued to carry them *amid waves like mountains* (Q.11:42). Noah – peace be upon him – called: *O my son! Come ride with us* (Q.11:42), and his son replied: *I shall betake me to some mountain that will save me from the water* (Q.11:43).[258] Noah – peace be upon him – said: *This day there is none that saveth from the commandment of Allah save him on whom He hath had mercy* (Q.11:43), and these were the people of the Ark. Noah's supplication: *Leave not one of the disbelievers in the land* (Q.71:26) had preceded and was granted. Whoever had taken refuge on the mountain and everyone who was not in the Ark drowned. Then came the call from the Unseen, from the 'He', for the One who calls does not mention Himself,[259] and He spoke without the vocative particle because of nearness.[260] The earth swallowed its

255. For the gnostic, the *basmalah* ('In the Name of Allah') is equivalent to God's existence-generating word 'Be!' See, for example, *Fut.*II.640.

256. Arabic: *fāra al-tannūr*. Ibn 'Arabī points out in *Fut.*I.493 (Chap. 69) that this expression commonly meant the breaking of dawn. The verb *fāra* can apply equally to water, in which case it means 'to boil', and fire, in which case it means 'to flare up'.

257. Reminiscent of the apocalyptic Q.99:2: 'When the earth throws up her burdens.'

258. Sura 11 is the only one that mentions this son of Noah. There was considerable speculation as to the identity of this son. Al-Ṭabarī and others give his name as Canaan, known to the Arabs as Yam. See Martin, 'Noah in the Qur'an', pp.272–3.

259. The verse states simply '*qīla*' ('it was said').

260. The next few sentences describe the commands from the 'Word', who calls for the flood's end and for the wrongdoers' departure. 'Then the word went forth: "O earth, swallow up thy water, and O heaven, withhold [thy rain]!" and the water abated, and the matter was ended. The Ark rested on Mount Jūdī, and the word went forth: "Away with those who do wrong!"' (Q.11:44). Following these addresses from the 'Word', Noah calls to his Lord with-

الأرضُ ماءها وأقلعت السماءُ وانتقص الماء واستوت سفينة النجاة على الجوديّ إشارةً إلى الجود الالهي. وقال هذا القول من هذا المقام ﴿بُعْداً لِلْقَوْمِ الظَّالِمِينَ﴾ (هود ٤٤) وهم الذين سخِروا.

٣٩ فاعلم أن الله – عز وجل – أيّها[٢٣٥] السرَّ اللطيف الذي أقامه الحق في هذه المنزلة منزلة نبيّه نوح، عليه السلام، قد سوّى سفينتك وصنعها بيديه ووحيه، وكانت عند وحيه بعينه يعني محفوظة بحيث أراها. (35) يقول الله: فمن أنت حتى ينزل الحق لك هذا النزول ولا سيّما من مقام الأنانية.[٢٣٦] ثم إن نفسك الأمارة بالسوء وشيطانك ودنياك وهواك لم يزالوا يسخَرون بك ما دُمْتَ تُنشئ هذه السفينة، نشأة النجاة. والتنوّر محل النار إلى جانبك، تقول لهم: منه يخرج الماء. وهم قد تحقّقوا أن المقابل من جميع الوجوه لا يستحيل لمقابله أصلاً، فسخروا وقالوا: إنك ناقص العقل. فما فرّقوا بين محل النار والماء، وذلك لجهلهم بجوهر العالم وصُوَره. فلو علموا أن النار صورة في الجوهر والماء أيضاً صورة

٢٣٥ ل، ظه: إنها؛ ط: انهى؛ ش: وقد علم انها

٢٣٦ ظه: الأنانية؛ ش، ل، ط: الإنابة

water, the heaven ceased raining, and the water subsided. The Ark of salvation came to rest on Mount Jūdī, as an allusion to the divine generosity.[261] And this Word said from this station: *Away with those who do wrong!* (Q.11:44) – those who had mocked.

§39 Know, O subtle secret, which the Real has affirmed in this waystation, the waystation of His prophet Noah, peace be upon him, that God – may He be magnified and glorified – has fashioned your Ark and has built it with His hands and His inspiration. At the time of the inspiration, the Ark was under his *eyes* (cf. Q.11:37),[262] meaning 'preserved' insofar as He made it seen [by Noah]. God said:[263] Who are you that the Real should descend to you in such a way, especially from the station of the divine solicitude? Your soul that commands to evil,[264] your Satan, your world, your passion, do not cease to mock you as long as you are constructing this Ark, the construction of salvation. The Furnace – the locus of fire at your side – says to them: 'Water will come forth', while they have verified that nothing can in any way ever be transformed into its opposite. So they mocked and said: 'You are weak in intellect.' They did not distinguish between the locus of the fire and that of the water because of their ignorance concerning the world's substance and its forms. Had they known that fire is a form within substance and that water is also a form

out the vocative particle (*yā*), using simply the shortened form for Rabbī (my Lord): 'Rabbi', replacing the long form Rabbī (long *ī*) with the short form Rabbi (short *i*).

261. Arabic: *jūd* to correspond with the name of the mountain, Jūdī. There is always a connection with God's giving existence (*wujūd*) underlying the mention of this word.

262. Q.11:37: 'Build the ark under Our eyes and by Our inspiration.' See also Q.54:14: 'She floats under Our eyes, a recompense to one who had been disbelieved.' In a poem found in *Fut.*III.114 (Chap. 330), Ibn 'Arabī also interprets 'under Our eyes' as being under God's protection: 'An ark constructed of planks of salvation/and palm fibres/it sails under the eye of His protection/as a promise to one who was disbelieved.'

263. The speech that follows is not Qur'anic. Ibn 'Arabī is attributing this speech to God based on his own interpretation of the verse. Hence what follows is a remarkable example of divine speech on the tongue of the Shaykh al-Akbar. It is impossible to distinguish one voice from the other in the passage that extends to the end of Para. 39.

264. Arabic: *al-nafs āl-ammāra* [*bi-l-sū'*] – the 'commanding [to evil] soul'. See Q.12:53: 'Nor do I absolve my own self: the soul is certainly prone to evil, unless my Lord do bestow His Mercy. But surely my Lord is Oft-forgiving, Most Merciful.' The speaker is the Prophet Joseph.

في الجوهر لَمَا سخروا. وإنما تخيّلوا أَن الماء جوهر وأن النار جوهر، ثم تقابلا تقابُلاً فأحالوا ما قال وسخروا منه.

وأنت مشتغل بإنشاء سفينتك أي سفينة نجاتك واستعدادك لأمر الله عن أمر الله، وهو الأنا. فقل للساخرين: إنهم إن هلكوا في شيء، فهم لما هلكوا فيه، لا يخرجون منه أبداً وزيادة.

فاركبْ في سفينتك بالباء التي هي اسم الله، وأقِمْ ألف التوحيد بين الباء وسين باسم، (36) فإنك لا ترى في هذه الرحمن الرحيم. فنحن نتخلّف عن سفينتك، فإنّ جريانها بالباء وهي الحافظة،[٢٣٧] وبالباء مرساها بساحل الجود الالهي فإن بالجود ظهر الوجود، فظهر بالجُوديّ ما كان في السفينة. وألْقِ في سفينتك ﴿مِنْ كُلٍّ زَوْجَيْنِ اثْنَيْنِ﴾ للتوالد والتناسل، فإن بضرب[٢٣٨] العالم العُلوي في العالم السُّفْلي تتكوَّنُ أنت والمولَّدات كلها، فلا بد من تحصيل الزوجين في هذا السفر فإنه سفر هلاك.

٤٠ ولما كان الماء يماثل العلم في كون الحياة عنهما حِساً ومعنىً، لهذا أُهلكوا بالماء لِرَدِّهم العلمَ، وكان من التنور لأنهم ما كفروا إلا بماء التنور وما ردّوا إلا العلم الذي شافههم

٢٣٧ ك: الخافضة

٢٣٨ ط: تضرب

within substance, they would not have mocked. They imagined that water is a substance, and that fire is a substance, and that they were mutually opposed, so they declared what Noah said impossible and mocked him.[265]

You are concerned with constructing your Ark – namely, the Ark of your salvation – and with your preparation for God's command, because of God's command, which is the 'I.' So say to the mockers that they will perish in some affair, and in addition, when they perish in it, they will never emerge from it.

Embark on your Ark with the *bāʾ* – which is the Name of God – and set up the *alif* of *tawḥīd*[266] between the *bāʾ* and the *sīn*: *bi-smi.*[267] You will not see 'the All-Merciful, the All-Compassionate' in this for We are behind your Ark. Their course is set with the *bāʾ* – which is the particle of preservation[268] – and their anchoring on the shore of divine generosity is also with the *bāʾ*. For through generosity (*jūd*), existence (*wujūd*) becomes manifest, and upon Mount Jūdī the contents of the Ark became manifest. Cast out of your Ark *two of every kind* (Q.11:40) for the sake of engendering and procreation, for it is with the conjoining of the higher world with the lower world that you and all engendered beings have been engendered. So pairs must be obtained in this voyage, for it is the voyage of destruction.[269]

§40 Water is like knowledge in that life comes from both with respect to the sensible and the suprasensible. Therefore, Noah's people perished by water because of their rejection of knowledge. And their destruction came from the Furnace because they disbelieved only in the water of the Furnace, and rejected the knowledge that Noah had

265. See Commentary for a discussion of Ibn ʿArabī's ideas about substance.

266. The declaration of God's unity.

267. This reference is to Q.11:41: 'In the Name of Allah (*bi-ismi-llāh*) be its course and its mooring.' As Gril points out (*Dévoilement*, p.43, n.95), the *alif* of *ism* (Name) in this formula is suppressed. It represents the hidden Essence. Also see *Fut.* (Chap. 5) on the secrets of this formula.

268. Arabic: *ḥāfiẓa*. In MS. K the word is *khāfiḍa*, 'lowering', which is also true of the particle *bi-*.

269. See Commentary.

به على لسان تنور جسمه. وما علموا أنه مترجِم عن معناه الذي هو النور المطلق، فانحجبوا بماء التنور عن التنور، وما علموا أنه النور دخلت عليه تاء تمام النشأة بوجود الجسم فعاد تنوراً أي نوراً تامَّ المُلك، فهو نور التاء ومَظهرُه.[٢٣٩]

وأما إحالة[٢٤٠] الاستحالة فصحِبَهم فيها[٢٤١] جهلٌ، وذلك لو[٢٤٢] نظروا إلى التنور لرأوْه يُنْبع الماء،[٢٤٣] وليس بينهما تقابُلٌ من جميع الوجوه، فإن البرودة جامعة، فقد جهلوا سرّ الله في الطبيعة وسر الله في اختصاص التنور فهلكوا. وما هلك كل من شافهه بالخطاب إلا بماء التنور خاصة لأنهم ما رَدُّوا سواه. وسائر العالم إنما هلك بماء التنور وماء السماء. فأما ماء السماء فهو ماء الدولاب الدائر، فإنه يُقَطَّر[٢٤٤] في إنْبيق الزمهرير، وأنه عاد

٢٣٩ ط: النار مظهره
٢٤٠ ش، ل، ظه: حالة
٢٤١ ط: فيما
٢٤٢ ط: + أنهم
٢٤٣ ط: + منه
٢٤٤ ب: يقْطُر؛ ل، ط: مقطر

conveyed to them orally[270] upon the tongue of the Furnace of his body. They did not know that he was translating its meaning, which was unqualified light.[271] They were veiled from the Furnace by the Furnace's water, and did not know that it was light (*nūr*) to which the *tā'* of the completion (*tamām*) of the human constitution had been added by the existence of the body. So it became a *tannūr*, that is to say, a light that completed the Kingdom,[272] for it is the light of *tā'* and its place of manifestation.

Those who claim transmutation is impossible are ignorant.[273] If they had looked at the Furnace, they would have seen that it is the source of water and that the two did not oppose each other in any way, for coldness is something that brings together.[274] They were ignorant of the secret of God in Nature and the secret of God in the special status of the Furnace, so they perished. Everyone whom Noah addressed orally perished only through the water of the Furnace specifically, because they rejected only it. The rest of the world perished by the water of the Furnace and the water of heaven. The water of heaven is the water of the revolving wheel,[275] for it condenses in the alembic of the *Zamharīr*[276] and returns to the

270. Arabic: *shāfahahum*, from *shāfaha*, 'to speak mouth-to-mouth'. The word appears to have derived from *shafa*, 'lip'.

271. In this interpretation, Ibn 'Arabī is following the fourth caliph/first imam, 'Alī, for whom the word had to do with the illumination of dawn (*tanwīr al-ṣubḥ*). It has special significance in regard to the supererogatory prayer of dawn and the beginning of the time of fasting during Ramadan. See *Fut.*I.493 (Chap. 69) and I.608 (Chap. 71), as well as Gril, *Dévoilement*, p.41, n.92.

272. Arabic: *mulk*. Ibn 'Arabī uses this term generally to represent the phenomenal world, or the 'world of witnessing', as opposed to the suprasensible worlds of the *malakūt* and *jabarūt*. See Commentary on *tannūr*.

273. Arabic: *iḥālat al-istiḥāla*. There is a play on words here, based on two forms of a root that have different meanings: *istiḥāla* (= transmutation) and *iḥāla* (= is impossible).

274. In the sense that coldness contracts.

275. Arabic (probably derived from Persian): *dūlāb*. The first syllable of '*dūlāb*' (*d-w-l*) calls to mind words associated with this Arabic root: for example, *dawla* (alternation, change, especially in time or fortune; dynasty, and so forth). Hence one is left with the image of the wheel of fortune, the ever-turning cycle of existence. See *Fut.*II.453 (Chap. 198, section 30).

276. The sphere of *Zamharīr* is a place of extreme cold that is prepared for the unbelievers in Gehenna. See Q.76:13 where the comfort of the blissful in the Garden is contrasted with the fate of the wretched: 'Reclining on raised thrones they will see there neither a sun['s excessive heat] nor [a moon's] excessive cold.' Iblīs will be punished primarily in the *Zamharīr*

إلى ما منه انتشاء.[٢٤٥] وإهلاك الله – عز وجل – بالنار لكن هنا واسطة الرسالة، فأَدْرَجَ النار في الماء لما لم يُكْشَفْ عن الساق. فأخرج النارُ الرطوبات والبخارات وأخذ عُلُواً، وقد عاد النارُ بُخاراً فأخذ في الجو أخذ الدولاب إذا خرج من الماء، فما زال يصعد حتى يبْلُغَ[٢٤٦] دائرة الزمهرير، فتقاطر مطراً بتقدير العزيز العليم. فليست إلا دوائر التقدير في كُرَة الانشاء، لا تزال أبداً في الدنيا ولا في الآخرة.

فنتج هذا السفر وقف الحكمة الالهية مع القدرة النافذة في التناسل على الزوجين. ونتج له أن الالهية إذا لم تكن علوية فليست بصحيحة النسب،[٢٤٧] ونتج له أن الجود عليه[٢٤٨] تكون النجاة. ألا ترى أن موسى، عليه السلام، لما أراد أن يدعو على قومه بالهلاك دعا عليهم بالبخل فلما بخلوا هلكوا. وتبيَّن أن كل كون في العالم لا بد أن يتوجه عليه القول فتارة بغيب[٢٤٩] الغيب إذا جاء القول على بناء ما لم يُسمَّ فاعلُه مثل: ﴿وَجِيءَ يَوْمَئِذٍ بِجَهَنَّمَ﴾ (الفجر ٢٣) ﴿وقِيْلَ بُعْداً ... وَقِيلَ يَا أَرْضُ ابْلَعِي مَاءَكِ﴾ (هود ٤٤) وتارة بالانّا كقوله: ﴿إذْ قلنا﴾ وتارة بالألوهية مثل: ﴿قال الله﴾ وتارة بالربوبية مثل: ﴿قال ربك﴾ فكل قول بحسب الاسم الذي يُضاف إليه.

٢٤٥ كذا في ك، ب، ظ؛ ش، ل: انتشا؛ ط: انتشار

٢٤٦ ش، ل، ط، ظ: بلغ

٢٤٧ ط: + عليه

٢٤٨ ط: علة

٢٤٩ ي: بدون النقط؛ ش، ط: يغيب

place from whence it arose. God – may He be magnified and glorified – causes destruction by fire,[277] but here, through the mediation of the prophetic mission, fire was introduced into the water, for 'the leg had not yet been uncovered.'[278] Fire extracts wetness and vapours, and begins to rise. Fire becomes vapour again and begins to act in the air like the wheel when it emerges from the water. It continues to ascend until it reaches the sphere of the *Zamharīr*. It condenses as rain by *the determination of the All-Mighty, All-Knowing* (Q.6:96; 36:38; 41:12). The cycles of determination in the sphere of origination never cease in this world or the next.

This voyage results in the cessation of the divine wisdom despite the effective power in the couple with respect to procreation. It results in the knowledge that if divine [wisdom] is not supernal in nature then it is not correct. It results in the knowledge that salvation depends on generosity. Do you not see that when Moses – peace be upon him – wanted to call down destruction upon his people, he called down avarice upon them, and when they became avaricious they perished?[279] It is clear that the Word must direct its attention to every creature in the cosmos, sometimes from the unseen of the Unseen, when the Word comes with a grammatical construction in which its agent is not named, such as: *He will be led on that day to Gehenna* (Q.89:23); *it was said 'banished' … and it was said: 'O earth, swallow your water'* (Q.11:44); and sometimes with the 'We', as in His saying: 'Since We said'; and sometimes with the Divinity, such as: 'God said' and sometimes with the Lordship, such as: 'Your Lord said.' Every Word accords with the name to which it is attached.[280]

---

because it is the contrary of his fiery nature (*Fut.*I.300). See also *Fut.*I.290 (Chap. 58), I.297 (Chap. 61), II.207 (Chap. 124), III.26 (Chap. 306), III.440 (Chap. 371).

277. Reference to Q.71:25: 'Because of their sins they were drowned, then made to enter a Fire.'

278. See Q.68:42: 'The Day that the shin shall be laid bare, and they shall be summoned to bow in adoration, but they shall not be able.' The meaning is that the Hour had not arrived, revealing what was concealed, or exposing the panic of those fleeing the events of the Last Day.

279. A reference to Q.71:21: 'They have disobeyed me and followed one whose wealth and children increase him in naught save ruin.'

280. Ibn 'Arabī bids us pay attention to the pronouns used when God addresses us. See

فمن سافر سفر نوح فإنه سيعرف من العلوم البرزخية والكونية شيئاً. وفي هذا السفر تُتَعلَّم الصنعةُ، ولهذا آخِرُها الجود فإنها من أجل الجود وُجِدَتْ. ويكفي هذا القدر من سفر نوح، عليه السلام، فإن سرَّه يطول.

٤١ سفر الهداية وهو سفر إبراهيم الخليل، عليه السلام

﴿إِنِّي ذَاهِبٌ إِلَى رَبِّي سَيَهْدِينِ﴾ (الصافات ٩٩) فأضافه بفِداء ابنه لما نزّل عليه لأن اللذة إنما تعظُم على قدر الغُصّة. ثم إنه لما بُشِّرَ بإجابة[٢٥٠] دعائه في قوله: ﴿رَبِّ هَبْ لِي مِنَ الصَّالِحِينَ﴾ (الصافات ١٠٠) ابْتُلِيَ فيما بُشِّرَ به لأنه سأل من الله سواه، والله غيور، فابتلاه بذبحه وهو أشدّ عليه من ابتلائه بنفسه. وذلك أنه ليس له في نفسه منازعٌ سوى نفسه،

٢٥٠ ط: في إجابة

Whoever goes on Noah's voyage will know something of the sciences pertaining to the *barzakh* and to existence. In this voyage one learns about the Work[281] and therefore, its end is generosity; for it is for the sake of generosity that the Work has been brought into existence.

This much suffices concerning the voyage of Noah; divulging more of its secret would take too long.

§41 The Voyage of Guidance, which is the Voyage of Abraham, the Intimate Friend, peace be upon him

Lo! I am going unto my Lord. He will guide me (Q.37:99). He connected it[282] to the ransom of his son when He sent down revelation upon him, because pleasure increases in accordance with the amount of agony.[283] Then when he was given the good news that his prayer – in which he said: *My Lord! Grant me a righteous [son]* (Q.37:100) – had been answered, he was tested with what he had been given the good news about, because he had asked God for something other than Him. God was exceedingly jealous and tested him with the sacrifice of his son. This was more difficult for him than the trial of his own soul. That is because he had no adversary in himself other than his soul, and with the slightest of thoughts he was able to repulse it

al-ʿAbādila, p.42 and Chodkiewicz's discussion of this subject in *Ocean Without Shore*, p.36. See also *Fut.*II.278 (Chap. 167), III.531 (Chap. 386).

281. Arabic: *ṣanʿa*. This word may refer both to God's workmanship and the alchemical Work.

282. The passage starts out on a note of ambiguity, since not only are the subjects of the verbs not specified but also the verb *aḍāfa* can mean to receive as a guest as well as to relate, annex or connect. Abraham is associated with hospitality in all three monotheistic religions.

283. Arabic: *ghuṣṣa*. This is a particularly graphic word to describe the agony Abraham feels, for it literally means something that obstructs the throat, choking the individual. It often means by extension the strangulation of death. See Lane, *Lexicon*, vol. 6, p.47. The word occurs in Q.73:11–13: 'And leave Me those in possession of the good things of life, who deny the Truth; and bear with them for a little while. With Us are fetters and a fire, and a food that chokes, and a penalty grievous.'

فبأدنى خاطر يردّها، فيقلّ جهاده. وابتلاؤه بذبح ابنه ليس كذلك لكثرة المنازعين فيه، فيكون جهاده أقوى. ولما ابتُلِيَ بذبْح ما سأله من ربه، وتحقق نسب[٢٥١] الابتلاء، وصار بحكم الواقعة كأنه[٢٥٢] قد ذُبِح وإن كان حيّاً بشِّرَ بإسحاق، عليهم[٢٥٣] السلام، من غير سؤال، فجمع له بين الفداء وبين البدل مع بقاء المبدَل منه، فجمع له بين الكسب والوهب. فالذبح مكسوب من جهة السؤال، موهوب من جهة الفداء، فإن فداءه لم يكن مسؤولاً، وإسحاق موهوب. ولما كان إسماعيل قد جُمِعَ له بين الكسب والوهب في العطاء، فكان مكسوباً موهوباً لأبيه، فكانت حقيقته[٢٥٤] تامة[٢٥٥] كاملة. لذلك كان محمد، صلى الله عليه وسلم، في صلبه. بل لكون محمد، صلى الله عليه وسلم، في صلبه، صح الكمال والتمام لاسماعيل. فكانت في شريعتنا ضحايانا فداءً لنا من النار.

٢٥١ ط: نسبة؛ ش، ل، ظ: بسبب

٢٥٢ ط: فكأنه

٢٥٣ ش، ل، ط: عليه

٢٥٤ ل، ط: حقيقة

٢٥٥ ط: - تامة

with little effort. The trial of sacrificing his son was not like that because of the many adversaries involved in it, so the effort was more intense.[284] When he was tested with the sacrifice of what he had asked for from his Lord, and verified the origin of the trial, and came under the judgement of the event, it was as if he himself had been sacrificed, even though he remained alive. Then he was given the good news of Isaac – upon him be peace – without having asked.[285] He[286] brought together for him ransom and substitution, while the one for whom he was a substitute remained alive. And H/he[287] brought together for him acquisition and bestowal, for the sacrifice was acquired from the viewpoint of request, bestowed from the viewpoint of the ransom, for his ransom was not requested, and Isaac was bestowed. Since Ishmael brought together for him acquisition and bestowal in the gift, he was acquired by and bestowed upon his father. Thus his reality was complete and perfect. For this reason, Muhammad – God's blessing and peace be upon him – was in his loins. By virtue of Muhammad's being in his loins, perfection and completeness are correctly attributed to Ishmael. In our Law, our sacrificed animals are a ransom for us from the Fire.[288]

284. There is no mention of adversaries in the Qur'anic narratives about Abraham, and his son not only does not oppose him but offers himself as a willing victim. An account in the exegetical literature, however, tells of a succession of encounters along the way with Satan, who, in the form of an old man, tries to stop Abraham from carrying out God's command. The ritual of casting stones at Satan during the *ḥajj* is thought to stem from this extra-Qur'anic tale. It is possible that Ibn 'Arabī also presumes that Abraham's family, friends and the Law itself opposed the intended sacrifice.

285. See Q.37:112.

286. The pronoun 'he' in the following two sentences is ambiguous. In the first case, it could refer to either God bringing together ransom and substitution for Isaac or to Isaac bringing them together for Abraham: ransom in the form of the ram and substitution in the form of another son.

287. This second case appears to refer to Ishmael, whose near sacrifice results in both his acquisition and bestowal.

288. See *Fut.*I.596 (Chap. 70, On the Secrets of *Zakāt*). See also *Fuṣūṣ*, chapter on Isaac (trans. Austin, *Bezels*, p.100).

٤٢ فمن طلب سفر الهداية من الله فليتحقَّقْ عالم خياله فإن الحقائق لا بد أن تنزل عليه فيه، وهو منزل صعب لأنه مَعْبَر ليس مطلوباً لنفسه وإنما هو مطلوب لما نصب له ولا يَعْبُره إلا رجل،[٢٥٦] ولهذا سُمِّيَ تأويل الرؤيا عبارة لأن التفسير[٢٥٧] يعبر منها إلى ما جاءت له كما عبر النبي، صلى الله عليه وسلم، من القيد إلى الثبات في الدين ومن اللبن إلى العلم، (37) فإذا وصل وجد. فلو عبر الخليل،عليه السلام، من ابنه إلى الكبش لرأى الفداء قبل حصوله. وكان يمتثل الأمر فارغ القلب لمعرفته بالمآل ولكن ظلمة الطلب والسؤال من ربه غيرَ ربِّه منعه من العبور لأن الظلمة يتعذر العبور فيها لأنه لا يدري أين يضع قدمه. ولم تكن أيضاً تحصل له تلك اللذة التي حصلت له

٢٥٦ ك: الرجل.

٢٥٧ ب: المعبر؛ ش، ل، ط، ظ: المفسر

§42 Whoever seeks from God the voyage of guidance, let him verify the world of his imagination,[289] for it is in imagination that the realities must descend upon him. It is a difficult waystation because it is a passageway[290] that is not sought for its own sake; it is sought only for what it is set up to signify. Only the spiritually adept Man[291] can pass through it.[292] For that reason, dream interpretation[293] is called an 'act of passage',[294] because the interpreter[295] passes from the dream-form to what it elicits [namely, the meaning], just as the Prophet – God's blessings and peace be upon him – 'passed' from the form of a fetter to its interpretation as firmness in religion, and from the form of milk to its interpretation as knowledge.[296] When he arrived, he found.[297] If the Intimate Friend – upon him be peace – had 'passed' from the form of his son to its interpretation as the ram, he would have seen the ransom before its occurrence, and he would have obeyed the command with an unconcerned heart because of his inner knowledge of the final outcome.[298] However, the obscurity of the request and his asking his Lord for something other than his Lord prevented him from 'passing', since darkness hinders passage because one does not know where to put one's foot. Then, however, he would not have attained the pleasure which he attained or the

289. The world of the imagination is located between the sensible and the suprasensible worlds. In it the forms of the material world become spiritualized and the immaterial spiritual realities become corporealized.The classic treatment of imagination in Ibn 'Arabī remains Corbin, *Creative Imagination*.

290. Arabic: *ma'bar*. Yet another word derived from the significant root *'-b-r*, to cross over, to interpret. See Commentary.

291. Arabic: *rajul*. Ibn 'Arabī does not mean by this term here the ordinary man but the spiritually adept human being, whether male or female.

292. Arabic: *lā ya'buruhu*.

293. Arabic: *ta'bīr al-ru'yā*. The second-form verbal noun of *'abbara*, again from the root *'-b-r*, is concerned primarily with dream interpretation.

294. Arabic: *'ibāra*. See Commentary for a discussion of this term.

295. Arabic: *mufassir*. This is the technical term for Qur'anic commentator. Here it is used to apply to the decipherer of dreams.

296. These are interpretations made by the Prophet attested to in numerous hadith.

297. It is possible that Ibn 'Arabī's obscure statement refers to the Prophet's finding the correct interpretation and meaning of the dream vision.

298. Abraham's failure to interpret, and hence his anxiety, are also recounted in the *Fuṣūṣ*, chapter on Isaac.

ولا ذاك الامتنان الالهي المشهود. وكان الفداء بالحَمَل الذي هو بيت شرف الوسط وروح العالم لأنه أشرف البيوت، فكان بدلاً من جسده لا من روحه لاشتراكهما في النسبة، فإن الذبح لا يقع إلا في الجسم، والهدم والخراب لا يقع إلا في البيوت.

٤٣ فإذا سافر الانسان في عالم خياله جازه إلى عالم الحقائق فرأى الأشياء على ما هي عليه، وحصل له الوهب المطلق الذي لا يتقيَّد بكسب، وصار يأكل من فوقه بعد ما كان يأكل من تحت رِجْله.
(38) ولما كان الوهب يُبْقِيك بخلاف المشاهدة كان سَحْقاً ولم

divine favour which he contemplated. The ransom was made with the Ram [Aries], a zodiacal house of nobility, which is in the centre and is the spirit of the world, for it is the most noble and elevated of the zodiacal houses.[299] The ram was a substitute for his body, not for his spirit, because of the similarity between the two. Sacrifice takes place only with respect to the body, while desolation and demolition take place only with respect to houses.[300]

§43 When the human being voyages in the world of his imagination,[301] he 'passes through' it to the world of the realities, so he sees things as they really are and obtains unqualified bestowal, which is not restricted by any acquisition. He begins to eat 'from above him' after his having eaten 'from below his feet'.[302] Since bestowal gives you subsistence rather than contemplation, it is pulverization[303] not

299. Aries is the first of the zodiacal houses, or signs, in astrology. It is the most noble (*ashraf*) because 'The first day that was appointed for the earth when the sphere began to move was in the Ram [Aries]' (*Fut.*III.461). It is also highest (also *ashraf*) because of its place in the heavens.

300. Perhaps a reference to Q.27:52: 'Now such were their houses, in utter ruin, because they practised wrong-doing. Verily in this is a Sign for people of knowledge.' Ibn 'Arabī is drawing an analogy between the celestial and terrestrial realms when he makes the earthly ram correspond to the son's body and the heavenly ram, the noble first-born sign of the zodiac, correspond to his spirit. It is only the former that can be offered as a sacrifice. As for the desolation and demolition that occurs in houses, it may be that Ibn 'Arabī means here both terrestrial houses and celestial ones, as the progression of time causes one astrological house /sign to replace another. See also *Fut.*I.675 (Chap. 72), where the word '*ifsād*' is used for the destruction of the body, as it was used in the Voyage of Enoch to describe the changes that occur with the movement of the celestial cycles (see Para. 33).

301. See n.79.

302. See Q.5:66: 'If only they had stood fast by the Law, the Gospel, and all the revelation that was sent to them from their Lord, they would have eaten from above them and below their feet.' According to Ibn 'Arabī, one sense of eating from above has to do with inspiration, while eating from below has to do with acquired sciences. See *Fut.*II.488 (Chap. 206), II.594ff. (Chap. 276), III.439 (Chap. 371). For other references to this verse, see Commentary.

303. Arabic: *saḥq*. Play on words with 'Isḥāq' (Isaac) and conveniently rhyming with *maḥq* (effacement). The Shaykh here and in the following lines exploits nearly the full range of the root *s-ḥ-q*, which includes the personal name Isḥāq, the words meaning 'pulverizing', 'crushing' or 'abrading', and the words meaning 'distancing', 'removing' and 'estranging.' See Lane, *Lexicon*, vol. 4, pp. 1318–19. The root *s-ḥ-q* is found in the Qur'an twice, excluding the mention of the Prophet Isḥāq, both times with the meaning of 'distancing' or 'far off'. Q.22:31: 'Whoever associates partners with Allah [it is] as though he had fallen from the sky and birds had snatched him or the wind had blown him to a place far off' (*saḥīq*). Q.67:11: '… so away

يكن مَحْقاً، فإن المسحوق مُفَرَّق[٢٥٨] الأجزاء فهو أبعد من حال المحق. ولولا ما علّق السؤالَ أولاً بقوله: ﴿هَبْ لي من الصالحين﴾ لكانت البُشْرى بالمشاهدة لا بإسحاق. فأسحَقَ[٢٥٩] إسحاق[٢٦٠] السائلَ بسؤاله الكون عن محق العين أي أبعده. فكانت[٢٦١] إشارة إلى مقام البُعد المحال، فإن الأمور الالهية لا تنزل أبداً إلا بحسب الاستعداد، والمحل هنا غيرُ متجرّد إليه، فكيف يَهَبُه[٢٦٢] العينَ وهو غير قابل، والواهب عليم حكيم، والوقت قاضٍ، والابن من عالم التبديد.[٢٦٣]

٢٥٨ ش: مفرد

٢٥٩ ط: فاسحاق

٢٦٠ ش، ظ: - اسحاق

٢٦١ في سائر النسخ ما عدا ي: وكانت

٢٦٢ ط: بهبة

٢٦٣ ط: التبديل

obliteration,[304] for the parts of what is pulverized are separated;[305] thus it is more dispersed[306] than the state of obliteration. If Abraham had not begun his supplication by saying: *Grant me a righteous [son]* (Q.37:100), the good news would have been contemplation rather than Isaac/pulverization.[307] Isaac estranged/pulverized[308] the petitioner who asked for a creature from the obliteration of his essence; that is, he distanced him. It was an allusion to the station of impossible distance, for divine affairs only descend in accordance with preparedness, and the locus here was not completely devoted to Him. How could He bestow the essence upon him when he could not receive it? The Bestower is All-Knowing, All-Wise. The Moment is a judge and the son is from the world of dispersal.[309]

---

with (*fa-suḥqan*) the Companions of the Blaze.'

304. Arabic: *maḥq*. See *Fut*.II.554ff. (Chap. 255, On Knowledge of Effacement). The root also includes the meaning of waning or voiding of the moon. See *Fut*.III.110 (Chap. 330).

305. Arabic: *mufarraq*. This participle is from the same root as *furqān*. See Commentary, pp. 187–90.

306. Arabic: *abʿada*, which is a synonym of *asḥaqa*. The root *b-ʿ-d* is a near homophone of *b-d-d*, 'separate', which we will encounter as the final sentence in the chapter: 'The son is from the world of dispersal' (*tabdīd*).

307. *Isḥāq* can mean either the individual Isaac or 'pulverizing'.

308. Arabic: *asḥaqa Isḥāq*, which is, of course, a play on words. Since *asḥaqa* means both 'to pulverize' and 'to estrange or distance', the phrase can be read in two ways.

309. Arabic: *tabdīd*. The second-form verb *baddada*, from which the noun above derives, means to divide, distribute; remove, eliminate; waste, squander. Another word from the same root, *budda*, means escape. Another meaning attested to in the ancient sources is 'substitute' – something 'given … received … or done, instead of, in the place of, or in exchange for, another thing; compensation' (Lane, *Lexicon*, vol. 1, p. 198), which fits in nicely with the trope of substitution of ram for son in the story of Abraham's sacrifice. In this latter sense, it brings to mind the near homophone *badala*, to substitute.

٤٤ سفر الاقبال وعدم الالتفات
وهو سفر لوط إلى إبراهيم الخليل، عليهما السلام

واجتماعه به في اليقين. (39) الخبر المروي في ذلك معلوم محفوظ عند العلماء، وروحه فينا هو المطلوب لنا في الاعتبار.

اعلم أن اسم لوط أعني هذه اللفظة اسم شريف جليل القدر لأنه يعطي اللصوق (40) بالحضرة الالهية، ولهذا قال: ﴿أَوْ آوِي إِلَى رُكْنٍ شَدِيدٍ﴾ (هود ٨٠) يريد القبيلة لأني لا أستطيع الانتقال من الركن الالهي إلى الركن الكوني. وقد شهد له رسول الله، صلى الله عليه وسلم، بذلك فقال: "يرحم الله أخي لوطاً لقد كان يأوي إلى ركن شديد." (41) فنِعْمَ الشاهدُ والمشهودُ له. فلاسْتِناده إليه ولصوقِه به في علم الله سُمِّيَ لوطاً، لم يُضَفْ إلى غيره. وجعل له السُّرَى لأنه سفرٌ في الغيب إذ لفظ السرى لا يُطْلَق إلا على سير الليل، ففي الاعتبار لا في التفسير قيل له: [ف]

§44 *The Voyage of Approach and No Turning Back,*[310] *which is the Voyage of Lot towards Abraham, the Intimate Friend, peace be upon him*

His meeting with him is in 'Certainty'.[311] The tradition reported concerning this is well known and preserved by the religious scholars, but we should seek to interpret its spirit esoterically.

Know that the name Lot – I mean, this expression – is a noble name of majestic value, for it means attachment[312] to the Divine Presence. For that reason, he said: ... *or had some strong support* (Q.11:80)[313] – he meant the tribe – 'because I cannot pass from divine support to creaturely support.'[314] The Messenger of God – God's blessing and peace be upon him – bore witness to him in that regard when he said: 'God have mercy on my brother Lot, who sought refuge in a strong support.'[315] How excellent are the witness and the one for whom he bore witness, for he sought to rely upon Him and to cling to Him with respect to knowledge of God. He was called 'Lot' and this name was not attributed to anyone but him. God made him journey by night[316] because he voyaged in the Unseen, since the expression *surā* is only applied to night travel. In esoteric interpretation, not in exoteric explication, it was said to him: *Journey by night*

310. Arabic: *iltifāt*. Lot's direct course towards 'Certainty' contrasts with the lagging behind, and turning back towards Sodom of Lot's wife, who met her fate in a shower of brimstone.

311. Arabic: *yaqīn*. This is also the name of the town located between Jerusalem and Hebron to which Lot was reported to have fled to avoid the destruction of Sodom. A shrine was built there that Ibn 'Arabī visited in 1206. He composed a short treatise, *K. al-Yaqīn*, at the site where Lot prostrated and said: 'I have the certitude that the promise of God is true.' See Gril, *Dévoilement*, p. 48, n. 108.

312. Arabic: *luṣūq*. Ibn 'Arabī connects the name Lūṭ to the word *lāṭa*, to cling or adhere to.

313. The entire verse reads: 'Would that I had strength to resist you or had some strong support (*rukn*).'

314. The unitalicized part of this statement is Ibn 'Arabī's addition.

315. Al-Bukhārī, *Ṣaḥīḥ*, *anbiyā'* LX.51; *Ṣaḥīḥ* Muslim, *īmān* I.289; *faḍā'il* XLIII.6291 (USC-MSA XXX.5845); Ibn Māja, *Sunan*, *fitan* XXXVI.4161; al-Tirmidhī, *Jāmi'*, *tafsīr* XLVII.3404.

316. For this term see pp. 17–18, 168–9.

﴿أَسْرِ بِأَهْلِكَ﴾ (هود ٨١) أي بجميع ذاتك، فشاهِدِ الحقائقَ كلها ﴿إلا امْرَأَتَكَ﴾ فاعتبرْناها فينا الأمرَ بترك نفسه الأمّارة بالسوء التي لا حظَّ لها في المعارج العُلى المعنوية. وسار إلى اليقين وهو موضع معروف سُمِّي بهذا الاسم، وفيه كان ينتظره إبراهيم الخليل، عليه السلام، لأنه موطنه. ولهذا قال، عليه الصلاة والسلام: "نحن أولى بالشك من إبراهيم" (42) لعلمه بأن إبراهيم الخليل[٢٦٤] في اليقين. فحصل ذلك المقام للنبي لوط، عليه السلام. وفي الصبح جاء اليقين له لأنه طلوع الشمس وكشف الأشياء عيناً بعد ما كانت غيباً، فأعطت اليقين بلا شك ولا ريب.

٤٥ فهذا أُنموذج من ذلك، أي حظّنا من سفر لوط، وكذلك كل سفر أتكلّم فيه إنما أتكلم فيه في ذاتي لا أقصد التفسير، تفسير القصة الواقعة في حقّهم. وإنما هذه الأسفار قناطر وجسور موضوعة نَعْبُر عليها إلى ذواتنا وأحوالنا المختصة بنا فإنّ فيها منفعتنا إذ كان الله نصبها مَعْبَراً لنا ﴿وَكُلًّا نَقُصُّ عَلَيْكَ مِنْ أَنْبَاءِ الرُّسُلِ مَا نُثَبِّتُ

٢٦٤ ط: - لعلمه ... الخليل

with your family (Q.11:81) – namely, with your entire essence – and contemplate all of the realities, *except thy wife* (Q.11:81). We interpret it[317] in ourselves as the command to leave his soul that commands to evil,[318] which has no portion in the supernal suprasensible ascents. He betook himself to al-Yaqīn [= Certainty], which is a place well known that is called by that name, and in it he awaited Abraham the Intimate Friend – peace be upon him – who was staying there. For this reason, the Prophet – God's blessing and peace be upon him – said: 'We have more reason to doubt than Abraham',[319] because of his knowledge that Abraham the Intimate Friend was in 'Certainty'. The prophet Lot – peace be upon him – obtained this station. In the morning, certainty came to him, because when the sun rose and unveiled things to his eye after they were hidden it provided certainty without doubt or equivocation.[320]

§45 This is an example of that – that is, our share in Lot's voyage and also in every voyage that I have spoken about. I speak about it only as far as my own self is concerned. It is not my intention to explicate the actual story in each case. These voyages are only bridges and pontoons that are placed for us to 'cross over'[321] to our essences and the states that are specific to us. There is utility for us in them, since God has set them up as passageways[322] for us. *And all that We relate unto thee of the story of the messengers is in order that thereby We may*

317. The Arabic again uses the root *ʿ-b-r*, meaning to cross or pass over from the surface meaning to the inner one.

318. Arabic: *al-nafs al-ammāra bi-l-sūʾ*. See Q.12:53: 'Indeed the soul is an enjoiner of evil, unless my Lord bestows His Mercy. Indeed my Lord is Oft-forgiving, Most Merciful.' The words are the Prophet Joseph's.

319. Muslim, *Ṣaḥīḥ*, *īmān* I.289; Ibn Māja, *Sunan*, *fitan* XXXVI.4161; al-Bukhārī, *Ṣaḥīḥ*, *anbiyāʾ* LX.51: 'We are more liable to be in doubt than Abraham when he said: "My Lord! Show me how You gave life to the dead."' See Q.2:260: 'And [mention] when Abraham said, "My Lord, show me how You give life to the dead." [Allah] said, "Have you not believed?" He said, "Yes, but [I ask] only that my heart may be satisfied."'

320. See Q.11:81 and 54:34–5. It is in the morning that the people of Sodom are destroyed and Lot and his people realize both the truth of God's threat and the grace of His deliverance.

321. Another instance of the word *ʿabara*. See Commentary.

322. Arabic: *maʿbar*, another use of the root *ʿ-b-r*.

بِهِ فُؤَادَكَ وَجَاءَكَ فِي هَذِهِ الْحَقُّ وَمَوْعِظَةٌ وَذِكْرَى [لِلْمُؤْمِنِينَ]﴾ (هود ١٢٠) فما أبلغ قوله – تعالى: ﴿وجاءك في هذه الحق﴾ وقوله: ﴿وذكرى﴾ لما فيك وما عندك بما نَسِيتَه، فيكون هذا الذي قصصتُه عليك يُذكِّرُك بما فيك، وما نبَّهتُك عليه، فتعلم أنك[٢٦٥] كل شيء وفي كل شيء ومن كل شيء.

فإني وإن كنت من كل شيء — فإني مع الحق في كل شيء
فإني ظلٌّ به ظاهر — وإن كنت ظلاً فإني لفي
فعين هبوطي صعودي إليه — بسعد السعود لدى كل حي
فقد زاد رُشْدي على كل رشد — كما زاد غيي على كل غي
كما هو مع كل ميْت وحي — كذا هو في كل نَشْرٍ وطي

﴿وَاللَّهُ يَقُولُ الْحَقَّ وَهُوَ يَهْدِي السَّبِيلَ﴾ (الأحزاب ٤).

٤٦ سفر المكر والابتلاء فيذكر يعقوب ويوسف، عليهما السلام

اعلم[٢٦٦] إذا أكرم الله عبداً سافر به في عبوديته. يقول – عز وجل: ﴿سُبْحَانَ الَّذِي أَسْرَى بِعَبْدِهِ﴾ فما سمّاه إلا بأشرف أسمائه عنده لأنه ما

٢٦٥ ل: + مع؛ ط: + على
٢٦٦ زائد في كل النسخ ما عدا ي: أنه

make firm thy heart. And herein hath come unto thee the Truth and an exhortation and a reminder for the believers (Q.11:120). How eloquent the Most High's saying: *And herein hath come unto thee the Truth* and His saying: *and a reminder* of that which is within you and with you which you have forgotten. What I have recounted to you is to remind you of what is within you and what I have called your attention to, so that you will know that you are everything, in everything and part of everything.

Even if I am part of everything,
I am with the Real in everything.
I am a shadow that becomes manifest through Him,
And, if I am a shadow, I am an afternoon shadow.[323]
My very fall is my ascent to Him,
With the star that is most auspicious[324] for every living being.
My being guided on the right path has exceeded every other
guidance,
And my straying has exceeded every other straying.
Just as He is with every dead and living one,
So too is He in every disclosure and concealment.

And Allah speaks the truth and He guides on the Path (Q.33:4).

§46 The Voyage of Ruse and Trial in the Account of Jacob and Joseph, peace be upon them

Know that when God honours a servant, He makes him voyage in his servanthood. He – may He be magnified and glorified – says: *Glorified be He who made His servant voyage by night* (Q.17:1), so He called him only by the most noble of his names,[325] for a servant is not

323. Arabic: *fay'*. As Gril (*Dévoilement*, p.50, n.113) explains, *ẓill* is shadow in general, *fay'* is the specific kind of shadow that extends with the sun's declination.

324. Arabic: *saʿd al-suʿūd*. The twenty-fourth lunar mansion, considered the most favourable of the cluster of stars known as *suʿūd*. Note also the play on words between *ṣuʿūd* (ascent) and [*saʿd al-*] *suʿūd*.

325. The most noble name a person can be called is, for Ibn ʿArabī, 'servant'.

تحسّن عبدٌ بحُسْن أحسن ولا أزين من حُسْن عبوديته لأن الربوبية لا تَخْلَع زينتها إلا على المتحققين بمقام العبودة.[٢٦٧]

يا مُشبِهاً يوسف في حسنه رفقاً على مُشبِه يعقوبِ
إن له صبراً على نأيكم يقصر عنه صبر أيوبِ
لولا لحوق النقص قلنا رضىً وإنه ليس بمطلوبي
وإنما مطلبي منه الذي يعلمه[٢٦٨] فذاك مرغوبي
فالأمر ما بيني وبين الذي أسأله الوصل بمحبوبي

واعلم أن الذين تحققوا بمقام العبودة[٢٦٩] يُعرّض[٢٧٠] بصاحبه[٢٧١] للبلاء. ثم إنه[٢٧٢] من شأن هذا الموطن أنه لا يكمل فيه عزٌ لأحد ولا راحة. ولما وهب الله عزاً لحسن يوسف، عليه السلام، ابْتُلِيَ بذل الرِقّ. ومع ذلك الحُسن العالي الذي لا يقاومه شيء بيع ﴿بِثَمَنٍ بَخْسٍ دَرَاهِمَ مَعْدُودَةٍ﴾ (يوسف ٢٠) من ثلاثة دراهم إلى عشرة لا غير، وذلك مبالغة في الذلة تقاوم مبالغته عزة الحسن.

ثم سلب الرحمة من قلوب الاخوة والحسن مرحوم أبداً بكل وجه. فظهر أن الأمر الالهي لم يكن بيد الخلق منه شيء سوى التصريف تحت القهر. فزال بهذا الذل العظيم عز[٢٧٣] ذلك الحسن العرضي، فبقي في سفره طيِّبَ النفس عزيزاً بالعزة الالهية لا غير. والقصة معروفة فلا معْنَى لذكرها في عالمها، ولكن الفائدة في ذكرها في عالمنا أعني عالم الانسان[٢٧٤] في نفسه.

٢٦٧ كذا في ي و ك، وفي سائر النسخ: العبودية.
٢٦٨ ي: بدون النقط؛ ف: تعلمه
٢٦٩ كذا في ي وك وط، وفي سائر النسخ: العبودية
٢٧٠ ط: تعرض
٢٧١ ش: صاحبه؛ ط: لصاحبه
٢٧٢ ش، ط: إن
٢٧٣ ش، ل، ط، ظ: عن
٢٧٤ ط: العالم الانساني

embellished with anything more fine or beautiful than the beauty of his servanthood, because the beauty of lordship is conferred only upon those who have realized the station of servanthood.

> O you who resemble Joseph in his beauty,
> Be kind to him who resembles Jacob.
> His patience with your distance
> Surpasses even Job's patience.
> Were it not for our shortcoming,
> We would declare ourselves content.
> But this is not what I seek.
> What I seek from him is what only he knows: that is my desire.
> What separates me from what I ask him
> Is union with my Beloved.

Know that those who have realized the station of servanthood are exposed to trial. Furthermore, it is a characteristic of this homeland that no one can have perfect honour or rest in it. When God bestowed ~~the~~ honour of beauty ~~upon~~ Joseph – peace be upon him – he was tried with the humiliation of being a slave. Despite that superior beauty which nothing could resist, he was sold *for a low price, a number of dirhams* (Q.12:20), from a mere three to ten. That is the utmost humiliation when measured against the utmost superiority of his beauty.

God stripped mercy from the hearts of his brothers; beauty is always in every respect the object of mercy. It appears that nothing of the divine order is in the hand of the creatures save the disposal to act under His subjugation. Thus, through that great humiliation, He removed the honour of that accidental beauty. In his voyage, Joseph remained good of soul, distinguished with divine superiority and nothing else. The story is well known, so we do not intend to mention it in its particular world. But the utility lies in mentioning it in our world – I mean the human world with respect to the soul.

٤٧ فاعلم أن الله – تعالى – لما أراد من النفس المؤمنة أن تسافر إليه اشتراها من إخوتها الأمارة واللوامة بثمن بخس من عَرَض العاجلة، وحال بينها وبين العقل الذي هو أبوها، فبقي العقل حزيناً لا تفْتُر له دمعةٌ، فإن الالهام الالهي والامداد الرباني إنما كان لهذا[٢٧٥] النفس. فكان[٢٧٦] العقل يتنزه في الحضرة الالهية بوجود هذه[٢٧٧] النفس. فلما حيل بينه وبينها لم يزل يبكي حتى كُفَّ بصرُه. وذلك أن البصر وإن لم يكن مكفوفاً صاحبه، فإن الظلمة إذا تكاثفت وحجبت المُبْصَرات، صار صاحب البصر أعمى وإن كان البصر موجوداً يبصر به الظلمة. ولما كان الحزن ناراً والنار تعطي الضوء لذلك قيل ﴿وَابْيَضَّتْ عَيْنَاهُ مِنَ الْحُزْنِ﴾ (يوسف ٨٤) فجاء بالبياض، فإن البياض لون جسماني كما أن الضوء نور روحاني.

٤٨ ثم إنه لما وقع البيع وحصل في المِلْك، قيل للمرأة التي هي عبارة عن النفس الكل:[٢٧٨] ﴿أكْرِمي مَثْواه﴾ (يوسف ٢١). فمن كرامتها به أن وهبتْ نفسها له. ورأته النفوس الجزئية خارجاً عنها فقالت: ﴿مَا هَذَا بَشَراً إِنْ هَذَا إِلَّا مَلَكٌ كَرِيمٌ﴾ (يوسف ٣١) لما رأته من تقديسه نفسَه عن الشهوات الطبيعية، وهذا مما يدلّك على عِصْمته من أن يهمّ بسوء، فإن المَلَك ليس من السوء في شيء، ولهذا صوَّبت النفس الكل[٢٧٩] قولهم بقولها:[٢٨٠] ﴿فاستعْصَمَ ولئِن لمْ يفعلْ﴾ (يوسف ٣٢) لأسجننه، فعندما ﴿همَّ بها﴾ (يوسف ٢٤) ليأخذ منها ما أودع الله من الحقائق فيها

٢٧٥ ش، ظ، ل: هذه
٢٧٦ ش، ل، ط، ظ: وكان
٢٧٧ ك: هذا
٢٧٨ ش، ط: الكلي؛ ظ، ظه: الكلية
٢٧٩ ط: الكلي؛ ظ، ظه:الكلية
٢٨٠ ط: لها

§47 Know that when God the Most High wants the soul of the believer to voyage towards Him, He buys it from its brothers – the soul that commands to evil[326] and the soul that blames[327] – *for a low price* (Q.12:20) – the accidents of temporal existence. He separates it from the intellect, which is its father, and the intellect continues to grieve; its tears do not let up. Divine inspiration and lordly support is only for this [righteous] soul. The intellect is distinguished in the Divine Presence only because of the existence of this soul. So when the intellect is separated from the soul it does not cease weeping until it loses its sight. Even if the possessor of vision has not lost his sight, when darkness becomes thick and the objects of vision become veiled, he becomes blind. Even if he has vision he sees only darkness with it. Since grief is a fire and fire gives brightness – as it was said: *And his eyes were whitened with sorrow* (Q.12:84) – this grief produced whiteness. Whiteness is a corporeal colour just as brightness is a spiritual light.

§48 Then when he was sold and became his Master's possession, it was said to the woman, who is interpreted as the Universal Soul: *Receive him honourably* (Q.12:21). From her generosity to him she gave herself to him. The particular souls saw him outside themselves and said: *This is not a human being. This is no other than some noble angel!* (Q.12:31) when they saw that he had purified himself of natural desires. This was one of the things that indicated his safeguardedness from desiring evil, for the angel never desires evil. For that reason, the Universal Soul corrected their speech by saying: *He proved continent, but if he does not do [what I command]*[328] *he verily shall be imprisoned* (Q.12:32). When *he desired her* (Q.12:24), in order to take from her the realities that God had deposited in her,

326. See n.264.
327. Arabic: [*al-nafs*] *al-lawwāma*. See Q.75:2: 'I call to witness the blaming soul.'
328. The bracketed words are missing in all the MSS.

من غير أمر إلهي له بذلك، غار الحقُّ أن يتصرّف عبده في شيء من غير أمره. فأظهر له في سرِّه برهانَ عبوديته. فتذكَّر عبوديته، فامتنع من التصريف بغير أمر سيده. فحبستْهُ النفسُ في سجن هَيْكَله، فلم يزل يناجي في سره سيدَه بالعبودة، حتى أقرَّتِ النفس أنها الطالبة، لا هو. فأثبت له السيد الحفظ والأمانة. ولو هَمَّ بسوء لم يكن أميناً، ولو فعل لم يكن حفيظاً. ولهذا قال: ﴿لِنَصْرِفَ عَنْهُ السُّوءَ وَالْفَحْشَاءَ﴾ (يوسف ٢٤) والهمّ بالسوء من السوء وهو مصروف عنه أعني السوء، فلم يكن يهم بسوء. فولّاه الملك والسيادة بدلاً من العبودية الكونية الظاهرة التي كان فيها قبل ذلك.

٤٩ ثم أجدب محل العقل الذي هو الأب، وسمّع بالرخاء الذي في مدينة ابنه وهو لا يعلم أنه ابنه لأنه أعمى. فبعث إليه بالرَّحِم المتّصِلة ليُنيلَه شيئاً مما أُمِّنَ عليه، فبعث إليه بثوبه الذي فيه رائحته وهو على صورته. فلما استنْشَقَ الرائحةَ وألقاه على وجهه أبصر قميصه. فأخذ في الرحلة إليه ابتداءً في عزٍّ، يناقض سفر ابنه. فلما دخل عليه سجد لأنه معلِّمه الذي يَهَبُه من الله ما تقوم به ذاتُه ويتنعَّم به وجودُه.

فقد تبين أن النفس هنا بمنزلة يوسف من وجوه:[٢٨١] أحدها ما ذكرناه من وقوع البيع والشراء، ومنها قوله: ﴿رَبِّ قَدْ آتَيْتَنِي مِنَ الْمُلْكِ﴾ (يوسف ١٠١) والملك فيه المطيع والعاصي والموافِق والمخالِف. وفي النفس قيل: ﴿فألْهَمَها فُجورَها وتَقْواها﴾ (الشمس ٨). ومنها أيضاً قوله:

٢٨١ ش، ظ، ظه: في وجوه؛ ط: بوجوه

without having received a divine command to do that, the Real became jealous that His servant might exercise free disposal in something without His command. So He made a demonstration of his servanthood appear to him in his secret self. Joseph remembered his servanthood and refrained from exercising free disposal without a command of his Master. So the Soul imprisoned him in the prison of his bodily frame. He did not cease silently beseeching his Lord with his servanthood until the Soul was made to acknowledge that she was the one who had sought him, not he who had sought her. The Master affirmed his safeguardedness and his fidelity. Had he desired evil, he would not have been faithful, and had he done the deed, he would not have been someone who guards himself. For this reason, He said: *That We might ward off from him evil and lewdness* (Q.12:24). Desire for evil is itself an evil. It – I mean evil – was warded off from him, hence he could not desire evil. God invested him with dominion and masterhood as a substitute for the apparent existential servanthood he had possessed before that.

§49 Then the locus of the intellect, which is the father, experienced drought. He heard of the prosperity in his son's city, although he did not know that he was his son, since he was blind. Through the bond of kinship, Joseph sent something to him, so that he might be given something that he had entrusted him with. So he sent him his shirt that held his scent, for it was in his form. When Jacob inhaled the scent and cast it upon his face, he saw that it was Joseph's shirt. He began to journey towards him, setting forth with nobility, the opposite of the voyage of his son. When he entered into Joseph's presence, he prostrated himself, because Joseph was his teacher, who bestowed upon him from God that by which his essence subsisted and that by which his existence was made joyful.

It has been made clear that the soul here stands for Joseph in several respects. One of them is what we mentioned concerning the selling and buying. Another is His saying: *O my Lord! Thou hast given me [something] of sovereignty* (Q.12:101) – sovereignty includes the obedient and the disobedient, the complying and the opposing.

﴿وَعَلَّمْتَنِي مِنْ تَأْوِيلِ الْأَحَادِيثِ﴾ (يوسف ١٠١). وقال: ﴿هَذَا تَأْوِيلُ رُؤْيَايَ مِنْ قَبْلُ﴾ (١٠٠). والرؤيا إنما تكون من عالم الخيال وهو العالم الوسط وهو بين عالم العقل وعالم الحِسّ. وكذلك النفس بين عالم العقل وعالم الحس، فتارة تأخذ من عقلها وتارة تأخذ من حِسّها هكذا. ولهذا دُفِعَتْ[٢٨٢] للمرأة[٢٨٣] لغلبة الأنوثة، وإن كان تأنيثها[٢٨٤] غير حقيقي مع ذلك الحسن.[٢٨٥] فلو كانت الذُكورية غالبة لم تدفع النفس من أجل المودّة والرحمة التي يسكن بها الذَّكَر للأُنْثى والأنثى للذكر بخلاف الأنثى للأنثى والذكر للذكر فإن المودة لا تثبُت بينهما. ولولا الشَّبَهُ الذي ظهر في الغِلْمان بالاناث ما حنَّ إليهم أحدٌ، فالحنان إنما وقع على الحقيقة للأنثى، إمّا بالحقيقة أو بالشبه. ولهذا إذا بَقَلَ وجهُ الغلام وطَرَّ شاربُه رحلت المودة والرحمة التي كانت تُوجِب السكونَ إليه ولهذا قيل:

وقالوا العِذارُ جناح الهوى   إذا ما استوى طار عن وَكْرِه

هذا البيت أَنْشدَنيهِ قائلُه وهو الكاتب الأديب أبو عمرو بن مهيب بإشبيلية، عمله في حمو بن إبراهيم بن أبي بكر الميرغي[٢٨٦] وكان أجمل أهل زمانه، رآه عندنا زائراً وقد خط عذاره. فقلت له: يا أبا عمرو،

٢٨٢ ش: اوقعت

٢٨٣ ش، ط: المرأة

٢٨٤ ط: ثانيها

٢٨٥ ب، ط: الحس

٢٨٦ ش: الفرعي؛ ط: الهدنجي

It is said concerning the soul: *And inspired it with what is wrong for it and what is right for it* (Q.91:8). Also regarding it is His saying: *Thou hast taught me [something] of the interpretation of dreams* (Q.12:101), and *This is the interpretation of my dream of old* (Q.12:100). Dream-vision derives only from the world of the imagination, which is the intermediate world between the world of the intellect and the world of sense perception. Similarly, the soul is between the world of the intellect and the world of sense perception. Sometimes it takes from its intellect and sometimes it takes from its sense perception. Thus the soul [= Joseph] warded off the woman because of the predominance of the feminine in it, even though its femininity is not real,[329] in spite of that beauty. If masculinity had been dominant in Joseph's soul, it would not have warded off the Universal Soul, because of the love and mercy that the male feels for the female and the female for the male. This is in contradistinction to the love of the female for the female and the love of the male for the male, for love is not established between them. Were it not for the similarity to women that young men manifest, no one would feel any tenderness for them. Tenderness, in reality, only takes place for what is feminine, either in reality or because of some resemblance. Thus when the face of a young man sprouts a beard and moustache, love and mercy, which were the cause of attraction to him, depart.[330] For this reason it is said:

They say that cheek-fluff[331] is the wing of desire:
When it alights, desire flies from its nest.

This couplet was recited to me by its author, the secretary and belle-lettrist Abū ʿAmr b. Mahīb, in Seville. He composed it regarding Ḥamū b. Ibrahīm b. Abī Bakr al-Mīraghī, the most beautiful person of his time. Abū ʿAmr saw him when he was visiting us and his cheek-fluff had begun to appear. I said to him: 'O Abū

329. The word *nafs* (soul) is grammatically feminine.

330. For the temptations and trials attendant to companionship with beardless young men, see *Fut.*II (Chap. 108).

331. Arabic: *ʿidhār*. It is related to words of the same root meaning virginity (*ʿudhra*) and excuse (*ʿudhr*).

أما ترى إلى هذا الحَسَنِ الوجهِ؟ فعمل الأبيات في ذلك وهي:

وقالوا العذار جناح الهوى إذا ما استوى طار عن وكرِهِ
وليس كذلك فخبِّرْهم[287] قياماً بعذري[288] أو عذرِهِ
إذا كمُلَ الحسن في وجْنةٍ فخاتمه ويك من شَعْرِهِ

وقد ورد أن في وجوه الغلمان لمحاتٍ من الحور العين. فيا أيتها النفس المنيعة، احذري في سفركِ، أن تغفُلي عما يجب عليكِ لسيدكِ من الوقوف عند حدوده والحفظ لحُرَمه، فإنك إذا فعلت ذلك سيُنيلك حُرْمَتَه بحرمته، ويهبك نعمته بنعمته.

٥٠ سفر الميقات الالهي لموسى، عليه السلام

يقول الله – عز وجل: ﴿وَلَمَّا جَاءَ مُوسَى لِمِيقَاتِنَا ... [الآية]﴾ (الأعراف ١٤٣)

وأبْرَحُ ما يكون الشوقُ يوماً إذا دَنَتِ الدِّيارُ من الديارِ[289]

اعلم أن العبد إذا كان عبداً حقيقةً وفى[290] الجناب الالهي السيادي ما يستحقّه من الأدب والخدمة، وكان معه أبداً على قدم الحذر والمراقبة لأنفاسه لعلمه بأنه ﴿يَعْلَمُ السِّرَّ وَأَخْفَى﴾ (طه ٧) فلا

٢٨٧ ل، ط: فخيرهم
٢٨٨ ب: بعذرك؛ ط: لعذري
٢٨٩ ش: الخيام من الخيام
٢٩٠ ط: ووفى

'Amr! Don't you see his beautiful face?' And he composed a verse regarding that. It is:

They say that cheek-fluff is the wing of desire:
When it alights, desire flies from its nest.
But it is not like that. Tell them,
To establish my excuse[332] or his:
When the face's cheek has become perfect,
Its conclusion is: Woe unto you from its hair!

It has also been reported that the faces of young men contain glances from the eyes of houris. O impregnable soul! Beware during your voyage of being distracted from what you must do for your Master, halting at His limits and preserving what He has made sacred. If you do that, He will confer His protection with its protection and will bestow upon you His favour with its favour.

§50 *The Voyage of the Divine Appointment of Moses, peace be upon him*

God – may He be magnified and glorified – said: *And when Moses came to Our appointment* … (Q.7:143).[333]

Desire was more agonizing than ever one day
When the abodes approached the abodes.[334]

Know that the servant, if he is really a servant, treats the divine, masterly Dignity with the courtesy and service He deserves. He always adheres to caution[335] and watchfulness over his breaths with Him, because of his knowledge that *He knows the secret and the more*

332. Arabic: *ʿudhrī*. A play on words with *ʿidhār* (cheek-fluff).

333. Arabic: *mīqāt*. Derived from the root *w-q-t*, this term may include not only the time of an appointment but also the place. One of its meanings is the place where a pilgrim on the *ḥajj* or *ʿumra* enters into the ritual state of *iḥrām*.

334. One should keep in mind that the root of *dār* (abode), *d-w-r*, generally has to do with circling. This verse is also found in the *Futūḥāt*'s Chapter on Love (II.340, Chap. 178).

335. Arabic: *ḥidhr*. This word describes Moses' final journey. See *Isfār*, Para. 68.

يطمع في شيء منه البتة، فلا يزال جامداً لا تقوم به حركة عن موطن عبوديته، ولا شوقٌ إلى مِنْحة من مِنَح سيده، فكيف إلى مجالسته أو محادثته أو مسامرته غير أن الشوق كامنٌ في فِطْرة العبد بما هو إنسانٌ كالنار في الحجر.

النارُ في أحجارها مخْبوءةٌ لا تُصْطَلى ما لم تُثِرْها[٢٩١] الأزْنُدُ

فلا يظهر إلا بشيء غريب زائد على ذاته. فإن وعد السيدُ عبدَه بمحادثته[٢٩٢] أو مجالسته ثار الشوق الكامن بين ضلوعه، وحنّ إلى وعْد ربه، لكن لا يدري متى يفجأه الوعد[٢٩٣] لكونه غيرَ مربوط بحدٍّ وأجل، فإن كان الوعد بضرب ميقات، هاج الشوق وعظُم غَلَيانُه لانقضاء المدة، فأعطى العجلة عند العبد وهو قوله: ﴿وَمَا أَعْجَلَكَ عَنْ قَوْمِكَ يَا مُوسَى﴾ (طه ٨٣) وكان معذوراً فقال: ﴿وَعَجِلْتُ إِلَيْكَ رَبِّ لِتَرْضَى﴾ (طه ٨٤).

٥١ ثم إن المواقيت لما كانت آجالاً كان حكمها حكمَ الآجال، وحكمُ الآجال كما قد سمعتَ في قوله – تعالى: ﴿ثُمَّ قَضَى أَجَلاً وَأَجَلٌ مُسَمًّى عِنْدَهُ﴾ (الأنعام ٢). كذلك قال: ﴿وَوَاعَدْنَا مُوسَى ثَلَاثِينَ لَيْلَةً﴾ (الأعراف ١٤٢) فهذا ميقات. ثم قال: ﴿وَأَتْمَمْنَاهَا بِعَشْرٍ فَتَمَّ مِيقَاتُ رَبِّهِ أَرْبَعِينَ لَيْلَةً﴾ وهذا الميقات المضروب ميقاتُ غيبٍ فإنه[٢٩٤] ليليٌّ إذ كان الأمر الذي لأجله[٢٩٥] ضُرِبَ الميقاتُ غيباً أيضاً فإن المدلولات أبداً تُطابِق أدِلّتَها.

٢٩١ ط: يثرها

٢٩٢ ط: لمحدثته

٢٩٣ ظ: الوحي

٢٩٤ ك: لأنه

٢٩٥ ط: اجل

hidden (Q.20:7). He craves nothing from Him whatsoever but remains inert, undertaking no movement away from his homeland of servanthood, and desiring no gifts from his Master. Much less does he desire to sit with Him or converse with Him or engage in night-conversation with Him! Nevertheless, in the servant's original nature, inasmuch as he is a human being, desire is hidden like fire in the rock.

Fire in rocks is hidden; it does not burn
Unless the fire-drill draws it forth.

Desire does not become manifest in a human being until something extraneous is added to his essence. If the Master promises His servant that He will converse with him or sit with Him, the secret desire between his ribs is aroused. He longs for His Lord's promise but does not know if the promise will come upon him unexpectedly, for it is not linked to any limit or term. If the promise is fixed for a given time, desire for the time's fulfilment is stirred up and its ferment increases. It gives haste to the servant, which is His saying: *What hath made thee hasten from thy folk, O Moses?* (Q.20:83). He made excuses, saying: *I hastened unto Thee that Thou mightest be well pleased* (Q.20:84).

§51 Then since fixed times are terms,[336] their authority is that of terms, and the authority of the term is as you have heard the Most High say: *He has decreed a term for you, and a fixed term is with Him* (Q.6:2).[337] Similarly He said: *And We did appoint for Moses thirty nights* (Q.7:142) – this is a fixed time – then He said: *And We added to them ten, and he completed the whole time appointed by His Lord of forty nights* (Q.7:142). This appointed fixed time is the fixed time of the Unseen, because it takes place at night, since the affair for the sake of which the fixed time was appointed was also unseen, because objects of signification

336. Arabic: *ājāl*. Fixed terms are commonly associated with the time God has appointed for a person's lifespan: 'He hath decreed a term for you, and a fixed term (*ajalun musamman*) is with Him' (Q.6:2). There is no extending this term once it reaches its conclusion.

337. Arabic: *'indahu*. The sense is 'in His Presence'.

فلما تعيّنت المدة بالثلاثين ولم يُخَوِّفْه أولاً بالأربعين لئلا يطولَ عليه أو يحْدُسَ في سرّه بذكر الأربعين[٢٩٦] التي هي أربعُ من العقد، أن ذلك إشارة إلى انقضاء هيْكله المربَّع فيَعظُمَ أسفُه. ولا تقُلْ:[٢٩٧] وأين الأربعون من الأربعة؟ فاعلم أن هذا الهيكل إنما قام من الأربعة المركَّبة وهي الأربعون. والأربعة لا تركيبَ فيها فإنها بسائط ولكن[٢٩٨] هي أصل الأربعين. فكذلك هذا الهيكل لم يَقُمْ من البسائط الأربعة التي هي الحرارة والبرودة واليبوسة والرطوبة، وإنما قام من المركبة التي هي السوداء والصفراء والبلغم والدم. وكل واحدة من هذه مركبة من حرارة ويبوسة كالصفراء، وحرارة ورطوبة كالدم، وبرودة ويبوسة كالسوداء، وبرودة ورطوبة كالبلغم.

٥٢ فكان الوعد المسمى بالأربعين عنده، وجاء الذكر بالثلاثين لِمَا ذكرْناه. ولم يكن المراد بالأربعين إلا هذا أو مثْلَه مما يُطابِقه، فإن الأمر الحاصِل بعد الميقات لا يُبقى رسْماً للعبد عند العبد. فإن كانت محادثة فالعبد أُذُنٌ كلُّه، وإن كانت مشاهدة فالعبد عيْنٌ كلُّه. فقد زال عن حكم ما تقتضيه ذاته مع أنه تقتضيه ذاته ولكن لا لِعيْنِها. ولم يكن قبل ذلك ذاق هذا المقام ولا شاهد هذه الحال، فبالضرورة كان يبعد عنده، ولذلك

قال: إذا ما تجلَّى لي فكلِّي نواظِرٌ   وإن هو ناداني فكلِّي مسامعُ

٢٩٦ ك: - لئلّا يطولَ عليه أو يحْدُسَ في سرّه بذكر الأربعين

٢٩٧ ط: يقل

٢٩٨ ك: - ولكن

always correspond to their signifiers. The time was specified as thirty at first so as not to alarm him with forty, so that the time would not seem too long or so that he would not intuit in his inner heart by the mentioning of the forty – which are four tens – that it is an allusion to the termination of his fourfold bodily frame, which would have increased his sorrow. Do not ask: What does the forty have to do with the four? Know that this bodily frame stands only upon four composite principles, which are the forty.[338] There is no composition in the four, for they are simple principles but they are the root of the forty. Similarly, this bodily frame is not built from the four simple principles, which are: heat, cold, dryness and wetness. It is only built from four composites, which are: black bile, yellow bile, phlegm and blood, each one of these being composed of: heat and dryness, such as yellow bile; heat and wetness, such as blood; cold and dryness, such as black bile; and cold and wetness, such as phlegm.[339]

§52 The promise called 'the forty' was *with Him* (Q.6:2).[340] The 'thirty' were mentioned for the reason we mentioned, and the intended meaning of 'the forty' was only this or something similar that is equivalent to it. What took place after the appointment left no trace of the servant with the servant. If it involved conversation, the servant became all ear; and if it involved contemplation, the servant became all eye. He had abandoned the property that his essence demanded,[341] despite the fact that his essence demanded it, but not for its own sake. Before that he had not tasted that station or contemplated that state, so necessarily he was far from Him. For this reason, Moses said:

When He disclosed Himself to me, all of me became seeing,
And when He called me, all of me became hearing.

338. As he specifies below, these four composite principles are: black bile, yellow bile, phlegm and blood.

339. See Commentary.

340. Again, the sense of *'indahu* is 'in God's Presence'. The entire verse reads: 'He hath decreed a term for you, and a fixed term is with Him (*'indahu*)' (Q.6:2).

341. In other words, servanthood.

٥٣ فلمّا أكمل الثلاثين، وهو الميقات الأول، حرّكه بالتطهير لاظهار تمام الميقات فاسْتاكَ فأتمّ الميقات من أجل السِّواك. ولو أتمه[٢٩٩] من غير أن يجعل تمامه مشعراً بعقوبة لحزن موسى – عليه السلام – وظن أنه أيضاً يَعِدهُ بعد العشر بوعد آخر. فلما جعل لذلك سبباً وهو تطهير الفم (43) لجأ إلى التحفُّظ فلم يتحرّك في شيء من غير أمر إلهي. وأيضاً لما أوقع التقديس خرج عن عبوديته، والحضرة المقدَّسة[٣٠٠] لا تقبل إلا العبد، والعبد ليست له القُدُّوسية. فغارت أن يدخل عليها المُنازِع لها في صفتها من التقديس ولا سيّما بغير أمر إلهي.

فإن العزيز لا يراه ذو عِزّة وإنما يراه الذليل لأنها ما تجد[٣٠١] ما تمنحه.[٣٠٢] فالعزيز إذا دخل على العزيز ليس له ما يمنحه إلا العزة، وبها دخل عليه، فما يمنحه. فلا سبيل إلى دخوله عليه إلا بما تقتضيه حقائق العبودة.[٣٠٣] فلهذا أيضاً أتمّ له عشراً ليزول عنه التقديس الذي ابتغاه. وهذه كلها أسبابٌ إلهية وضعها الحق في العالم لاظهار حكمته في كونه.

فإذا تمّ الميقات، وتحرّر العبد بتمامه من رِقّ الأوقات، ولم يبْقَ عبداً إلا له – تعالى – وفّاه وعده، فناجاه وكلّمه. فبعد أن وفاه

٢٩٩ ك: انه

٣٠٠ ط: الالهية

٣٠١ ش، ظ، ظه: لأنه لا يجد

٣٠٢ ي: غير منقوطة؛ ش، ل، ط: يمنحه

٣٠٣ ب، ش، ط، ظ: العبودية

§ 53 When Moses had completed the thirty nights, which was the first appointment, God roused him to purify himself in order to show that the appointment was completed. He used the *siwāk*[342] and completed the appointment on account of the *siwāk*. If he had completed it without making its completion a source of awareness of punishment, Moses – peace be upon him – would have become sad. He thought that after the ten additional days, God would renew another promise for him. Having made a means for that – which was the purification of his mouth – he took refuge in restraint and made no movement without a divine command. Also, since sanctification had taken place, he had departed from his servanthood. The Sanctified Presence does not accept anyone but the servant, and the servant does not have sanctity. The Sanctified Presence is too jealous to allow anyone who contends with it over its attributes of sanctity to enter into its Presence, especially without a divine command.

A possessor of might does not see the Mighty One, only the humble one sees Him, because [the Presence][343] does not find anything to give to him. When the mighty one enters into the presence of the Mighty One, He has nothing to give him but might. He enters into His Presence with it, so what can He give? There is no way to enter into His presence save with what the realities of servanthood demand. For this reason also, God made Moses complete ten more nights so that the sanctification he was seeking would be removed from him. All of these are divine causes that the Real deposited in the cosmos in order to manifest His wisdom in His creation.

When the fixed time is completed and the servant is completely freed from the bondage of the Moments[344] and there remains no servant save of God the Most High, He fulfils His promise and delivers him and speaks to him. After He has fulfilled His promise

342. The *siwāk* is a kind of large toothpick used for cleaning the teeth. It is a sunna of the Prophet to use the *siwāk*, and the permissibility of using the *siwāk* during the month of Ramadan is a subject of Islamic law. Ibn ʿArabī discusses this at some length in his chapter in the *Futūḥāt* on the Secrets of Fasting. See Commentary.

343. The pronoun is feminine singular, hence it appears to refer to the Sanctified Presence (*al-ḥaḍra al-muqaddasa*) mentioned earlier.

344. Arabic: *awqāt*. See Commentary for a discussion of this term.

الوعد حظَّه وقدّس سَمْعَه ولَفْظَه، وأعطاه الكلام الكل كما أعطاه السمعَ الكل فإنه كما كان أذناً كله عند سماعه كان لساناً كله عند مراجعته. فعرف ذوقاً ومشاهدةَ عين أن الكل يقبل الكل، وأنه واحدٌ في كل حضرة يتميّز.[٣٠٤] فهذا سفر غيْبيّ معْنويّ زمانيّ ظهر في اللسان المحمدي بقوله "من أخلص لله أربعين صباحاً ظهرت ينابيع الحكمة من قلبه على لسانه" (44) فيسمع أوّلاً قلبه ثم ينطق لسانه بما وعاه بسمع[٣٠٥] قلبه.

٥٤ ولكن صاحب هذا السفر لا بد أن يخلُف في قومه من ينوب منابه. وقد ذكرنا المسافر. فانظر أنت يا أخي في النائب حتى يكون لك في المسألة مدخل بوجهٍ ما. وعند التجلي يكون سفر الجبال، منهزمة أمام جلال المتجلي إذ لا طاقة للجبال على مشاهدة الغيب أصلاً.[٣٠٦] ولهذا قال ﴿لَوْ أَنْزَلْنَا هَذَا الْقُرْآنَ عَلَى جَبَلٍ لَرَأَيْتَهُ خَاشِعاً مُتَصَدِّعاً مِنْ خَشْيَةِ اللهِ﴾ (الحشر ٢١). هذا مع التنزُل، فكيف مع سماع الكلام برفع الوسائط؟ فكيف مع[٣٠٧] الرؤية؟ فتحقّقْ هذا الفصل تشهدْ علماً كثيراً والحمد لله.[٣٠٨]

٣٠٤ ي: بدون النقط

٣٠٥ ك: وسمع

٣٠٦ ط: أهلا

٣٠٧ سقط من: ط

٣٠٨ ش: + وحده؛ ل: + تعالى؛ ط، ظ: - والحمد لله

– his portion – and has sanctified his hearing and his expression, He gives him speech in its totality just as He gives him hearing in its totality. Just as he is all ear when he listens to Him, he is all tongue when he repeats. He knows by taste and by eye-witnessing that the all receives the all, and that it is one in every presence that is distinguished. This is a hidden, suprasensible time-linked voyage that appears in the Muhammadan tongue with his saying: 'He who devotes himself exclusively to God for forty mornings, the founts of wisdom will spring from his heart and upon his tongue.'[345] thus he hears first of all with his heart, then his tongue speaks what his heart has retained and heard.

§ 54 However, the companion of this voyage must leave behind with his people someone who can be his deputy.[346] We have already mentioned the voyager, so regard, O brother, the deputy so that you will have some way to enter into this question. At the time of the Self-disclosure, the mountains voyaged, put to flight before the majesty of the Self-Discloser, since the mountains had no power whatsoever to contemplate the Unseen. For that reason, He said: *If We had caused this Qur'an to descend upon a mountain, thou verily wouldst have seen it humbled, rent asunder by the fear of Allah* (Q.59:21). If this is what occurs when the Qur'an descends, imagine how it is to hear the Speech when intermediaries are removed! And how it is to see!

Verify this chapter and you will contemplate ample knowledge, praise be to God!

345. A hadith that is found in the canonical collections. See also *Fut.*III.97 (Chap. 326): 'From this waystation [of discussion and dispute] wisdom is given to the one who has made himself pure for God for forty mornings, for he witnesses God in all his states, just as the Messenger of God – peace and blessings upon him – mentioned God in all his moments.'

346. In Moses' case, it was his brother Aaron.

٥٥ سفر الرضى

وهو قوله – عز وجل – عن موسى عليه السلام: ﴿وَعَجِلْتُ إِلَيْكَ رَبِّ لِتَرْضَى﴾ (طه ٨٤) حين قال له: ﴿وَمَا أَعْجَلَكَ عَنْ قَوْمِكَ يَا مُوسَى﴾ (طه ٨٣).

عجلتُ إلى ربّيَ لِيرْضى لِسُرعتي ... فلما وصلنا قال لِمَ عَجِلَ العبدُ
فقلتُ له الوعد الكريم أتى بنا ... إليك ولكن ما أرى صدق الوعدُ
فقال لي الرحمن كمِّلْ شروطه ... كما قد أُمِرْتم فانتفى القرب والبُعدُ

ومن ذلك

أن الرضى هو أصلي ... الذي خُلِقْتُ عليه
وحدي ولم أرَ غيري ... يؤول فيه إليه

مواهب الله لا نهاية لها، فما لها آخِرٌ ترجع إليه فتنقضي. والعبد ما يُوَفِّي[309] فيما كلّفه الله وُسْعَه ولا حقَّ استطاعته فصحّ وثبت رِضَى اللهِ عنهم ومنهم[310] فيما أتوْا به من الأعمال ورضُوا عنه ورضوا بما وهبهم

٣٠٩ ط: توفى

٣١٠ ش، ط: - ومنهم

§55 The Voyage of Good Pleasure[347]

This is His – may He be magnified and glorified – saying, on the part of Moses:

I hastened unto Thee that Thou mightest be well pleased (Q.20:84), *when He asked him: What hath made thee hasten from thy folk, O Moses?* (Q.20:83).

I hastened to my Lord so that He would be pleased with my
    swiftness.
When I arrived, He asked: Why did the servant hasten?
I answered Him: The generous promise brought us to You,
But I do not see the veracity of the promise.
The All-Merciful said to me: 'Complete its conditions
As you have been commanded.'
Then proximity and distance were abolished.

And, on this subject:

Good pleasure is my root; upon it I was created –
Myself alone – and I have seen none but myself
Return in Him to Him.

God's bestowals are infinite; there is no terminal point they can reach and then disappear. The servant cannot fulfil to his full extent or his true capability what God has imposed upon him, thus God's good pleasure from and with[348] His servants is validated and affirmed in the deeds that they have accomplished.[349] And they are well pleased with Him and with what He has given them from Himself, which

347. Arabic: *riḍā*. It may also be translated as 'satisfaction'. See *Fut.*II.212 (Chap. 128): On Knowledge of the Station of Good Pleasure, and *Fut.*II.213 (Chap. 129): On Abandoning Good Pleasure.

348. There is a distinction that is marked by two prepositions *min* and *ʿan*, which is also alluded to in *Fut.*II (Chap. 128).

349. Ibn ʿArabī cites a number of Qur'anic verses to this effect in Chap. 128 of the *Futūḥāt*: 'Keep your duty to Allah as best you can' (Q.64:16); 'Allah tasketh not a soul beyond its scope' (Q.2:286); and 'Allah asketh naught of any soul save that which He hath given it' (Q.65:7).

مما عنده مما لا يتناهى كثرةً فـ ﴿رَضِيَ اللهُ عَنْهُمْ وَرَضُوا عَنْهُ﴾ (المائدة ١١٩) فالرضى من صفات الحق، والرضى من صفات الخلق بما ينبغي للحق وبما يليق بالمخلوق وإن كان لا يستغني عن الامداد[٣١١] الالهي لأنه فقير بالذات، محتاج على الدوام لبقاء وجوده وإبقائه عليه. وفي رضاي عنه رضاه عني. وأنا حكيم وقتي، عليّ يدور الوجود ويخدمني.

إن الحكيم الذي الأكوان تخدمه ... لأنه ينزِل الأشيا مَنازلَها
يَبدو إلى كل ذي عين بصورته ... لا يقول بأن الحق نَازَلَها
فإن تبدّتْ إلى عيني حقيقتُه ... يكون كوني بلا شكٍ مُنَازِلَها

٥٦ واعلم أن الانسان إذا جهل حالَه فقد[٣١٢] جهل وقته، ومن جهِل وقته جهل نفسه، ومن جهل نفسه جهل ربه، فإن رسول الله، صلى الله عليه وسلم، يقول: "من عرف نفسه عرف ربه" إمّا بالنقيض كالمعرفة العامة،

٣١١ ط: الابتداء

٣١٢ ط: - فقد

is infinitely abundant. Hence *Allah is satisfied with them and they are satisfied with Him* (Q.5:119). Good pleasure is one of the attributes of the Real, and good pleasure is one of the attributes of the creature, in a way befitting the Real and in a way that is appropriate for the creature, since he cannot dispense with divine support; for the creature is poor essentially, perpetually needing the Real for the subsistence and preservation of his existence. In my good pleasure with Him is His good pleasure with me. I am the Sage of my time; existence revolves around me and is in my service.

The Sage is he whom the creatures serve,
For he makes things descend to their proper places.[350]
He appears in His[351] form to everyone who has an eye
And does not assert that the Real is the One who descends
to them.[352]
If His reality appears to my eye,
My being, without doubt, will go to meet it.

§56 Know that when the human being is ignorant of his state he is ignorant of his Moment;[353] and whoever is ignorant of his Moment is ignorant of himself; and whoever is ignorant of himself is ignorant of his Lord. The Messenger of God – God's blessing and peace be upon him – said: 'Whoever knows himself knows his Lord',[354] either negatively,[355] like common knowledge, or through the form, like elite

350. See *Fut.*III.35–6 (Chap. 309, On the Waystation of the Malāmiyya) for a similar formulation.

351. The pronoun here is ambiguous. Does he appear in God's form or in his own?

352. This much of the poem is also found in *Fut.*IV.435 (Chap. 559).

353. Arabic: *waqt*. In *Fut.*II.64 (Chap. 73, Question 33), Ibn ʿArabī does not hold out much promise that this knowledge is attainable: 'The Moment (*waqt*) [here connected with *taqdīr*, determination, decree] is the most inaccessible (*aʿazz*) station with respect to denying or conceiving any knowledge of it; it is never attained.' Nonetheless, it is the Moment that governs the state of the servant and bestows upon him what his preparedness is capable of receiving. See *Fut.*II.539 (Chap. 238: On the Moment).

354. This hadith is not considered sound by the traditional sources but Ibn ʿArabī attests to its authenticity by way of unveiling. A thorough study of this hadith has been made by Altmann in 'The Delphic Maxim'.

355. Presumably by the *via negativa*, determining what God is not gives a certain knowledge of Him. See also *Isfār*, Para. 69, which spells out this mode of knowing/not knowing.

وإمّا بالصورة كالمعرفة الخاصة، وهي التي عوَّل عليها أهل الخصوص من الجماعة. ونحن وإن كنا نقول بذلك فمعرفة العامة عندنا أرجح، فإنها الجامعة بين الابتداء والانتهاء وإليها الرجوع ولا بد عامة وخاصة.

فاعلم ذلك، وكن على بصيرة من أمرك في ذلك وعلى بينة من ربك، عسى يتلوك شاهدٌ منك (45) فيكون سبب سعادتك[٣١٣] به، إن شاء الله! فتكون ممن سبقتْ له الحسنى من الله – جل ثناؤه وعز جلاله.

٥٧ ولما قال الله – عز وجل – لموسى – عليه السلام: ﴿وَمَا أَعْجَلَكَ عَنْ قَوْمِكَ يَا مُوسَى﴾ (طه ٨٣) أضرب موسى – عليه السلام – عن الجواب وجوابه أن يقول: أعجلني كذا وكذا ويبين فقال: ﴿هُمْ أُولَاءِ عَلَى أَثَرِي﴾ (طه ٨٤) يشير إلى حكم الاتّباع ثم ذكر عَجَلته فقال: ﴿عَجِلْتُ إِلَيْكَ رَبِّ لِتَرْضَى﴾ إني سارعتُ إلى إجابة دعائك حين دعوْتَني وقومي على أثري. فقال الله – عز وجل – له:[٣١٤] ﴿فَإِنَّا قَدْ فَتَنَّا قَوْمَكَ مِنْ بَعْدِكَ﴾ (طه ٨٥) أي اختبرْناهم ﴿وأضلَّهُمُ السامريُّ﴾ بالعِجْل الذي قال لهم في شأنه ﴿هَذَا إِلَهُكُمْ وَإِلَهُ مُوسَى﴾ (طه ٨٨). وسبب ذلك أنه لما مشى مع موسى، عليه السلام، كشف الله عن بصره حتى أبصر

٣١٣ ط: فتكون سعادتك به

٣١٤ سقط من سائر النسخ ما عدا ي

knowledge, which is that upon which the elite among the majority rely.[356] As for us, although we profess the latter, we prefer the knowledge of the commoners, for it brings together the beginning and the end to which both commoners and elite must necessarily return.

Know that. Be upon insight from your affair regarding that, and be upon a clear proof from your Lord. Perhaps a witness from you will follow you and will be the cause of your felicity,[357] God willing! You will be one of those for whom *kindness hath gone before* (Q.21:101) from God – may His praise be glorified and His majesty be magnified.

§ 57 When God – may He be magnified and glorified – said to Moses – upon whom be peace – *What hath made thee hasten from thy folk, O Moses?* (Q.20:83), Moses avoided giving the answer 'My haste was because of this or that', rather he explained his haste by saying: *They are close upon my track* (Q.20:84), alluding to [his people's] following [him]. Then he mentioned his haste, saying: *I hastened unto Thee that Thou mightest be well pleased* (Q.20:84) – I came swiftly to answer Your call when You called me, and my people are upon my track. God – may He be magnified and glorified – said to him: *Lo! We have tried thy folk in thine absence* (Q.20:85) – in other words, We have put them to the test, *and al-Sāmirī*[358] *hath misled them* (Q.20:85) with the calf,[359] saying to them: *This is your God and the God of Moses* (Q.20:88). The reason for this is that when the Sāmirī walked with Moses – upon whom be peace – God ~~veiled~~ unveiled his sight until he saw the

356. '[The servant] knows necessarily that if he were similar to Him or like Him he would know it in himself. He knows by his dependence that someone who depends upon Him cannot resemble Him. So he knows that he is not like his Lord, even if God has established him as vicegerent and has brought him into existence upon the [divine] form.' *Fut.* III.301 (Chap. 361).

357. See Q.11:17: 'Is he [to be counted equal with them] who relieth on a clear proof from his Lord, and a witness from Him reciteth it, and before it was the Book of Moses, an example and a mercy?'

358. 'Sāmirī' is generally translated as 'Samaritan'. Polemicists have pointed out that the Samaritans did not exist at the time of Moses and cite this Qur'anic story as proof of the inaccuracy of the Qur'an. Without entering into this (to my mind, pointless) debate, I think it is of some interest that the Samaritans themselves have claimed descent from the Joseph tribes of Ephraim and Manasseh (see 'Samaritans', *Encyclopaedia Judaica*, vol. 17 [2007]).

359. Arabic: *'ijl*, from the same root as *'ajal*, haste.

المَلَك الذي هو على صورة الثَّوْر من حملة العرش فتخيّل أنه[٣١٥] إله موسى الذي يكلِّمه. فأخرج لقومه[٣١٦] العجل، وكان قد عرف جبريل حين جاءه وأنه لا يمر بشيء إلا حَيِيَ بمروره. فقبض قبضةً[٣١٧] من أثر فرس جبريل ورمى بها في العجل، فحيي العجل وخار لأنه عجل والخوار صوت البقر. (46) وقال لهم: ﴿هَذَا إِلَهُكُمْ وَإِلَهُ مُوسَى﴾ (طه ٨٨) ونسي السامري إذا سأله عابِدوه أنه لَا ﴿يَرْجِعُ إِلَيْهِمْ قَوْلاً وَلَا يَمْلِكُ لَهُمْ ضَرًّا وَلَا نَفْعاً﴾ (طه ٨٩) فقال لهم هارون، عليه السلام: ﴿وَإِنَّ رَبَّكُمُ الرَّحْمَنُ فَاتَّبِعُونِي وَأَطِيعُوا أَمْرِي﴾ (طه ٩٠) فقال لهم ما ذكر الله في كتابه عنه أنه خاطبهم به.

٥٨ سفر الغضب والرجوع

قال الله – تعالى: ﴿وَلَمَّا رَجَعَ مُوسَى إِلَى قَوْمِهِ غَضْبَانَ أَسِفاً﴾ (الأعراف ١٥٠ وانظر طه ٨٦).

غضِبْتُ على نفْسي لنفْسي فلم أجِد سواه فقلتُ الذنْبُ لِلْمُتقدِّمِ
فما زلتُ مسروراً وما زلتُ قارعاً[٣١٨] لما كان مني فيه سنُّ[٣١٩] التندُّمِ
فلو كنتُ حقاً لم أكنْ واحداً[٣٢٠] به ولو كنت خلْقاً لم أقلْ بالتقدّمِ

"غضبان" على قومه، "أسفاً" عليهم لما فعلوه من اتخاذهم العجل إلهاً. وإنما كان عجلاً لأن السامري لما مشى مع موسى،

٣١٥ ط: - أنه
٣١٦ ط: لهم
٣١٧ ط: قبضته
٣١٨ ل: فارغا
٣١٩ ش: يئس؛ ط: سر
٣٢٠ ل: واجداً

angel among the Bearers of the Throne,[360] who has the form of a calf, and he imagined that it was the god of Moses who spoke to him. Thus he fashioned the calf for Moses' people and, having recognized Gabriel when he came to him and knowing that everything comes to life as he passes, he took a handful of earth from the hoof print of Gabriel's horse and threw it on the calf.[361] The calf came to life and lowed, since it was a calf and lowing is the sound of cattle. He said to them: *This is your God and the God of Moses* (Q.20:88). But when its worshippers asked him, the Sāmirī *forgot* (Q.20:88)[362] that *it returneth no saying unto them and possesseth for them neither hurt nor use* (Q.20:89). Aaron – upon him be peace – said to them: *Your Lord is the All-Merciful, so follow me and obey my order* (Q.20:90), and told them what God had mentioned in His Book.[363]

§58 The Voyage of Anger and Return

God the Most High said: *And when Moses returned to his people, angry and grieved …* (Q.7:150).

I was angry with myself because of my self;
But, finding none but Him, I said:
The sin belongs to the one who has precedence.
I remained joyful, but kept on striking myself
For what I did, having reached the age of regret.
If I were a Real, I would not be one through Him;
And if I were a creature, I would not claim precedence.

He was *angry* with his people, *grieved* for their sake over what they had done by taking the calf as a god, when it was only a calf, for

360. Ibn ʿArabī devotes Chapter 13 of the *Futūḥāt* to the Bearers of the Throne. The Throne is the seat of the All-Merciful.

361. See *Fuṣūṣ*, chapter on Jesus.

362. The pronoun is ambiguous. In some translations, such as that by Yūsuf ʿAlī, the referent is given in brackets as Moses.

363. It is unclear what Book Aaron is referring to since the Qurʾan had not yet been revealed.

عليه السلام، في السبعين الذين مشوْا معه، (47) كشف الله عنه غِطاء بصره. فما وقعتْ عينه إلا على الملك الذي على صورة الثور وهو من حملة العرش لأنهم أربعة: واحد على صورة أسد، وآخر على صورة نَسْر، وآخر على صورة ثور، ورابع على صورة إنسان. فلما أبصر السامري الثور تخيّل أنه إله موسى الذي يكلمه، فصوّر لهم العجل وقال لهم:[٣٢١] ﴿هَذَا إِلَهُكُمْ وَإِلَهُ مُوسَى﴾ (طه ٨٨) وصاغه من حُلِيِّهم لتتبع[٣٢٢] قلوبُهم أموالَهم لِعلْمه أن المال حُبُّه مَنوطٌ بالقلب، وعلم أن حب المال يحجبهم أن ينظروا فيه هل يضرّ أو ينفع أو يردّ عليهم قولاً إذا سألوه.

٥٩ وقال لهم هارون: ﴿يا قَوْمِ إنما فُتِنْتُمْ﴾ أي اخْتُبِرْتم ﴿به﴾ لتقوم الحجّة لله عليكم إذا سُئِلتم ﴿وَإِنَّ رَبَّكُمُ الرَّحْمَنُ﴾ ومن رحمته بكم أنه أمْهلكم ورزقكم مع كونكم اتّخذتم إلهاً تعبدونه غيره – سبحانه – ثم قال لهم: ﴿فاتَّبِعوني﴾ لما علم أن في اتّباعهم إيّاه الخير ﴿وَأَطِيعُوا أَمْرِي﴾ (طه ٩٠) لكون موسى، عليه السلام، أقامه فيهم نائباً عنه فـ ﴿قَالُوا لَنْ نَبْرَحَ عَلَيْهِ﴾ يريدون عبادة العجل ﴿عَاكِفِينَ﴾ أي ملازمين ﴿حَتَّى يَرْجِعَ إِلَيْنَا مُوسَى﴾ (طه ٩١) الذي بُعِثَ إلينا وأُمِرْنا بالايمان به. فحجبهم هذا النظر أن ينظروا فيما أمرهم به هارون، عليه السلام.

٣٢١ سقط من ط

٣٢٢ ط: يتبع

when the Sāmirī went with Moses – upon him be peace – among the seventy who walked with him,[364] God unveiled the covering from his eyes, and his eye fell upon nothing but the angel who was in the form of the bull. It was one of the Bearers of the Throne,[365] because there are four: one in form of a lion, another in the form of an eagle, another in the form of a bull and the fourth in the form of a human being. When the Sāmirī saw the bull, he imagined that it was the God of Moses who spoke with him, so he formed the calf for them and said: *This is your God and the God of Moses* (Q.20:88). He fashioned it from their jewellery so that their hearts would follow their possessions, because of his knowledge that love of possessions is connected with the heart. He knew that love of possessions veiled them from seeing whether the calf would harm them or benefit them or answer them when they spoke or asked it something.

§ 59 Aaron said to them: *O my people! Ye are but being seduced* (Q.20:90), namely, put to the test *by him* (Q.20:90), in order that the proof against you be established by God, when you are asked. *And your Lord is the All-Merciful* (Q.20:90) and, because of His mercy towards you, He has granted you a delay and has provided for you despite your having taken a god to worship other than He – may He be glorified! Then he said to them: *So follow me* (Q.20:90), because he knew that there was good in their following him, *and obey my order* (Q.20:90), for Moses – upon him be peace – had set him up among them as his deputy. *They said: We shall by no means cease* (Q.20:91) – meaning in their worship of the calf – *to be devoted* (Q.20:91) – namely, attached, *until Moses return unto us* (Q.20:91), the one who was sent to us and commanded us to have faith. This view veiled them from contemplating what Aaron – peace be upon him – had commanded them.

364. Q.7:155: 'And Moses chose seventy of his people for Our place of meeting …'.

365. 'And the angels will be on the sides thereof, and eight will uphold the Throne of thy Lord that day, above them' (Q.69:17). In this world, the Bearers of the Throne are four angels in the shape of a man, a bull, an eagle and a lion – archetypes drawn from the Revelation of St. John in the New Testament. In the next world, according to a hadith of Ibn 'Abbās, there will be eight bearers.

فلما رجع موسى إلى قومه وجدهم قد فعلوا ما فعلوا فـ ﴿أَلْقَى الْأَلْوَاحَ﴾ من يده ﴿وَأَخَذَ بِرَأْسِ أَخِيهِ يَجُرُّهُ إِلَيْهِ﴾ (الأعراف ١٥٠) عقوبةً له بنائبه[٣٢٣] في قومه. فناداه هارون، عليه السلام، بأمه فإنها محلّ الشفقة والحنان ﴿قَالَ يَبْنَؤُمَّ لَا تَأْخُذْ بِلِحْيَتِي وَلَا بِرَأْسِي﴾ ولقد خشِيتُ لما وقع ما وقع من قومك أن تلومني على ذلك و﴿تَقُولَ فَرَّقْتَ بَيْنَ بَنِي إِسْرَائِيلَ وَلَمْ تَرْقُبْ﴾ أي تلزم ﴿قَوْلِي﴾ (طه ٩٤) الذي أوْصَيْتُك به.

٦٠ ثم ردّ وجْهَه إلى السامري فقال له: ﴿فَمَا خَطْبُكَ﴾ أي ما حديثك ﴿يَا سَامِرِيُّ﴾ (طه ٩٥)، فقال له السامري ما رآه من صورة الثور الذي هو أحد حَمَلة العرش، فظنّ أنه إله موسى الذي يكلِّمه. فلذلك صنعْتُ لهم العجل، وعلمتُ أن جبريل ما يمرّ بموضع إلا حيِيَ به لأنه روح. فلذلك ﴿قبضْتُ﴾ ﴿من أثره﴾ - لعلمه[٣٢٤] بحياة تلك[٣٢٥] القبضة - ﴿فنبذتُها﴾ (طه ٩٦) في العجل، فخار. فما فعله السامري إلا عن تأويل، فضلَّ وأضلَّ فإنه ما كلُّ تأويلٍ يصيب مع علمه أن التجلّي في الصُّوَر[٣٢٦] جاءتْ به الشرائع مع التنزيه.

فقَبِلَ موسى عُذْر[٣٢٧] أخيه فـ ﴿قَالَ رَبِّ اغْفِرْ لِي وَلِأَخِي وَأَدْخِلْنَا فِي رَحْمَتِكَ وَأَنْتَ أَرْحَمُ الرَّاحِمِينَ﴾ (الأعراف ١٥١). وأمّا الذين عبدوا العِجل فما أعطَوْا النظرَ الفكري حقَّه للاحتمال الداخل في

٣٢٣ ل: بنيابته؛ ط: بتأنيه
٣٢٤ ك: لعلمي
٣٢٥ ط: بتلك
٣٢٦ ط: الضوء
٣٢٧ ط: حذر

When Moses returned to his people and found them doing what they were doing, *he cast down the tablets* (Q.7:150) from his hand, *and seized his brother by the head, dragging him towards him* (Q.7:150) in order to inflict a punishment on his deputy among his people. Aaron – peace be upon him – called to him, mentioning his mother, for she is the place of compassion and tenderness, *and he said: Son of my mother! Clutch not my beard nor my head. I feared lest* (Q.20:94) when what took place happened, you would blame me for that, and *thou shouldst say: Thou hast caused division among the Children of Israel and hast not waited for my word* (Q.20:94) – that is, adhered to *my word*, with which I entrusted you.[366]

§60 Then Moses turned his face to the Sāmirī and said to him: *And what hast thou to say* (Q.20:95), that is, what have you to tell, *O Sāmirī?* (Q.20:95). The Sāmirī told him what he had seen of the form of the bull, which is one of the Bearers of the Throne, and that he had thought it was the God of Moses who spoke with him: 'Therefore, I formed the calf for them, since I knew that Gabriel does not pass by any place but that it comes to life, for he is a spirit. For that reason, I took a handful from his footprint' – because of his knowledge of the life in that handful – '*and then threw it* (Q.20:96) on the calf, and it lowed'. The Sāmirī had only acted from an interpretation,[367] so he was misled and led others astray – for not every interpretation hits the mark – despite the fact that he knew that the Laws have mentioned divine Self-disclosure in forms alongside His transcendence.

Moses accepted the excuse of his brother. *He said: My Lord! Have mercy on me and on my brother; bring us into Thy mercy, Thou the Most Merciful of all who show mercy* (Q.7:151). As for those who worshipped the calf, they did not grant reflective speculation its due as the story

366. See also *Fut.*II.277 in which Aaron counsels the Muhammadian follower to exercise gentleness with his companion the philosopher, based on his own humiliation at the hands of his brother despite his innocence. Ibn 'Arabī claims that had Moses not let the Tablets fall from his hands, he would have seen that they were inscribed with 'guidance and mercy' (Q.7:154).

367. Arabic: *ta'wīl*. As in the case of Adam, the Sāmirī exercised his reason improperly by drawing false conclusions. See Para. 27.

القِصّة، فما عذرهم الحقُّ ولا وفّى عابِدوه النظرَ في ذلك، فثبت بهذه الآية النظر العقلي في الالهيات حتى يَرِدَ الشرعُ بما يَرِدُ في ذلك. وأما الذلة التي نالتْ بني إسرائيل في الدنيا[٣٢٨] فمشهودة إلى اليوم. ما أقام الله لهم عَلَماً، وما زالوا أذِلّاء في كلّ زمان وفي كلّ ملة. وجعل الله ذلك جزاءَ المُفْتري على الله حيث نسب إليه من غير ورود شرعٍ ما لا يليق في النظر الفكري أن يكون عليه الاله المعبود من الصفات. ﴿وَاللهُ يَقُولُ الْحَقَّ وَهُوَ يَهْدِي السَّبِيلَ﴾ (الأحزاب ٤).

٦١ سفر السعي على العائلة

لقد فُزْتُ بالسعي الجميل على أهلي ... بربِّي فجلَّى لي العناية في شُغْلي
فلولاهم ما كُنتُ عبْداً مقرَّباً ... ولا كنت من أهل السيادة والفضلِ
ولا سلكتْ نفسي إذا ما زجرْتُها ... عن الشغل بالأكوان في أقْوَم السُّبْل
وكنت مع[٣٢٩] المختار في ظل عرشه ... إذا كانت الأنصار تأتي مع الرُّسْلِ

قال الله – تعالى: ﴿إِنِّي آنستُ ناراً لَعَلِّي آتِيكُمْ مِنْهَا بِقَبَسٍ أَوْ أَجِدُ عَلَى النَّارِ هُدًى﴾ (طه ١٠). فانظر ما أعْجبَ قوّةَ النبوّة لأنه وجد الهدى.

٣٢٨ سقط من سائر النسخ ما عدا ي
٣٢٩ ط: من

admits,[368] so the Real did not excuse them. The worshippers of the calf were not endowed with speculation concerning that. Rational speculation in divine science has been affirmed by this verse unless the Law brings what it brings concerning that. As for the humiliation that the Children of Israel have obtained in this world, it is well known to this day. God did not establish a sign for them,[369] and they continue to be humiliated in every time and among every religious community. God made that the recompense of those who fabricate lies against God, attributing to Him, without reference to Law, attributes that are not fitting for reflective speculation to attribute to a God that is worshipped. *And Allah speaks the truth and He guides on the Path* (Q.33:4).

§61

The Voyage of Striving on Behalf of One's Household[370]

Through my beautiful striving on behalf of my people,[371]
I came upon my Lord. He showed me solicitude in my concern.
Were it not for them, I would not be a servant, brought near,
Nor would I be a person of mastery and excellence.
Had I held my soul back[372] from concern for creatures,
It would not have travelled the straightest of paths.
I was with the chosen one,[373] in the shadow of His Throne,
When the Helpers came with the Messengers.

God the Most High said, reporting the speech of Moses: *I see a fire afar off. Peradventure I may bring you a brand therefrom or may*

368. With this Ibn 'Arabī demonstrates that there is a role for rational speculation and that Moses' people did not go far enough in using their reason.

369. Unlike Noah, for whom God established the sign of the *tannūr*. See Para. 37.

370. Arabic: *'ā'ila*. People one is responsible for supporting, those who depend on one for sustenance.

371. Arabic: *ahl*. In its most specific sense it is one's wife, but in its extended sense it refers to one's family, folk, people or followers.

372. Or 'rebuked', 'upbraided'.

373. Arabic: *al-mukhtār*. An epithet for Muhammad.

وهذا يدلّك على أنه ما قطع مما[٣٣٠] أبصر أنه نار ولا بدّ. وكل نار فهو نور إذا اشتعل، والأنوار مُحرِقة بلا شك في الأجسام القابلة للاحتراق والاشتعال. ورد في الخبر الصحيح "لأحرقتْ سُبُحات وجهه ما أدركه بصرُه مِن خلْقه" (48) والسبحات الأنوار. وأخبر أن السبحات تبلغ أشِعّتها مبلغ ناظر العين في الادراك.

٦٢ واعلم أن الأمر الواحد قد تكون له وجوهٌ مختلفة، فيكون[٣٣١] من كونه كذا عنه كذا، ومن كونه كذا أيُّ حُكْمٍ آخَرَ يكون عن ذلك أمر آخر. فالأمر من كونه يُرى ما هو[٣٣٢] كونه يُعْلِمُ، ومن كونه يُعْلَمُ[٣٣٣] ما هو[٣٣٤] كونه يُسْمَعُ، وإن كان الأمر الذي يُدرك به أمرٌ واحدٌ في عينه وتختلف تعلُّقاتُه به. فنقول[٣٣٥] فيه بالنظر إلى الأمر الواحد أنه يسمع بما به يبصر بما به يتكلّم إلى غير ذلك. وبعض النُظّار يجعل لكل حكم إدْراكاً خاصاً غير الادراك الآخر فيُعدِّدُ،[٣٣٦] وإن كنّا لا نقول بذلك ولكن سُقْناه ليعلم السامع أنّا قد علمْنا أنّ ثَمَّ من يقول بهذه المقالة وإن كُنّا لا نرْتضيها. وإنما اختلفت[٣٣٧] التعلُّقات لاختلاف المتعلَّق لا لاختلاف المتعلِّق اسم فاعل.

فالعين واحدةٌ والحكم مختلِفٌ والقائلون بذا قومٌ لهم نظرُ
الله أعظم أن تُدْرى مقاصده في خلقه بل له الآيات والعبرُ

٣٣٠ ي: بدون النقط؛ ف، ل، ط: فيما
٣٣١ ط: - فيكون
٣٣٢ ط: + من
٣٣٣ ط: - يعلم
٣٣٤ ط: + من
٣٣٥ ي: بدون النقط
٣٣٦ ش، ط: فتعدد
٣٣٧ ط: اختلف

find guidance at the fire (Q.20:10). Contemplate how wonderful is the power of prophecy, for Moses found guidance. This indicates to you that he was not certain that what he saw was a fire. Every fire must be a light, since it blazes; there is no doubt that lights burn in bodies that accept burning and blazing. It has come in a sound tradition: 'The Glories of His Face would burn everything the sight of His creatures perceives.'[374] The Glories are lights. The tradition reports that the rays of the Glories have a similar effect to the glance of the eye with respect to perception.[375]

§62 Know that the same thing can have different aspects.[376] From its being in a certain way, x will appear from it; and from its being another way – some other determination – y will appear from it. The thing's being seen is not the same as its being known; and its being known is not the same as its being heard. Even if that thing which is perceived is one in itself, it is varied and different in its relationships; thus with respect to that one same thing, we say that one hears by what one sees by what one speaks, and so forth. Some speculative thinkers make for every property a specific perception that is different from another perception, so that perception becomes multiple. Even if we do not profess that doctrine, we cite it so that the hearer will know that we know that there are those who profess this doctrine, even if we do not approve of it. The relationships differ only because what they are related to differs, not because the thing that relates them differs.

The essence is one but the property differs;
Those who profess this are people of perception.
God is too great for anyone to perceive His intentions
Concerning His creatures,

374. The entire hadith reads: 'God has seventy – or seventy thousand – veils of light and darkness; were they to be removed, the Glories of His Face would burn away everything perceived by the sight of His creatures.' Found in Muslim *Ṣaḥīḥ*, *īmān* I.293; Ibn Māja, *Sunan*, Muqaddima 13.

375. See *Fut.*II.110: 'The Glories of the Face are lights belonging to the Essence.'

376. Or 'faces'.

جلّ الاله فلا عقلَ يُحصّله وعزّ قدْراً فما يَحْظى به بشرُ
لكن له صُوَرٌ فينا محقّقةٌ جاء الخطاب بها في ضِمْنها صُوَرُ
تَعْنو لصورة من تُعْزى[٣٣٨] له صوَرٌ فما ترى صوراً إلا لها سوَرُ

٦٣ واعلم أن كل خير في السعي على الغير، والسعي على الأهل من ذلك، وشرف الأهل بشرف من يُضاف إليه. ورد في الحديث في أهل القرآن أنّ "أهل القرآن هم أهل الله وخاصته" (49) فما عَظُمَ[٣٣٩] أجرُ من سعى في حق الله إلا من أجل الأهلية فافهم. إذا كانت عناية الله بأهل البيت النبوي المحمدي ما ذكر الله لنا في كتابه في قوله – تعالى: ﴿إِنَّمَا يُرِيدُ اللهُ لِيُذْهِبَ عَنْكُمُ الرِّجْسَ أَهْلَ الْبَيْتِ وَيُطَهِّرَكُمْ تَطْهِيراً﴾ (الأحزاب ٣٣) فإن[٣٤٠] الفرّاء (50) لما سُئِل عن الرجس ما هو قال القَذَر. فإذا كان الله – [تعالى] – مع أهل بيت النبوة يريد ذهاب الرجس وحصول التطهير فما ظنك بأهل القرآن الذين هم أهله وخاصته، فالحمد لله الذي جعلني منهم. وأقلّ الأهلية في ذلك حمل حروفه محفوظةً في

٣٣٨ ط: يعزى
٣٣٩ ب، ش، ط: أعظم
٣٤٠ ش، ل، ط، ظ: قال

But He does have signs and exemplary lessons.[377]
The Divinity is majestic – no intellect can attain It –
and mighty in power – no mortal can achieve It –
But It does have forms that are realized in us –
Divine discourse has come regarding them –
Within which are forms, humbly submitting[378] to the Form
Of the One to whom all forms are attributed.
You will not see any form unless it has a sura.[379]

§63 Know that every good derives from striving for the other, and striving for one's family is part of that. A family's nobility derives from the nobility of the one it is attributed to. It has come in the hadith regarding the people of the Qur'an that 'the people of the Qur'an are the people of God and His elite.'[380] The recompense is great for someone who strives for what is due to God, if only for the sake of belonging to His people. So understand. God's solicitude for the People of the House of the Prophet Muhammad is as He has mentioned to us in His Book, saying: *Allah's wish is but to remove uncleanness far from you, O People of the House, and to purify you completely* (Q.33:33). When al-Farrā'[381] was asked what was 'uncleanness', he responded: 'It is soiling.' If God the Most High[382] wanted to remove uncleanness from the People of the House of the Prophet and for them to obtain purity, what do you think about 'the people of the Qur'an who are His people and His elite'?[383] Praise be to God who made me one of them! The least degree of belonging to His people is to bear the Qur'an's letters as something preserved in the

377. Arabic: *al-āyāt wa-l-'ibar*. See Commentary, p. 169.

378. See Q.20:111: 'Faces shall be humbled before the Living, the Subsisting.'

379. Play on words between *ṣūra* (form) and *sūra* (chapter of the Qur'an). This juxtaposition of *ṣūra* and *sūra* can also be found in the last two lines of the poem that begins Chap. 174 of the *Futūḥāt*, On Knowledge of the Station of the Voyage and Its Secrets (II.293), as well as in numerous other poems by the Shaykh.

380. Ibn 'Arabī cites al-Tirmidhī as the source for this hadith. See *Fut.*I.196 (Chap. 29).

381. Abū Zakariyyā' Yaḥyā b. Ziyād al-Farrā' (761–822), one of the most important grammarians and philologists of the Kufan school.

382. Missing in holograph MS. Y.

383. See also *Fut.*I.196 (Chap. 29).

الصدور، فإن تخلّق بما حمل وتحقّق به وكان من صفاته فبَخٍ على بَخ.

ولقد بلغني عن أبي العباس الخشّاب (51) من أصحاب أبي مدين [رضي الله عنه] بمدينة فاس أن رجلاً دخل عليه وبيده كتاب من كتب الطريق، فقرأ عليه ما شاء الله وأبو العباس ساكتٌ، فقال له الرجل: يا سيدي لِمَ لا تتكلم لي عليه، فقال له أبو العباس: اقْرَأْني، فعَظُم على الرجل هذا الكلام. فدخل على شيخنا أبي مدين فقال له: يا سيّدنا كنتُ عند أبي العباس الخشاب وقرأت عليه كتاباً في الرقائق ليتكلّم لي عليه، فقال لي اقْرَأْني. فقال الشيخ: صدق أبو العباس، على ما كان يحوي ذلك الكتاب؟ فقال: على الزهد والورع والتوكل والتفويض وما يقتضيه الطريق إلى الله. فقال له الشيخ: فهل كان فيه شيء ما هو حالٌ لأبي العباس الخشاب؟ قال لا، فقال له الشيخ: فإذا كانت أحوال الخشاب جميع ما يحوي عليه ذلك الكتاب، ولم تتّعِظْ بأحواله ولا تخلّقتَ بشيء من ذلك فما فائدة قراءتك عليه وسؤالك أن يتكلم لك، وقد وعظك بحاله، وأفصح في ذلك ونصح.

breast.[384] If someone assumes the character of what he bears and realizes it so that it becomes one of his attributes, then so much the better!

The following report reached me concerning Abū al-ʿAbbās al-Khashshāb,[385] one of the companions of Abū Madyan[386] – may God be pleased with him[387] – in the town of Fez. A man came to visit him, with one of the books concerning the Path in hand. He read a bit to him, but Abū al-ʿAbbās remained silent. The man said to him: 'My master, why don't you speak to me about it?'

Abū al-ʿAbbās said to him: 'Read me.' This speech was distressing to the man, so he paid a visit to our shaykh Abū Madyan, and said to him: 'O my master, I was with Abū al-ʿAbbās al-Khashshāb and read to him a book concerning subtle spiritual points so that he would talk to me about it, and he said to me: "Read me."'

The shaykh answered: 'Abū al-ʿAbbās spoke the truth. What did that book contain?'

He said: 'Asceticism, scrupulousness, trust in God, commitment and what the path to God demands.'

The shaykh said to him: 'Was there anything in it that was not a state belonging to Abū al-ʿAbbās al-Khashshāb?'

He answered: 'No.'

The shaykh said to him: 'If the spiritual states of al-Khashshāb are everything that that book contains and you did not find counsel in his states or assume the character traits of any of them, there is no use in your reading it or asking him to speak to you about it. He has counselled and advised you through his state – and so eloquently!'

384. Meaning: to memorize it.

385. See *Fut.*II.21 (Chap. 73), where Abū al-ʿAbbās al-Khashshāb is mentioned as one of those Men who converse with God.

386. Abū Madyan (*c.*1126–97) was one of the greatest Maghribī Sufi Masters. Although Ibn ʿArabī never met him in corporeal form, he considered him one of his teachers and mentions him often in his writings. In the *Futūḥāt*'s Chap. 73, in the section devoted to the categories of Men of God (*rijāl*), Abū Madyan is said to have been one of the eighteen Men of his time with great spiritual power, who manifest things by and from the command of God. See Cornell, *Abū Madyan*; Addas, 'Abū Madyan and Ibn ʿArabī'; Addas, *Quest*; Hirtenstein, *Unlimited Mercifier*, pp.80–2; Abrahamov, *Ibn al-ʿArabī and the Sufis*, pp.157–64.

387. Absent from holograph MS. Y.

فخجل الرجل وانصرف. أخبرني بهذه الحكاية عنه الحاج عبد الله المَوْرُوري[٣٤١] (52) بإشبيلية في جماعة.

فانظر يا وليي إلى حُسْن طريقتهم ما أعْجَبها، جعلنا الله منهم وألحَقَنا بهم إنه وليُّ ذلك والقادر عليه.

٦٤ سفر الخوف

فررْتُ مني إليه إذ خفت منه عليه
وذاك من جهل نفسي بما تؤول إليه

قال تعالى: ﴿فَفَرَرْتُ مِنْكُمْ لَمَّا خِفْتُكُمْ فَوَهَبَ لِي رَبِّي حُكْماً وَجَعَلَنِي مِنَ الْمُرْسَلِينَ﴾ (الشعراء ٢١) وقال - تعالى: ﴿فَخَرَجَ مِنْهَا خَائِفاً يَتَرَقَّبُ﴾ (القصص ٢١).

ما مرّ يومٌ[٣٤٢] علينا إلا بَكَيْتُ عليه إذا مشى وتقضَّى بما[٣٤٣] نؤول إليه
إنِّي رأيتُ أموراً وكلها في يديه تجري على حكم وقتي فالحكمُ فيَّ لَدَيه

الخوف من مقام الايمان قال الله - تعالى: ﴿فَلَا تَخَافُوهُمْ وَخَافُونِ إِنْ كُنْتُمْ مُؤْمِنِينَ﴾ (آل عمران ١٧٥). وقال في حق الملائكة

٣٤١ ش: الموروي؛ ل، ظ: الموروزي؛ ط: المروزي
٣٤٢ ش، ل، ظ: يوماً
٣٤٣ ش، ل: مما

The man was ashamed and went away. Al-Ḥājj ʿAbd Allāh al-Mawrūrī[388] told me this story in Seville in an assembly of Sufis.

So observe, my friend, the beauty of their way, how wonderful it is! May God make us one of them and attach us to them! He is the One who takes charge of this and has power over it.

§64 The Voyage of Fear[389]

I fled[390] from myself to Him
Since I feared Him on account of Him.[391]
That was because of my soul's ignorance
Of its eventual return[392] to Him.

God the Most High said in the words of Moses to Pharaoh: *I fled from [all of] you when I feared you; then My Lord bestowed authority upon me and made me one of His Messengers* (Q.26:21); and the Most High said: *So he departed from thence, fearing, vigilant* (Q.28:21).

Not a day passed by but that I cried over it
When it passed and decreed that to which we are returning.
I saw that things – and all of them are in His hands –
Follow the ruling property of my Moment,[393]
But the ruling property in me is with Him.

Fear is one of the stations of belief. God the Most High said: *Fear them not; fear Me, if ye are believers* (Q.3:175). He said in the case of the

388. An Andalusian disciple of Abū Madyan and friend of Ibn ʿArabī. In *Fut.*IV.76 (Chap. 462), Ibn ʿArabī calls him 'the Pole of those who trust in God (*al-mutawakkilūn*)' of his time. See also Austin, *Sufis*, pp. 100–10; Addas, *Quest*, pp. 130–1.

389. Arabic: *khawf.* Further on in the text, a near homophone with the word *khafāʾ* (hidden/manifest) will be made.

390. Arabic: *farartu*. See Commentary for a discussion of this type of movement.

391. Two prepositions are used here in conjunction with the verb 'to fear': *min* and *ʿalā*. The verse recalls the well-known hadith: 'I seek refuge in Your satisfaction from Your anger, in Your clemency from Your punishment, in You from You.' See Muslim, *Ṣaḥīḥ*, *ṣalāt* 222.2.51.

392. The root of the word used here is *ʾ-w-l*, which is also the root of *taʾwīl*, interpretation.

393. Arabic: *waqt*. See Commentary for a discussion of this term. See also n. 353.

﴿يَخَافُونَ رَبَّهُمْ مِنْ فَوْقِهِمْ وَيَفْعَلُونَ مَا يُؤْمَرُونَ﴾ (النحل ٥٠) وأفعالهم أفعال الخائفين. وقال في حق طائفة يمْدَحهم: ﴿يَخَافُونَ يَوْماً تَتَقَلَّبُ فِيهِ الْقُلُوبُ وَالْأَبْصَارُ﴾ (النور ٣٧). فلكل موطن خوفٌ يخصه إذا حققت ذلك[٣٤٤] فما متعلّق كل خوف إلا ما يكون من الله وهو مُحْدَث. فما الخوف إلا من المحدَثات، والله يُوجِد[٣٤٥] ذلك، فتعلق خوفُنا بالموجد لذلك، وهذا قوله ﴿وَخَافُونِ إِنْ كُنْتُمْ مُؤْمِنِينَ﴾ (آل عمران ١٧٥) فجعل الخوف نتيجة الايمان فإنه موقوف على الخبر[٣٤٦] الالهي الذي يأتي به الصادق من عند الله، فإن العلم من غير إيمان لا يعطيه ولا سيما وقد دل الدليل أن العالم مصنوعٌ[٣٤٧] لله – تعالى – وثبت أنه تعالى عليم حكيم. فخرج العالم على أحسن صنعة من عالِم، فما ثَمَّ ما يدل على فساده، لكن ينتقل من حال إلى حال، ومن منزل إلى منزل، هذا غير محال. ولهذا الانتقال حصل الخوف عند الرجال من الله لأنهم[٣٤٨] لا يعرفون مراد الله فيهم ولا أين ينقلهم ولا في أي صفة وطبقة يميزهم، فلما أُبْهم[٣٤٩] الأمر عليهم عظم خوفهم منه.

٣٤٤ ط: - ذلك

٣٤٥ ط: + في

٣٤٦ ط: العلم

٣٤٧ ب، ل: الله

٣٤٨ ط: - لأنهم

٣٤٩ ك: استبهم، وفي هامش النسخة: انبهم

angels: *They fear their Lord above them, and do what they are commanded* (Q.16:50). Their actions are the actions of the fearful. And He said in the case of a certain group, praising them: ... *who fear a day when hearts and eyes will be overturned* (Q.24:37).[394] To each homeland belongs a fear that is specific to it, if you have realized that. Every fear is connected only to what derives from God; it is something temporally originated. There is only fear of temporally originated things. God is the One who brought them into existence, so our fear is actually connected to the One who brings things into existence. This is His saying: *Fear Me, if ye are believers* (Q.3:175). Thus He made fear the effect of belief;[395] it is based on the divine report, which the Veracious One Muhammad transmitted from God's presence,[396] for knowledge excluding belief does not result in fear,[397] especially when proof indicates that the cosmos is a work of God the Most High; and it has been affirmed that God the Most High is All-Knowing, All-Wise, hence the cosmos has emerged as the most beautiful product of an All-Knowing One. There is nothing that indicates that it is corrupt. It is transferred, however, from state to state and from waystation to waystation; this is not impossible. From this transference, fear of God comes to humankind because they do not know God's intention concerning them, or where He is transferring them to, or with what attribute or level He will distinguish them. Since the affair is obscure, their fear of Him becomes great.

394. These are people 'whom neither traffic nor merchandise can divert from the Remembrance of Allah, nor from regular Prayer, nor from the practice of regular Charity' (Q.24:37).

395. Ibn 'Arabī begins his chapter on fear in the *Futūḥāt* with this line: 'Fear God if you have faith.' See *Fut.*II.184 (Chap. 100).

396. It is noteworthy that Ibn Arabī does not cite the following in connection with fear and knowledge: 'Those truly fear Allah, among His servants, who have knowledge' (Q.35:28). In *Fut.*II.193 (Chap. 110) he writes: 'Self-disclosure gives knowledge, and knowledge gives fear.'

397. As Ibn 'Arabī points out in *Fut.*II.186 (Chap. 103, on abandoning hope), knowledge destroys belief, for when you know something you no longer believe in it but have certainty of its existence.

٦٥ و[٣٥٠]أما خوف الملائكة فهو خوف نزول[٣٥١] عن مرتبة إلى مرتبة أدنى ولا سِيَّما وقد رُوي أن إبليس كان من أعبد الخلق لله – تعالى – وحصل له الطرد والبعد من السعادة التي كان يرجوها في عبادته من الله – تعالى – لما حقَّتْ عليه كلمة العذاب عاد إلى أصله الذي خُلِق منه وهو النار، فما عُذِبَ إلا به. فسبحان الحَكَم العدل.

ورجال الله يخافون من الاستبدال وهذا[٣٥٢] الذي يدعوهم إلى تفقُّد أحوالهم مع الله – عز وجل – في كل نَفَس ولا سيما والله يقول ﴿وَإِنْ تَتَوَلَّوْا يَسْتَبْدِلْ قَوْماً غَيْرَكُمْ ثُمَّ لَا يَكُونُوا أَمْثَالَكُمْ﴾ (محمد ٣٨) يعني فيما وقع منهم من المخالفة لأمر الله بل يكونون على أتمِّ قَدَمٍ وأقواه في طاعة الله.

فلولا الله ما عُرِفَ المقام ولا وُجِدَ الوراءُ ولا الأمام

٦٦ فبالله وُجِدْنا وإليه دُعينا ورُدِدْنا ﴿أَلَا إِلَى اللهِ تَصِيرُ الْأُمُورُ﴾ (الشورى ٥٣). ولما أقامني الله في مقام الخوف كنت أخاف من ظِلِّي أن أنظر إليه لئلا يحجبني عن الله – تعالى[٣٥٣]. ومع[٣٥٤] هذا كله فما هي الدنيا دار أمان. ولو بُشِّرَ الانسان بالسعادة فإنها محل نقص الحظوظ. وسبب ذلك إنما هو التكليف الشرعي. فإذا زال التكليف الذي هو خطاب الشارع بالأمر والنهي ارتفع عن العبد الخوف العرضي وبقيت له الهيبة، فيكون خوفه

٣٥٠ ط: - و
٣٥١ ط: يزول
٣٥٢ ك: وهو
٣٥٣ ط: - تعالى
٣٥٤ ط: على

§65 As for the angels' fear, it is the fear of descending from one level to a lower level, especially when one sees that Iblīs was one of the creatures who most worshipped God the Most High. He was rejected and distanced from the felicity that he hoped for with respect to his worship of God the Most High.[398] When the word of chastisement was meted out against him, he returned to the root upon which he was created, which is fire; so he was punished only with it. Glorified be God, the just Judge!

The Men of God fear being replaced. This is what incites them to examine their states with God – may He be magnified and glorified – in every breath, especially since God says: *And if ye turn away, He will exchange you for some other folk, and they will not be the likes of you* (Q.47:38), meaning, with respect to the opposition to God's command that takes place on their part; rather, these others will be upon the most perfect and firm foot in obedience to God.

> Were it not for God, the station would not be known,
> Nor would 'behind' and 'before' be found.

§66 Through God we have come into existence and to Him we are called and returned: *Do not all things reach Allah at last?* (Q.42:53). When God made me stand in the station of fear,[399] I was afraid when I looked at my shadow that it would veil me from God the Most High. And with all this, this world is not an abode of safety, even if a person receives good tidings, for it is a place where fortunes are diminished. The reason for that is the imposition of the Law. Were the imposition – which is the Lawgiver's addressing us with positive and negative commands – to disappear, accidental fear would disappear from the servant and there would remain only awe. His fear would

398. For some Sufis, Iblīs was a radical monotheist. He refused to bow down to Adam, a mere creature of stinking mud.

399. Fear (*khawf*), when it is a station not a state, is not a transitory mood occasioned by an accidental occurrence or passing state of mind. It accompanies the wayfarer always and may be described as more akin to awe than to fright. Ibn 'Arabī has devoted two chapters in the *Futūḥāt* to Fear (II.184, Chap. 100) and the Abandoning of Fear (II.184–5, Chap. 101), trans. Chittick, *SDG*, pp. 162–3. See Commentary.

هيبةً للمشهد الالهي. قال الشاعر يصف جلال[٣٥٥] حضرة في حق قوم:[٣٥٦]

كأنما الطير منهم فوق أرؤسهم   لا خوف ظلم ولكن خوف إجلال

جعلنا الله من أهل الهيبة والتعظيم، فإن ذلك لا يكون إلا من استيلاء العظمة بسلطانها على قلب العبد المعتنَى به في المشاهد القدسية الالهية.

٦٧ واعلم أن الخفاء في اللسان هو الظهور. قال امرؤ القيس:

خفّاهن من أنفاقهن(53)

أي أظهرن يعني اليرابيع، فإن اليرابيع تجعل لجحرتها[٣٥٧] التي تتخذها في الأرض بابين. إذا جاء الصائد من الباب الواحد خرج من الباب الآخر. ويُسمَّى ذلك الجُحْر النافِقاء، ومنه سمي المنافق منافقاً لأن له وجهين:

٣٥٥ ط: اجلال

٣٥٦ ل: - يصف ... قوم

٣٥٧ ك: بجحرتها

become awe of the divine contemplation. The poet said, describing the majesty of a certain tribe's presence:

> As if the bird among them, above their heads,
> Had no fear of injustice, but fear of majesty.[400]

May God make us one of the people of respectful awe and magnification! That stems only when magnificence seizes with its power the servant who devotes his attention to Him in the holy and divine places of contemplation.

§67 Know that *khafā'*[401] in the Arabic language means manifestation. Imru'l-Qays[402] said:

> He made them emerge from their tunnels . . .

In other words 'he made them manifest themselves', meaning the jerboas;[403] for the jerboas make two doors for their burrows which they utilize. When the hunter comes to one door, they go out through the other door. This burrow is called *nāfiqa*, and from it the hypocrite is called *munāfiq*, because he has two faces: one face

400. These lines are also found in *Fut.*I.130 (Chap. 8) and II.12 (Chap. 73). I have been unable to find the original source.

401. In Arabic, this word also means 'hiddenness'. It is probable that this is a reference to God's divine hidden ruse (*makr*), which, as Gril points out (*Dévoilement*, p. 72, n. 142), serves to heighten the servant's fear. Note the near homophone with *khawf* (fear), although they come from different roots, *kh-w-f* and *kh-f-y*. See Commentary for a discussion of God's divine hidden ruse.

402. The most famous Arabic poet of the pre-Islamic period, d.*c.*544. Ibn Manẓūr defines *khafā* as above and gives Imru'l-Qays' complete verse in *Lisān al-'Arab*, XVIII 256. The line reads:

> He made them emerge from their tunnels
> As if rain from a massive cloud had made them emerge.

Ibn Manẓūr describes the animals in question not as jerboas, however, but mice.

403. Jerboas, found in the deserts of Asia and North Africa, belong to the rodent family. They are nocturnal creatures, sleeping by day in their burrows. They actually build four kinds of burrows, the more permanent ones containing many entrances, not just two as Ibn 'Arabī has it. See http://en.wikipedia.org/wiki/Jerboa, accessed May 2014. They construct their burrows with emergency exits on one end near the surface in order to escape from enemies. See Burton and Burton, *International Wildlife Encyclopedia*, p. 1323. For the relevance of these creatures to this chapter and the *Isfār* in general, see Commentary.

وجهاً يقابل به المؤمنين ويظهر أنه معهم، ووجهاً يقابل به الكفار ويظهر أنه معهم، فجعلوا لمن هذه صفته اسم المنافق. والله يقول في حق من قال: ﴿نَفَقاً فِي الْأَرْضِ﴾ (الأنعام ٣٥). يقول: إن طلبك الأعداء من جانب واحد[358] خرجت من الجانب الآخر طلباً للسلامة منهم ﴿وَلَوْ شَاءَ اللهُ لَجَمَعَهُمْ عَلَى الْهُدَى﴾ (الأنعام ٣٥) فيكونون[359] أهل باب واحد. وكان المنافقون في زمان رسول الله، صلى الله عليه وسلم، يأتون إلى المؤمنين بوجه يظهرون به أنهم معهم ويأتون المشركين بوجه يظهرون به أنهم معهم ويقولون: ﴿إِنَّمَا نَحْنُ مُسْتَهْزِئُونَ﴾ (البقرة ١٤). وأخبر الله أنه – تعالى – ﴿ يَسْتَهْزِئُ بِهِمْ﴾ (١٥) بذلك الفعل الذي يفعلونه مع المؤمنين وهم لا يشعرون. فهذا من مكر الله بهم وهو قوله – تعالى: ﴿وَمَكَرُوا مَكْراً وَمَكَرْنَا مَكْراً وَهُمْ لَا يَشْعُرُونَ﴾ (النمل ٥٠) فإن شعر به فليس بمكرٍ.

٦٨ سفر الحذَر

لقد جاءني الوحي العزيز بأن أسْرِي بنفسي وأهلي عالم الخلق والأمر

بأن[360] الاله الحق ربي قد قضى بموت عدو الدين في غمة البحر

٣٥٨ ط: - واحد

٣٥٩ ي: بدون النقط؛ ك: فيكونون؛ ب: فيكونون من؛ ط: فتكون

٣٦٠ ك: فإنّ

with which he faces the believers and shows them that he is with them, and another face with which he faces the unbelievers and shows them that he is with them. So they have devised the name *munāfiq* for someone who has this attribute. God says in the case of someone who says: *a burrow in the earth* (Q.6:35), that if enemies are seeking you from one side you can leave through the other side, seeking safety from them. *If Allah willed, He could have brought them all together to the guidance* (Q.6:35);[404] you will be among the people of one door. The hypocrites in the time of the Messenger of God – God's blessing and peace be upon him – came to the believers with a face that showed that they were with them and they came to the unbelievers with a face that showed that they were with them, saying: *Verily, we did but mock* (Q.2:14). God informs us that He, the Most High, *doth mock them* (Q.2:15) for the way they acted with the believers, although *they perceived not* (Q.27:50). This is one of God's ruses concerning them, as God the Most High says: *So they plotted a plot; and We plotted a plot, while they perceived not* (Q.27:50), for if it is perceived, it is not a plot.

§68 The Voyage of Caution[405]

The noble[406] revelation came to me
To take myself[407] and my family
On a night journey
In the world of creation and command.[408]
For the Divinity, the Real, my Lord, has decreed

404. The entire verse reads: 'If their spurning is hard on thy mind, yet if thou wert able to seek a burrow in the earth or a ladder to the skies and bring them a sign, [what good would it do?]. If Allah willed, He could have brought them all together to guidance, so be not thou amongst those who are swayed by ignorance.'

405. Arabic: *ḥadhar* or *ḥidhr*. May also be translated as 'warning'.

406. Arabic: *ʿazīz*. Also means 'mighty', 'venerable'.

407. May also be translated as 'my soul'.

408. 'His, verily, is all creation and command. Blessed is Allah, the Lord of the Worlds' (Q.7:54). The world of creation is the material universe, the world of command the spiritual one.

يقول الله – تعالى – حكاية عن قول شخص ﴿وَإِنَّا لَجَمِيعٌ حَاذِرُونَ﴾ (الشعراء ٥٦) والحذر نتيجة خوف. يقول – تعالى: ﴿خُذُوا حِذْرَكُمْ﴾ (النساء ٧١) فإنه من أخذ حذره من شيء لم يؤْتَ عليه منه، وأكثر ما يؤتَى على الشخص من مَأْمَنه، أي من الجهة التي يأمن على نفسه منها. فينبغي للعاقل أن لا يأمن إلا من الجهة التي أمنه الله منها. فإن قوله – سبحانه – هو الصدق الذي ﴿لَا يَأْتِيهِ الْبَاطِلُ مِنْ بَيْنِ يَدَيْهِ وَلَا مِنْ خَلْفِهِ﴾ (فصلت ٤٢) وهو الصادق – سبحانه. وهذا الحذر إن ساعد القدَرُ، حينئذ ينفع فإنه ورد "لا يُنْجي حَذَرٌ مِنْ قَدَر"[54] إلا أن يكون ذلك الحذر من القدر، حينئذ تكون به النجاة. ولقد بالغنا في ذلك بقولنا:

يا حذري من حذري لو كان يُغْني حذري

Death to the enemy of religion
In the gloominess[409] of the sea.[410]

God the Most High recounted a story about the speech of a certain individual: *And lo! We are all amply warned* (Q.26:57).[411] Warning is the fruit[412] of fear. God the Most High says: *Take your precautions* (Q.4:71),[413] for whoever is warned of anything is not taken by surprise by it; and what takes an individual by surprise most often is what comes from his place of safety,[414] that is, from the direction where he believes that he is safe. The intelligent person must only feel safe from the direction which God has made safe, for His Word – glorified be He! – is true: *No falsehood can approach it from before or behind it* (Q.41:42),[415] and He is the Truthful – glorified be He! This caution is useful then, if predestination[416] assists, for it has come in a Prophetic tradition that: 'Caution does not save from predestination'[417] unless that caution is part of the predestination; then there will be salvation. We have expressed that in our saying:

O my caution of my caution!
If only my caution sufficed me!

409. Arabic: *ghumma*. The root also has the meaning of 'to veil, to cover'.

410. The Qur'anic reference is to Pharaoh, who was drowned in the sea while pursuing the Israelites. For Ibn 'Arabī's controversial interpretation of Pharaoh's character, see *Fuṣūṣ*, chapter on Moses, and Gril, 'Le personage coranique'.

411. Again, this individual is Pharaoh, who, feeling threatened by the small band of Israelites, is poised to pursue them. This verse follows shortly upon God's revelation to Moses to 'journey by night with My servants' (Q.26:53).

412. Arabic: *natīja*, as in the Arabic title of this book.

413. The entire verse reads: 'O ye who believe! Take your precautions, and either go forth in parties or go forth all together.'

414. Arabic: *ma'man*. This could also be translated as 'place of faith'.

415. The entire verse reads: 'No falsehood can approach it from before or behind it: It is sent down by One full of wisdom, worthy of all praise.' The reference is to the Noble Qur'an.

416. Arabic: *al-qadar*. Ibn 'Arabī frequently refers to 'the secret of predestination' in his writings, which is, in his opinion, very obscure and knowable only if God reveals it to an individual. He associates it with the Qur'anic verse: 'None of us there is, but has a known station' (Q.37:164). See *Fut.*I.259 (Chap. 47).

417. Ibn Ḥanbal, *al-Musnad* V 234.

٦٩ فأبلغ الحذر إنما هو في الحذر من الحذر أن تتخذه[٣٦١] سنداً.[٣٦٢] ومن رحمة الله – تعالى – بنا أن حذّرنا نفسَه وأبلغ من هذا ما يكون فقال – تعالى: ﴿وَيُحَذِّرُكُمُ اللهُ نَفْسَهُ وَاللهُ رَءُوفٌ بِالْعِبَادِ﴾ (آل عمران ٣٠). ومن رأفته أن حذّرنا نفسه فإنه مَن ﴿لَيْسَ كَمِثْلِهِ شَيْءٌ﴾ (الشورى ١١) لا يُعْرَف أبداً إلا بالعجز عن معرفته. وذلك أن نقول ليس كذا وليس كذا مع كوننا نُثبِت له ما أثبته لنفسه إيماناً لا من جهة عقولنا ولا نظرنا، فليس لعقولنا إلا القبول منه فيما يرجع إليه. فهو الحي ﴿الَّذِي لَا إِلَهَ إِلَّا هُوَ الْمَلِكُ الْقُدُّوسُ السَّلَامُ الْمُؤْمِنُ الْمُهَيْمِنُ الْعَزِيزُ الْجَبَّارُ الْمُتَكَبِّرُ﴾، ﴿عَالِمُ الْغَيْبِ وَالشَّهَادَةِ ... الرَّحْمَنُ الرَّحِيمُ﴾، ﴿الْخَالِقُ الْبَارِئُ الْمُصَوِّرُ﴾، ﴿الْحَكِيمُ﴾ (انظر الحشر ٢٢-٢٤). بهذا وأمثاله أخبرنا عن نفسه فنؤمن بذلك كله على[٣٦٣] علمه بذلك لا على تأويل منا لذلك فإنه ﴿لَيْسَ كَمِثْلِهِ شَيْءٌ وَهُوَ السَّمِيعُ الْبَصِيرُ﴾ (الشورى ١١) فلا ينضبط لعقلٍ ولا لناظرٍ.[٣٦٤] فما لنا من العلم به من طريق الاثبات إلا ما أوصله إلينا في كتبه وعلى ألسنة رُسُله المترجِمين عنه، ليس غير ذلك. ونسبة هذه الأسماء إليه غير معلومة عندنا. فإن المعرفة بالنسبة إلى أمرٍ ما موقوفة على علم المنسوب إليه، وعلمنا بالمنسوب إليه ليس بحاصل، فعلمنا بهذه النسبة الخاصة[٣٦٥] ليس بحاصل، فالفكر والتفكر والمتفكر

٣٦١ ب، ش، ط، ظ: يتخذه

٣٦٢ ش، ل، ط: مستندا

٣٦٣ ط: عن

٣٦٤ ب: العقل ولا الناظر

٣٦٥ ش، ط، ظ: الحاصلة

§69 The most extreme caution is caution of taking caution: that you take it as a support. Among God the Most High's mercy towards us is that we are cautious of Him Himself. There is nothing more cautious than this. The Most High said: *Allah biddeth you be cautious of Him. And Allah is full of compassion for [His] servants* (Q.3:30). Part of His compassion is that He made us be cautious of Him, for He is the One of whom it is said *nothing is as His likeness* (Q.42:11).[418] He is known only through the inability to know Him. So we say: 'He is not such and such' while affirming what He affirms of Himself through faith, not from our intellects or our speculation. Our intellects have only what we receive from Him concerning what refers to Him. He is the Living, *He is Allah, than whom there is no other god, the Knower, the King, the Holy One, Peace, the Keeper of Faith, the Guardian, the Majestic, the Compeller, the Superb* (Q.59:23); *Knower of the Unseen and the Witnessed, the All-Merciful, the All-Compassionate* (Q.59:22); *the Creator, the Shaper out of naught, the Fashioner* (Q.59:24); *the Wise* (Q.59:24) and similar things. He has informed us about Himself and we believe in everything He has taught us about that, not on the basis of our own interpretation[419] of it. For *nothing is as His likeness, and He is the All-Hearing, the All-Seeing* (Q.42:11).[420] He cannot be apprehended by intellect or speculation, for we cannot know Him by way of affirmation, save what He has caused us to receive in His Books and upon the tongue of His Messengers, those who interpret[421] on His authority; there is nothing other than that. The relationship of these Names to Him is not known to us, for the knowledge of the relationship to a certain affair depends upon the knowledge of the thing to which it is related; and our knowledge of the thing to which it is related cannot be attained. Hence our knowledge of this specific relationship cannot be attained. Thought, reflection and the one

418. Here the Shaykh gives the first part of this oft-cited verse, mentioning only the transcendent, incomparable aspect of God (*tanzīh*).

419. Once more this type of interpretation is the Arabic *ta'wīl*. See n.45 above and Commentary for a discussion of this term.

420. Here the Shaykh completes the verse mentioned above, giving it its sense of immanence and likening (*tashbīh*).

421. Arabic: *al-mutarjimīn ʿanhu*. The root meaning is 'to translate'.

يضرب في حديد بارد. جعلنا الله وإياكم ممن عقل ووقف عند ما وصل إليه منه – سبحانه – ونُقِلَ.

٧٠ واعلم أن سفر الحذر يُخْرِج صاحبَه من المحسوس إلى المعقول، ومن النعيم إلى العذاب، ومن الستر إلى التجلي، ومن الموت إلى الحياة القائمة بالأكوان التي تنتجها معرفتنا بالعالم.

ويؤدي إلى العلم بالنشأة الانسانية ومن أين صدرت من حيث جسميته وبالحركة المستقيمة دون المنكوسة والأفقية وإن عرفهما فبحكم التبعية.

ويعلم كل مقام يقتضي له الزيادة والشفوف[٣٦٦] على غيره، والنضرة[٣٦٧] في كل ما يبصره[٣٦٨] ويأتيه، فله فيه تفكُّهٌ ونعيم.

ويقف من هذا المقام بهذه الصفة على علم التوارث وفي ماذا يقع وما الذي يورَث وممن يورِّث ومن يرث.

ومن هذا السفر تُعْرَف[٣٦٩] مشارق الأنوار ومطالع أهلّة الأسرار، فيحذرون من إدراك الصفات التي تُفنيهم[٣٧٠] عن ذواتهم والنعيم بها إلا أنه تكون النجاة

٣٦٦ ش، ل: الشفوق

٣٦٧ ط: البصيرة

٣٦٨ ل، ظ: والنصرة على ما ينصره

٣٦٩ ش، ط، ظ: يعرف

٣٧٠ ط: تغيبهم

who reflects are futile.[422] May God make us and you among those who are rational and halt at what has come from Him – glorified be He! – and what has been transmitted.

§ 70 Know that the voyage of caution moves the voyager from the sensible to the intelligible, from favour to chastisement,[423] from the Veil to Self-Disclosure, and from death into the life subsisting in the beings that our knowledge of the cosmos produces.[424]

It leads to knowledge of the human constitution: from where it stems with respect to its corporeality with its vertical movement, not the movement that is curved or horizontal, even if these are known subsequently.[425]

One comes to know every station that demands that one be superior or inferior[426] to others, and that one enjoy all that he sees and that comes to him, so that he has delight and bliss in it.

In this station, with this attribute, one learns the science of transmission by inheritance, in what it occurs, what one inherits, from whom one inherits and who inherits.

From this voyage one knows the dawning places of the lights and the risings of the crescent moons of secrets.[427] The companions of this station take precautions against perceiving the Attributes that annihilate them from their essences and the enjoyment of them. Nevertheless, their outcome with respect to all of this will be salvation from what they take precautions against. No matter what

422. Arabic: *yaḍrib ḥadīd bārid.* Literally: 'beat a cold iron'.

423. Arabic: *ʿadhāb.* The root of this word also means 'sweetness'.

424. It is unclear exactly what Ibn ʿArabī means here.

425. See Commentary regarding these three types of movement.

426. Arabic: *shufūf.* A variant gives *shufūq*, which is a possibility since the dot is missing in the holograph MS. (although the shape of the letter suggests a *fāʾ* rather than a *qāf*). In the latter case, the meaning would be concern or anxiety over others.

427. Arabic: *mashāriq al-anwār wa-maṭāliʿ ahillat al-asrār.* Note the similarity of this phrase to the title of Ibn ʿArabī's *Mawāqiʿ al-nujūm*. See also Gril, 'Journey', pp.4–6. In bringing together this reference to lights and secrets, Ibn ʿArabī may be alluding to the east/west axis of exoteric/esoteric knowledge and practice, since he calls the gnostics of the Maghrib 'the people of secrets' and the gnostics of the eastern Islamic lands 'the people of the lights'. See Hirtenstein, 'Land of the Olive'.

لهم عقيب هذا كله مما[٣٧١] يحذرون منه. ولو كان العدوّ ما كان من القوة فإنهم الغالبون بنصر الله، فإنه – سبحانه – لا يُقاوَم ولا يغالب، فإنه العزيز الرحيم. وهذه الصفة إذا قامت بالعبد فإن الله يأخذ بيده في جميع أموره ويهديه إلى ما فيه نجاته.

وله من خرق العوائد: المشي على الماء، والنجاة من الأعداء، أعداء الأرواح والبشر، وهلاك الأعداء.

وينتج هذا السفر القرب الالهي المقرون به سعادة الأبد.

وفي هذا المقام يأمن صاحبه في سفره فيه من كل ما يحذره من القواطع التي تحول بينه وبين سعادة الأبد.[٣٧٢] ولو صال عليه جميع من في الأرض غلبهم[٣٧٣] وظهر عليهم.

ويحصل لصاحبه المتصف به من الكشف ما يقف به على غوامض الأسرار إذ كان نوره يُنَفِّر[٣٧٤] كل شبهة وجهل، ويُبطِل كل تمويه وزور. ويُورث النفس شجاعةً وإقداماً وقوةً، فيفعل بالهمة ما لا يقدر على فعله بالأجرام ولا بالعدد، غير أن صاحب هذا السفر يحصل له في أول دخوله فيه هَلَعٌ طبيعي وضيق صدر وخوف لما يراه في أول طريقه من ضعفه[٣٧٥] وقوة هذا المقام، وهذا الضعف والذلة القائمة به تورثه العزة والقوة. ويكشف له علم الظاهر والباطن فلا يخفى عليه شيءٌ.

ويتولاه الله بنفسه في خروجه إلى الارشاد والهداية فيكون مُعاناً. وتحصل له البشرى من الله حتى يأمن، فتتوفّر[٣٧٦] داعيته إلى

٣٧١ ط: - مما

٣٧٢ ب، ل، ط، ظه: سعادته الأبدية

٣٧٣ ل، ط: عليهم

٣٧٤ ط: يقر

٣٧٥ ط: ضعف

٣٧٦ ب، ش، ل، ط: يتوفر

power the enemy has, they are victorious with God's help, for He – glorified be He! – is not overpowered or overcome. He is the All-Mighty, the All-Compassionate. If these attributes are established for the servant, God takes his hand in all his affairs and guides him to that in which lies his salvation.

Among the charismatic gifts[428] the voyager has are: walking on water, salvation from enemies – whether they are spirits or human beings – and the destruction of enemies.

This voyage results in divine proximity to which eternal felicity is connected.

In this station, the voyager is safe in his voyage from all the brigands,[429] against whom he takes precaution, who might come between him and his eternal felicity. Even if everyone on the earth should assault him, he will overcome them and triumph over them.

The voyager attributed with this attains from unveiling that by which he learns things that are obscure in the secrets, since its light dispels every doubt and abolishes all falsification and lies. The soul is bequeathed courage, boldness and power. He effects with his spiritual power[430] what he cannot do with bodies or instruments.

Nevertheless, when the voyager begins to set out on this voyage, he experiences a natural impatience, a tightening of the chest and fear when he sees his weakness at the beginning of his path and the power of this station. This weakness and humility subsisting in him nonetheless make him the heir of might and power. Knowledge of the exoteric and esoteric dimensions is unveiled to him, and nothing is hidden from him.

When leaving this station, God takes charge of him to rightly direct and guide him. He will be assisted. He attains good tidings from God so that he will be reassured. His motivation to transmit His message will be sufficient, for fear inhibits and cowardice turns

428. Arabic: *kharq al-ʿawāʾid*. Literally: what breaks the habitual. Among the many references to these saintly miracles in the *Futūḥāt*, see in particular II.371ff. (Chap. 186), which is dedicated to this subject, and *Mawāqiʿ al-nujūm*.

429. Arabic: *qawāṭiʿ*. Literally: things that cut off – in this case, the road.

430. Arabic: *himma*. See Jaffray, 'Ibn ʿArabī on *Himmah*'.

التبليغ، فإن الخوف مانعٌ والجُبْن صارف، غير أن الحق يؤيّد صاحب هذا السفر تأييداً يعرفه ويأنس به ويركن إليه لا بد من ذلك. ويُعْطَى الحجة والقوة والظهور على خصمائه.

﴿وَاللهُ يَقُولُ الْحَقَّ وَهُوَ يَهْدِي السَّبِيلَ﴾[٣٧٧] (الأحزاب ٤).

٣٧٧ ي: + (في الهامش) سماعا لاسماعيل [إسماعيل ابن سودكين النوري] صفر سنة ثمان و ثلاثين و ستمائة.
ك: + هذا آخر الاسفار والحمد لله حق حمده والصلاة على رسوله محمد وآله الطيبين، نسخ في أواخر شهر جمادى الأول من سنة ثلاث وستين وستمائة بمدينة قونية حماها الله تعالى على يد الفقير إلى الله تعالى(؟) المروري عفا الله عنه وغفر له ونفعه بما فيه منقول من خط الشيخ مؤلفه رضي الله عنه.
ب: + هذا آخر الاسفار والحمد لله حق حمده والصلاة والسلام الإتّمان على سيدنا محمد وآله وصحبه وعترته أجمعين. واتفق إتمام نسخ النسخة صحيحة يوم الخميس من شهر ربيع الأول لسنة ست عشرة وسبعمائة هجرية بمدينة قيصرية (وفي الهامش: بلغت المقابلة ...)
ش: + تم والله أعلم. تم كتاب الاسفار عن نتائج الأسفار بحمد الله وعونه وحسن توفيقه، والحمد لله رب العالمين. كتبه عبد الكريم بن أبي بكر المرني(؟).
ل: + تمت الرسالة.
ط: + وصلى الله على سيدنا محمد وعلى آله وصحبه وسلم والحمد لله رب العالمين.
ظ: + تم كتاب الاسفار عن نتائج الأسفار للشيخ الامام سلطان المحققين محيي الملة والدين محمد بن علي بن العربي رضي الله عنه وعنا به على يد محبه محب الله بن سيد محمد الشترندي(؟) بجوار حضرت شيخ {= حضرة الشيخ} المؤلف عفى عنهما ولوالديهما ونفعهما بهذا وأدخلهما في الجنة.
ظه: + وصلى الله على سيدنا محمد وآله وصحبه أجمعين والحمد لله رب العالمين وقد تم كتاب الاسفار في نتائج الأسفار الذي ألفه سيدنا الأبهر سلطان العارفين شيخ {= الشيخ} الأكبر إمام المحققين أبو عبد الله سيدي محمد بن علي بن عربي الحاتمي الطائي الأندلسي قدس الله سره ونفعنا به والحمد لله على التمام تمت بيوم السبت 21 في ربيع ثاني ١٣١٨. اللهم افتح علينا بركة الشيخ قدس الله سره العزيز وأمدنا الله بمدده آمين.

one away. However, God assists this voyager with an assistance by which he recognizes Him, is intimate with Him and is dependent upon Him, as he inevitably is. He is given proof, power and triumph over his enemies.

And Allah speaks the truth and He guides on the Path (Q.33:4).

التعليقات

(1) يشير إلى قصة موسى والخضر عليهما السلام، انظر سورة الكهف ٦٠-٨٢ وصحيح البخاري، تفسير سورة الكهف ٦/ ١١٠: "إن موسى قام خطيباً في بني إسرائيل فسئل أي الناس أعلم؟ فقال: أنا. فعتبه الله عليه إذ لم يرد العلم إليه، فأوحي الله إليه: إن لي عبداً بمجمع البحرين هو أعلم منك ..." انظر بقية القصة.

(2) انظر سورة البقرة ٢٤٩.

(3) انظر سورة الكهف ٨٣-٩٨.

(4) انظر سورة الشعراء ١٩٢-١٩٤.

(5) انظر سورة فاطر ١٠.

(6) انظر سورة الأنعام ٥٩، ٦٣، ٩٥؛ الاسراء ٧٠؛ الروم ٤١. وانظر إلى القصة التي يرويها الشيخ في الفتوحات ٥٦٢\١ و ٢٦٢\٢.

(7) سورة يونس ٢٢-٢٣: ﴿هُوَ الَّذِي يُسَيِّرُكُمْ فِي الْبَرِّ وَالْبَحْرِ ۖ حَتَّىٰ إِذَا كُنتُمْ فِي الْفُلْكِ وَجَرَيْنَ بِهِم بِرِيحٍ طَيِّبَةٍ وَفَرِحُوا بِهَا جَاءَتْهَا رِيحٌ عَاصِفٌ وَجَاءَهُمُ الْمَوْجُ مِن كُلِّ مَكَانٍ وَظَنُّوا أَنَّهُمْ أُحِيطَ بِهِمْ ۙ دَعَوُا اللَّهَ مُخْلِصِينَ لَهُ الدِّينَ لَئِنْ أَنجَيْتَنَا مِنْ هَٰذِهِ لَنَكُونَنَّ مِنَ الشَّاكِرِينَ. فَلَمَّا أَنجَاهُمْ إِذَا هُمْ يَبْغُونَ فِي الْأَرْضِ بِغَيْرِ الْحَقِّ ...﴾ وسورة الشورى ٣٣-٣٤: ﴿إِن يَشَأْ يُسْكِنِ الرِّيحَ فَيَظْلَلْنَ رَوَاكِدَ عَلَىٰ ظَهْرِهِ ۚ إِنَّ فِي ذَٰلِكَ لَآيَاتٍ لِّكُلِّ صَبَّارٍ شَكُورٍ. أَوْ يُوبِقْهُنَّ بِمَا كَسَبُوا وَيَعْفُ عَن كَثِيرٍ.﴾ ففي هذه الآيات إشارات إلى أن المسافر بالبحر يتعرض لخلف الوعد وكفر النعمة من وجه وللهلاك لأجل ذنوبه من وجه آخر.

(8) انظر مثلا صحيح البخاري، تهجد ١٤، ٦٣/٢: "ينزل ربنا تبارك وتعالى كل ليلة إلى السماء الدنيا حين يبقى ثلث الليل الآخر يقول من يدعوني فأستجيب له ..."

(9) انظر ما يقول الشيخ عن الخلاء الذي خلق الله فيه العالم في الفتوحات ٢/١٥٠ باب ٧٨.

(10) انظر ذكر هذه الأطوار في القرآن الكريم: غافر ٦٧، المؤمنون ١٢-١٤، النجم ٤٦-٤٧، النحل ٧٠.

(11) هو المكان الذي يجتمع فيه الناس لرؤية الله عز وجل في جنة عدن وهي أعلى الجنان، انظر الفتوحات ٣١٩/١ باب ٦٥.

(12) فرقد السبخي (من سبخة البصرة أو الكوفة) من صالحي التابعين، توفى سنة ١٣١. انظر ابو نعيم، حلية الأولياء ٤٤/٣-٥. وابن حجر العسقلاني، تهذيب التهذيب ٢٦٢/٨-٢٦٤.

(13) انظر سنن أبي داود، ملاحم ١٧، ١٢٣/٤؛ سنن ابن ماجة، فتن ٢١، حديث ٤٠١٤ وجامع الترمذي، تفسير القرآن ١١/٥، شرح تحفة الأحوذي ٩٩/٤-١٠٠ وهذا لفظه: "... عن ابي أمية الشعباني قال أتيت أبا ثعلبة الخُشَني قال قلت: كيف تصنع في هذه الآية؟ قال أية آية؟ قلت: يأيها الذين امنوا عليكم أنفسكم لا يضركم من ضلَّ إذا اهْتَدَيْتم (المائدة ١٠٥) قال: أما والله لقد سألت عنها خبيراً سألتُ عنها رسول الله - صلى الله عليه وسلم - فقال: بل ائْتِمروا بالمعروف وتناهوْا عن المنكر حتى إذا رأيتَ شُحاً مطاعاً وهوىً متّبعاً ودنيا مؤثرة وإعجاب كل ذي رأي برأيه فعليك بخاصة نفسك ودع العوام فإن من ورائكم أياماً الصبر فيهن مثل القبْض على الجمْر للعامل فيهن مثل أجر خمسين رجلاً يعملون مثل عملكم."

(14) انظر جامع الترمذي، فتن ١٩، شرح تحفة الأحوذي ٢١٣/٣: "عن أبي سعيد الخدري قال: قال رسول الله – صلى الله عليه وسلم –: والذي نفسي بيده لا تقوم الساعة حتى تكلِّم السباعُ الانسَ وحتى يكلم الرجل عذبة سوطه وشراك نعله وتخبره فخذه بما أحدث أهله بعده" وانظر سبب ورود الحديث في مسند أحمد بن حنبل ٨٣/٣-٨٤.

(15) انظر صحيح البخاري، مناقب ٢٥، ٢٣٩/٤: "... أن عبد الله بن عمر – رضي الله عنهما – قال سمعت رسول الله – صلى الله عليه وسلم – يقول: تقاتلكم اليهود فتُسلَّطون عليهم ثم يقول الحجر: يا مسلم هذا يهودي ورائي فاقتلْه" وانظر كذلك ببعض الاختلاف في الألفاظ: جامع الترمذي، فتن ٥٦، شرح ٢٣٤/٣ وسنن ابن ماجة فتن ٣٣ والمسند ٦٧/٢ الخ ...

(16) انظر حديث الولي في صحيح البخاري، الرقاق ٣٨، ١٣١/٨: "من عادى لي ولياً ..." إلى قوله: "وما ترددت عن شيء أنا فاعله ترددي عن نفس عبدي المؤمن يكره الموت وأنا أكره مساءته." وانظر أيضا رواية عائشة في المسند ٢٥٦/٦ وكذلك رواية وهب بن منبه التي أوردها أبو نعيم في حلية الأولياء ٣٢/٤: "إني أجد في بعض كتب الأنبياء – عليهم الصلاة والسلام – أن الله – تعالى – يقول: ما ترددت عن شيء قط ترددي عن قبض روح المؤمن يكره الموت وأكره مساءته ولا بد له منه."

(17) انظر مثلا صحيح مسلم، صلاة ٢٢٢، ط. الآستانة ١٣٢٢ ٥١/٢. "عن عائشة قالت: فقدت رسول الله – صلى الله عليه وسلم – ليلة من الفراش فالتمستُه فوقعت يدي على بطن قدميه وهو في المسجِدَ وهما منصوبتان وهو يقول: اللهم أعوذ برضاك من سخطك وبمعافاتك من عقوبتك وبك منك لا أحصي ثناءً عليك أنت كما أثنيت على نفسك" وللحديث روايات عديدة؛ انظر المعجم المفهرس لألفاظ الحديث النبوي ٤٢٧/٤.

(18) انظر المسند ٣٩١/١. "عن عبد الله [بن مسعود] قال، قال رسول الله – صلى الله عليه وسلم –: ما أصاب أحداً قط همٌّ ولا حزن فقال: اللهم إني عبدك ... أسألك بكل اسم هو لك سميت به نفسك ... أو استأثرت به في علم الغيب عندك أن تجعل القرآن ربيع قلبي ... إلا أذهب الله همه وحزنه ..."

(19) انظر شرح قول أبي بكر في الفتوحات ٣٧١/٣ باب ٣٦٩، ٤٢٩ باب ٣٧١؛ ٤٣/٤ باب ٤٣٠.

(20) انظر سورة فصلت ٩-١٠.

(21) انظر ما يذكر عنه الشيخ الأكبر في روح القدس، تحقيق محمود محمود غراب دمشق ١٩٨٦ ص ٦٦-٧١.

(22) انظر الفتوحات ٢٠/٢ باب ٧٣، ١٩٥ باب ١١٠؛ ٩٤/٣ باب ٣٢٥؛ ٧٨/٤ باب ٤٦٣.

(23) "إن الله أدبني فأحسن أدبي ..." رواه السلمي في جوامع آداب الصوفية، تحقيق أيتان كولبرغ، القدس ١٩٧٦ ص ٣. انظر أيضا السمعاني، أدب الاملاء والاستملاء، تحقيق فيسفيلر، ليدن ١٩٥٢ ص ١.

(24) انظر تفسير طه ١١٤ في الفتوحات ٣٨/١ باب ٢.

(25) جزء من حديث حارثة، انظر نور الدين الهيثمي، مجمع الزوائد ٥٧/١.

(26) لهذا الحديث روايات منها: المسند ١٦٣/٦، ١٨٨، ٢١٦؛ صحيح مسلم مسافرين ١٣٩ ١٦٩/٢ إلخ ... وابن ماجة أحكام ١٤.

(27) انظر تفسير هاتين الآيتين في الفتوحات ٤٢١/١، ١٥٣/٢ باب ٨٠، ١٦٦ باب ٨٨.

(28) "حفت الجنة بالمكاره والنار بالشهوات". رواه المسلم في الصحيح، الجنة ١، ٨/١٤٢. وانظر كذلك المعجم المفهرس ٤٧٩/١.

(29) إشارة إلى سورة الحديد ١٣: ﴿فَضُرِبَ بَيْنَهُمْ بِسُورٍ لَهُ بَابٌ بَاطِنُهُ فِيهِ الرَّحْمَةُ وَظَاهِرُهُ مِنْ قِبَلِهِ الْعَذَابُ.﴾

(30) انظر الحديث: "استوصوا بالنساء فإن المرأة خلقت من ضلع وإن أعوج شيء في الضلع أعلاه فإن ذهبت تقيمه كسرته وإن تركته لم يزل أعوج فاستوصوا بالنساء" رواية البخاري، أنبياء ١ ٤/١٦١.

(31) انظر سورة الأعراف ٢٦: ﴿يَا بَنِي آدَمَ قَدْ أَنْزَلْنَا عَلَيْكُمْ لِبَاساً يُوَارِي سَوْآتِكُمْ وَرِيشاً وَلِبَاسُ التَّقْوَىٰ ذَٰلِكَ خَيْرٌ ...﴾

(32) قارن بما رواه السراج في اللمع، القاهرة ١٩٦٠ ص ٣٩١ عن أبي سليمان الخواص: "كنت راكباً حماراً لي يوماً وكان يؤذيه الذباب فيطأطئ رأسه فكنت أضرب رأسه بخشبة كانت في يدي فرفع الحمار رأسه إلي وقال اضرب فإنك هو ذا تضرب على رأسك."

(33) انظر ما يقول الشيخ عن حركات الأفلاك السريعة والبطيئة في الفتوحات ٤١٧/٣ باب ٣٧١.

(34) أي قوله تعالى: ﴿وَقِيلَ يَا أَرْضُ ابْلَعِي مَاءَكِ ...﴾ إلى آخر الآية (هود ٤٤).

(35) يريد قوله تعالى: ﴿وَاصْنَعِ الْفُلْكَ بِأَعْيُنِنَا وَوَحْيِنَا﴾ (هود ٣٧).

(36) أي ﴿بِسْمِ اللهِ مَجْرَاهَا وَمُرْسَاهَا﴾ (هود ٤١).

(37) انظر صحيح البخاري تعبير ١٤-١٥ و ٢٤ ٩/٤٥ و ٤٧-٨٤.

(38) يريد قوله تعالى في سورة المائدة ٦٦: ﴿وَلَوْ أَنَّهُمْ أَقَامُوا التَّوْرَاةَ وَالْإِنْجِيلَ وَمَا أُنْزِلَ إِلَيْهِمْ مِنْ رَبِّهِمْ لَأَكَلُوا مِنْ فَوْقِهِمْ وَمِنْ تَحْتِ أَرْجُلِهِمْ ...﴾.

(39) يقول الهروي في الاشارات إلى معرفة الزيارات، تحقيق جانين سورديل، دمشق ١٩٥٣ ص ٢٩-٣٠: (في الطريق من القدس إلى الخليل) ياقين قرية بها مقام لوط عليه السلام ... وسميت ياقين لأنه لما سار بأهله ورأى العذاب قد نزل بقومه، سجد في هذا الموضع وقال: أيقنت أن وعد الله حق ... وقد ألف الشيخ في مسجد لوط رسالة سماها كتاب اليقين سنة ٦٠٢ هـ.

(40) لاط يلوط: لصق.

(41) انظر الطبري، جامع البيان تحقيق محمود شاكر ٤١٩/١٥-٢٢٤.

(42) انظر الطبري ٤٩٠/٥ في تفسير البقرة ٢٦٠.

(43) ورد في السواك: "مطهرة للفم مرضاة للرب" رواه البخاري صوم ٢٤ ٣٨/٣.

(44) رواه أبو نعيم في الحلية وابن حنبل في الزهد؛ انظر السخاوي، المقاصد الحسنة، بيروت ١٩٨٥ ص ٦٢٠-٦٢١ والعجلوني، كشف الخفاء ٢٢٤/٢.

(45) انظر سورة هود ١٧.

(46) انظر سورة طه ٩٦ والأعراف ١٤٨ وطه ٨٨.

(47) انظر الأعراف ١٥٥.

(48) انظر سنن ابن ماجة مقدمة ١٣ رقم ١٩٦.

(49) نفس المرجع، مقدمة ١٦ رقم ٢١٥، المسند ١٢٧/٣-١٢٨.

(50) م ٧٠٢ هـ من علماء اللغة.

(51) ذكره الشيخ في المحدِّثين، انظر الفتوحات ٢١/٢ باب ٧٣.

(52) مـن أصحـاب أبـي مديـن أيضـا، ذكـره الشـيخ فـي الفتوحـات ٧٦/٤ بـاب ٤٦٢ وفـي روح القـدس ص ٩٧-١٠٢.

(53) انظـر لسـان العـرب ٢٥٦/١٨. "قـال امـرؤ القيـس يصـف فرسـاً: خفاهـن مـن أنفاقهـن كأنمـا * خفاهـن ودق مـن سـحاب مركـب."

(54) انظـر مـا رواه فـي المسـند ٢٣٤/٥: "لـن ينفـع حـذر مـن قـدر ولكـن الدعـاء ينفـع ممـا نـزل وممـا لـم ينـزل فعليكـم بالدعـاء عبـاد اللـه."

فهرس المخطوطات

ي: يوسف آغا ٤٨٥٩، ١٢–٤٨، في خط الشيخ

ك: كوبرلو ٧١٣، ٣٠–٤٤، ٦٦٣٥

ب: بايزيد ٣٧٨٥، ٩٢–١٢٩، ٧١٦٥

ش: شهيد علي ١٣٤٠، ١٥٣–١٨٠، ٧٨٩٥

ل: المكتبة البرطانية ٨٣٤٨، ١–١٤

ط: طبعة حيدرآباد

ظ: ظاهرية ٩٢٠٥،١٣٤–١٥١

ظه: ظاهرية ٩٦٥٥، ١–٢٧، ١٣١٨٥

ف: فخر الدين الخرساني ٥٨٧–٦٠٠، ٨١٤٥

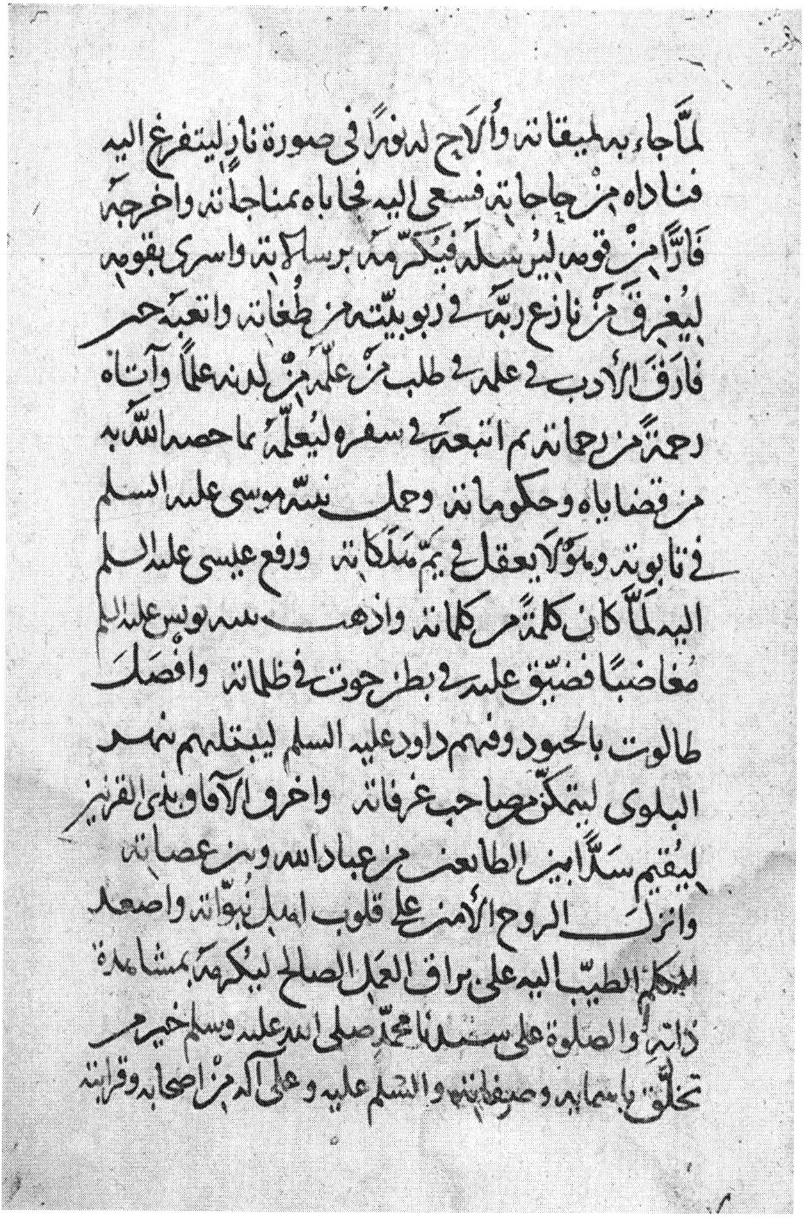

لما جاء به لميقاته وألاح له نوراً في صورة نار ليتفرغ اليه
فناداه من جانبه فسعى اليه فحاباه بمناجاته واخرجه
فاراً من قومه ليرسله فيكرمه برسالاته واسرى بقومه
ليغرق من نازع ربه في ربوبيته من طغاته واتبعه خضر
فارق الأدب في علمه في طلب من علمه من لدنه علماً وآتاه
رحمة من رحماته ثم اتبعه في سفره ليعلمه بما خصه الله به
من قضاياه وحكوماته وحمل نبيه موسى عليه السلم
في تابوته وهو لا يعقل في يم ممكناته ورفع عيسى عليه السلم
اليه لما كان كلمة من كلماته واذهب نبيه يونس عليه السلم
مغاضباً فضيق عليه في بطن حوت في ظلماته وافضل
طالوت بالجنود وفهم داود عليه السلم ليبتليهم بنهر
البلوى ليتمكن بصاحب غرفاته واخرج الآفاق بذي القرنين
ليقيم سداً بين الطاغين من عباد الله وبين عصاته
وانزل الروح الامين على قلوب انبيائه بنبواته واصعد
الكلم الطيب اليه على براق العمل الصلح ليكرمه بمشاهدة
ذاته والصلوة على سيدنا محمد صلى الله عليه وسلم خير من
تخلق باسمائه وصفاته والسلم عليه وعلى آله من اصحابه وقرابته

Folio 95a from Beyazit MS. 3875, dated 716 H.

COMMENTARY

The Title of the Book: al-Isfār ʿan natāʾij al-asfār

The Arabic title of the treatise, *al-Isfār ʿan natāʾij al-asfār*, is based on a play of words and intertwined meanings. In Arabic script, the words *isfār* (unveiling) and *asfār* (voyages/books) appear the same unless vocalized. This particular play on words is not Ibn ʿArabī's invention but was already part of the Sufi stock of sayings, as witnessed by Abū Naṣr al-Sarrāj (d. 988) in his classic *K. al-Lumaʿ*[1] and al-Qushayrī[2] in perhaps the most popular of all Sufi manuals, *al-Risāla*: 'They [namely, the Sufis] say: *Safar* [= voyage] is so called because it unveils (*asfara*) the characters of the men.'[3]

It is also connected – both in its sense of travel and in its sense of removing a veil – with danger: the former because of the obvious perils of setting out on a journey and the latter because, in times and places where it is customary for a woman to veil her face, if a woman unveils herself it is a sign warning of something untoward.[4] One is reminded here of the startling vision Ibn ʿArabī had in Mecca of the Kaʿba lifting her veils, appearing as a beautiful young girl and threatening the Shaykh.[5] The descent of the Qurʾan, we might point out, is also sometimes called a descent of warning. It descends to the

1. *K. al-Lumaʿ*, p. 188.

2. *Al-Risāla*, trans. Knysh; see also von Schlegell, *Principles of Sufism*.

3. The word used is *rijāl* as opposed to the more general *insān*, human being. *Rajul/rijāl* is a technical term for Ibn ʿArabī, meaning a very special group of spiritually advanced individuals, which includes women.

4. See *Isfār*, Para. 17; *Fut.*II.293 (Chap. 174). See also the poem that begins Chap. 174 and the remarkable lines of Poem VII of Ibn ʿArabī's *Tarjumān al-ashwāq*: 'As I kissed the Black Stone, friendly women thronged around me; they came to perform the circumambulation with veiled faces. They uncovered the (faces like) sunbeams and said to me, "Beware! for the death of the soul is in thy looking at us"' (trans. Nicholson, p. 61). See also *Tarjumān*, Poem XLII, p. 127: 'I boded ill from her unveiling ...'.

5. See *Fut.*I.700–1 (Chap. 72).

reciter/interpreter not all at once but fragmented, unveiling itself in stages.[6] Its message is often one of warning and admonishment. Among other meanings derived from this root, something that is *sāfir* is plain and obvious, and *isfār* also is the word Ibn ʿArabī uses to describe the first light of dawn, marking the end of the intimate night conversation of prayer.[7] The root *s-f-r* also has the meaning 'book' (*sifr*, plural: *asfār* – thus spelled the same as the word meaning 'voyages'), especially with reference to the Scriptures, or a volume in a series. The *sufarāʾ* are mediators and envoys, human or angelic,[8] from the Real to the created world.[9]

Finally, although there is no overt reference to this type of operation being performed on the root *s-f-r* in this particular text, when the letters are transposed, as Ibn ʿArabī often does in his poetry for rhetorical effect, it yields the root *f-s-r*, which has to do with interpretation and commentary – the word for Qurʾanic commentary is *tafsīr* – and *f-r-s*, which has to do, among other things, with physiognomy and perspicacity, *firāsa*. Ibn ʿArabī was apparently well acquainted with the works of the grammarian Ibn Jinnī (d. 1002), who championed this method, which he called *ishtiqāq akbar*, or 'major [etymological] derivation'. By rearranging the three letters of select Arabic roots, he gives every possible arrangement in order to arrive at some sort of general etymology.[10] Thus the notions of voyage, veiling and unveiling, danger, light, Scripture and interpretation of word and sign are all present in this one Arabic root.

As for the other word in the title, *natāʾij*, which we translate as 'results', it comes from an Arabic root with basic meanings of bearing young, resulting in, manufacturing and concluding in. Thus *natāʾij* are the fruits of some activity, whether natural or fabricated.

6. See Q.25:32: '… We have rehearsed it to thee in slow, well-arranged stages, gradually.'
7. See *Fut.*I.396 (Chap. 69).
8. In modern parlance, they are ambassadors.
9. See *Fut.*II.259 (Chap. 160).
10. See *al-Khaṣāʾiṣ fī ʿilm uṣūl al-ʿArabiyya*, II, pp. 133–9. P. Beneito has delivered lectures on this theme at the Muhyiddin Ibn 'Arabi Society's UK and US Symposia: 'Unified Vision – Unified World?'

They are also the conclusions of syllogisms in logic,[11] a process that Ibn ʿArabī often compares to producing offspring by a coupling of terms.[12] In the *Isfār*, almost every chapter among the chapters devoted to the prophets ends with a list of the results of that specific voyage. In some cases the connection with the narrative in question is clear, but generally it is not. In this, the catalogue of 'results' concluding these chapters resembles the sometimes quite extensive lists of sciences attained from the verses of the Qurʾanic suras given in the 114 chapters of the *Futūḥāt* devoted to the waystations[13] and the gnomic chapter summaries provided in Chapter 559 of that same work.

No doubt the Shaykh wanted his students to realize these results for themselves experientially rather than conceptually, at which point the connections that to the reader appear obscure would become apparent.

> When the shaykhs were asked what something was, they did not answer by providing essential definitions. On the contrary, they answered with the result (*natīja*) of the station in him who is qualified by it. Their very answer proved that they had acquired that station through tasting and state. How many there are who know its essential definition but have no whiff of it in themselves! Such a person stands far apart from it. Indeed, he may not even have faith in the first place, but he knows both its essential and its imperfect (*rasmī*) definition. So all have agreed that answering them through results and state is more complete, since the stations have no profit if they do not produce effects within the individual. They are desired for that reason, not for themselves.[14]

11. See *Fuṣūṣ*, chapter on Ṣāliḥ (trans. Austin, *Bezels*, p. 142).
12. See, for example, *Fut.*I.170–1 (Chap. 21).
13. Chaps. 270–383.
14. *Fut.*II.143 (Chap. 74), trans. Chittick, *SPK*, p. 279.

Reference to the Isfār in the Futūḥāt

As we have mentioned when considering the date of the *Isfār*'s composition, Ibn ʿArabī refers to the *Isfār* several times in the *Futūḥāt*. In Chapter 182, for example, he refers to it in connection with Moses' flight: 'I have called this flight of Moses the voyage of seeking (*safar al-ṭalab*)';[15] however, we find no such chapter in the *Isfār* under that name. He seems to be referring to the Voyage of Fear, which delves into the reasons for, and results of Moses' flight from Pharaoh. The discrepancy is difficult to account for. It is quite possible that the *Isfār* circulated in more than one recension.

Another mention comes at the end of Chapter 190, a chapter devoted to voyaging that we will discuss more fully below. In it, Ibn ʿArabī quotes the Qurʾanic verse *Glorified be Him who carried His servant by night from the Inviolable Place of Worship to the Far Distant Place of Worship [...] that We might show him of our signs* (Q.17:1), then remarks 'We have mentioned this voyage in a treatise of ours called *al-Isfār ʿan natāʾij al-asfār*.'[16]

Interestingly, one of the most intriguing mentions of the title is in Part 4 of the *Futūḥāt* Chapter 337, where it is given not as a title but as one of the sciences that one gains stemming from Sūrat Muḥammad: 'In [this sura/waystation] is knowledge of the unveiling of the results of the voyages.'[17] In Part 4, which, as we have seen,[18] is devoted to the *manāzil*, or suras/waystations, the sciences gained from the various *manāzil* are all connected with verses from that particular sura. In Sūrat Muḥammad there are several references to travel, the most relevant here being Verse 10: *Do they not travel through the earth, and see what was the end of those before them?*[19] Although the verse

15. *Fut.*II.155 (Chap. 82).

16. *Fut.*II.383 (Chap. 190).

17. *Fut.*III.146 (Chap. 337).

18. See Introduction, p. 15.

19. There is a reference to the 'way of Allah' in Verses 1, 4, 32, 34 and 38; to His guidance in Verses 5, 17, 25 and 32; and to His giving a firm foothold in Verse 7. Sūrat Muḥammad is also notable for its insistence upon the lessons that can be learned from the stories and

concludes with: *Allah brought utter destruction on them, and similar [fates await] those who reject Allah* (Q.47:10), Ibn ʿArabī typically does not quote the verse to its end.[20] Instead, he connects this verse with another one that mentions the word 'consider', or 'cross over to' as he chooses to interpret it, based on the Arabic root *ʿ-b-r*, another loaded word for Ibn ʿArabī, which we will discuss below.[21]

The Prologue [Para. 1]

The Prologue (*Khuṭba*) follows the standard format of medieval Arabic religious treatises, giving praise to God followed by praise to His Prophet. It also serves here to introduce the themes of the book: creation of earth and heaven (Paras. 10–12); the voyage of the Qurʾan (Paras. 18–21); the voyage of the planets (Paras. 13–17); the voyage of Muhammad (Paras. 22–5); the voyage of Adam (Paras. 26–31); the voyage of Enoch (Idrīs) (Paras. 32–6); the voyage of Noah (Paras. 37–40); the voyage of Abraham (Paras. 41–3); the voyage of Joseph and Jacob (Paras. 46–9); the voyage of Lot (Paras. 44–5); and the voyages of Moses (Paras. 50–7, 60–7). It also mentions the voyages of other Qurʾanic figures: Jesus, Jonah, Saul, Dhū al-Qarnayn; the Angel Gabriel; and the excellent word's[22] return to God on the Burāq of the righteous deed, although these receive but passing mention in the *Isfār*.

examples of former communities and peoples who turned back or strayed from Allah's way; for example, 'Thus does Allah set forth for human beings their lessons by similitudes' (Q.38:3).

20. For example, *Fut.*II.382 (Chap. 190, On Knowledge of the Voyager).

21. The chapter also includes a section on Adam's 'fall' and suggests an unstated parallel between Muhammad and Moses, who both reached a high waystation because of their quests on behalf of community and family, respectively. See *Fut.*III.141 (Chap. 337); *Isfār*, Paras. 61–3.

22. A reference to Muhammad's Night Journey but by extension to the mystic who imitates the Prophet in his righteous conduct and visionary voyages.

This is the content of the Prologue. But what is most striking about the Prologue is what Ibn ʿArabī manages to convey through its form. The Prologue is written in rhymed prose (*sajʿ*), which is not uncommon in treatises of the day. However, when we isolate the final words describing each enumerated voyager, we see that all end with the rhyme *–āti*, indicating in most cases a feminine plural inanimate noun with the third person singular possessive pronoun 'his' in the genitive case, a case that Ibn ʿArabī associates with humility and servanthood, attached. Each final word acts as a kind of talisman and *aide-mémoire* for that particular voyage. The list runs as follows:

Muhammad – *āyātihi* (His signs)
Adam – *ladhdhātihi* (his pleasures)
Idrīs – *darajātihi* (his degrees)
Noah – *najātihi* (his salvation)
Abraham – *hidāyatihi* (his guidance) and *karāmātihi* (his grace / charismatic gifts)
Joseph – *bishārātihi* (his good news)
Lot – *niqamātihi* (His vengeance)
Moses – *mīqātihi* (his appointment), *ḥājātihi* (his need), *munājātihi* (his intimate conversation [with God]), *risālātihi* (his missions)
Moses' folk / Pharoah – *ṭughātihi* (his idol-worshipping)
Khiḍr – *raḥamātihi* (His mercies) and *ḥukūmātihi* (His wisdoms)
Moses (again) – *halakātihi* (his destruction)
Jesus – *kalimātihi* (His words)
Jonah – *ẓulumātihi* (his darknesses)
Saul – *ghurafātihi* (his ladlings)
Dhū al-Qarnayn (Alexander the Great) – *ʿuṣātihi* (His disobeyers)
The Trustworthy Spirit – *nubuwwātihi* (his prophethood)
The Good Words that ascend – *dhātihi* (His Essence)
Muhammad (again) – *banātihi* (his daughters) and *ṣifātihi* (His Attributes)

We also note in the Prologue the emphasis on verbs – especially the energetic form two (*faʿʿala*) and form four (*afʿala*) verbs connected with God's actions. It is God who is creating, making, causing and acting, while the voyagers all play a passive role. God makes His servant Muhammad journey by night and causes him to see some of His Signs; He sends Adam down to earth; He raises Enoch from the earth, then makes him dismount at his place in the heavens; He carries Noah in his Ark; He accompanies Abraham on his departure from his homeland; He takes Joseph away from his father Jacob and makes Jacob follow him to Egypt; He causes Lot to journey by night to escape His wrath; He spurs Moses on to his appointment at the Mount, makes him see the light in the Burning Bush, causes him to flee Pharaoh, makes his people journey by night across the Red Sea, makes him follow Khiḍr on three significant journeys, carries him in his ark when he is a small boy; He raises Jesus; He makes Jonah set out on his voyage within the whale; He splits the heavens; He sends down the Holy Spirit and causes the Good Words, namely Muhammad, to ascend.

Although many prophets are enumerated in the Prologue, the main body of the *Isfār* confines itself to only nine: Muhammad, Adam, Enoch (Idrīs), Noah, Abraham, Lot, Joseph, Jacob and Moses. With the exception of Muhammad, all are Old Testament/Hebrew Bible prophets.

The principal points the Shaykh wishes to emphasize in the Prologue are that in reality God is the only Actor and that the human being is a servant of, and totally dependent on God.

The Three Voyages [Paras. 2, 6][23]

Ye shall surely travel from stage to stage (Q.84:19).

The three voyages enumerated in the *Isfār* are largely determined by the directional prepositions attached to them: from (*min 'inda*) God, to (*ilā*) God, and in (*fī*) God. A foreshadowing of these three voyages can already be discovered in the book's Preface, as the first three prophetic voyages enumerated can be described as: in God (Muhammad), from God (Adam), and to God (Enoch).

The voyage 'from God' is described in this paragraph in an extremely terse and ambiguous way, complicated by the conflicting vocalization found in the manuscripts. The result, or gain, of this voyage is either what exists (*mā wujida*) or what he, the voyager, finds (*mā wajada*). Since we do not have the folios from the autograph of this paragraph, we are left in doubt as to what the author intended. The voyage 'from God' is described in more detail in Paragraph 7 of the *Isfār* when the three kinds of voyager 'from God' are discussed.

The voyage 'to God' in effect includes everyone and everything, for all are on a path to God whether they are aware of the fact or not: *To Allah We belong, and to Him is our return* (Q.2:156). In Paragraph 7 of the *Isfār*, the division into three kinds of voyager is made on the basis of the idea one has of God. The ones who corporealize Him, the ones who strip Him of every attribute that would liken Him to human beings, and those who are safeguarded from either of these extremes.

'In God' is the voyage of wandering and bewilderment. It has no end. In some parts of the *Futūḥāt* wandering is connected to wayfaring since it does not have a stated goal (although elsewhere it seems more directed and moves on a straight line). This would correspond to the Second Path of the *Futūḥāt* Chapter 337, the path 'that has no end so that it drives the wayfarer (*sālik*) into nonexistence. In this Second Path the wayfarer wanders aimlessly,

23. See the many superb articles in Mercer (ed.), *Journey of the Heart*. Especially relevant is Chodkiewicz, 'Endless Voyage'. See also Gril, Introduction to *Dévoilement*, and Morris, *Reflective Heart*.

for nonexistence cannot be determined or tied by a limit.'[24] Any goal other than the Real, who alone has Being, leads to nonexistence and wandering in a state of bewilderment without end. The Real is the only real goal; other aims are nonexistent mirages, will-o'-the-wisps, flickering phantoms appearing here and there on the landscape that the wayfarer – the *sālik* – if he is among the wretched, may pursue without ever reaching the 'resting place' (*mustaqarr*) of Mercy. There is hope in this situation for other wayfarers, however, as Ibn 'Arabī points out. There is a chance that the wayfarer becomes so lost that he cries out to his Lord to guide him; he aligns his actions with God's Law/Path and devotes himself to *dhikr*, both of which practices evoke God's mercy. With God's help, he finds his halting place 'at' God. The state of wandering does, after all, have its positive side, as its lack of a fixed aim seems to connect in some way to the station of no station, the waystation of the Muhammadians, or people of Yathrib, which is a very high station.

The Voyage 'with God' [Para. 2]

The Shaykh limits the prepositions involved in the spiritual voyage in the *Isfār* to three: 'from', 'to', 'in', inexplicably omitting the preposition that adheres to every voyage and is absent from none: *bi-* (or *ma'a*) ('with'). God, who is *closer to [the human being] than the jugular vein* (Q.50:16), *with you wheresover ye may be* (Q.57:4), *surrounding everything* (Q.41:54) is the eternal Companion on the voyage.[25] As S. Hirtenstein has noted: 'God is simultaneously ever-present and the end-point of the spiritual journey.'[26] It is unthinkable that Ibn 'Arabī has simply forgotten to make this one of his voyages, since he includes it in his answer to al-Tirmidhī's Question 12 in the *Futūḥāt* regarding the way that those going to the sessions of prayer proceed

24. *Fut.*III.141 (Chap. 337).
25. As in the hadith 'You are the Companion of the voyage and the vicegerent in the family.'
26. *Four Pillars*, pp.3–4.

to these sessions: 'They include the one whose going (*sayr*) is in (*fī*) Him with His Names. He is the companion of going from (*min*) Him, to (*ilā*) Him, in (*fī*) Him, and with (*bi-*) Him.'[27]

Also, we see in the Introduction (*muqaddima*) to the *Futūḥāt* that one of the principles of the elite among the people of God is the following tenet: 'He who desires to arrive at Him (*ilayhi*) will not arrive at Him except with Him (*bi-hi*) and with you – with you with respect to your seeking Him, and with Him because He is the place of your quest.'[28]

> He the Most High is with us wherever we are: in the state of His 'descending to the nearest heaven in the last third of the night', in the state of His being 'seated upon the Throne' (Q.5:20), in the state of His 'being in the Cloud', in the state of His being 'upon the earth and in heaven' (Q.43:84), and in the state of His being 'closer to the human being than his jugular vein' (Q.50:16).[29]

Perhaps Ibn 'Arabī does not mention the voyage 'with' God in the *Isfār* because he believes it is too obvious to mention. We are always travelling with Him. In Chapter 191 of the *Futūḥāt*, On the Voyage and the Path, which, as we shall see, bears many similarities to passages in the *Isfār*, God's accompaniment on the voyage is made explicit:

> There is a voyage with (*bi-*) the Real and a voyage with the creatures. The voyage with the Real consists of two kinds: a voyage of essence and a voyage of attribute. The Perfect Human Being voyages upon all these voyages, so he voyages with his Lord upon a divine unveiling and a verified 'with-ness', in which he is with the Real just as the Real is with us wherever we are. ... If the servant is with Him, h/He voyages with H/his voyage. Thus He discloses to him that he is He, just as He disclosed to him that he is not He.[30]

27. *Fut.*II.49 (Chap. 73). These four voyages are related to the four postures of *ṣalāt*. See our discussion of the word *sayr* below.

28. *Fut.*I.41 (*Muqaddima*).

29. *Fut.*III.340 (Chap. 367). Emphasis mine.

30. *Fut.*II.384 (Chap. 191).

The Modes and Perils of the Voyage [Para. 2]

We have learned that we are people of voyaging. We traverse by the watering places with the breaths, a journey of winter and summer,[31] in order to taste hunger. We believe in fear because it is what provides you with protection.[32]

The modes of voyage mentioned by Ibn ʿArabī in his Prologue are the land voyage, the sea voyage and the combination of land and sea. As was the case of the three kinds of voyagers, the two modes of travel are alluded to in the opening Prologue of the *Isfār*. The voyage of Noah is a sea voyage while that of Abraham is a land voyage.

In the Qur'an, when the two kinds of voyage are mentioned together, land is always given first place. From that Ibn ʿArabī deduces that land voyage is preferable to sea voyage. The terrors of the sea are frequently detailed in the Qur'an, such as in Sura 10:23 with its description of raging storms and towering waves. In Ibn ʿArabī's time, sea travel was considered much more dangerous than land travel and this opinion is reflected in both the *Isfār* and the *Futūḥāt*.[33] Denis Gril recounts Ibn ʿArabī's story in the *Futūḥāt* about a man from Kairouan who had to choose between voyaging by land or by sea.

> A man from Kairouan wanted to make the pilgrimage. He was vacillating between making the journey by the overland route, or by sea. Sometimes the land route seemed preferable, and at others, he preferred the sea. He said: 'The day after tomorrow, in the morning, I will ask the opinion of the first man I meet. Whatever he thinks is the best thing to do, I will decide.' The first man he met was a Jew. It was hard for him, but he overcame his discomfort and said:[34] 'By God, I certainly shall ask his opinion.'

31. See Sūrat Quraysh.

32. *Fut.*IV.163 (Chap. 521).

33. See Ibn ʿArabī's comments in *Fut.*III.19 (Chap. 304) where he mentions the possibilities of shipwreck, confiscation of goods, enslavement or imprisonment, and death.

34. See our later comments (pp.176–8) on the Jew and the thorn bush regarding attitudes and polemics of the time.

> 'O Jew', he said, 'I would like to ask your advice regarding this voyage; should I go by land or by sea?'
>
> 'Glory be to God', exclaimed the Jew, 'Why are you asking me a question like that? Do you not know that in your own Book God is telling you: "It is He who makes you go by land and by sea" (Q.10:22)?[35] He mentioned the land before the sea. If there were not a secret meaning intended by God, and one to which it would be best to conform, He would not have mentioned it first. The sea comes second, in case one does not have the means of travelling by land.'
>
> I was amazed by his words, and took the overland route. Never have I experienced a trip of the sort, by God! The Lord provided me with more goodness than ever I could have wished.[36]

All voyages are potentially dangerous and involve considerable risk, and in Ibn ʿArabī's day to set out on any kind of voyage was even more daunting. Pilgrims travelling to Mecca for the *ḥajj* were often gone for years at a time, and it was not uncommon for the pilgrim to die *en route*. But Ibn ʿArabī does not limit himself to warning of the dangers of physical travel. He 'crosses over' to the spiritual landscape, transposing these three kinds of voyages to the symbolic plane. It is through *sulūk* (and *safar*) that the seeker approaches God, and in this pursuit God guides through His being Light:

> 'It is He who maketh the stars for you, so that you might be guided by them in the dark places of the earth' – which is the external wayfaring through the actions of the body – 'and of the sea' (Q.6:97) – which is the inner spiritual wayfaring through the actions of the soul.[37]

Occasionally in the *Futūḥāt*, the 'sea voyage' means simply this: spiritual wayfaring through the actions of the soul, which seems easy enough to understand. But in Chapter 521 of that same work, in which he confirms Q.2:197's assertion that the voyager's best provision is God-fearing (*taqwā*), he goes into further detail, clearly

35. It is notable that the Jew is able to quote from the Qur'an.

36. *Fut.*II.262 (Chap. 161), trans. Gril, *Dévoilement*, p.4, n.13; and Gril, 'De la Proximité', pp.344–5. The same story is told in the *Futūḥāt*'s Chap. 70, on *Zakāt*: *Fut.*I.562.

37. *Fut.*I.192 (Chap. 27).

taking the trope of voyaging here as rational speculation. The utmost danger lies in speculating on God's Essence, which in any case has been forbidden by the authorized sources. Enemies – the 'jinn' of egotistical thoughts are singled out for reprobation – abound, ready to cut off the road at every turn. The 'sea voyage' here represents rational speculation on intelligibles and matters pertaining to the law. Dangers come from two sides: from doubt, symbolized by the sea itself into which the voyager is plunged, and from the arch enemy – interpretation (*ta'wīl*) – which is a sort of pirate who robs them when they are far from land.

Again, sometimes the 'land voyage' means precisely what it says: external wayfaring through the body's actions, or confining oneself to the exoteric aspect of the law. Such voyagers have only one enemy: an excessive dependence on outer form. Those who combine the two forms of travel (by 'sea' and 'land'), the people of God and the verifiers among the Sufis, must confront three enemies: their land enemy is God's Self-Disclosure in form, and their two sea enemies are their own shortcomings and their interpretation (again *ta'wīl*) of what has been disclosed to them.[38] 'Whoever is safe from the authority of Self-Disclosure in form, from the shortfall that reverses gain, and from interpretation of what has been disclosed to them, is safe from enemies. ... His trade is profitable.'[39]

In seeking to interpret a book whose subtext is itself interpretation of a Book, we can carry these references to the law over to the Qur'an and the types of interpretation of it that involve risk. 'Sea voyage' or rational speculation is practised primarily by the philosophers and theologians (*mutakallimūn*) who were in constant danger of falling into doubt because of their rejection of what made no sense to their intellects or could be confirmed by demonstration; at best what intellect considered impossible could be consigned to the realm of allegory. On the other hand, 'land voyage' appears to be a case of restricting interpretation to the literal form of the text. Hence there

38. *Fut.*IV.164 (Chap. 521).
39. Ibid.

is a need to navigate between the Scylla of transcendence (*tanzīh*) and the Charybdis of immanence (*tashbīh*). The skilled interpreter must face both these dangers; he must be cautious not to strip the revelation of its concreteness, rendering it a bloodless abstraction, not to mention failing to acknowledge the inability of his intellect to grasp what transcends it without divine assistance; and he must beware of his own tendency to restrict the revelation to a single literal interpretation and God to a single sensible form of disclosure.

Movement [Paras. 3–5]

... movement is for love, there being no movement
in existence except for love.[40]

Movement is a central theme in Ibn ʿArabī's writings, and it is amazing to see how many kinds of movement he discusses. In reality, movement in all its dimensions begins and ends in God. 'Not an atom moves but to Him and from Him.'[41] All movement is considered by the Shaykh to be straight (*mustaqīm*) – although, as we shall see, this straightness perhaps should be translated more as 'correct', 'upright' or 'righteous', not all paths being geometrically straight – since God is the Creator of all the paths and all the beings who travel along these paths.

Below we will discuss several of the kinds of movements that Ibn ʿArabī deals with, drawing predominantly from the *Isfār* and *Futūḥāt*.

Circular Movement/Orbits

Circularity plays such a primal role in Ibn ʿArabī's work that he does not hesitate to call 'what is' 'the Circle of Existence.' He dedicated an early treatise *Inshāʾ al-dawāʾir*[42] to the subject and we find numerous

40. *Fuṣūṣ*, chapter on Moses (trans. Austin, *Bezels*, p.258).

41. *Fut.*I.36 (*Muqaddima*).

42. Trans. Fenton and Gloton as 'Description of the Encompassing Circles', and *La Production des cercles*.

circular diagrams drawn throughout the *Futūḥāt* and elsewhere.

God created the celestial spheres within the 'circular' Cloud and set them in their 'floating' orbits.[43] From the circularity of celestial movement, the cosmos came into existence, hence circular movement is the first movement of the universe.

> The first shape that the body received was circularity; it is called a sphere, or a circle. From the movement of that sphere came into manifestation the world of the bodies, high and low.[44]

The way of all things leading from their beginning from God to their return to God (*al-mabdā' wa-l-ma'ād*) follows a circular trajectory, since: *to Him returns the affair, all of it* (Q.11:123), and: *ye were without life, and He gave you life; then will He cause you to die, and will again bring you to life; and again to Him will ye return* (Q.2:28).

> Things proceed from God and return to Him. ... In the world of shape the affair inevitably takes the form of a circle, since [a circle] does not return to God by the path on which it emerged from Him; rather it extends until it reaches its place of origin. This does not happen in a straight line or it would never go back to Him. But it does go back to Him. Hence there is no escape from circularity, in both the suprasensory and sensory domains. It is because He created the cosmos in His form that His creation is circular in shape.[45]

43. See *Fut.*III.420 (Chap. 371).

44. *Fut.*III.119 (Chap. 332). The entire chapter is an exposition of inclination/curvature – both physical and metaphoric, as in affection, concern, sympathy (*'aṭf/ḥunuww/mayl*) – and circularity (*dawr/kawr*). In it are several wonderful Akbarian plays-on-words; for example, in the opening poem of the chapter, the mountain where Moses was called to meet with God, Mount Ṭūr, is connected through the root *ṭ-w-r* with the stages (linear/consecutive) of development (*ṭawr*). And the affection (*ḥunuww*) of Moses for his wife is connected with her being made from a curved rib.

45. Ibid. Trans. Chittick, *SDG*, p.224, slightly modified.

Another form of circular movement involving God and human being is the circular dance of repentance, which in Arabic uses the same root as the word 'turning'. As Ibn 'Arabī says, echoing the Qur'an, God turns to us first and then we turn to Him.[46] This turning brings us back to our root of servanthood and humbleness after our having strayed, seemingly, from His straight path. But as we shall see illustrated in Ibn 'Arabī's recounting of the story of our exemplary predecessor Adam, the path of repentance and turning, though circular, is really a straight one. Through our inevitable turning away from God comes the overwhelming desire to turn back to Him, and in desiring proximity to Him we indeed approach Him. Sin is the goad that sets the heart back on the path to nearness, thus even our distancing becomes a drawing close.

Circular movement is also apparent in time: 'Time, through a complete circular movement returns to its initial point.'[47]

> The Real – exalted is He – has united forever the posterior with the anterior, so that time is cyclical and rotation is incessant both with respect to spirits and with respect to bodies, and between both [domains, both bodily and spiritual] there are extraordinary and amazing formal correspondences (*ashkāl*).
>
> 'And to the moon We have assigned mansions/waystations [which it must pass through] until it becomes once more [thin and curved] like the dry palm' (Q.36:39).
>
> Thus the day turns around and succeeds the night, and the night succeeds the day; the sphere turns and the created world turns; the word, letters, and names go round; happiness goes round; summer and winter, autumn and spring go round; and the star goes round [in its orbit]. 'This is how you have been created, and this is the way you will have to return' (Q.7:29) 'and truly you have known the original creation' (Q.56:62).[48]

46. 'Then turned He unto them that they might turn [repentant to Him]' (Q.9:118).

47. Refers to a hadith concerning how the end and beginning of the cycle of this world coincide. Hence the birth of the Prophet Muhammad corresponds to the beginning of the cycle with Adam. See Vâlsan, 'L'Investiture', p. 305, n. 3.

48. *Ayyām al-sha'n* in *Rasā'il Ibn 'Arabī*. Trans. Beneito, slightly modified, in 'Ark of Creation', p. 52.

Ibn ʿArabī often discusses the solar and lunar cycles in a symbolic sense as well.[49] The latter has unparalleled significance in Ibn ʿArabī's estimation, both in itself and as a symbol for the Perfect Human Being. Just as the moon appears to travel along an arc of manifestation from crescent to full, then along an arc of concealment from waning to void, the Perfect Human Being journeys through the cycles of existence.

> He coined this example [for the gnostics] in actuality so that they will derive a lesson from it (*li-yaʿtabirū fīhi*) by 'crossing over' (*ʿubūr*)[50] to the knowledge of the Perfect Human Being and of God because of [the Perfect Human Being's] existence in the form that He set up, and the alteration of states upon [him] through the alteration of levels in which he becomes manifest. The Most High said: 'And for the moon We have appointed waystations' (Q.36:39).[51]

As time moves through its cycles, the birth of Muhammad – or his becoming manifest in bodily form, as his unseen spiritual form existed 'when Adam was between water and clay'[52] – coincides with the point of the cycle where Adam's cycle began.

Circularity is also manifest in the encirclement of mercy, embracing everything, like ribs encircling the vital organs.

The angels are said to circumambulate the heavenly Temple, and in imitation of the cosmic principle of circularity, human beings have ever engaged in ritual circumambulations and round dances. Notable in the Islamic context is the pilgrims' circumambulations of the Kaʿba and, returning once again to the invisible domain, the mystic's circumambulation of the heart.[53]

49. See *Fut.*III.111 (Chap. 330) for the symbolic relation between sun (as 'lamp') and moon (as 'light').

50. See below for our discussion of this important term.

51. *Fut.*III.111 (Chap. 330).

52. Some Muslim scholars, such as Ibn Taymiyya in his *al-Istighātha fī radd ʿalā al-Bakrī*, consider this hadith spurious and think that it should say, 'between body and spirit'.

53. See, for example, *Fut.*I.50ff. (Chap.1) and I.666 (Chap. 72). S. Hirtenstein presented an illuminating talk on this subject, entitled 'The Mystic's Kaʿba'.

Vertical and Horizontal Movement

As we have noted above, all movement – even circular movement – is in reality straight (*mustaqīm*) since all movement begins and ends in God, and God is 'upon a straight path' (*ṣirāṭ mustaqīm*). The word *mustaqīm* really has more the sense of correct than of straight here, since even crooked movement is *mustaqīm* if it is the movement appropriate to the being and state in question. The movement of a bow, for example, is *mustaqīm*, even though it is bent.

Within the great Circle of Existence, the various genera have movements that are proper, or *mustaqīm*, to them. Among the elements, the proper movement of fire and air is to rise upward while the proper movement of earth and water is to seek lowness.

Minerals and other 'inanimates' have a special status with Ibn ʿArabī since they do not move of their own accord but only when moved by an agent. One has only to recall the high regard given to the Kaʿba's Black Stone. In his discussion of the rocks Ṣafā and Marwa, between which the *ḥajj* pilgrim runs as part of the fulfilment of the requirements of the pilgrimage rites, Ibn ʿArabī has the highest of praises for the inanimates:

> The inanimates are more knowing of God and more worshipful of God than the rest of the generated beings. They are created in a knowledge that has no reason, desire, or free disposal, for they are directed by others, not themselves. There is no director but God, so they are directed by God's direction. ... The inanimate does not have highness as [its] natural movement but when it is thrown high and departs from its nature it seeks lowness, which is the reality of servanthood. ... It sinks through fear of God [cf. Q.2:74].[54]

Ibn ʿArabī goes on to add that it is this quality in the human being, the stone nature, that is highest, since servanthood is his root as well.

Plants, while unable to engage in locomotion, are not devoid of movement: they grow upwards while sinking their roots downwards

54. *Fut.*I.710 (Chap. 72).

in the earth in a movement that is the inverse of the human movement.[55] Exceptions are the vegetation in the Garden, in particular the Tree of Life, which is vertical as are humans, and liminal plants such as the date palm, said to be sensate hence combining horizontal and inverted movement.

The animal, for its part, is aligned with the horizontal plane, which is its particular 'straight movement'. If the animal walked on two legs, says the Shaykh, it could not be ridden or carry burdens, which are part of its benefit to humankind.[56]

The human being is so configured as to stand upright and maintains his vertical axis while moving in the six directions: forwards, backwards, right, left, up and down. Straightness and verticality are essential qualities for the human being; in his function as spiritual Pole (*quṭb*), his standing upright is described as being like a tent peg keeping the heavens from collapsing upon the earth. When the microcosmic Human Being is transferred to the next world, the heavens will come tumbling down upon the earth.[57] It is interesting, however, to note that the movement Ibn 'Arabī associates with woman is the curve. Taken from the curved rib of Adam, she is often described as inclining, bending in mercy.[58]

Among the suprasensible entities, the proper movement for the angel is to descend with messages and inspiration and then ascend to the supernal realm – the angel does not move along a horizontal axis and cannot incline[59] – while the proper movement for the human being is to ascend in knowledge and descend in servanthood.[60]

As for demonic entities, they can move in only four directions – forwards, backwards, right and left – but not in six, which is the number associated with humankind: they cannot approach from

55. See *Fut.*II.217 (Chap.132); see also *Fut.*II.464ff. (Chap. 198, section 33).

56. *Fut.*II.217 (Chap. 132).

57. See *Fut.*I.125 (Chap. 7). See also *Fuṣūṣ*, chapter on Adam (trans. Austin, *Bezels*, pp. 51–2).

58. See *Fut.*I.124–5 (Chap. 7).

59. See *Fut.*I.54 (Chap. 2). Inclination is associated with deviation (*inḥirāf*), and the angel cannot deviate.

60. Ibid.

above or below.[61] As Satan in the Qur'an states: *Then we will come to them from before them and behind them and from their right and from their left* (Q.7:17).

The Lord Himself has described Himself as descending to the Throne of the All-Merciful and again to the lowest heaven – the heaven of this earth – in the final third of the night in order to receive the petitions of His servants. As a refutation of the practice of stripping God of all attributes, God also describes Himself as 'sitting' on the Throne, 'wavering' before taking the soul of His fearful believing servants, and 'rushing' to meet those who approach him running.[62]

Thus there is a veritable chessboard of movements in existence, all of which, when adhering to their essential root, are both 'straight' (correct) and 'circular' (returning to their Lord).

It is not only corporeal or quasi-personified beings who have movements. The Qur'an descends upon the hearts of its reciters. Acts ascend on the mounts of their performers.[63] Spiritual energies (*himam*, sing. *himma*) ascend. It is with these energies that the people of God travel (*sayr*) to the sessions of prayer.[64] The 'Good Words' ascend.

One of the most salient features of Arabic morphology is the animating of the fixed form of the consonantal three (or in rarer cases two or four) letter roots by the addition of vowels – *ḥarakāt*. The word '*ḥaraka*' itself means movement. Thus by means of the 'broken' *kasra* ('i') which 'lowers' (*khafḍ*), the 'inclusive' *ḍamma* ('u') which 'raises' (*rafʿ*), and the 'opening' *fatḥa* ('a'), which 'erects'

61. See *Fut.*I.157 (Chap. 16).

62. 'If My servant approaches Me by a hand's breadth, I will approach him by an arm's length; and if he approaches Me by an arm's length, I will approach him by a cubit; and if he comes to Me walking, I will come to him running.' Hadith mentioned in the canonical collections of al-Bukhārī, Muslim and Ibn Māja.

63. Ibn ʿArabī's discussion of the waystation equivalent to Sūrat Muḥammad has a section about deeds personified, taking their performers as mounts. If we examine Sūrat Muḥammad itself, we see that deeds are frequently mentioned. This sura's importance *vis-à-vis* notions of travel and admonitory exempla has been discussed earlier. See n.19.

64. *Fut.*II.48–9, question 12 (Chap. 73).

(*naṣb*),[65] a number of grammatical operations supplying meaning can be obtained.

Movement can be either voluntary or involuntary, active or passive. Involuntary movements in human beings include sneezing, shivering and the like. Ibn ʿArabī also mentions planetary movement as being voluntary or not, or 'willingly or loth' to quote the noted passage in Qur'an 41:11: *He said to [the heaven] and to the earth: Come ye together, willingly or loth. They said: We do come willingly, obedient.*[66]

A very special kind of movement is embodied in the Muslim prayer, consisting of the four basic postures of standing, bowing, prostrating and sitting. Prayer itself is likened to a voyage. A wonderful analogy is set up using the Qur'anic injunction (Q.20:12) to Moses at the Burning Bush to doff his sandals because he is in a holy place. According to Ibn ʿArabī, the command came because Moses had reached a station in which he could speak to God face-to-face without mediation, represented by the two sandals, made from the dead skin of a donkey (= lack of understanding, pure externality and foolishness). But the one who prays, says Ibn ʿArabī, is commanded to don his sandals, because when he is praying he is 'walking' and engaged in intimate conversation with his Lord.

> It indicates that the one who prays walks in his prayer and in conversation with his Lord, in the verses that save him, waystation by waystation. Every verse is a waystation and a state. ... The companion said: 'When I descended at this waystation, we were commanded to pray in sandals.' That is his pointer from God the Most High that he is walking in waystations, which are the verses of the Qur'an he recites in his prayer, since the sūras are waystations according to the [Arabic] language.[67]

65. This word is also connected with appointment and investiture.

66. See *Fut.*I.123 (Chap. 7). It seems that the heavens were more willing to move out of obedience to God's command than the earth, which moved willingly only when it realized it was compelled, hence Ibn ʿArabī says it moved 'willingly unwillingly'.

67. *Fut.*I.192 (Chap. 27).

The two sandals represent the two realities taking part in the prayer: the Real and the servant. In the case of Moses, there was but one reality: Moses had become annihilated in the Real. But the one who engages in the obligatory ritual prayer is described as setting out on a journey (*yarḥal*), crossing back and forth from the waystation of speech to the waystation of listening as Lord and servant engage in the dialogue of the 'two halves of the prayer'. It is a speaking and a listening between two parties, conversing intimately. God is said to have divided the *Fātiḥa*, which opens every ritual prayer, into halves: half belonging to Him and half to His servant. Once the *Fātiḥa* is completed, the servant departs on another journey as he goes from standing to bowing, then to prostrating, then to sitting – each movement accompanied by a prayer having an inner meaning. 'All of these are in actuality waystations and watering holes in the prayer, for [the one who prays] is a voyager from state to state. How can one say to one whose state is a constant voyage: "Don thy sandals!?"'[68] Doubt and distraction, stumbling on the meanings of obscure verses, are thorns and debris on the road. The servant must protect his two feet – his internal and external dimensions – by donning his two sandals – the Holy Book and the Sunna of the Prophet – to protect himself as he travels.

As for prostration itself, even God is said to prostrate Himself by equating Himself with the sick or needy servant in a *ḥadīth qudsī*:

> The divine prostration is the most magnificent of divine descents that the Real has Himself made [to] the waystation of His servant. It is His saying: 'I was sick and you did not come to visit Me; I was hungry and you did not feed Me; I was thirsty and you did not give Me to drink.' There is nothing greater than this divine descent. Then He interpreted it by [saying]: So-and-so was sick, and so-and-so was hungry, and so-and-so was thirsty. So He Himself descended to their waystation through their states and connected all that to Himself by His attributing Himself with those states.[69]

68. *Fut.*I.192–3 (Chap. 27).
69. *Fut.*I.481 (Chap. 69).

Words Relating to Voyaging[70]

As M. Chodkiewicz has pointed out in his article 'The Endless Voyage', Islamic discourse is thoroughly saturated with terms relating to voyaging that have taken on metaphorical meaning:

> Even a brief semantic analysis is sufficient to show how Islam's religious vocabulary constantly reminds man of his condition as *viator*, pilgrimage being the ritual expression of this condition. A number of times in each of the five daily prayers – a total of seventeen times per day – the Muslim asks God to lead him along the straight path (*ṣirāṭ mustaqīm*) .... The first meaning of the very word to denote Divine Law – *sharīʿa* – is the road that leads to the watering place .... The term that normally is translated by 'brotherhood' or 'mystical order' – *ṭarīqa* – belongs to the same semantic domain: a *ṭarīqa* is a road and, more specifically, a road to perfection, an *itinerarium in Deum*. He who sets out on the road, the *sālik* – the 'walker' – does so under the direction of a *murshid*, a 'guide'.[71]

One of the Five Pillars of Islam, the *ḥajj*, or pilgrimage to Mecca during the appointed season, is incumbent upon every Muslim who possesses the means to do so. This often involved a journey of many months, a once-in-a-lifetime grand voyage. Islam itself was truly born when the Prophet emigrated (*hijra*) from Mecca to Medina and then returned to Mecca in triumph as ruler and pilgrim (*ḥājj*). Pilgrimage to the tombs of holy individuals (*ziyāra*) was also a common practice and continues to this day.

Below we will discuss some of the terms related to voyaging that we find in Ibn ʿArabī's works, including the *Isfār*.

70. See also Morris, 'He Moves You', and *Reflective Heart*, pp. 12–14. Also highly recommended is Wilson's marvellous 'Caravan of Summer'. The *Encyclopaedia of Islam* has a number of relevant articles concerning travel in Islamic history and thought. See, for example, Toorawa, 'Trips and Voyages'; Gordon, 'Journey'.

71. Chodkiewicz, 'Endless Voyage', p. 71.

Sayr

Sayr is a general term for going, moving, setting out, departing, travelling, flowing, following (a behaviour), proceeding and acting. *Sīra* (from the same root as *sayr*) can also be a kind of biography, especially of the Prophet Muhammad. Words based on this root are mentioned 'some twenty-seven times' in the Qur'an.[72] We translate it as 'going'.

The Shaykh often uses it for planetary motion:

> [God] made these heavens unmoving (*sākina*) and created planets in them. With respect to their going (*sayr*) and their floating in these heavens, He made measured movements, neither excessive nor deficient, and He made them rational, hearing, and obeying: 'He revealed in every heaven its command' (Q.41:12). Then when God made the planets float in these heavens, paths arose from their going – for every planet a path. It is His saying: 'By the heavens possessing orbits' (Q.51:7). These paths are called 'spheres'. The spheres originate with the going of the planets.[73]

In an extraordinary group of passages in Chapter 73 of the *Futūḥāt*, a chapter in part dedicated to answering questions posed by the noted Sufi al-Tirmidhī, Ibn 'Arabī discusses the ritual prayer in terms of travelling and participating in an assembly or session. Question 12 asks: 'How is the manner of their going (*sayr*), namely, to these assemblies where the speech [= prayer] begins?' The Arabic root used throughout his response is *s-y-r*. The answer includes such notions as spiritual aspiration (*himma*), which is a kind of intense concentration and direction of energy towards the spiritual world, and purification exercises involving *dhikr* (devotional practice of remembrance) and retreats. A distinction is made between

72. Morris, *Reflective Heart*. The reader is advised to look at Morris's discussion of this term on pp.14–16, in which the author singles out those Qur'anic verses in which *s-y-r* appears that are most applicable to Ibn 'Arabī's thought, for example, Q.22:46; 29:20; and 30:42.

73. *Fut.*III.416 (Chap. 371).

the people of knowledge and the people of faith, the ideal situation being a combination of the two. People of knowledge cannot 'go' to the 'sessions' without intermediaries. The Messenger of God is their 'veil keeper' and precedes them on the path. People of faith 'go' directly to God without intermediaries.[74] Best of all are those who 'go' with both knowledge and faith, and whose four movements 'from', 'to', 'in' and 'with' God correspond to the four movements of prayer: standing, bowing, prostrating and sitting; the four 'states of spiritual quaternity':

> Because of this, the 'delight of the Prophet's eye' was in the ritual prayer, for he was whispering with Him despite the diversity of the states that are restricted to standing, bowing, prostrating, and sitting. ... These are the states of spiritual quaternity, so they are similar to the [four material] elements. ... The forms of the meanings are temporally created from the mixture of these four states, just as the forms of the corporeal, natural progeny are temporally created from the mixing of the elements.[75]

If the order of prepositions corresponds to the order of the prayer postures, then 'going from' corresponds to standing, 'going to' corresponds to bowing, 'going in' corresponds to prostration and 'going with' to sitting. Salient too is the notion of quaternity, which we will find later in the passage devoted to Moses' first voyage.

Safar[76]

We translate *safar* here as 'voyaging' in order to distinguish it from going (*sayr*), wayfaring (*sulūk*), travelling (*riḥla*) and roaming or wandering (*siyāḥa*). It appears only twelve times in the Qur'an; for example, in the verses on shortening the prayer and on the exemption from fasting when voyaging. These all mention *safar*, not *sulūk*

74. Included in this group are ʿAbd al-Qādir, Abū al-Suʿūd ibn al-Shibl and Rābiʿa al-ʿAdawiyya.

75. *Fut.*II.49 (Chap. 73).

76. See Peters, 'Safar'; Morris, *Reflective Heart*, pp.16–17, and 'He Moves You', p.45.

or any of the other terms mentioned above. The hadith 'You are the Companion on the voyage' also uses this word.[77] J.W. Morris points out that Ibn ʿArabī uses this term with less frequency in the *Futūḥāt* than some others, perhaps because

> it always refers primarily to something that human beings do by themselves, to the result of their own limited purposes and intentionality. ... [T]he particular semantic focus of this term on our conscious goals and intentions, even in supposedly spiritual contexts, sharply limits its appropriateness for expressing the metaphysical ideas and deeper kinds of spiritual awareness that Ibn ʿArabī is usually seeking to communicate in his discussions of the spiritual journey.[78]

As we have noted previously, the root conveys, in addition to the meaning of 'voyaging', the following senses: uncovering, the glowing whiteness of pre-dawn and pre-sunset, and book. Ibn ʿArabī makes full use of the entire spectrum of this root in both the *Isfār* and the *Futūḥāt*.

In his definition of Sufi technical terms, embedded in the *Futūḥāt*'s Chapter 73, the Shaykh says:

> The heart, when it heads in the direction of the Real, the Most High, by *dhikr* of the Real or the self, however it may be, is called the 'voyager' ... [or] 'one who voyages through reflecting upon intelligibles.'[79] It is 'crossing over' (*iʿtibār*) with respect to the Law, so that he crosses (*ʿabara*) from the shore of this world over to the further shore. He is the agent, the wayfarer (*sālik*).[80]

Ibn ʿArabī explains the connection of the two words *isfār* and *asfār* and relates them to salient themes in the *K. al-Isfār* in the context of his discussion of various rules pertaining to fasting when voyaging:

77. For example, *Fut.*IV.267 (Chap. 558).

78. Morris, *Reflective Heart*, pp.16–17, and 'He Moves You', p.45.

79. See *Fut.*II.382 (Chap. 190), IV.163ff. (Chap. 521).

80. *Fut.*II.134 (Chap.73). See also English translation of 'al-Iṣṭilāḥāt al-Ṣūfiyya' by Bayrak and Harris, p.90.

> [God] said: 'As for one among you who is ill or upon a voyage, [he should fast] a number of other days' (Q.2:184) … 'Or upon a voyage' [refers to] the people of wayfaring (*sulūk*) on the Path to God in the stations and the states. '*al-safar*' is from '*al-isfār*', which is 'making manifest' because *al-safar* is only called '*safar*' because in it is unveiled the character of the Men.[81] The stations and states in this wayfaring unveil to them that action does not belong to them, even if they do it; rather it is God who is the Agent through them, as the Most High said: 'You did not throw when you threw, but Allah threw' (Q.8:17).[82]

Thus aside from the reference to unveiling of character during the voyage, an important hint regarding the passive nature of the Perfect Voyager, who moves only when moved, is also presented in this passage.

In the *Futūḥāt*'s Chapter 190, On Knowledge of the Voyager, the goal of the voyager – here seen as someone who proceeds on the basis of rational speculation rather than blind faith – is clearly determined. It is to know and to do: to know God insofar as this is possible and to do what He has commanded, increasing in belief from the bare proof of His existence to the stage where God is seen everywhere and worship of Him is constant and essential. The stages in which this coming to full maturity in faith is accomplished are well served by the metaphor of the voyage. The voyager in reflection progresses in stages, seeking first of all proofs for the existence of God. He finds in himself only the sign of his own possibility to either be or not be, dependent on the One who wills his existence or his nonentity. From there he voyages onward, discovering about the One that He is transcendent and necessary of being through Himself. At another stage, he finds that this Transcendent and Necessary Being cannot not be; further stages prove to him that He is not temporally originated, or a substance possessing dimensions, and that He has knowledge, will,

81. As we have seen, this expression was a common Sufi maxim.
82. *Fut.*I.628 (Chap. 71).

power, life, speaking, hearing and seeing. Then he voyages further and it is disclosed to him that this Being has sent messengers, that these messengers are veracious. He follows their law until, in the end, he sees God in everything. At this point, 'he desires to throw down the staff of the voyage and to remove from himself the name "voyager". Then his Lord instructs him that the actual affair has no end, whether in this world or the hereafter.'[83] There is, in effect, no cessation to the voyage. This is the voyage in knowledge.

To voyage in deeds is to fulfil the obligations of the law in this world. When the legal prescriptions cease in the hereafter, the voyager still remains engaged in worship, but then it will be an essential worship, not one that is the result of a command.

A special kind of voyage is the voyage of the breath. The breath, says Ibn 'Arabī, emerges from the heart and passes from the sound-element *alif*, 'aa', which is called the essential He-ness (*huwiyya dhātiyya*) through the spirits to the *wāw*, which extends the breath with its sound of 'oo'. From here it descends to the lower world through the prolongation of the *yāʾ* with its sound of 'ee'. Angelic revelation stems from the level of the *wāw*, which is a connector, and human revelation stems from the level of the *yāʾ*, since it is the sign of lowering – that is, humility. The *alif* remains upon its root, as the Divine Essence, the *huwiyya*, remains transcendent of the worlds.[84] These are the only vowel sounds in the Arabic language.

The points of articulation are halting places where the consonant sounds from the least voiced *hāʾ* to the most voiced *wāw*[85] are produced, forming twenty-eight letters to correspond with the twenty-eight 'mansions' or 'waystations' the planets pass through on their course through the heavens. The movement of the planets, called into action by the Divine Speech 'Be!' (*kun*) gives rise to the life-engendering energies affecting the cosmos, hence the bond

83. *Fut.*II.383 (Chap. 190).

84. See *Fut.*II.391 (Chap. 198).

85. Hence we see that the combination of these two letters, forming the word '*huwa*' – the third person singular pronoun denoting the absent or unseen individual – gives the totality of the powers of the letters, with all that that entails.

between breath actualized in language and creation through the articulations in the Breath of the All-Merciful is a close one.

For the human being, the phrase *bismillāh al-Raḥmān al-Raḥīm*, in the Name of God the All-Merciful, the All-Compassionate, is the equivalent of God's saying '*Kun*!' (Be!), hence it holds extraordinary power. For this reason, as we shall see, Noah is enjoined to set sail in his Ark accompanied by the *basmalah*.[86]

Because of its engendering qualities, the human being should, to the best of his ability, remain aware of the breath and the essential quality of mercy that pervades it. 'The shortest and closest distances are the most difficult for him. It is what is between two breaths. Whoever's distance consists of his breaths, he is upon the most difficult voyages, but when he is safe, his gains are great.'[87]

Riḥla[88]

My journey (*riḥla*) was only within me,
and my guidance was only to myself.[89]

The word '*riḥla*' seems to have been originally connected with the actual saddling up of, and mounting a camel or other riding beast for the sake of travel. It appears four times in the Qur'an, once in its own right and three times in the derivative form meaning 'saddlebag'. Addressing this latter usage first, we find reference to the saddlebag (*raḥl*) in the story of Joseph (Q.12:62, 70, 75), when Joseph hides the drinking cup in his brothers' saddlebag. The one Qur'anic instance is found in Q.106:2 (Quraysh): *[For the taming/civilizing/assembly/union (al-īlāf) of Quraysh], for their taming, [We cause] the caravans to set forth (riḥla) in winter and summer.* When Ibn 'Arabī discusses this verse in his exegesis of the Sura in Chapter 278 of the *Futūḥāt*, however, he uses the word *safar* rather than *riḥla*.

Travel of the sort mentioned in the famous travelogues by Ibn

86. *Isfār*, Para. 38.
87. *Fut.*IV.163 (Chap. 521).
88. See Netton, 'Riḥla', and its bibliography.
89. *Fut.*III.350 (Chap. 367).

Jubayr (1145–1217) and Ibn Baṭṭūṭa (1304–68 or 77) is generally known as *riḥla*, as is the travel encouraged by the Prophetic injunction: 'Seek knowledge as far as China', which gave birth to a genre of travel: *al-riḥla fī ṭalab al-ʿilm*, for the sake of studying with sundry masters.[90]

Ibn ʿArabī also uses *riḥla* to describe other types of travel. There is, for example, his use of the word *riḥla* to describe the movements of the ritual prayer, in which the 'donning of sandals' we have already discussed takes place, unless one is in a state of complete annihilation, when 'doffing the sandals' is appropriate.[91]

Sometimes the Shaykh uses *riḥla* as an equivalent of *safar, sulūk* and *siyāḥa*, as in when he says: 'The journey (*riḥla*) of the one He chooses is only *from* Him and *to* Him and *in* Him',[92] which is one of the categories he uses for wayfaring (*sulūk*).

Siyāḥa[93]

Siyāḥa, which we translate as 'wandering' or 'roaming', generally means a kind of itinerant dervishhood of a severely ascetic nature. The root *s-w-ḥ* is found three times in the Qurʾan: *Those that turn in repentance; that serve Him, and praise Him; that* wander *in devotion to the cause of Allah; that bow down and prostrate themselves in prayer; that enjoin good and forbid evil; and observe the limit set by Allah* (Q.9:112); *It may be, if he divorced you, that Allah will give him in exchange consorts better than you, who submit, who believe, who are devout, who turn to Allah in repentance, who worship, who* wander, *and fast ...*' (Q.66:5); and: Wander *throughout the land for four months but know that ye cannot cause failure to Allah and that Allah will disgrace the disbelievers*

90. See Elmore, 'The Flight of the Fabulous Gryphon', *Journey of the Heart*, p.91.

91. See also Ibn ʿArabī's extraordinary claims in *Kitāb al-kutub* regarding his own ascent, in which the 'doffing of the sandals' at the Divine Footstool (eighth celestial sphere), *à la* Moses at Mount Ṭūr, takes place. *Rasāʾil Ibn ʿArabī*, pp.10–11, trans. Elmore, 'Flight of the Fabulous Gryphon', pp.92–3.

92. *Fut.*IV.366 (Chap. 559).

93. See Morris, *Reflective Heart*, pp.17–18, 38–43, and 'He Moves You', pp.64–8 (partial trans. of *Fut.*, Chap. 174).

(Q.9:2)[94] (emphasis ours).[95] Despite Qur'anic approval, *siyāḥa* did not always find favour with the more conservative among Muhammad's *umma* (community). Aḥmad b. Ḥanbal, for example, stated: '*Siyāḥa* has nothing to do with Islam.'[96] And 'Ā'isha is reported to have said: 'The *siyāḥa* of this nation is fasting.'[97]

Ibn 'Arabī uses the term often. He says Jesus was one of those who practised *siyāḥa*[98] and he himself practised it at the outset of his spiritual path.[99]

In Chapter 174 of the *Futūḥāt* – somewhat misleadingly named 'On the Station of the Voyage' (*safar*), since the entire chapter deals with the notion of *siyāḥa* – the *sā'iḥ* is depicted as a roamer through the deserts and uninhabited lands, whose chief intent is to flee from other members of his species in order to be alone with God and to avoid the claim that others have on him.[100] He seeks exclusive closeness and intimacy with his Lord and finds society inimical to this pursuit. Ibn 'Arabī says that the people of God generally do not go roaming about the earth in a state of utter poverty unless they are troubled by excessive intercourse with other human beings.

In addition, *siyāḥa* is specifically connected with *i'tibār*, inner consideration, reflecting on one's experience, crossing over from the observed to the contemplated, or 'spiritual insight',[101] which as we shall see below, is another kind of voyaging.

94. Morris quite charmingly and accurately gives the last part as 'know that you-all cannot get away from God' ('He Moves You', p.47; *Reflective Heart*, p.18).

95. I have changed the translations of Yusuf Ali (first two quotations) and Sahih International (last translation) from 'travel' to 'wander' to reflect the distinction I make between the various sorts of travelling.

96. Melchert, 'Piety of the Hadith Folk, p.431.

97. al-Ṭabarī, *ad* Q.9:112, *Jāmi' al-bayān*.

98. *Fut.*II.49 (Chap. 73, Question 14).

99. See *Fut.*I.196 (Chap. 29).

100. For more on the recourse to flight, see Commentary, pp. 277–82.

101. Morris, *Reflective Heart*, p.38, and 'He Moves You', p.64.

Sulūk[102]

[Wayfaring is] moving with knowledge from station to station, from Name to Name, from Self-Disclosure to Self-Disclosure, and from breath to breath.[103]

We have already discussed the word *sulūk*, here translated as wayfaring, at some length in our Introduction in connection with the manuals devoted to the Sufi path. It is a highly ascetic and rigorous self-discipline that both fulfils and goes beyond the letter of the law, inducing action when action is commanded, and restraint when it is prohibited. As Ibn ʿArabī states in his poem opening the *Futūḥāt*'s Chapter 189, *sulūk* derives from a root giving the concrete meaning of entering into, hence the passage of a needle in the process of stringing pearls[104] and the entering of a traveller onto a path. Although elsewhere it is sometimes connected with *ḥayra* – bewilderment – and *tayyāh* – getting lost, wandering, becoming perplexed (derived from *tīh*, the desert, the trackless wilderness), as well as the idea of perishing and becoming proud, the opening poem mentions the straightness of this threading: 'Wayfaring is the straightest (*aqwām*) path; If you keep straight, then you are a wayfarer on it.'[105]

The most complete treatment Ibn ʿArabī gives to *sulūk* is in Chapter 189 of the *Futūḥāt*, and much of the material in that chapter may be used to fill out some of the remarks the Shaykh has made in the opening paragraphs of the *Isfār*. For example, here we have a fuller treatment of the kinds of voyagers and voyages, here called, in keeping with the designation of the chapter, wayfarers and wayfarings.

As for wayfarers, here there are four kinds distinguished by the company they keep: 'a wayfarer who wayfares with his Lord; a wayfarer who wayfares with himself; a wayfarer who wayfares with a group; and a wayfarer/not wayfarer. Their path is distinguished

102. Ibid. p.46.
103. *Fut.*II.381 (Chap. 189).
104. *Fut.*II.380 (Chap. 189).
105. Ibid.

in accordance with the wayfarer's goal and rank in knowledge of God.'[106]

The first wayfarer is he for whom God is his hearing, seeing and all his faculties. When he carries out his acts of obedience to his Lord, it is his Lord who is carrying them out through him. The second wayfarer is a striver who seeks to come close to his Lord through obligatory and supererogatory acts, the undertaking of which he realizes are personally incumbent upon him, so that his Lord will love him and will become, as in the first wayfarer, all his faculties. This he seeks to know by tasting, not by report. The third wayfarer has experienced what the first two have experienced and knows how all his faculties are commanded in particular so that they function as a group united in the obedience of God. The fourth wayfarer sees that he is a locus for wayfaring and that he cannot be distinguished from wayfaring itself as long as God is associated with it. The way appears to him underfoot as he moves with his faculties through the realm of legal prescription. Then he comes to see that, as a locus for the manifestation of wayfaring, he has no existence. He then realizes the paradoxical truth of God's saying '*You did not throw* when you threw, but Allah threw' even to the point where the addition of 'and He did not throw'[107] would be perfectly correct.

The modes of these wayfarers exceed by far the three that are mentioned in the *Isfār.* They include eight modes:

> the wayfarer <u>from</u> Him <u>to</u> Him; the wayfarer <u>from</u> Him <u>to</u> Him <u>in</u> Him; the wayfarer <u>from</u> Him <u>to</u> Him <u>in</u> Him <u>with</u> Him; the wayfarer <u>from</u> Him but neither in Him nor to Him; [5] the wayfarer <u>to</u> Him but neither from Him nor in Him; [6] the wayfarer neither from Him nor to Him nor in Him – he is described as a wayfarer and as wayfaring; [7] the wayfarer who does not voyage; and [8] the <u>wayfarer–voyager</u> (*al-sālik al-musāfir*).[108]

Excluding the last two, one of which is not treated at all, and one

106. *Fut.*II.381 (Chap. 189).
107. Q.8:17.
108. *Fut.*II.382 (Chap. 189); our emphasis.

of which is treated in the subsequent chapter on the Voyager, the wayfarings are briefly described as follows: the wayfarer from Him to Him moves from Self-Disclosure to Self-Disclosure. The wayfarer from Him to Him in Him wayfares from a Divine Name to a Divine Name in a Divine Name. The wayfarer from Him to Him in Him with Him wayfares with a Divine Name from a Name to a Name in a Name. The wayfarer from Him but not in Him or to Him is the one who departs from God's Presence in creation to creation. The wayfarer to Him but not from Him or in Him is the one who flees to Him in creation from creation, like Moses' flight.[109] The wayfarer neither from Him nor in Him nor to Him is the ascetic/renunciate non-gnostic who moves in righteous deeds from this world to the next world.

Isrāʾ

Another term which we have discussed in our Introduction is *isrāʾ*, a nocturnal journey, in a general sense. As Ibn ʿArabī and others have pointed out, to add 'by night' to this word is superfluous since it pertains exclusively to night journeys; hence the addition is generally taken to have special significance. In the Qur'an, it is not only connected with Muhammad's Night Journey and Ascent but also with Moses and his exodus from Egypt: *We revealed to Moses that he should journey by night with My servants* (Q.20:77; 26:53), and with Lot, who is told to travel by night from Sodom (Q.15:65).

It is only the highest of human beings, such as the Prophet Muhammad, who are taken on the Night Journey and *miʿrāj* in both body and spirit; and this is the only case where one can be sure no satanic delusion enters in. It is possible for people to have spiritual ascents where they are shown many marvels by their demonic guides.[110]

Other words for night travel, which are not used, however, in the *Isfār*, are *iddlāj/adlaja* – to set out at nightfall – and *isʾād* – being hasty

109. See below, pp. 277–81, for a discussion of the term 'flight', and *Isfār*, Para. 64.
110. *Fut.*II.622ff. (Chap. 283).

in journeying, especially at night.[111] Ibn ʿArabī connects *iddlāj* to God's descent to the lowest heaven every night in the third part of the night.[112] Muhammad is also called '*mudlij*' in the Prologue of the *Futūḥāt*.

ʿAbara

The basic root of this word means to cross, traverse, pass from one side to another – as in crossing a valley or river.[113] It has extended meanings of auguring from the flight of birds and considering, meditating on, or pondering the meaning of – as in pondering a book or a sign. The second verbal form *ʿabbara* means 'to interpret [a dream]', which might have derived from the art of prognosticating by observing the passage of birds in the sky. It also means to explain, state clearly and so forth. The eighth verbal form *iʿtabara* is to be taught a lesson, take as an example, to consider and so forth. The noun *ʿibra/ʿibar* means 'lesson', 'example', 'admonition'.

The various permutations of this root and its meanings weave through the entirety of the *Isfār* as well as the Shaykh's other works. Seekers are constantly advised to take lessons and warnings from all they experience with their senses as they pass through this world. They are told to 'cross over' from the forms seen in their dreams to higher, more spiritual meanings, as did the Prophet Muhammad when he interpreted his dream of a fetter as firmness in religion and milk as knowledge. In the *Futūḥāt*, even the rulings of the Shariʿa are first presented in their exoteric form, then 'crossed over' to an esoteric meaning that yet manages to leave the plainer meaning intact.

111. See *Fut.*I.278 (Chap. 54).

112. See *Fut.*I.468 (Chap. 69).

113. A cognate is found in Hebrew: '*ivri*' is the adjective meaning 'Hebrew'. 'In its etymological meaning, 'Hebrew', *ivri*, implies an experience of passage. Abraham passed, he passed from one world to another, from one shore to another.' Neher, *L'Existence juive*, p. 134, quoted in Ouaknin, *Zeugma*, p. 194.

Naqala

The root *n-q-l* means to move, travel, roam and so forth, but also to transmit, to extend the meaning of words, to translate, to copy (for example, a manuscript) and to communicate. *Naql* is also traditional learning transmitted from ancient sources.

Ibn ʿArabī uses this word frequently, most often perhaps to describe the movement from state to state, from breath to breath and from Divine Name to Divine Name. These are unavoidable movements that, even if the person makes no effort to pursue them, pass through him regardless. Just as every day God is in some task, at every instant and in every breath we are subject to a never-ending fluctuation of states and the constant influence of a Divine Name.

Naql is also the word used when Ibn ʿArabī speaks of the *miʿrāj* in the *Futūḥāt*'s Chapter 367: 'God does not *move* a servant from place to place in order to see Him, rather to make him see His signs that were hidden from him. ... And likewise, when God moves the servant in his states – also to make him see some of His signs – He moves him in His states.'[114]

Often the word is also used to describe the movement of the individual from this world to the next world and the voyage of the soul through the stages of the next world. In one significant passage, the Shaykh describes the wanderers (*sāʾiḥūn*) who make their homes in caves, and the Prophet himself, who never built a dwelling for himself, because of their awareness that before long they will be transferred to the next world:

> [T]hey see this world as a bridge set up of wood, over a great river, and they are crossing it, travelling upon it. Have you ever seen anyone build a dwelling on a wooden bridge? No, by God! Especially when one knows that the rains will come down and that the river will become great with the flood that comes, and that bridges are cut off. Everyone who builds upon a bridge will only bring ruin upon himself.[115]

114. *Fut.*III.340 (Chap. 367).
115. *Fut.*I.212 (Chap. 33).

Paths

When we turn to the various words used for the path, road or way, we find *ṭarīq*, *minhāj*, *nahj*, *sharīʿa*, *ṣirāṭ*, *sabīl* – each with its particular flavour. Ibn ʿArabī mentions the path in virtually every chapter of the *Futūḥāt*, at the very least concluding nearly every chapter with the verse from Q.33:4: *And Allah speaks the Truth and He guides on the Path.* In the *Isfār* this verse appears five times, at the end of Paragraphs 17, 25, 45, 60 and 70 (which marks the end of the book). Paragraph 17 is the final paragraph of the Voyage of Creation and Command; Paragraph 25 is the final paragraph of The Voyage of the Vision among the Outer Signs and Inner Signification (corresponding to Muhammad's *miʿrāj*); Paragraph 45 is at the end of Lot's Voyage to Certainty; Paragraph 60 concludes Moses' Voyage of Anger and Return.

Ibn ʿArabī depicts the paths in various ways, presenting different facets and focal points throughout his works. For example, in the *Futūḥāt*, Chapter 337, he describes three paths associated with ontological considerations. Into the first enter all those who follow the doctrine of being, whether they are professors of *tawḥīd*, believers, polytheists or infidels. The second path has no limit and drives its wayfarer into nonexistence. This path belongs to those 'who divest God of any definite point'. A middle, *barzakhī* – or liminal – path exists, the third path, whose goal is neither existence nor nonexistence, which Ibn ʿArabī connects to the states [= attributes] in the science of *Kalām* (dialectical theology).

> As for the *barzakhī* Path, it is only wayfared upon by those in particular who know God, those whom the Real affirmed and obliterated in this very affirming them, and made them subsist in the state of their annihilation. They are those who neither die nor are they kept alive (Q.20:74)[116] until God judges between the servants. Then they will take the right-hand path to the path of the Existent

116. The verse reads: 'Verily he who comes to his Lord as a sinner, for him is Hell: therein shall he neither die nor live.'

the Real. They have acquired an attribute from the reality of that path and have acquired a configuration that manifests upon them in the waystation of the Existent the Real, by which they recognize each other, and which the people of the other two paths do not recognize. This is an example like the example that the Real made for the people of God so that they would learn from it the levels of guidance and bewilderment and of the guided and the misguided. God makes for them a light, or rather, lights, by which they are guided in the 'darknesses of the land' of their nature, in the darknesses 'of the sea' of their reflective thoughts, and in the darknesses of their rationally speaking souls – both the land and the sea of these souls, because of what they are upon in their configuration. For the rationally speaking souls are generated between pure light and sheer, unsullied, elemental nature.[117]

Staying Still

We cannot leave this section without discussing the words pertaining to staying still, not moving or travelling of one's own accord. It is a concept that is as important to Ibn ʿArabī as travelling; in fact it may accompany the journey if the journey is an *isrāʾ* and/or *miʿrāj*. It may be the supreme irony in a book devoted to movement of all kinds that in reality there is no movement at all. M. Haj Yousef has explained that in a cosmos that is created anew in every instant there can be no movement. Ibn ʿArabī explains:

> So it would be fine to call this change 'motion', although we know there is nothing but the embodied thing itself, the place, and the fact that it occupied a place next to that which it occupied before. But those who claim that there is some [real] thing called 'motion', which got into the embodied thing and caused it to change from one place to another, they have to prove it![118]

117. *Fut.*III.141 (Chap. 337).
118. *Fut.*II.457 (Chap. 198), trans. Yousef, *Time and Cosmology*, p.42.

We have already noted the high position the inanimate rock has in Ibn ʿArabī's thought. With no will of its own, it accepts being moved by its Creator, and if displaced upwards, it returns to its root of lowness and utter servanthood.

There are several terms related to unmoving that Ibn ʿArabī uses, such as *iqāma* (settling, standing), *thubūt* (fixity) and *mawqif* (halting), but we will confine our discussion to one term of singular importance, *sukūn*.

Sukūn

The root *s-k-n* has to do with being or keeping silent, still, at rest, stationary. It includes words that involve dwelling, residing, inhabiting, as well as trusting and feeling calm. It is also a root that is used in grammar to describe a quiescent, unvocalized ('unmoving') letter. One of its meanings, expressed by the words *maskana* (the state) and *miskīn* (the individual), also involves lowliness and humility, even abasement and utter destitution. The connotation is positive in meaning for the pious, who quote the Prophet Muhammad's supplication: 'O God, make me to live lowly (*miskīn*), make me to die lowly, and gather me among the congregation of the lowly.'[119] The word *sakīna* has a special meaning in the Qur'an (Q.2:248), as it is the Divine Presence or source of tranquillity that is said to dwell in the Ark of the Covenant.[120] *Sukkān* is the rudder of a ship, used to guide and calm its movement. Ibn ʿArabī uses this word in connection with Noah's Ark in *Kitāb al-Isrā'*: 'I then saw an Ark of spiritual essence ... whose rudder (*sukkān*) is the stillness (*sukūn*) of the heart.'[121]

119. Cited in Lane, *Lexicon*, vol. 4, p. 1395.

120. Oddly enough, the *sakīna* is thought by some early Arab lexicographers to have the head and tail of a cat, or to be in the image of a cat (see Lane, *Lexicon*, vol. 4, p. 1304). I include this note for the benefit of my beloved feline companions: Finjan, Louie, Bilqis, Marjan, Zorby, Kippie, Mimi, Toby, Tiki, Mitzi, Mazi, Edi and Avi.

121. Trans. Beneito, 'Ark of Creation', p. 42.

Chapter 175 of the *Futūḥāt* speaks of those who abandon the voyage, supporting the superior wisdom of staying still with two Qur'anic verses: *It is He who, out of His bounty, has settled us in an abode wherein neither toil nor weariness affect us* (Q.35:35) and *He is with you wherever you are* (Q.57:4). To voyage is to invite toil and weariness, which in any case is pointless, since the God who is the goal of the voyage is with us anyway, whether we go or stay. 'He has a facing in every direction, so why should I roam?[122] Moving in order to attain Him is an indication of lack of finding stillness.'[123]

In the extraordinary passage that follows, Ibn 'Arabī, in the voice of the quiescent servant, compares himself to one of the waystations or mansions (*manzila*) of the moon, sought not seeking:

> His Names seek me; I do not seek them; the Lights seek me; I do not seek them. I halt with the One for whom neither movement nor transfer [from place to place] is possible. The companion of the voyage is with His saying: 'Our Lord descends every night to the lowest heaven', and the companion of staying still is with His saying: 'The All-Merciful sits upon the Throne' (Q.20:5). Remaining still is preferable to moving.[124]

When we remain still, God becomes our trustee (see Q.73:9), bringing us whatever it is that He in His wisdom has decreed for us.

> So even if what befalls the servant is voyaging and moving (*intiqāl*), let the Real be the one who bears him on the litter of divine solicitude – while the servant remains in that condition of stillness where he is. Then he will not even experience any tiring movement, being in repose, shaded and served [by God]. This is the voyage of one who has abandoned voyaging, even while he is destined to voyage.[125]

Finally, mention must be made of those beyond moving and staying put. As Ibn 'Arabī says in the opening poem to Chapter 270:

122. The Arabic word used here is from the root *j-w-l*, which is synonymous with *r-ḥ-l*.

123. *Fut.*II.294 (Chap. 175).

124. Ibid.

125. Ibid. Trans. (with minor alterations) Morris, 'He Moves You', p.69, and *Reflective Heart*, p.44.

The waystation of the Pole and the Imamate
Is a waystation that has no mark.
He who rises above going and standing still possesses it.[126]

The Voyagers [Para. 7]

Three kinds of voyagers are described as voyaging 'from' God, or 'from His Presence' (*min ʿindahu*). The first kind is, in effect, banished from God's Presence and includes Iblīs and those who associate partners with God. The second group, while not banished, consists of sinners who cannot stand to be in God's Presence because of the shame they feel. The third kind is a very elite group, made up of envoys and heirs of the prophets who, having voyaged to the Presence of God, return to the world of the creatures in order to guide them.

Three kinds of voyagers voyage 'to' God. The first kind consists of polytheists and those who give God a body or make Him similar to creatures in any way. These folk will never see Him. The second group consists of those who strip God of all attributes. When these voyagers arrive they will be reproached but not subjected to eternal punishment. The third kind – God's elite – are safeguarded and feel no fear since they are already accepted into the Divine Presence.

Two kinds of voyagers voyage 'in' God. The first voyage in their intellects and inevitably lose their way if this is their sole guide. The other group, containing once more God's elite, are made to voyage in Him – the passive form of the verb *safara* is used to show that they do not undertake this voyage relying on their own rational powers but allow themselves to be guided by God to His Presence.

126. *Fut.*II.571 (Chap. 270).

Knowledge vs. Practice: Towards the Eschaton [Para. 8][127]

Ibn 'Arabī claims that the 'early ones', that is, the companions of Muhammad, excelled in practice, while the 'latter ones', Ibn 'Arabī's contemporaries or near contemporaries, excelled in knowledge. There is a definite apocalyptic thrust to this, not so much in terms of the end of time as we know it but in the etymological sense of the Greek word *apokaluptein*: to 'uncover, reveal'. In Ibn 'Arabī's view, with the death of the Prophet Muhammad we entered into the last third of the night of the cosmos's existence, a time when certain hitherto concealed esoteric knowledge becomes more abundant and manifest in the fewer people prepared to receive it.

In the first part of the night, which in Ibn 'Arabi's works alludes to the time preceding the birth of Islam's Prophet, the balancing of the elements and domination of the animal soul were present in the cosmos. In the middle part of the night, during Muhammad's lifespan, the cosmos received its spirit and rational faculty, which became dormant after his decease. We, in the third part, are like sleepers, awaiting the dawn of the Hour, when we will awaken in the fullness of our faculties. Because we are now 'asleep' we have access, through dreams and vision events, to the Imaginal World of the Barzakh – the liminal world that is neither purely spiritual nor exclusively material but partakes of both. These windows of perception grant the later generations knowledge of the unseen and the hereafter that the former generations did not have, while they, on their part, were able to enjoy and more completely imitate the Prophet's example:

> Since the Self-Disclosure of the Real in the last third of the night [gives] complete benefits, sciences, and kinds of knowledge in their most perfect aspects, since they stem from the Self-Disclosure that

127. Beneito has delivered a lecture on the subject of this paragraph entitled 'Past and Future of Knowledge'. See also his article 'The Time of Deeds'.

is closest – [that of] the lowest heaven, the knowledge belonging to the latter part of this community after the death of the Messenger of God – peace and blessings upon him – is more complete than the knowledge belonging to the middle or the first parts of it; because when God sent the Prophet – peace and blessings upon him – polytheism was firmly established and unbelief was manifest. He did not call the first generation, which was the generation of the Companions, to anything in particular other than belief, which was more evident to them than what they had of hidden knowledge. The Noble Qur'an was sent down to him and he began to interpret it in a way in which the general populace of that century could understand it. He made representations and similitudes, and used attributes belonging to temporally originated things. Everything that he said in describing his Creator was equivalent to a sensible, well-fashioned, evenly balanced form. Then he blew into that narrated form a spirit in order to manifest the perfection of the configuration. It was the spirit of 'nothing is as His likeness' (Q.42:11); 'glory be to your Lord, the Lord of might, over what they describe' (Q.37:180). Every verse is a glorification in the Qur'an, for it is the spirit of the form of the configuration of the address. So understand, for it is a wonderful secret.

To the elite of the first century but not to the common people, indeed to some of the elite from behind the discourse of transcendence, great secrets appeared. But despite this, they did not reach the place the latter ones of this community reached, because they took it from the material letters of the Qur'an and the prophetic reports. In this they were equivalent to the people of night conversation who converse in the first part of the night before they go to sleep. When the time of the third part of this night arrives – which is the time that we are in until the rising of the dawn, the dawn of the Resurrection, the Uprising, the day of Resurrection and Gathering, the Real will disclose Himself in the third of this night which is our time, giving sciences, secrets, and gnostic knowledges to the hearts by disclosing what the letters of the reports do not give, for He will give them without any matter, indeed as meanings devoid [of all matter]. They [the moderns] are more perfect in knowledge while

> the first [generation] was more perfect in practice. As for belief, they are equal [in that].[128]

The Prophet's contemporaries had his physical form to contemplate and it was more difficult for them to grasp the hidden dimensions of the revelation that his message contained. The later generations had to be content with what was written and heard in the authoritative sources, already a step removed from the actual presence of the Prophet. On the other hand, the generation of the Prophet was particularly disposed to envy, self-aggrandizement and resistance to authority. Overcoming these vices occupied much of their attention and the result was a people strong in their belief and practice but deficient in gnostic knowledge: *They know a manifest side of the life of this world, but of the last world they are heedless* (Q.30:7).

In another passage, Ibn ʿArabī gives a more cosmological explanation of the relation between the practice of the ancients and the knowledge of the moderns:

> [Muhammad's physical] manifestation occurred with the Scale [= Libra], which is justice with respect to being, and it is balanced because its nature is hot and wet. It is part of the property of the Hereafter. The movement of the Scale is connected with the last world and [continues] until the entrance into the Garden and the Fire. For this reason, knowledge in this community is more abundant than with those who were among the 'first ones'. Muhammad – peace and blessings upon him – received 'the knowledge of the first ones and the last ones' because the reality of the Scale gives that. Unveiling is swifter in this community than it was in others because of the predominance of coldness and dryness over the rest of the communities before us, even though there were wise ones and scholars, thus individual people were designated, in contradistinction to how people are today.
>
> Do you not see that this community is the interpreter of all the sciences of the nations? ... This community knows the science of those who preceded [it, as well as] being singled out for sciences

128. *Fut.*III.188 (Chap. 346).

> that the predecessors did not have – [alluded to] by [the Prophet's] saying: 'I learned the knowledge of the first ones' – who are those who preceded him. Then he said: 'and the last ones' – and this is the knowledge of what the predecessors did not have. It is what his community after him knows until the Day of Resurrection. He notified [us] that we have sciences that did not exist before. ... For masterhood of knowledge in this world was affirmed of him – peace and blessings upon him.[129]

Although both generations shared in the benefits accruing to the descent of the All-Merciful in the last third of this night when He asks if there is anyone who repents who can be forgiven and anyone who supplicates who can be answered, the later generation has the advantage of fuller Self-Disclosure. It will not be cut off at 'dawn' with the resurrection.

The Jew and the Gharqad Bush [Para. 8]

This shocking – and, to many, offensive – hadith comes from the canonical collections of hadith.[130] The reference is to an apocalyptic battle between the Jews and the Muslims at the end of time. The *gharqad* is a boxtree that looks, in fact, rather like how one imagines Moses' Burning Bush. Ibn 'Arabī employs this hadith here less as invective directed against the Jews than as a sign of the end times. This is not the only time he uses this hadith. It appears twice in the *Futūḥāt* in Chapters 317 and 357 as well as in his treatise on cosmology, *'Uqlat al-mustawfiz*.[131] In Chapter 357, he writes:

129. *Fut.*I.144 (Chap. 12).

130. At the time of the Second Intifada this hadith took on new life and a search for '*gharqad*' on the internet will give some indication of the tenor of recent exegesis. Jewish settlers, for example, were accused of planting fences of *gharqad* bushes as a form of protection against the Palestinians.

131. Nyberg, *Kleinere Schriften*, p. 92.

> And it is established on his authority with respect to the killing of the Jews at the end of time, when the Jews hide behind the tree.[132] The tree will say: 'O Muslim! This is a Jew who is hiding behind me. Kill him!' The tree was the thorn bush (*gharqad*). It was cursed for informing who among the Jews had sought its protection. Here there is a wonderful divine secret. It is well known that among the trees there was one that watched over the claim of anyone seeking protection with it, relying upon that tree for God's mercy and the fulfilling of the claim of the neighbour. This is one of the praiseworthy attributes in every sect and religious community. The Messenger of God – peace and blessings upon him – said to the daughter of his uncle, Umm Hānī: 'We have granted refuge to him whom you have granted refuge, Umm Hānī.'[133] And he was a polytheist. The Jews are People of the Book in any case, so they deserve more to have their claim as neighbour fulfilled.[134]

In Chapter 317, the emphasis is more on the generally unacknowledged fact that creatures other than human beings have rational speech. After naming the various body parts that will testify against their owners on the Day of Resurrection, he continues:

> Through [this intrinsic life], trees will speak at the end of time when Jews hide behind them and Muslims are seeking to slay them. A tree will say to a Muslim, when it sees him hunting for the Jew, 'O Muslim, there is a Jew behind me, so slay him', so he will slay him. But the thorn-bush will conceal the Jew when he comes to it, which is why the Messenger of God cursed it. Nor can it be said that the tree only felt pity toward him who relied upon it, like people of noble character, since you should know that God's right has more

132. Muslim, *Ṣaḥīḥ*, *fitan*, 41.84: 'Abū Hurayra reported Allah's Messenger (may peace be upon him) as saying: The last hour would not come unless the Muslims will fight against the Jews and the Muslims would kill them until the Jews would hide themselves behind a stone or a tree and a stone or a tree would say: Muslim, or the servant of Allah, there is a Jew behind me; come and kill him; but the tree Gharqad would not say, for it is the tree of the Jews.' See also Ibn Majā, *fitan* 33.

133. For this hadith, see *Ṣaḥīḥ* al-Bukhārī (1.8.353; 4.53.396; 8.73.179) and *Ṣaḥīḥ* Muslim (Book 4).

134. *Fut.*III.258 (Chap. 357).

> claim to be observed and that it is more necessary for a person of faith to employ a noble character for God. Do you not see that He says, 'In the matter of God's religion, let no pity for them seize you' (Q.24:2)?[135]

This is not the place to discuss Ibn 'Arabī's various comments about the People of the Book. The Shaykh lived at a time and in places of intense and equally distasteful polemics among Jews, Christians and Muslims, some of it connected, as this hadith is, to apocalyptic events. But perhaps to counter the severity of the above hadith, we can mention Ibn 'Arabī's citation of another report concerning a Jew:

> Do you not see that the Prophet rose to his feet before the casket of a Jew? Someone said to him, 'That is the casket of a Jew.'
>
> He replied, 'Is it not a soul?' Hence he assigned the cause only to the soul's essence. Hence he rose up to assert the majesty and greatness of the soul's eminence and its placement. How could the soul not have eminence, since it is inblown from the spirit of God? It derives from the most eminent, angelic, spiritual world, the world of purity.[136]

135. *Fut.*III.67 (Chap. 317), trans. Chittick, 'Two Chapters from the *Futūḥāt al-Makkiyya*', p.99. The Qur'anic verse reads *in toto*: 'The woman and the man guilty of adultery or fornication, flog each of them with a hundred stripes: let not compassion move you in their case, in a matter prescribed by Allah, if ye believe in Allah and the Last Day: and let a party of the Believers witness their punishment.'

136. *Fut.*III.263 (Chap. 358), trans. Chittick, *SDG*, p.287.

The Lordly Voyage from the Cloud to the Sitting on the Throne,[137] Assumed by the Name the All-Merciful [Paras. 10–12]

Between the Cloud and the Sitting [on the Throne]
The intellects that possess understanding wander bewildered.[138]

The 'beginning' of this voyage is the locus of the Real's 'whereness' as posed to the Prophet Muhammad in the famous hadith of the Cloud: 'Where was our Lord before He created His creation?', to which he answered: 'He was in a Cloud above which and below which there was no air.'[139]

In the *Isfār*'s Paragraph 10, Ibn ʿArabī describes the Cloud as a barrier, as a 'pavilion' or 'surrounding wall of an enclosure'[140] and elsewhere as a 'veil of inviolable incomparability' (*ḥijāb al-ʿizza al-aḥmā*),[141] which prevents any relationship between the Ultimate Reality (true Being) and creation (possible existence). 'There is nothing existent save Him in the Cloud', says Ibn ʿArabī in the *Futūḥāt*;[142] or as the Prophet Muhammad says in a hadith: 'God was/is, and nothing was/is with Him.'[143] In His essential He-ness (*huwiyya*), which both conceptually and grammatically falls into the category of the absent, hence hidden, person, God cannot be known. But God desired to be known, as the well-known hadith tells us: 'I was a Treasure but was not known. So I loved to be known, and I created the creatures and made Myself known to them.'[144]

137. See also *Fut.*III.429 (Chap. 371, section I).

138. *Fut.*II.131 (Chap. 73).

139. Hadith found in: al-Tirmidhī, *Jāmiʿ*, *Tafsīr* Sūra 11, 1; Ibn Majā, Muqaddima 13; Aḥmad IV.11,12.

140. 'And We have made the heavens as a canopy (*saqf*) well guarded' (Q.21:32).

141. See, for example, *Fut.*I.4 (Khuṭba).

142. *Fut.*I.111 (Chap. 5).

143. A variation of the hadith found in al-Bukhārī, *Ṣaḥīḥ*: 'God was, and there was nothing other than He.'

144. Trans. Chittick, *SPK*, p.66.

The Cloud is 'the first divine locus of manifestation through which God manifested Himself; in it the essential Light began to flow, as is manifest in His words: *Allah is the light of the heavens and the earth* (Q.24:35).[145] The Cloud is at the all-embracing apex of a 'horn of light' that extends to the earth, where it reaches its most constricted point.[146] Also described as 'the Ocean of the Cloud', it is a *barzakhī*, or liminal, field where a number of suprasensible events take place, including the possibility of Creator–creature interface: the human being's assumption of Divine Names, such as Knowing and Willing, and the Real's qualification with human attributes such as laughter and surprise.[147] When the Lord makes His voyage of descent from the Unseen Cloud as a bright beam of total Generosity, saturating this 'ocean' or 'horn' with light, it is to establish Himself – to 'sit' as a king would – upon the Throne of all-encompassing existence. Since the movement of descent is to bring the possible things into existence through pure mercy, this king is called the All-Merciful and His solicitude towards the creatures is absolute and all-encompassing.

Ibn 'Arabī explains in the *Futūḥāt* that the Cloud and the Throne are to be distinguished by the Divine Name associated with them. When one reads that the 'Lord' descends, as the appellation of this voyage suggests, the point of origination is in the Cloud. Thus when in another famous hadith the Lord is said to descend to the lowest heaven in the last third of the night, the 'place' He descends from is the Cloud. When one reads about the 'All-Merciful', the locus of this Name is the Divine Throne. Ultimately, however, all Divine Names are really One, since the Named is One.[148] Thus the All-Merciful is also said to descend along with the Lord to the lowest heaven in the last third of the night, in that the continuation of the hadith shows the attributes of All-Mercy as He asks: 'Is there anyone who turns in repentance so that I can turn towards him? Is there

145. *Fut.*I.148 (Chap. 13).
146. See *Fut.*I.149 (Chap. 13).
147. See *Fut.*I.41 (*Muqaddima*).
148. See, for example, *Fut.*IV.196–7 (Chap. 558).

anyone seeking forgiveness so that I can forgive him? Is there any supplicator so that I can give to him? Is there anyone who is praying so I can answer him?'[149]

The relationship between the Cloud and the All-Merciful must also be seen in terms of the movement of breath. For example, Ibn 'Arabī describes the existence of the Cloud as stemming from the exhalation of the Breath of the All-Merciful as it relieves the immutable possible entities of the constriction of their nonexistence, giving form and existence to all creation: 'The first form assumed by the Breath of the All-merciful was the Cloud. So it is an All-merciful Vapour within which there is mercy; or rather, it is mercy itself.'[150] The Cloud, then, is a kind of womb in which creation is engendered:

> The Cloud is the root of all things and forms. It is the first branch that appeared from the root. It is a grass, not a tree. Then from it the command and the creation, which is the earth, branched out ad infinitum. This is by the determination of the Mighty, the All-Knowing.[151]

The elect of God, the 'Muhammadians' or 'people of Yathrib', who are in the waystation of 'place' – that is, 'with God'[152] – are able to contemplate Him in the Cloud and upon the Throne:

> *They contemplate Him in the Cloud with the same eye through which they contemplate Him sitting [upon the Throne], with the same eye through which they contemplate Him in the lowest heaven, with the same eye through which they contemplate Him on earth, with the same eye*

149. al-Bukhārī, *Ṣaḥīḥ*, *tahajjud*, XIV 1094.

150. *Fut.*III.430 (Chap. 371), trans. Chittick, *SPK*, p. 132.

151. *Fut.*III.420 (Chap. 371).

152. This is actually the 'station of no station'. The term 'Muhammadians' is not some inept equivalent of 'Muslims'. The Muhammadians are those who like Abū Yazīd al-Bisṭāmī have divested themselves of all personal attributes and thus 'when they are seen, God is remembered'. Ibn 'Arabī states: 'In this path only two individuals are called "Muhammadian": a person who has been singled out for inheriting knowledge of a ruling that did not exist in any law before Muhammad, or a person who brings together all the stations, then emerges from them, entering "no station", like Abū Yazīd and his equals. This person is also called a "Muhammadian", but everyone other than these two is ascribed to one of the prophets' (*Fut.*I.223, Chap. 36).

through which they contemplate Him in the 'with-ness', and with the same eye through which they contemplate Him in 'Nothing is as His likeness' (Q.42:11).[153]

The Voyage of Creation and Command [Paras. 13–17]

[T]he origin [of all motivation] is the movement of the Cosmos out of its state of nonexistence in which it was [latently] until its existence, it being, so to speak, a stirring from immobility [rest]. The movement that is the coming into existence of the Cosmos is a movement of love.[154]

God's creative activity in this paragraph is given two words, *khalq* 'creation', and *ibdāʿ*, the latter often translated as 'origination' to distinguish it from other words pertaining to God's creation, making and fashioning of the cosmos: *khalq*, *barʾ*, *inshāʾ*, *iḥdāth*, *taṣwīr*, *jaʿl* and so forth. Origination is the creation of something that has no likeness, which in effect is everything, for 'origination is nothing but the specific face that He has in everything and by which it is distinguished from other things.'[155]

The 'voyage of creation' is primarily an exegesis of a passage in Sura 41 in which a parallel is set up between God's origination of the cosmos and His origination of the human being writ large, the microcosmos. In fact, in translating his commentary it becomes difficult to fix upon a pronominal referent for he is speaking about the two – human being and cosmos – simultaneously. This becomes clear when the various referents in the Qurʾanic passage that indicate the cosmos are given equivalents in the human being: breath = vapours; stars and lamps = eyes; seven heavens = seven faculties: sense perception, imagination, reflection, intellection, recollection, memory and supposition; the seven planets ('floating stars') =

153. *Fut.*II.386 (Chap. 194).
154. *Fuṣūṣ*, chapter on Moses (trans. Austin, *Bezels*, p.257).
155. *Fut.*IV.315 (Chap. 558).

the seven divine attributes: Living, Knowing, Willing, Powerful, Speaking, Hearing and Seeing.

Another sura, not mentioned here but suggested by the context, is Q.65:12: *Allah is He who created seven heavens and of the earth a similar number. His command descends among them: that ye may know that Allah has power over all things, and that Allah comprehends all things in knowledge.* The interpretation of this verse was said to be of such a perilous nature that Ibn 'Abbās, a companion of the Prophet, was reported to have remarked: 'If I were to explain its true meaning, you would stone me for being an unbeliever.'[156] Ibn 'Arabī claims to have given some of Ibn 'Abbās' interpretation of this verse in Chapter 11 of the *Futūḥāt*, entitled 'On knowledge of our Fathers, the High Things and our Mothers, the Low Things'.

The Voyage of Creation parallels in many ways the Voyage that follows it, that of the Noble Qur'an, in that both are likenesses of the Perfect Human Being. For Ibn 'Arabī, the cosmos itself is a great scroll that is recited by the Real in a continual and ever-renewed way[157] and 'the Universal Human Being in reality is the Noble Qur'an'.[158]

At the end of this section comes a reference to the intriguing story of the Bedouin woman, Laylā, lowering her veil to inform her lover of the danger that his approach would surely occasion from the hostility of her tribe. The thwarted lovers, in actuality, were the noted Umayyad poets Laylā al-Akhiliyya and Tawba b. Humayr. Tawba had asked Laylā's father for her hand but he refused and married her to someone else. The lovers continued to meet and were ultimately found out. Members of Laylā's tribe waited one day in concealment near the lovers' accustomed trysting spot in order to kill Tawba. Laylā discovered this and, through her unaccustomed unveiling, was able to signal to Tawba that something was amiss. Ibn 'Arabī liked the story so much that he used it twice in his book

156. See Hirtenstein, *Four Pillars*, p.6. See also Ibn 'Arabī, *K. al-Fanā' fī al-mushāhada*.
157. See *Fut.*I.101 (Chap. 5).
158. *Isfār*, Para. 21.

of poems *Tarjumān al-ashwāq* (The Interpreter of Desires),[159] as well as in the *Futūḥāt* in Chapter 174, on the Voyage. Here the story is used metaphorically to refer to the voyage unveiling the character of the voyager, but it also suggests the risk one takes in approaching too near to God's inviolable precincts, for example, seeking to know His Essence, or trusting in one's reason to interpret what God wished to remain concealed of the meaning of His Books.

The Voyage of the Noble Qur'an [Paras. 18–21]

We have dealt with some of what this section contains, in particular the nature of recitation, in our remarks in the Introduction about *tafsīr.*[160] Here we will address the issue of *qur'ān* and *furqān*[161] in connection with how the Qur'an descends upon the hearts of its reciters.

The revelation to Muhammad has two aspects to it, one being the comprehensive: the suras gathered and collected, as the root meaning of the word *qur'an* conveys. The other aspect is detailed and particular: the suras taken separately, the verses considered individually, the words and concepts distinguished.

In Paragraph 18, Ibn ʿArabī cites the Qur'anic commentators as saying that the Qur'an descended all at once in its totality to the nearest heaven and from there to the heart of Muhammad intermittently, in fragmented form.[162] In this he follows Ibn ʿAbbās, who claimed: 'The Qur'an was sent down all at once to the heaven of this world, and then God, Exalted is He, sent it down to the Prophet in instalments of five verses at a time, or more or less than this. ... The Qur'an did not come down in one month or two, nor in a year or two; the time between the first revelation and the last was twenty

159. *Tarjumān*, pp.61, 127.
160. See Introduction, pp. 18–23.
161. See Translation, n.137.
162. The word used is *nujūman*, which is also the word employed for stars and grasses.

years, or as [many] as God willed.'[163] Its piecemeal descent in its guise as *furqān* (usually translated as 'Criterion' or 'Discriminator') seems to be at variance with later statements in the same paragraph which say that it descends all at once to the heart and that Muhammad already possessed the Qur'an in its totality before the angel Gabriel told him to recite it. For that reason, he was told not to hasten in its coming (see also Q.20:114).

In the *Futūḥāt*, Ibn ʿArabī says:

> We know by way of unveiling that the *furqān* was attained by the Messenger of God – God's blessings and peace be upon him – as an undifferentiated Qur'an (*qurʾān mujmal*), not separated into verses and sūras. For that reason, he would hasten its coming when Gabriel descended to him with it in a *furqān*. It was said to him: 'Do not hasten the coming of the Qur'an' (Q.20:114), which you know [already], so that you would receive it as undifferentiated and it would not be understood from you 'before its revelation has been completed' (Q.20:114) as a *furqān*. 'And say: My Lord, increase me in knowledge' (Q.20:114) in the detailing of the meanings that You brought together in me.' [The Real] has alluded to certain secrets, saying: 'Lo! We revealed it on a [blessed] night' (Q.44:3). He did not say 'some of it'. Then He said: 'In which every wise command is made clear' (Q.44:4) – this is the revelation of the *furqān*, which is the other of the two faces.[164]

There is, in fact, no discrepancy between possessing the whole and receiving the parts. In many places scattered throughout the *Futūḥāt*, and indeed in several places of the *Isfār*, the idea of the perfect servant's embodiment of the entire Qur'an is presented. Because of the complete receptivity of some hearts, the Qur'an descends upon them not as words or even meanings but as tasting (*dhawq*). This was the case of Muhammad, of whom his wife ʿĀ'isha said: 'His character was the Qur'an', as well as that of Abū Yazīd al-Bisṭamī, Sahl al-Tustarī and others. It is a principle also exemplified later on in the

163. *Tafsīr al-Tustarī*, p.5.
164. *Fut.*I.83 (Chap. 2).

Isfār when the Shaykh tells the student who was expecting verbal elucidation of a spiritual text to 'Read me!'[165] Those who manifest the qualities of utter humility, whose hearts never lift their heads from prostration, are Qur'ans. This is whether they have actually memorized every word of the text or not, indeed whether they even understand the Arabic language!

> If the Qur'an descends upon the heart, it brings comprehension with it: the being in question understands that which is being recited even if he does not understand the language of the Revelation; he knows the significance of that which is being recited even if the meaning that the words have outside of the Qur'an are unknown because they do not exist in his own language; he knows what these words mean in his recitation, and at the very moment that they are being recited.[166]

These people are said to know the 'inimitability of the Qur'an' – said to be the 'Speech of the Real' – and to be among the 'unlettered' (*ummiyyīn*),[167] even if they can read and write. They receive this knowledge as a divine gift.[168]

> In our opinion, being unlettered (*ummiya*) is not incompatible with memorizing the Qur'an or memorizing prophetic reports; but for us, being unlettered [applies to] someone who turns away from his reflective speculation and rational judgement in deducing meanings and secrets that [the Qur'an and hadith] contain, [rejecting] what rational proofs give him regarding knowledge of divine things and what juristic proofs, analogies and causal explanations give to the legal scholars who use independent reasoning (*mujtahidīn*) regarding the determinations of the Law.
>
> When the heart is safe from the knowledge of reflective speculation, with respect to Law and reason, it is 'unlettered' and is

165. *Isfār*, Para. 63.
166. *Fut.*III.93–4 (Chap. 325).
167. This epithet was given to the Prophet Muhammad: 'It is He who has raised up from among the unlettered people a Messenger from among them' (Q.62:2).
168. *Fut.*I.227 (Chap. 37).

> receptive to the divine opening in the most perfect way possible – quickly, without any tardiness. [The heart] is provided with knowledge from God (*ladunī*) of everything, whose measure no one knows except for a prophet or one of the saints who has tasted it.[169]

Since the Human Being is a *qur'ān*, he brings together all good things, which is the first stage of revelation.[170] This stage is connected with courtesy, just as Muhammad refrained from hastening the coming of the Qur'an, which he already possessed, out of courtesy. Ibn 'Arabī, with his typical fascination with etymology, claims: 'Courtesy (*adab*) is derived from 'banquet' (*ma'daba*), which is to come together for food. Likewise courtesy is to bring together all good.'[171] The best that the human being can gather in his lifetime is knowledge of the Divine Names and the assumption of their praiseworthy character traits. The second stage of revelation is one of *furqān*: 'Having united you with Him through the Qur'an, He then "discriminates" you, such that you are distinguished from Him by means of the "Discriminatory" Book.'[172] The individual thus contains a host of opposing attributes and diverse properties while nonetheless remaining one in essence.

Even if people may not be prophets or messengers, what they receive is nonetheless revelation: 'Whoever has learned the Qur'an by heart, prophecy has entered between his two sides',[173] unlike the Prophet, who received the revelation in his heart. Because of this, Ibn 'Arabī says, 'our prophecy is veiled from us, despite our being a locus for it'.[174]

As an appendix to this voyage of the Qur'an, Ibn 'Arabī inserts a 'section' [Paragraph 21], that, by its being set apart at the end of the chapters dealing with cosmological and revelatory voyages and

169. *Fut.*II.644 (Chap. 289).
170. See *Fut.*II.640 (Chap. 288).
171. Ibid.
172. *Fut.*I.629 (Chap. 71).
173. Prophetic tradition, cited by Ibn 'Arabī in *Fut.*II.194 (Chap. 110).
174. Ibid.

before the chapters devoted to Muhammad's Voyage of Vision and the voyages of the various prophets, suggests that this may indeed be the focal point of the entire treatise. In it, we find an echo of what was mentioned above: the Universal Human Being is not said to be <u>like</u> the Qur'an but is said to <u>be</u> the Qur'an that descends from himself to the Presence of the One who brought him into existence. And he is the 'Blessed Night' on which it was revealed.

The Voyage of the Vision in the [Outer] Signs and Inner Signification [Paras. 22–5]

> Glory be to Him, who carried His servant by night from the Inviolable Place of Prostration to the Far Distant Place of Prostration, the neighbourhood whereof We have blessed, that We might show him of Our signs! (Q.17:1)

In this section, Ibn 'Arabī gives a word-by-word exegesis of the first verse of Sura 17 (*Banī Isrā'īl*, or *al-Isrā'*). M. Chodkiewicz calls this the most important bridge leading to our essential reality.[175] The central theme of the work, alluded to in the preceding section, can be seen here. The linguistic ambiguity of this verse's pronouns 'He/he' and 'We/Our' – a verse which mentions neither the Divine Name 'Allah' nor refers directly to the Prophet Muhammad – becomes the underlying motif of this paragraph. It begins with the Shaykh's cryptic opening poem, with its end-rhyme in the letter *hā'*, sign of the third person singular 'H/he'. Grammatically, this pronoun is marked with the vowel *kasra* indicating the brokenness, lowering and debasement ascribed to the servant by nature as well as the descent/condescension of the Most High to the level of the servant to bestow upon him mercy and revelation. It is a clear example of what occurs in the *munāzalāt* (mutual waystations) of the Qur'anic pathway, as the servant and Lord meet and assume each other's attributes while

175. Chodkiewicz, 'Endless Voyage', p. 82.

remaining servant and Lord.[176] These motifs are developed as the Shaykh explains the verse's exegesis.

Suffice it to say that the *isrāʾ* and *miʿrāj* were topics that Ibn ʿArabī dealt with quite often, with reference to the Prophet's Night Journey/Ascent and his own mystical ascents in imitation of the Prophet.[177] Ibn ʿArabī holds the position that Muhammad's experience as recounted in Suras 17 and 53 was both spiritual and physical while for his mystical imitators it was spiritual alone.[178]

Following the Shaykh's example, we will discuss below the individual components of this key verse.

Glorification

The Qurʾanic verse begins with the exclamation: *Subḥāna-Allāh*, glorified be God. The word *subḥāna* comes from the root *s-b-ḥ*. It is mentioned forty-one times in the Qurʾan.[179] As a *dhikr* it has different ramifications and benefits attendant to each mention.[180] Every creature in the universe glorifies God with praise in its own language (see Q.17:44), even if it is not understood by other creatures; it is both 'law' and 'natural disposition' for all existing things.[181]

The connection of glorification with the Night Journey, as explicitly stated in Q.17:1, found one of its earliest interpreters in Ibn Farghānī (Wāsiṭī) (d. 932), a companion of the more famous Sufis Junayd and al-Nurī. Concentrating on this word *subḥāna*, Wāsiṭī writes (as quoted by Sulamī): '[God] distanced Himself from anyone [else] having a movement or thought in sending out His Prophet – peace and blessings upon him – who would thus be a partner in the

176. See our previous discussion, p. 191.

177. See *Fut.*, Chaps. 167 and 367.

178. *Fut.*III.342 (Chap. 367).

179. The root *s-b-ḥ* also has to do with swimming or floating. The stars are often described as 'floating' in their spheres.

180. See *Fut.*IV.92ff. (Chap. 466) for a description of the Pole whose invocation is '*subḥān Allāh*'.

181. See *Fut.*II.672 (Chap. 294), IV.92 (Chap. 465).

night journey and the sending out.'[182] Other commentators, such as al-Ṭabarī (d. 923), also associate the word *subḥāna* with the notion of *tanzīh*. As F. Colby explains, with the word *subḥāna*, 'God distanc[es] Himself (*nazzaha nafsahu*) from any human conception.'[183] The thrust of the argument is that God alone was the agent of Muhammad's Voyage. It was not undertaken by God's Messenger as an act of individual will, and although secondary intermediaries were involved – Gabriel, Burāq, the *rafraf*[184] – God alone 'caused His servant to journey by night'.

Ibn ʿArabī defines glorification as 'declaring the incomparability (*tanzīh*) of the "Lord of inaccessibility above what they describe"' (Q.37:180), which 'requires that true knowledge of Him cannot be attained'.[185] Even the Names of God by which He describes Himself are excluded from the servant's glorification.

> Glorification is a declaration of incomparability. It is not a laudation through a positive quality. He cannot be lauded except through what is worthy of Him. But that which belongs to Him is not shared in common with anything. He can only be lauded through His Names, but every one of His Names known to us is assumed by the servant as his own trait (*takhalluq*).[186]

It demands a form of negative theology so extreme in its denial of any relationship of the Real to the temporally originated that it 'gives eminence to nonexistence', which is 'better at making known what is worthy of God'. Indeed the Shaykh concludes this passage with a statement shocking for its paradoxical formulation: 'nothing other than God makes God known with greater knowledge than does absolute nonexistence.'[187]

182. Colby, *Subtleties of the Ascension*, p. 33.
183. Ibid.
184. A kind of litter or cushion.
185. *Fut.*II.580 (Chap. 272). See also *Fut.*II.672 (Chap. 294).
186. *Fut.*III.148 (Chap. 338).
187. *Fut.*II.672 (Chap. 294).

A further remark may be made about transcendence of all similitude which opens up a link with the preceding chapter on the Voyage of Creation. In his subsection on the Divine Names in the *Futūḥāt*, considerable attention is given to the special properties of the Divine Name *al-Badīʿ*, the Originator. The Originator creates what has no likeness and there is nothing that is an exact likeness of any other thing, even if they may share certain properties. Even something as similar as the person's own reflection in a mirror is not an exact likeness. Thus every existing thing has a certain *tanzīh*.

But *tanzīh* implies distance; and God has described Himself as being closer to His servant than his jugular vein. Thus there is a counterpart to *tanzīh* in *tashbīh*, making (God) similar. God Himself makes Himself similar to His servants by taking on their attributes, even attributes of illness, as He states in the *ḥadīth qudsī*: 'I was sick and you did not visit Me; I was hungry and you did not feed Me; I was thirsty and you did not give Me to drink.'[188]

Thus by evoking the word '*subḥāna*', the ultimate inimitability of what is Singular is proclaimed while simultaneously setting the stage for its opposite: *Nothing is as H/his likeness, and H/he is the hearing, the seeing* (Q.42:11).

Carried

They will come to thee on foot and on every kind of camel, lean on account of journeys through deep and distant mountain highways (Q.22:27).

That the Prophet was <u>made</u> to voyage – in effect, he was carried – is an indication that the Prophet did not voyage of his own accord or initiative but was taken by God for a purpose: so that God could show him some of His signs, 'on the horizon and in himself'. It is a gift (not earned) and a solicitude on God's part towards his faithful servant. Muhammad was carried upon Burāq during his Night

188. *Ḥadīth qudsī*, narrated on the authority of Abū Hurayra and related by Muslim. See Hirtenstein and Notcutt, *Divine Sayings*, p.93. Also found in the New Testament Gospels, Matt. 25:41–5.

Journey; then he was carried closer to the divine presence by the *rafraf*. The Shaykh says:

> The temporally originated thing does not exist independently .... It must be carried. For this reason, the Messenger was taken on his Night Journey only upon Burāq, since the Night Journey was corporeal, sensed. If it were an imaginary Night Journey that could be interpreted as a vision, he would have either seen himself carried upon a mount or not carried upon a mount. But he knew that he was carried in the form in which he saw himself, since we know that his body was upon his bed and in his house asleep.[189]

Messengers, saints and believers are carried and know they are carried. In reality, as Ibn ʿArabī says, everything is carried. Nothing moves independently but not everyone knows that. The Prophet being carried in his corporeal form demonstrates his complete servitude in both soul and body. This is in stark opposition to ʿĀ'isha's claim that it was a vision and did not take place as a physical event. As M. Chodkiewicz points out, 'His body has already, in this world, acquired the privileges of the glorious body of the resurrected.'[190]

In Chapter 36 of the *Futūḥāt* Ibn ʿArabī writes about Muhammad being carried 'like a camel-rider' and asserts that the one who is carried is higher than the one who is not carried.[191] Drawing an analogy between Muhammad being carried by Burāq and the *rafraf* with the Divine Throne that is also carried, he claims that this being carried is a state of 'rest, glory and might' for the one carried.[192]

The 'camel-riders' are an elite group among the people of God, described in several chapters of the *Futūḥāt*.[193] These are folk one group of whom 'ride the camels of deeds in the dark night'[194] and the other group who ride the camels of effective spiritual power (*himma*).

189. *Fut.*IV.9 (Chap. 407).
190. Chodkiewicz, 'Endless Voyage', p. 83.
191. *Fut.*I.226 (Chap. 36).
192. Ibid.
193. Chaps. 30–2.
194. *Fut.*I.199 (Chap. 30).

They traverse great distances in the spiritual world without moving of their own accord in any way. When they are commanded, they move. When they are not commanded, they stay still. Also described as solitaries (*afrād*), they possess a knowledge so esoteric that both the fourth caliph/first imam ʿAlī and Ibn ʿAbbās, the companion of the Prophet, feared that were it to be revealed their lives would be in danger. Khiḍr is one of their number and it was he who taught Moses courtesy regarding what Moses had no knowledge of. Their constant invocation is: 'There is no power or strength save in God', which plays the part of their mount, and the verse they favour is: *You did not throw when you threw, but God threw* (Q.8:17), the verse of the perfect servant who has no attributes but God's. They are the ones who draw near to God through their supererogatory acts, and when they do, God loves them and safeguards them like sequestered houris in Paradise. They are described with the attributes of 'humility, incapacity, abasement, and weakness',[195] attributes of consummate servanthood.

Servant

Although Muhammad's name is not specifically mentioned in the relevant passage of the Qur'an, there was no question in the minds of the exegetes that he was the 'servant' referred to in Sura 17. Ibn ʿArabī emphasizes the 'servant' (*ʿabd*) aspect: Muhammad is not named except as a servant – in other words, he is the servant *par excellence*: 'No one has realized this station to its perfection like the Messenger of God, for he was an utter servant who renounced those states which would have removed him from the level of servanthood.'[196] Although the word suggests humility and lowness, this is in truth a very high station. Servitude (*ʿubūda*) corresponds to the human being's essential root, the reason for his very existence. God says: *I did not create jinn and human beings except to worship/serve*

195. *Fut.*I.202 (Chap. 31).
196. *Fut.*II.214 (Chap.130).

(*li-yaʿbudūn*) *[Me]* (Q.51:56) and, as Ibn ʿArabī says, explaining this verse: '… worship is a real name belonging to the servant, since it is his essence, his homeland, his state, his entity, his self, his reality, and his face.'[197]

Muhammad is the servant of the most transcendent/incomparable 'He' as well as the servant of the All-comprehensive Name 'Allah':

> God bears witness that he was a servant of Him both with respect to His He-ness and His All-comprehensive Name [= Allah]. He says concerning His Name: 'When *the servant of Allah* stood calling on Him' (Q.72:19); and He says concerning His He-ness: 'Glorified be He who carried *His servant* by night' (Q.17:1). So 'He' carried him by night as a servant.[198]

> The highest of waystations with God is for God to preserve His servant in the constant contemplation of his own servanthood, whether or not He has conferred upon him any of the lordly robes. This is the most eminent of waystations given to a servant. It is indicated in His words … .'Glorified be He who carried His servant by night' (Q.17:1). Note how He conjoined 'His servant' with the declaration of incomparability (*tanzīh*) [through the term 'glorification']. In this station, one of the lovers said:
>
> Address me not save with 'O her servant!'
> For that is the most eminent of my names.[199]

197. *Fut.*II.153 (Chap. 80).
198. *Fut.*II.214 (Chap.130). Emphasis mine.
199. *Fut.*III.32 (Chap. 308).

Night

Ibn ʿArabī notes that there is really no need to mention that the voyage was made at night since the word *isrā'* already includes the meaning of 'night'. So the 'repetition' of 'night' must perform some function or it would not be there. He gives several explanations for the emphasis.

First reason: to show that it was not Muhammad's spirit alone that went on the voyage as is the case with non-prophets. Ibn ʿArabī makes a grammatical point: since the additional qualifier 'at night' is not needed, time is not what is intended, rather the qualification pertains to the state/condition/circumstance of the servant. The body is equivalent to night.[200]

Second reason: night is the time for lovers, for being alone together and engaging in intimate conversation and prayer. Ibn ʿArabī has devoted many passages in the *Futūḥāt* to the special qualities of night and its 'folk', including an entire chapter – one of the Shaykh's most beautiful passages – devoted to these people who rise to pray while others sleep.[201] They are the people of revelation's descent, aspiration's ascent and constant roaming in the company of their Lord. In his chapter on the Secrets of Prayer, he notes that:

> [Night prayer] is the prayer of the lovers, the folk of secrets and abstruse knowledge, those sheltered by the veils. God gives them knowledges appropriate to this moment in the world. This is the moment of the ascents of the prophets, the messengers, and the mortal human spirits so as to see the imaginal signs of God and to gain spiritual nearness. It is also the moment when God descends from the station of Sitting [upon the Throne] to the heaven closest to us for the sake of those who seek forgiveness, repent, ask and supplicate. So it is an eminent moment.[202]

200. See also our Commentary on Noah, pp.225–6.
201. *Fut.*, Chap. 41. See Shamash, 'People of the Night'.
202. *Fut.*I.395 (Chap. 69), trans. Chittick, *SDG*, p.264, with slight modification.

Third reason: so that the extraordinary lights and signs would be more amazing to the viewer. If all this had taken place during the day, it would have been normal (light being a quality that belongs to day).

In fact, night plays an extraordinary role both in the *Isfār* and in Ibn ʿArabī's thought in general. It was on the Blessed Night of Power (*Laylat al-Qadr*) that the Qurʾan was revealed to Muhammad. It was at night that Muhammad made his *isrāʾ* and *miʿrāj*. It is in the last third of the night that the Lord descends to the Lowest Heaven. The *witr* (odd-numbered) prayer is often done at night during the night-vigil prayer (*tahajjud*). There are chapters in the *Futūḥāt* dedicated to those who spend the night in prayer (*al-mutahajjidīn*),[203] vigil, to people of the night and so forth.[204]

The Particle *bi-*

Ibn ʿArabī's attention to Arabic prepositions is a fascinating subject that really should have an entire study devoted to it. We have already seen the importance of prepositions for defining the three kinds of voyages. Examples abound in the *Futūḥāt*: The six particles: *fī*, *maʿa*, *ʿalā*, *bi-*, *min* and *ʿan*, connected to patience;[205] the definition of divine audition (*samāʿ*) as 'listening from (*min*) everything and in (*fī*) everything, and with (*bi*) everything.'[206] Jealousy in the Path of God is: 'for (*li-*) God, with (*bi-*) God, or from (*min*) God. Jealousy upon (*ʿalā*) God is impossible.'[207] Fear in one of the *Isfār*'s poems is from (*min*) God on account of (*ʿan*) God. The lights of Self-Disclosure include lights we run with, lights we run to, lights we run from and lights that are before us.[208] These are just a few examples among many.

203. Chap. 18.
204. See also *Fut.*I.394ff. (Chap. 69).
205. *Fut.*II.207 (Chap. 124). See also al-Ḥabashī, *K. al-inbāh*, pp.10–36.
206. *Fut.*II.367 (Chap. 182).
207. *Fut.*II.244 (Chap. 150).
208. *Fut.*II.485 (Chap. 206).

The particle *bi-* is an especially pregnant one for Ibn ʿArabī.[209] In the *Futūḥāt*'s Chapter 2, On the Letters, the Shaykh claims that particles and verbs consisting of one letter belong to the world of the angels and jinn – that is, to the realm of the inner dimension.

When the particle *bi-* is used in Arabic, it places the subject it is attached to – and it is always attached, never independent – into the genitive case, *khafḍ* (literally: 'lowering'), which normally requires the vocalization of the noun with the short vowel *kasra* (= '-i'), for example: *asrā bi-ʿabdi-hi*. The Arabic root *k-s-r* carries the basic meaning of 'brokenness', a quality that the Shaykh associates with the utter dejection resultant from the poverty and neediness of the servant. Hence the two words associated in Arabic with the genitive case also allude to what is humble, dependent and broken-hearted. God is said to be with those whose hearts are broken.[210]

Two Mosques

As in the case of the nameless 'servant' of this verse, the two mosques – the Sacred Mosque and the Furthest Mosque – are also not identified, and in interpreting where these mosques were, exegetes were

209. Perhaps there are no other particles as pregnant with significance as *bi-* and *li-*. Their mystical interrelation was already part of the Sufi lexicon at the time of al-Sulamī (d.1021), as he shows in his collection of Sufi traditions on the Prophet's Ascension: 'One of them said, 'When on the ascension the Prophet said, "I am with you (*bi-ka*)," the answer on the part of the Real was, "If you are with me, I am for you (*laka*)," since the [letters] L and B alternate with each other. One whose attribute is L, his description is B.' Colby, *Subtleties of Ascension*, p.92. See also Hirtenstein, *Four Pillars*, pp.19, 29–30: '[The people of the letter *Bā'*] Ibn ʿArabī calls people of wisdom and gnosis, who know that God is the tongue by which they praise Him, the hand with which they take and so on; [the people of the letter *Lām*] are people of authority and true knowledge, who know that God praises Himself by their tongue, that God Himself takes with their hand and so on. ... [B]oth these groups have realized servanthood, their utter indigence before God, but it is only the second, the people of *Lām*, who have penetrated to the fullest condition of realization – for they have relinquished the illusion of possessing not just their qualities and powers but even their very selfhood. They know who and what they truly are' (p.19). Moses' meeting with his Lord can perhaps be seen as his transition from being a man of the letter *bā'* to being a man of the letter *lām*. See our Commentary on Moses' first Voyage.

210. See, for example, *Fut*.II.149 (Chap. 77), III.481 (Chap. 376).

not always unanimous that the one was in Mecca and the other in Jerusalem. Some took the Furthest Mosque to be in the heavens. Most who took the *isrāʾ* to be from Mecca to Jerusalem – and they were in the majority – saw the first part of the narrative to be a horizontal movement: from one geographical locale to another, as opposed to *miʿrāj*, which ascends and which interpreters connected with the allusive verses of Qurʾan 53.

Masjid is a place name, the place where an action takes place, in this case prostration, the most excellent movement of prayer. Prostration is the servant's placing his face on the earth, which is the lowest element in creation and it is the stuff that Adam was made from.

The prostration of the heart was first associated with the Sufi Sahl al-Tustarī, who was shocked to discover that his heart, once it prostrated itself, never again arose. This is the true prostration of the gnostic. Even if he appears to raise his face from the ground, his heart remains prostrate.[211] Heart, says Ibn ʿArabī, is from the hidden dimension, face from the manifest one, hence the true gnostic does not raise his 'face' either, since that is a 'forgetting of God in things', neglecting to acknowledge God's presence in the manifest world. The true gnostic, like the first caliph Abū Bakr, does not see anything but that he sees God before it.[212]

The cosmos, with the exception of human beings and jinn,[213] is itself in continual prostration and did not need to be reminded that it was created to worship and serve God.

211. See *Fut.*III.302 (Chap. 362).

212. See *Fut.*IV.7 (Chap. 405).

213. Jinn are often interpreted by Ibn ʿArabī to be the hidden dimension of the human being as well as angels and 'genies'.

In the *Isfār*, the two mosques are given symbolic expression connected with their names 'inviolable' and 'distant'. Both are associated with the idea of servanthood, the first in preserving the utter transcendent holiness of the Godhead by adhering to the absolute root of nonexistence, and the second in distancing oneself from all attributes of lordship. This results in a concurrent raising and lowering of the servant: God's causing him to ascend brings about a certain likeness based, paradoxically, on the very stripping away of all likenesses: *Nothing is as His likeness* (Q.42:11) and nothing is as his likeness either! At the same time, this ascent brings about for the servant an even deeper descent into his roots of lowliness and dependence upon God. The true servant essentially has nothing to do with lordly attributes of might, independence and domination.

He/he

He is God; there is no god but He (Q.59:23).
So He began and ended with the He-ness.[214]

The *huwiyya*, He/he-ness, or, to give it its Latinized form, Ipseity, is an obscure and controversial topic. In Islamic spirituality, the third person singular pronoun (*ghā'ib* = 'absent') stands for a metaphysical principle of the Divinity at a level of Its own inner and completely concealed Self-Consciousness, 'before' the manifestation of the Divine Names and Attributes, 'before' the creation of all that exists. Indeed, it is on the exhalation of the All-Merciful *Hū*,[215] the relief from the cosmic constriction of nonexistence, that all that comes to exist is breathed into existence. For that reason, *Hū* is the highest of all *dhikr*s.[216]

The '*huwa*' contains the power of all the letters since it embraces the totality of the points of vocal articulation, beginning with the *hā'*, the nearly silent, hence 'weakest' first letter, and ending with

214. *Fut.*I.104 (Chap. 5).

215. The abbreviated pronunciation of *huwa*, emphasizing the long 'u' sound, used primarily in the *dhikr*, or invocation of God. They are spelled the same way.

216. See *Fut.*I.104 (Chap. 5).

the *wāw*, the final, most powerful of all letters, itself said to combine all the other letters.[217] 'Thus the He-ness/Ipseity (*huwiyya*) is the greatest of things in terms of effectiveness.'[218]

The Divine Name '*Huwa*' is even more inclusive than the comprehensive Name 'Allah', since it is indefinite enough to include all things that can be designated as him or it, whether existing or not existing – even the Name 'Allah'.[219]

The '*huwa huwa*' – 'H/he is h/He' or 'it is it': a perfect tautology, a complete S/self-Identification. In philosophical discourse this is what it connotes. In mysticism, however, as L. Massignon has indicated, it defines 'the state of the saint whose perfect personal unity testifies to divine unity in the world'.[220] Perhaps it can be best expressed by the hadith regarding God's friends, 'when they are seen, God is remembered.'[221] What is customarily hidden – the Real – is now manifest while what is usually apparent – the individual – is now absent. To paraphrase the Beatles: the inside is out while the outside is in. The paradox, however, lies in the fact that God has no likeness and cannot be seen. Thus what one is seeing is the H/he-not H/he.

In the *Isfār*, as well as in other places, Ibn 'Arabī stresses the fact that in Arabic the third person pronoun 'he' is known as the *ḍamīr al-ghayb*,[222] representing the absent or concealed individual.[223] He then takes this notion one step further by alluding to the *ghayb al-ghayb*, the unseen of the unseen; the H/he concealed within the he/He. This is the 'place' of the intimate night conversation, of that special 'mouth-to-mouth' discourse the Shaykh calls '*fahwāniyya*':[224] 'It is the address

217. *Fut.*II.395 (Chap. 198).

218. Ibid.

219. See *Fut.*III.514 (Chap. 382).

220. Massignon, 'Huwa Huwa'.

221. Ibn Māja, *Sunan*, *zuhd* 3: 'The best of you are those who, when they are seen, God is remembered.'

222. It should be noted that *ḍamīr* itself comes from a root (*ḍ-m-r*) that has connotations of secrecy, hiddenness, concealment.

223. See, for example, *Fut.*II.301 (Chap. 177), III.195 (Chap. 347).

224. See Elmore, 'Recent Editions', p.365, n.24: 'The term, *fahwānīya*, is cognate with *fūh* (mouth), which was chosen by Ibn al-'Arabī to represent this notion, I would suggest, in

of the Real face-to-face (*mukāfaḥa*) in the World of Similitudes. … It is to "worship God as if you see Him."[225] And from this you will know the He (*al-Huwa*).'[226] And how does the Shaykh define this *Huwa*? 'It is the essential Hiddenness (*ghayb*) which cannot be contemplated, for He is neither manifest nor a locus of manifestation.'[227]

When Ibn ʿArabī points out the fact that in this Qurʾanic verse it is the 'He' that carries His servant, he draws attention to the utterly transcendent and hidden Godhead who initiates this voyage, not the synthetic Name 'Allah' or any of the Divine Names in particular.

To Make See/to Show

The eye itself can only perceive things that are a mixture of light and dark. When there is too much light, the eye is blinded; when it is completely dark, the eye cannot see anything. There is a light that comes from the eye in the form of visible rays – this is an important thing to note here. If we compare God to Light we both see light and see by/with/because of light. 'By Thy light we see light' (Ps. 36:9). 'The object of vision, which is the Real, is light, while that through which the perceiver perceives Him is light. Hence light becomes included in light. It is as if it returns to the root from which it became manifest. So nothing sees Him but He.'[228]

---

part because of its usage in the well-known phrase describing intimate speech, *fāhu ilā fīya* (literally: 'his mouth next to mine', *mukāfaḥatan*), which reminded him of his very special relationship with Jesus as beloved confidant.'

225. Hadith found in the canonical collections, for example, al-Bukhārī, *Ṣaḥīḥ*, *Tafsīr* Sūra 31:2; *īmān* 37; Muslim, *imān* 1.

226. *Fut.*II.128 (Chap. 73). This and the following quotation come from Ibn ʿArabī's definitions of Sufi technical terms. It is illuminating in connection with this difficult subject to begin with the first technical term defined, secret of secrets, and to continue along the interlocked chain of definitions until one reaches *huwa*. This clarifies to some degree the notions of adornment with the Divine Names and Attributes, servitude vs. servanthood and equivalence (*sawā*), all of which are essential for understanding the relationship between the He and the he.

227. Ibid.

228. *Fut.*III.116 (Chap. 331), trans. Chittick, *SPK*, p.215.

God Himself is *al-Nūr*, the Light. When the Prophet was asked whether he had seen God, he replied: 'I saw Him as light. How should I see light?'[229]

The Qur'an is light. The Perfect Human Being is light.

Signs on the Horizon and in himself

First of all, it is essential to note that the word *āya* in Arabic means both 'sign' and 'Qur'anic verse'. That the Perfect Human Being is a kind of Qur'an – an assemblage, a synthesis of attributes, perceivable and hidden, just as the Qur'an has its clear and obscure verses – makes this analogy even more apposite.

At the most exoteric level of interpretation, the mysterious 'signs' that Muhammad saw during his Night Journey and Ascent are often connected with the equally mysterious visions, such as the Lote Tree of the Limit, described in Q.53:2–18.

In the *Futūḥāt*, Ibn 'Arabī points to the fact that the Night Journey has the intention of making the servant see the signs, as the hadith says, 'not [to make him voyage] to Me, for no place contains Me, and the relation of [all] places to Me is the same. For I am the One whom "the heart of My believing servant encompasses"; so how can he be made to voyage to Me when I am "at him" and "with him wherever he is?" (Q.57:4).'[230] In the *Isfār*, God's purpose in causing His servant to voyage by night is to remove ideas of corporeality, direction and so forth. This is done through the expression *subḥān-Allāh*, discussed above. This phrase declares God above and beyond any ideas of similitude.

Ibn 'Arabī emphasizes that the signs that the servant is made to see first when he is in retreat (*khalwa*) are those of the cosmos. These are then followed by the signs in oneself:

229. Hadith found in Muslim, *Ṣaḥīḥ*, *īmān* 1.291; al-Tirmidhī, *Jāmi'*, *Tafsīr* Sura 53:7.
230. *Fut.*III.340 (Chap. 367).

> The first thing unveiled to the companion of seclusion is the signs of the cosmos. This occurs before the unveiling of the signs of himself, for the cosmos comes before him, as the Most High said: 'We shall show them Our signs upon the horizons' (Q.41:53). Then after this He will show him the signs that he saw in the cosmos as being in himself. Were he to see them first in himself, then in the cosmos, perhaps he would imagine that his self is seen in the cosmos. So God removed this ambiguity from him by placing the vision of the signs in the cosmos first, just as it had occurred in existence, for the cosmos precedes the human being. How should it not precede him when it is his father! Hence the vision of those 'signs that are in the horizons and in himself' make clear to him that 'He is the Real', nothing else (Q.41:53).[231]

The chapter on Adam in the *Fuṣūṣ* has a clear exposition of this notion. In a way, God allows us to gain knowledge of Him not directly but through our knowledge of the macrocosm/world ('signs on the horizon') and microcosm/self ('signs in himself'). The attributes that we see in ourselves, aside from those of utter servanthood, are also ascribed to God; conversely, the Attributes we assign to God – with the exception of those pertaining to His complete Independence and Self-Sufficiency – we also assign to ourselves. 'He describes Himself to us through us. If we witness Him we witness ourselves, and when He sees us He looks on Himself.'[232] Creation as a whole and the human being specifically, he goes on to say, has an inner, spiritual, non-manifest aspect and an outer, material, manifest aspect. God too describes Himself as being Manifest and Non-manifest, Merciful and Wrathful, Beautiful and Awesome, Friend and Avenger. With 'two hands' He fashions His first Man, Adam, thus bequeathing him multiplicity and dynamic opposition. In his non-manifest dimension, the [Perfect] Human Being is 'upon the form' of God; in his manifest dimension, he is 'upon the form' of the cosmos.[233] At this level of knowledge, the signs that we contemplate

231. *Fut.*II.150–1 (Chap. 78).
232. *Fuṣūṣ*, chapter on Adam (trans. Austin, *Bezels*, p.55).
233. See also *Fut.*III.296 (Chap. 361).

on the horizons and in ourselves are polarized into opposites. But at a higher level, Ibn ʿArabī describes the 'secret signs' concealed in the gnostic: presence in absence, intoxication in sobriety, effacement in establishment. In other words, contradictory states, entwined in each other's embrace. All of God's signs, he says, are visible in what God gives or withholds, and all must be received with courtesy and gratitude. Ultimately, 'the knowledge that the gnostics have of Him does not come from seeing exterior and interior signs, since such signs indicate either a being conditioned in an absolute, or an absolute in a conditioned being. The gnostics see Him as the essential identity of all things.'[234]

Blessed

Fi-l-ḥaraka baraka: In movement there is blessing.[235]

The Arabic root here is *b-r-k*, which is not only connected with blessing but also with servanthood as the first form means 'to kneel down'. To kneel down before another is to lower oneself and to express humility. On the Night of Power, the Blessed Night, the Noble Qur'an comes down from its exalted position in the heavens to take form among God's creatures, similar to God's coming down in the last third of the night to listen to and answer prayers. With this movement downward comes restriction and dispersal as well as blessing.

It is a short step from *baraka* to *baraqa* – to shine, to flash, to emit lightning, and another short step to *barqaʿa* – to veil. And who can forget the fabulous flying steed Burāq, who carried the Prophet on his celestial voyage? Rearranging the letters of the original root, we get *rakaba* with all its connotations of mounting, riding, being carried, and the second form verb *rakkaba*, as in 'putting together': *In whatever form He wills, He puts thee together* (*rakkaba*) (Q.82:8).

234. *Fut.*IV.28 (Chap. 420).
235. Arabic proverb.

The inner heart lied not in what it saw (Q.53:11)

The inner heart of the human being is at rest with God and its vision is true beyond dispute. In this way, it can be compared to every instrument that guarantees certainty, such as the eye, unveiling and the true dream. It is only when interpretation oversteps its bounds and adds to direct contemplation of the thing 'as it is in itself' that error creeps in.

> If our unveiling opposes the unveiling of the prophets – peace be upon them – recourse is to be made to the unveiling of the prophets – peace be upon them. We know that a defect has occurred to the possessor of the unveiling through his having added to his unveiling a kind of interpretation (*ta'wīl*) through his unbelief; for he did not halt with his unveiling. [He is] like someone who has a dream-vision, for his unveiling is correct and he reports what he dreams, but the error comes with the interpretation,[236] not in the very thing that he dreamed. Unveiling is never wrong, while the one who speaks (*mutakallim*) about the object indicated (*madlūl*) [can be either] wrong or hit the mark, unless he is informed from God about that.[237]

The inner heart of the Prophet knows only certainty.

Adam: The Voyage of Trial [Paras. 26–31]

The relevant Qur'anic passages pertaining to Adam's 'disobedience' and 'fall' can be found in Q.2:35–8 and 7:19–25. We place the scare-quotes around 'disobedience' and 'fall' for a good reason: according to Ibn ʿArabī, Adam's voyage is only an apparent fall and distancing from God; in actuality, it is a fall that ennobles him. Adam's original state in the Garden is pure unveiling and unhampered satisfaction of desire. It is a state of the felicitous in the afterlife, but it is not

236. Literally: 'crossing over' (*taʿbīr*).
237. *Fut.*III.7 (Chap. 301).

the state that is suited to this world. When God appointed Adam as vicegerent on the earth, He knew that what would complete Adam's configuration as a Perfect Human Being is servanthood and subjection to the law.

The view that Adam's 'fall' was a necessary and ennobling event is also found in the *qiṣaṣ al-anbiyāʾ* literature, as we can see in this passage from Ibn Kathīr:

> Some people believe that the reason why mankind does not dwell in Paradise is that Adam was disobedient and that if it had not been for this sin, we could have been there all along. These are naive fictions because when Allah wanted to create Adam, He said to the angels, 'I shall make a vicegerent on the earth.' He did not say, 'I shall make a vicegerent in Paradise.' Adam's descent on earth, then, was not due to degradation but rather it was dignified descent. Allah knew that Adam and Eve would eat of the tree and descend to earth. He knew that Satan would rape their innocence. That experience was essential for their life on earth; it was a cornerstone of their vicegerency. It was meant to teach Adam, Eve, and their progeny that it was Satan who had caused them to be expelled from Paradise and that the road to Paradise can only be reached by obedience to Allah and enmity to Satan.[238]

This is also Ibn ʿArabī's view. Adam's fall to earth:

> was because of the vicegerency, not as the punishment of sin, because punishment is gained by the manifestation of evil deeds, while election and repentance are gained by the reception of the divine words. Descent remains only for the vicegerency, thus [his] falling is an honour and an ennobling, so that he returns to the next world with the abundant [and] numerous crowd of his sons, the felicitous ones from among the messengers, prophets, saints and believers.[239]

238. Ibn Kathīr, trans. Geme'ah, *Stories of the Prophets*, p. 14.
239. *Fut.*III.50 (Chap. 313).

Adam's – and for that matter, Eve's – 'punishment' for approaching the Tree was to descend to earth in the company of Iblīs.

> [God] said: 'Go down, all of you, from hence' (Q.2:38). ... Adam returned to his root from which he was created, for he was created from earth. God made him descend for the sake of the vicegerency, ... saying: 'Lo! I am about to place a vicegerent in the earth' (Q.2:30). [Adam] was not made to descend as a punishment for what happened. ... Eve was made to descend for the sake of procreation. But Iblīs was made to descend as a punishment, not as a return to his root. For [earth] is not his abode and he was not created from it.[240]

God's Pre-emptive Safeguarding from Sin and Disobedience

In traditional exegetical sources, exegetes struggled with the issue of apparent misbehaviour on the part of the paragons of humanity, the messengers, prophets and friends of God, as recounted in the Holy Writ; and Ibn ʿArabī likewise feels the need to account for such events as the apparent disobedience of Adam in the Qurʾanic narrative. For Ibn ʿArabī, the Perfect Human Being is incapable of disobeying. As controversial as this notion may appear, Ibn ʿArabī claims – with scriptural proof – that certain individuals have been forgiven their sins and acts of apparent disobedience before they have even been committed, and once committed they should not be reproached by the ignorant who are unaware of the Divine Judgement in these cases. Examples are the prophets, the People of the House,[241] certain individuals who have close proximity to God, such as Khiḍr, whose actions were morally repugnant to Moses, and the Muslim combatants at the Battle of Badr.[242] According to a hadith, this pre-emptive forgiveness even applies to the person who stays awake on the Night

240. *Fut.*III.143–4 (Chap. 337).

241. See our Commentary on Para. 63.

242. The Battle of Badr was between the Meccan pagans, said to number 1000, and the Muslims, greatly outnumbered at 319. Angels came to the assistance of the latter, hence the Muslim victory.

of Power.[243] These individuals have, in Ibn ʿArabī's words, experienced 'annihilation from acts of disobedience'.[244] They may 'transgress' because it has been preordained by God's decree (*qaḍāʾ*), but it is accompanied by forgiveness.

> This condition is equivalent to the 'good news' in His saying: 'That Allah may forgive thee thy faults of the past and those to follow' (Q.48:2). He has informed him of the actual sins that are forgiven, so they have no rule and no authority in him. When a time comes for their manifestation, the Name 'the All-Forgiving' accompanies them. Thus sins descend upon the servant and 'the All-Forgiving' veils their authority. So [these sins] are equivalent to someone who is thrown into the fire and is not burned, like Abraham – peace be upon him.[245]

In Chapter 220 of the *Futūḥāt*, such individuals are divided into two types: those who are the subjects of God's pre-eternal solicitude and those who know the divine decree. The first category consists of those who have been told: 'Do what you wish. I have already forgiven you.'[246] Acts which in others are deemed disobedient – and disobedience, says Ibn ʿArabī, is the greatest impurity – are permitted (*mubāḥ*) for these individuals. In the starkest of terms, the Shaykh declares: '[God] permits to them what is forbidden to others.'[247]

Later on in the *Futūḥāt*, Ibn ʿArabī discusses the relation between repentance and pre-eternal forgiveness, again using the Prophetic hadith as his prooftext:

243. See *Fut.*I.661 (Chap. 71).

244. *Fut.*II.512ff. (Chap. 220). See also *Fut.*II.23, 32 (Chap.73), 370 (Chap. 185).

245. *Fut.*I.233 (Chap. 39).

246. See, for example, al-Bukhārī, *Ṣukhā, jihād* 4.52.251; 314. The case involved a presumed hypocrite who assisted the enemy while professing Islam. His life was spared by the Prophet's remark that perhaps God had already forgiven the warriors who fought at Badr.

247. *Fut.*II.513 (Chap. 220).

> The gnostic turns to/repents to God with every breath in all acts issuing from him, with a repentance pertaining to the Law and a repentance pertaining to the Real. Repentance pertaining to the Law is for acts of disobedience while repentance pertaining to the Real involves becoming free from any power and any strength through God's power and strength. The gnostic continues to stand between the two [kinds of] repentance in the life of this world, [which is] the abode of legal prescription, even if he has a divine informing that it has been said to him: 'Do as you wish, I have already forgiven you', for that does not make him abandon his virtuous conduct. But after this informing no repentance pertaining to the Law remains for him, because he [stands] in [the legal categories of] permitted, recommended and obligatory; he has no share in [the legal categories] of disliked or forbidden, for the Law has removed this determination from him in the abode of this world. This has come in the sound report from God in a general sense and regarding the people of Badr in particular.[248]

As for the second group, those who have learned what God has decreed for His creatures,

> [t]hey have seen what has been determined for them: the carrying out of actions issuing from them as actions, not as something prescribed [by Law] for them to do by this or by that [ruling]. That [knowledge] is from the Presence of unadulterated Light, which the people of Kalām call the 'acts of God'. All of them are beautiful. There is no Agent but God and there is no act that is not God's.[249]

248. *Fut.*IV.49–50 (Chap. 437).
249. *Fut.*II.513 (Chap. 220).

Repentance

God is the oft-forgiving, or more literally, the oft-returning. In Chapter 327 of the *Futūḥāt*, Ibn 'Arabī speaks about Surat al-Tawba,

> the *sūra* of the divine return with mercy upon those servants with whom He was wrathful. For it is not an eternal wrath, rather wrath for a time; and God is the Oft-Returning (*al-Tawwāb*). He connected oft-returning to nothing but the All-Merciful in order to bring the objects of His wrath back to mercy or the Judge, in order to impose the period with respect to wrath and its authority in him for a set time. He returns to him with mercy after the completion of the time period.[250]

God turns first. God's turning to Adam in mercy and forgiveness both before and after his 'disobedience' is a foreshadowing of the condition of all humanity.

> Mercy preceded wrath at the first opening of existence, for mercy turned spontaneously to Adam before the punishment for eating of the Tree; then mercy was shown to him after that. So [there were] two mercies [bestowed upon Adam] with wrath in between them. The two mercies will seek to be mingled because they are alike. One will be added to the other and wrath will be made nonexistent between them, as someone said regarding the 'two [instances of] ease with hardship between them.'[251]

Giving the Divine Names Their Due

Islamic mysticism sees a split of Divine Attributes at the level of the Divine Footstool that lies beneath the all-encompassing Throne of Mercy.[252] It is here that polarization in the Names occurs, and we

250. *Fut.*III.100 (Chap. 327).

251. *Fut.*I.112 (Chap. 5). See Q. 94:5–6: 'Verily, with every hardship there is ease. Verily, with every hardship there is ease.'

252. It is much like the kabbalistic division of God's attributes below the all-encompassing *Keter/Ein Sof* into attributes of mercy (*Hesed*) and attributes of strict judgement (*Gevurah*).

find attributes of mildness confronting attributes of severity: the Exalter vs. the Abaser, the Helper vs. the Harmer, the Forgiver vs. the Avenger. There are certain Divine Names that God attributes to Himself that demand counterparts and relationships in this worldly abode. There can be no Lord without vassal; no Forgiver without transgressor. Names associated with God's forgiveness have no sphere of action or meaning without someone in need of forgiveness. Names involving vengeance and severity are pointless unless there are individuals whose actions elicit the manifestation of these Names.

> [The gnostic sees that] universal wisdom demands that the Divine Names be given their rights. And he sees that the Names Oft-Forgiver, All-Forgiver and their sisters have properties only because of disobedience. If no one committed acts of disobedience, some Divine Names would not receive their rights in this abode.[253]

Sin and evil – a result of transgressing God's command – are therefore necessary at this level of creation in order for God's forgiveness to become manifest.

Enoch/Idrīs: The Voyage of Might and Elevation in Place and Degree [Paras. 32–6]

Idrīs, one of the most intriguing figures in Islamic lore, is commonly thought to be equivalent to the biblical Enoch, the great-grandfather of Noah. In Q.21:85–6, he is placed in the company of Ishmael and Dhū al-Kifl as a man of 'constancy and patience ... admitted [to God's] mercy', one of the righteous. Sura 19:56–7, which is the passage that concerns Ibn 'Arabī in the *Isfār*, declares: *And make mention in the Book of Idrīs. Lo! He was a righteous man*[254] *and a prophet; and We raised him to a high position.* Idrīs also appears in numerous hadith recounting the Prophet's *miʿrāj*, most often encountered in

253. *Fut.*II.530 (Chap. 231).

254. Arabic: *ṣiddīq*. May also be translated as 'veracious'.

the fourth and, less commonly, in the second heaven.

Ibn 'Arabī associates Enoch with the art of writing,[255] the sun and Sunday, and the fourth, or middle, cosmic level.[256] He is one of the messengers whom God has kept alive, according to Islamic tradition. He is also one of the four celestial Poles, the other three being Jesus, Ilyās/Elijah and Khiḍr, who share with him the status of deathlessness. As the Pole occupying the central position, he is the 'Pole of the Universe'[257] and the Substitute (*badal*) who preserves the middle clime.[258] As T. Burckhardt points out, he is the 'transcendent', 'divine' man, 'historic prototype' of the spiritually complete human being – a counterpoint to Adam, the 'primordial man'.[259]

Enoch's traits of immortality and his connection with all things solar can both be traced back to Genesis 5: 18–25, where it is said that: 'All the days of Enoch were three hundred and sixty-five years; and Enoch walked with God' – 'walked with God' rather than dying, and the number 365 representing the days of a solar year. In actuality, the Enoch legend can be traced back even further than the Bible, for he bears remarkable similarity to the Akkadian seventh king, who is associated with the sun.

Enoch's invention of writing also has a long history.[260] Found in a plethora of Enochic literature: 1 and 2 Enoch, the Book of Giants, the Book of Jubilees and Merkabah texts, the scribal function attributed to him involved his being raised to the heavens to record both terrestrial and celestial events – astrological, meteorological and calendrical – in diverse languages.[261] Since he is associated with inventing

255. See *Fut.*I.326 (Chap. 67).

256. See *Fut.*I.155 (Chap. 15).

257. See Chodkiewicz, *Seal of the Saints*, pp. 93–4.

258. Ibid. p. 103.

259. *Mystical Astrology*, pp. 31–2.

260. A number of scholars have found parallels between Enoch as scribe and the even more ancient Mesopotamian scribe Nabu. See Orlov, *Enoch-Metatron*, p. 53, n. 57.

261. See, for example, Jubilees 4: 17, where he is said to have been the one who 'learned (the art of) writing, instruction, and wisdom and who wrote down in a book the signs of the sky ...'. VanderKam, *The Book of Jubilees*, cited in Orlov, *Enoch-Metatron*, p. 51. For additional material on Enoch, see VanderKam, *Enoch and the Growth of an Apocalyptic Tradition*, and *Enoch: A Man for All Generations*.

a system of recording speech so that it can be preserved and passed on, Enoch is closely connected with the science of letters, in particular their morphology, which as Ibn ʿArabī points out in numerous places, is not arbitrary. In addition, as the seventh biblical patriarch, he is associated with esoteric knowledge and divine secrets, acquired through visions, angelic conversations and reading celestial tablets.[262] Enoch also appears as a messenger–warner in 1 Enoch 12:3–4, sent to inform of impending divine punishment for the sins committed by the rebellious terrestrial brothers of the celestial watchers.[263]

Two of the most remarkable chapters in the *Fuṣūṣ* have to do with Idrīs and Ilyās (Elias) – Enoch and Elijah – whom the Shaykh conflates while devoting a chapter (Chapters 4 and 22) to each: 'Elias is the same as Idrīs [Enoch], who was a prophet before Noah whom God had raised to a high rank',[264] 'who was then raised up and sent down again [as Elias]. Thus God gave him two missions.'[265] The different meanings of the two similar words *makān* (place) and *makāna* (rank) in relation to Enoch's elevation are fundamental in the *Fuṣūṣ*' Chapter on Enoch, while of less importance in the *Isfār*, despite the designation of his voyage as one of being raised to a high place in the heavens and being accorded a high rank with respect to the knowledge he attained.[266]

Enoch/Idrīs also makes several appearances in the *Futūḥāt*. In connection with his being raised to a high rank, Ibn ʿArabī tells us that this is because the sun is the heart of the spheres.[267] The most intriguing mentions come in Chapters 14 and 15, devoted to him under the appellation of 'Healer of Wounds' (*madāwī al-kulūm*).[268]

262. Collins, 'The Sage', p. 345.

263. Orlov, *Enoch-Metatron*.

264. *Fuṣūṣ*, chapter on Elias (trans. Austin, *Bezels*, p. 229). It should be noted also that Robert Graves in *The White Goddess*, p. 143, remarks that the sun god Helios became St. Elias.

265. *Fuṣūṣ*, chapter on Elias (trans. Austin, *Bezels*, p. 229).

266. See also *Fut.*II.386 (Chap. 194).

267. *Fut.*II.170 (Chap. 90).

268. It is perhaps not coincidental that healing was attributed to the Greek god of the sun, Apollo, and his son Asklêpios. In Hermetic lore, Asklêpios is the son of Hermes, and, as noted by René Guenon, there is a connection between the healing powers of Asklêpios and the art of alchemy, the 'spagyric' medicine. See Guenon, 'Hermes'. One should also note

The healing he does seems to be primarily concerned with restoring elemental equilibrium, as an alchemist returns metals to their root as pure gold. He is the Pole who disseminates 'knowledge, wisdom and secrets not contained in any book', including knowledge of the aeon, alchemy, astrology, medicine, measurements, weights, life and death.[269] Like the angel Gabriel and the saint al-Khiḍr, he had the ability to make barren land fertile with his mere footstep.[270] In both the *Futūḥāt* and the *Isfār*, we find the story of Enoch's descent to the earth to instruct disciples in various arts and to inscribe on rocks and stones in order to preserve the ancient wisdom in the face of imminent global catastrophe.

Enoch is associated in the *Isfār* with astrology, one of the ancient arts, and as a bridge to the following chapter, he is credited with predicting the Flood of Noah. In Ibn 'Arabī's opinion, God has deposited ample wisdom in the heavens and indeed much of what occurs on the earth is a result of these secondary causes. Hence astrology has its place and those who eschew its study lose much benefit. There is no harm to religion in studying the stars, if one keeps in mind that God is the One who has *revealed in each heaven its command* (Q.41:12).

Of particular interest in the *Isfār* is the discussion of the opposition of contrary forces on a suprasensible level, which manifest in aversions and conflicts in the terrestrial realm. This, of course, is what we will see in the case of the flood where the conjunction of the planets will result in adverse effects for Noah's generation. Much is made, however, of the idea that, at their essential level, there is no enmity between these forces. The Starless Sphere, or the Heaven of the Zodiacal Towers (*burūj*), is beyond visible form and not subject to time. It is only in the Sphere of the Fixed Stars that forms come to be assigned to the twelve zodiacal signs. It is form that brings

both the linguistic and semantic connections between speech (*kalām*) and wound (*kalm*), which Ibn 'Arabī discusses in *Fut.*I.747 (Chap. 72). Both speech and wound have an effect on the body.

269. *Fut.*I.152 (Chap. 15).

270. *Fut.*I.153 (Chap. 15).

opposition into the picture. Forms include hotness, coldness, wetness and dryness, with heat opposing coldness and wetness opposing dryness. Using the elements of fire, which is hot and dry, and water, which is cold and wet, as an example in the chapter on Noah's voyage that follows this one, Ibn ʿArabī criticizes those who believe they are substances in their own right. For him, these elements are subsumed in the category of Substance: '[T]he Primal Substance is assumed in the case of every form, which, despite the multiplicity and variety of forms, springs in reality from a single substance, its primal substance.'[271] Hence fire and water are not essentially antagonistic and can come together as in the sign of the Furnace (*tannūr*). By extension, other seeming opposites and paradoxical statements can be resolved, as the Shaykh often points out.

Also of interest is the notion of hierarchy and submission as God subjects some to others at every level of creation, and the remark on the part of the Shaykh that there are heavenly affairs that are submitted to us.[272] In reality, even the Divinity is submitted to us since relationship entails dependence. In all of this, one needs to remain aware that the ultimate cause of celestial and terrestrial events is God, not the stars.

Undergirding the discussion of opposition versus coincidentia, hierarchy and submission, is a theme which appears like a leitmotif in all of Ibn ʿArabī's writings: that of unity and diversity. In some places it is tied in with the seeming opposition of both the myriad Divine Names and fixed entities to the singular Essence, or likened to a mirror and its reflections, the facets of a ringstone or the limbs and faculties of an individual body. When speaking of the distinctive zodiacal Towers and their relationship to undivided Reality in the *Isfār*, Ibn ʿArabī no doubt would like his reader to recall that 'the zodiacal Towers are equivalent to the Divine Forms in which the

271. Trans. Austin, *Bezels*, p.153 (chapter on Shuʿayb).

272. Nothing further is said about this in the *Isfār*, but see *Fut*.I.157 (Chap. 15) and *Fuṣuṣ*, chapter on Enoch.

Real appears',[273] and as such do not mar the essential unity and seamless harmony of the One.

Noah: The Voyage of Salvation [Paras. 37–40][274]

The anchors of the perfected one are not fast,
For he has no station in existence to contain him.
His Ark is floating and the wind drives him on.
In every state he is in, God sets his course.[275]

The story of Noah, his Ark, his paired animals and the paradigmatic first universal ecological catastrophe has intrigued countless generations of Jews, Christians and Muslims. Indeed the myth of a flood engulfing the entire earth figures prominently in many cultures, not only the so-named monotheistic ones. We have only to look at the Babylonian Epic of Gilgamesh to find one of the earliest accounts commemorated in literature.

For Jewish commentators, the biblical story of Noah raised questions of why the man was considered righteous when he really is not seen doing anything particularly good and, in fact, although obedient says nothing in response to God's address. The Zohar, for example, claims that Noah's silence was actually what brought about the Flood, called 'the waters of Noah'. Critics note that Noah can in no way be compared to Abraham, who prayed for the wicked in Sodom and Gomorrah, or to Moses, who prayed for his people after the incident of the Golden Calf.[276] In the Qur'an (71:28) this lack of concern for his contemporaries is reflected in Noah's cursing the wicked of his generation, praying only for the righteous, a prayer that backfires on him since his son is among the wicked.

273. *Fut.*II.435 (Chap. 198).

274. Perhaps one of the most intriguing analyses of Ibn 'Arabī's Noah can be found in Gilis, *Les Chatons*.

275. *Fut.*III.216 (Chap. 351).

276. See Zornberg, *The Murmuring Deep*, pp. 50–1.

Christian typologists focused on the Flood as a prefiguration of the End of Days and the Ark as the ark of baptism[277] or a symbol of the Church itself. In Roman Catholic and Eastern Orthodox sources, the Virgin Mary is also sometimes called the Ark of the New and Eternal Covenant, her womb the vessel of salvation.[278]

As literary critic Northrop Frye indicates:

> The Deluge itself is either a demonic image, in the sense of being an image of divine wrath and vengeance, or an image of salvation, depending on whether we look at it from the point of view of Noah and his family or from the point of view of everyone else. ... This episode suggests an additional symbolic dimension to the Deluge story, in fact to water imagery in the Bible in general. The question of what happened to the fish in the Deluge is an old puzzle: in one aspect of the symbolism, the flood has never receded and we are all fish in a symbolically submarine world of illusion. ... Hence both Noah's flood (I Peter 3:21) and the Red Sea crossing (I Corinthians 10:2) are regarded in the New Testament as types of the sacrament of baptism, where the one being baptized is symbolically drowned in the old world and awakens to a new world on the opposite shore. Similarly, there is a dimension of the symbolism in which the redeemed, after the apocalypse, are able to live *in* the water of life, as they now live in the air.[279]

Noah's story is told in seven different suras of the Qur'an: 7:59–64; 10:71–4; 11:25–49; 23:23–31; 26:105–22; 54:9–17; and 71:1–28. This last sura – Sūrat Nūḥ – is named for this prophet, and it is from this sura that Ibn ʿArabī draws most of his prooftexts in the Noah chapter of the *Fuṣūṣ*. In the *Isfār*, however, Ibn ʿArabī, with only one exception, uses the narration found in Sura 11.

In this chapter we will discuss some of the themes constellated in Noah, using the *Futūḥāt* and the *Fuṣūṣ* to fill in the outlines of

277. See 1 Pet. 3:20–1.

278. In this depiction, of course, the notions of the Ark of the Covenant and Noah's Ark are conflated.

279. Frye, *The Great Code*, p. 147.

this complex history. We will find very different interpretations and focuses in Ibn ʿArabī's treatment of Noah.

Noah the First Messenger

Noah is considered the 'second father' among the four 'fathers' of Islam: Muhammad (father of pure spirit), Adam (father of pure body), Noah (father of pure message) and Abraham (father of pure law). Noah is the 'father' who initiated the cycle of messengerhood.[280] Those who preceded him – and here we can mention Adam, his son Seth and Idrīs – were not messengers but prophets and warners whose law was not binding for their people as a whole, only for those who voluntarily submitted to it.

Ibn ʿArabī clarifies the misconception that if a messenger's call comes from his heart, his people will not fail to respond positively.[281] This was not the case with Noah, whose people put their fingers in their ears and covered themselves with their garments, becoming more obdurate than ever in their idol worship in the face of Noah's preaching. The messenger's place is but to deliver the message, no matter who the people are and no matter what their response.

Noah's Folk

Noah's folk receive considerable attention in the *Fuṣūṣ* and the *Futūḥāt*. The first in particular presents an extremely controversial picture of these individuals; indeed it was the chapter on Noah that most offended the 'orthodox' religious scholars and conservative thinkers such as Ibn Taymiyya for its turning Noah's polytheistic folk into gnostics *par excellence*, with global knowledge of God, worshipping Him in every form and manifestation, while Noah clung to a one-sided vision of Reality.[282] In addition, Ibn ʿArabī is accused

280. See *Fut.*III.50 (Chap. 313, On Knowledge of the Waystation of Crying and Lamenting [*naw*], which corresponds to Sūrat Nūḥ (Noah)).

281. See *Fut.*III.51 (Chap. 313).

282. 'Ibn ʿArabi's argument rests on his doctrine of divine manifestations, according to

of suggesting that Noah acted in ignorance, a state unbecoming of a prophet, in that he sought salvation for his unrighteous son while at the same time praying for the destruction of his people.[283] In Sura 11, Noah pleads for the Lord to spare his son, saying: *O my Lord, my son is of my family ... Said He, 'Noah, he is not of thy family; it is a work that is not righteous. Do not ask Me that whereof thou hast no knowledge. I admonish thee, lest thou shouldst be among the ignorant'* (Q.11:46). In the *Futūḥāt*, Ibn 'Arabī gives this as an instance of God teaching Noah courtesy,

> to ask for the unknown on the basis of knowledge. If he knows, and if he is one whose intercession and asking is accepted, then he should ask; but if he does not know, he should not ask. However, a father's mercy and natural, elemental sympathy overcame him, so he employed them other than in their proper place. Hence God let him know that this was an attribute of the ignorant. There cannot be any good with ignorance, just as there cannot be any evil with knowledge.[284]

This passage may be recalled when we turn to the stories of other fathers and sons: Abraham and his sons, and Joseph and Jacob.

In one version of the story, at issue is the imbalance between God's transcendence – or freeing God from any likeness to His creatures (*tanzīh*) – and His immanence – associating Him with others (*tashbīh*). The word in the *Fuṣūṣ* associated with Noah is *subbūḥiyya*, which is connected with ideas of glorification,[285] hence with *tanzīh*, transcendence. Noah's 'mistake' was calling his people to the path of

---

which God appears to the observer in both transcendent and immanent guises. In keeping with this doctrine, to discover the 'true' nature of God and His relationship with the world, the observer must renounce his rational outlook and give himself to the veridical 'direct vision' (*shuhūd*) and intuitive 'direct tasting' (*dhawq*). This new, higher knowledge can only be achieved by the human heart (*qalb*), an Arabic word whose lexical connotations point to 'motion', 'fluctuation' and 'transformation'. Knysh, '"Orthodoxy" and "Heresy" in Medieval Islam', p. 58.

283. See Knysh, *Ibn 'Arabī in the Later Islamic Tradition*, p. 106.

284. *Fut* II.617 (Chap. 281).

285. See our discussion on pp. 192–3 regarding *subḥāna*.

tanzīh, resulting in their engulfment and drowning, since pure *tanzīh* annihilates completely. Unadulterated *tanzīh* obliterates any knowledge of the Creator; this knowledge is possible for the human being only in relation to creation, knowledge of the signs on the horizon and in oneself ('He who knows himself knows his Lord') through the mediation of God's Attributes and Names. In declaring that '*Nothing is as His likeness*' (Q.42:11) and failing to complete the verse with '*and He is the Hearing, the Seeing*', Noah, in this account, places too much weight on God's unmanifest and unapproachable Essence. Although his call involves appeals to the people's outer senses and inner reason, association cannot be avoided. The worshipper of idols is at least aware that he is trying to get close to some aspect of God that is represented by those idols. But the suggestion here is that when Noah's people gave up their idols, they gave up knowledge of God altogether.

When we turn to the *Isfār*, we find an entirely different picture. There is no mention of punishment for the polytheists here, at least not in the first paragraph. It is entirely a cosmic matter. God has decreed a flood that seemingly has nothing to do with wiping out an evil people; it is instead part of the wisdom that God has deposited in the cycles of the heavens and which operates through these secondary causes. Suggested also in terms of cycles is the lunar, Adamic, cycle giving way to the solar, Muhammadan, cycle, in whose *barzakh*ian twilight/dawn – *isfār* – we now live – the last third of the night.

Later in the *Isfār*, when Ibn 'Arabī gives a symbolic interpretation of the Noah story based on personal internal transformation, Noah's people – the mockers – are for the most part internalized as the soul that incites to evil, the inner Satan, the world and the passions. They 'die' flooded by the knowledge that unites all opposites.

Noah's Ark

Noah's voyage is a sea voyage, the most dangerous of all journeys. The picture we get is of a large wooden vessel, tossed about between the teeming waters of the cloud-blackened heavens and the turbulent waters of the dark, unfathomable deep.

'Ark' is variously known in Arabic as *fulk*, *safīna*, *tābūt*, *markab* and *jāriya*.[286] The root *f-l-k* seems to have been associated first with the round whirl of the spindle and later came to be applied to a variety of round things. When the word *fulk* is used for ark or ship, it is typically associated with Noah's Ark because of the Qur'anic employment of this word.[287] In a passage of the *Futūḥāt*, Ibn 'Arabī likens the ark (*fulk*) to the Throne where the All-Merciful sits and claims it is the seat of the Perfect Human Being: 'Since sitting (*istiwā'*) on the Throne is an attribute belonging to the Real, and the human being was created upon His form, He made for him a vessel (*markab*) that He called an ark (*fulk*), just as the Throne is an ark. The ark is the seat (*mustawā*) of the Perfect Human Being.'[288] Although in other works Ibn 'Arabī also uses *fulk* for Noah's Ark, in the *Isfār* he never uses it in connection with Noah, but uses instead *safīna* (see below).

The root *f-l-k* is also associated with *falak*, celestial sphere. This word is used consistently in the *Isfār* with this meaning rather than ark.[289] There is an underlying connection between the turning of the spheres and the vessel that carries Noah to his salvation. Moreover, the *Isfār* appears to draw an implicit relation between Noah carried upon his ark and Enoch circling the heavens in his sphere.

The word *safīna* is used far less frequently in the Qur'an than *fulk*, a total of only four times – three in connection with Moses' sojourn with Khiḍr and only once in connection with Noah (Q.29:15). In

286. See Beneito, 'Ark of Creation', pp.25–7.

287. Used twenty-three times in the Qur'an.

288. *Fut.*III.162 (Chap. 341).

289. He does use it frequently, however, in the *Futūḥāt*, and the epigram heading this section of our commentary uses *fulk* for ark.

the *Isfār*, however, it is this word that is used exclusively in the Noah chapter. It is an open question why Ibn ʿArabī chose *safīna* as opposed to *fulk*. It could be that he is consciously making a distinction between the cases where he wants to associate Noah's voyage with heavenly ascent, such as in the *isrāʾ*,[290] and cases where he wants to emphasize other aspects such as the alchemical aspects of personal purification, and its concern with the elemental rather than the celestial. If this is true, we might note the similarity in sound between the words *safīna* and *ṣāfin* – meaning clear, pure, unadulterated – and see that by permutation of the root letters we get *nafs*, soul.

Tābūt, with the meaning of 'chest', 'trunk', 'ark' and even 'coffin', is used in the Qurʾan for the Ark of the Covenant, containing the *Sakīna* (Hebrew: *Shekhinah*) (Q.2:248). It is also the vessel that Moses' mother put him into in order to escape the fate of the other Israelite infants killed by Pharaoh (Q.20:39). Ibn ʿArabī uses *tābūt* in this sense in his prologue to the *Isfār*. It is not used for Noah's Ark.

Markab is a noun of place related to the root *r-k-b*, which means to convey, carry, ride. Hence it is sometimes used for ships. A cognate of the Hebrew word *merkabah*, the name given to the Chariot described by the Prophet Ezekiel, the Arabic *markab* suggests a variety of vehicles, including the cosmic Throne, the *rafraf* and the celestial steed Burāq of the Prophet's Ascension narrative.[291]

Although the root *j-r-y* is used numerous times in the Qur'an, primarily to refer to the rivers in paradise, only once does it refer to Noah' Ark as *jāriya* (Q.69:11). *Jāriya* carries the basic meaning of a moving or flowing (feminine) object.

The Ark = Body

G. Elmore notes that in the *ʿAnqāʾ Mughrib* 'the human body is apparently likened to Noah's ark adrift on the flood' and cites the following lines from the Shaykh's verse:

290. See Beneito, 'Ark of Creation', pp.25–7.
291. For a fascinating and detailed discussion of this term, see ibid. pp.21–5.

Stirred by a Western Wind laden with the Secrets,
While the Ark's Passenger (as long as it is driven
by the Wind of the Law) is preserved and blessed.[292]

Again, in Chapter 330 of the *Futūḥāt*, we find reference to the Ark as body in an extraordinary poem, based on the saga of Noah's Flood:

Your Ark is your bodies
On the overflowing sea of this world.
You are its riders and you are in danger;
You have no shore except decree and destiny
So beseech and make efforts:
There is no flight from God.[293]

The Ark, like the Cloud, is dark and womb-like, containing within itself the seed of generation until it comes to rest on Mount Jūdī, and its salvaged creatures, male and female, come out of their confinement to 'be fruitful and multiply' (Gen. 1:28).

In one reading of the transfer of the earth from the watery sign of Cancer to the fiery sign of Leo, Noah's earth – his physical form – is to be transferred to the other world, while his spiritual form is to attain salvation because of the preparations in this lifetime that he has made. It is a classic tale of initiatic death and rebirth, as so many interpreters have elucidated. Furthermore, it is a tale of death in life and life in death, two seemingly contradictory states that must be combined, like fire and water.

Alchemy (*al-kīmiyā'*/*'ilm al-ṣan'a*)

The *Isfār*'s paragraphs on Noah's voyage are imbued with alchemical references, such as the *tannūr* and the combination of fire and water. It is an alchemy that is not concerned with transforming base metals

292. 'Flight of the Fabulous Gryphon', p.96.
293. *Fut.*III.116 (Chap. 330).

into gold, except in a symbolic sense, but rather the transmutation of corporeal matter into pure spirit.

The word *'al-tannūr'* in early modern alchemy became *althanor* or the alchemical furnace, the agent of transformation. The Ark is a kind of retort, an alembic, a sealed vessel inside of which opposites – symbolized by the pairs of animals Noah takes with him – mingle to produce a single unity: the offspring of male and female energies and substances.

In terms of Aristotelian physics, the elements of fire and water are completely opposed to each other. Fire is hot and dry, water is cold and wet. Together they comprise the totality of the four natures. Ibn 'Arabī has many discussions of the four elements in his writings, but the passage in Chapter 279 of the *Futūḥāt* is particularly relevant for the coming together of the opposing elements of fire and water. In this chapter, the Shaykh discusses the hierarchy of the elements and how God in His wisdom placed intermediaries between the mutually antagonistic elements fire and water, air and earth. Hence between fire and water comes air. 'So when the Real wanted to transform water into fire, which is a natural repellent, He transformed it first into air then transformed that air into fire. He did not transform the water into fire until He transferred it to the air because of the compatibility.'[294]

The combination of fire and water had particular significance in alchemy.[295] In alchemical parlance, fire and water were equivalent to the active, masculine, rational principle sulphur[296] and the passive, feminine, psychic principle mercury, themselves the product of terrestrial exhalations, one emitted from earth when heated by the

294. *Fut.*II. 609 (Chap. 279).

295. The fire and water motif was also found in Jewish magical/alchemical sources. In Midrash, the word *shamayim* (heavens) was interpreted as consisting of *esh* (fire) and *mayim* (water). Alchemists used the symbol of two intersecting triangles – the six-sided Seal of Solomon or Shield of David – to signify the conjunction of fire and water. See Scholem, *Alchemy and Kabbalah*, p.93. We will return to the symbolism of the Seal of Solomon/Shield of David in connection with Moses' six voyages.

296. Note that the Perfect Human Being is known as the Red Sulphur (= Phoenix/ 'Anqā').

sun, the other cool and moist, under the influence of the moon. The former generated the uncoagulated sulphur component, the latter that of mercury. Sulphur thus was hot and dry, mercury cold and wet. Sulphur in early Greek alchemical texts was known as *theion hudor*,[297] meaning both divine and sulphur water. Mercury itself is sometimes described as igneous water or liquid fire and belongs to the liminal, *barzakhī* world. When it comes under the influence of sulphur, it passes out of its state of potentiality into actuality. The combination of mercury and sulphur causes crystallization to take place, resulting in salt, a symbol of stability, which plays the role of the body to sulphur's intellect and mercury's soul.[298] In the theory of the most prominent Arab alchemist, Jābir b. Ḥayyān,[299] all minerals are composed of these two substances in various degrees of purity and mixture; only gold, produced from pure mercury and pure sulphur, achieves the perfect balance. Hence through a process of purification, reduction, solution and re-composition, base metals could be 'cured' of their 'illnesses' by means of various elixirs and returned to their root of pure gold, gold being both the initial state and the end product.

Ibn ʿArabī, whose writings show more than a passing knowledge of Jabirean alchemy, found the theory eminently applicable to the transformation of the human being, naming one of his chapters in the *Futūḥāt* On Knowledge of the Alchemy of Happiness; 'happiness' with the sense of the ultimate felicity of the blessed.[300] In it, he personifies sulphur (*kibrīt*) and mercury (*zībaq*) as parents of the golden 'child' who may suffer various afflictions due to defects in the parents, compounded by environmental or temporal factors. Ibn ʿArabī takes a short step from here to the Prophetic tradition that

297. 'The name of the chemical solution *theion hudor* (divine water) or *theiou hudor* (sulfur water) is characterised by semantic ambiguity: the term *theion* means both "divine" and "sulfur," and Greek alchemists frequently play on this polysemy.' M. Martelli, 'Divine Water in the Alchemical Writings of Pseudo-Democritus', p. 5. Thanks to Stephen Hirtenstein for this reference.

298. See Guenon, *The Great Triad*.

299. See the incomparable work of Paul Kraus, *Jābir ibn Ḥayyān*.

300. Chap. 167.

the infant is born Muslim and it is the parents who make him or her 'deviate' into Jew, Christian or Zoroastrian.

In the *Isfār* we can see several of these symbols coming into play. In the first case, the earth itself is in a state of imbalance, fluctuation, dominated by water, symbolized by the zodiacal sign of Cancer. A fiery corrective in the form of Leo appears on the horizon. The immediate result is a return to chaos, a dissolution into a kind of liquid fire before the boiling waters subside and stability is achieved.

Analogously, in the human realm, the perfection of the human soul is preceded by a period of chaos in which the various elements dissolve into a black abyss, where the human being cannot survive without the Ark of Salvation, whatever this may symbolize for him. It is a 'dark night of the soul',[301] a 'night sea voyage'[302] that Ibn 'Arabī alludes to in the *Fuṣūṣ*' Chapter on Elias[303] and describes in more detail in his description of his own descent/ascent in the *Futūḥāt*.[304]

In a remarkable passage of the *Isfār*,[305] the Shaykh turns to address the seeker's 'subtle secret', the innermost part of his soul, encouraging this soul to follow the example of Noah. The seeker's 'Ark of Salvation' – symbol here of the human configuration – has been fashioned by God, and its perfecting is carried out under His 'eyes' and through His 'inspiration'. While the people mock – symbolic of everything that can distract the seeker from accomplishing his perfection, including not only worldly concerns, passions, Satan, but the seeker's own soul that commands to evil – the seeker must continue to trust in the signs and in his knowledge of what transformation entails. Distractions – akin to the brigands mentioned previously – must perish as the seeker sets sail as Noah did, accompanied by the *basmalah*: In the Name of Allah, the All-Merciful, the All-Compassionate, the formula that links the absolute abasement of

301. San Juan de la Cruz's '*noche oscura del alma*' (dark night of the soul).

302. 'The night sea journey is a kind of *descensus ad inferos* – a descent into Hades and a journey to the land of ghosts somewhere beyond this world, beyond consciousness, hence an immersion in the unconscious.' Jung, 'The Psychology of the Transference', 16, Para. 455.

303. *Fuṣūṣ*, chapter on Elias (trans. Austin, *Bezels*, p.235).

304. *Fut.*III.343, 345–6 (Chap. 367).

305. *Isfār*, Para. 39.

servitude with the burgeoning of divine generosity, symbolized by the conjunction of the animal pairs.

Thus on the microcosmic level, the transformation that takes place within the individual – Noah being the prototypical model – is a process of uniting the opposites in perfect balance: travelling on the straight path of essential surrender (*islām*), which paradoxically involves a cyclical journey from God to God in God through servanthood; annihilation of what is excessive and illusory – our tendency to assume in our own eyes God's attributes of grandeur – and increasing what is deficient – our lack of knowledge and practical virtue. Thus even if the ideas so prevalent in the Noah chapter of the *Fuṣūṣ* regarding *tanzīh* vs. *tashbīh* are not so much as mentioned in the *Isfār*, one can see that there too the goal is to achieve the perfect balance of the two, the equivalent of Muhammad's 'calling by night during the day and by day during the night',[306] the alchemical equivalent of which is the combining of fire and water in the *tannūr*.

The *Tannūr*

Tannūr is an unusual ancient Semitic word, evidently not Arabic in origin as a number of the early lexicographers noted. It appears in the Hebrew Bible with the meaning of 'oven' and other cooking sources.[307] Although it generally is taken to mean 'oven', 'furnace', 'kiln' or 'cauldron', it is also sometimes translated as 'the surface of the ground', 'the highest part of the ground', 'any place from which water pours forth' and 'the shining of the dawn'. The fourth Caliph and first Imam ʿAlī thus interpreted the Qurʾanic phrase '*fāra al-tannūr*' to mean 'and daybreak rose' or 'rises'.[308] Dawn is a

306. *Fuṣūṣ*, chapter on Noah (trans. Austin, *Bezels*, p. 77).

307. Gen. 15:17; Exod. 7:28; Lev. 2:4, 7:9, 11:35, 26:26; Isa. 31:9; Hos. 7:4, 7:6; 7:7; Mal. 3:19; Ps. 21:10; Lam. 5:10; Neh. 3:11, 12:38. One should note in particular the apocalyptic significance of the *tannūr* in Mal. 3:19. The *tannūr* is the furnace into which the wicked will be thrown. The most influential Andalusian Hebrew grammarian, Ibn Jannāh (d. *c.* 1050), classifies the root as *t-n-r*; *Sefer ha-riqmah*, vol. I, p. 234. I thank Jim Robinson for these references.

308. See Lane, *Lexicon*, vol. 1, pp. 318–19. Ibn ʿArabī is well aware of this meaning of *fāra*

liminal time for Ibn ʿArabī in that it is neither night nor day but an intermediate time partaking of both. For that reason, he believes that the Qurʾanic recitation performed at that time should be loud enough to be heard by the reciter but silent enough not to be heard by anyone else, hence partaking of both sound and silence.[309] The meaning of *fāra al-tannūr* as 'dawn rises' reminds the reader that the word '*asfara*' also has this as one of its meanings.

Ibn ʿAbbas, a prominent companion of the Prophet, reportedly said: 'The *tannūr* is the face of the earth.' Ibn Kathīr amplifies: 'This verse means that the face of the earth became gushing water springs. This continued until the water gushed forth from the *tanānīr*, which are places of fire. Therefore, water even gushed from the places where fire normally would be. This is the opinion of the majority of the *Salaf* (predecessors) and the scholars of the *Khalaf* (later generations).'[310] In some commentaries the *tannūr* is said to have belonged once to Adam.

Ibn ʿArabī performs a significant etymology of his own by deconstructing the word *tannūr* into the letter *tāʾ* and *nūr*. The latter is 'light', but the former has a rather strange association that gives only a clue to the esoteric meaning of this word. The Shaykh connects the *tāʾ* to the first letter of *tamām*, or completion, perfection. But it has an even more apparent association with the grammatical second person. When suffixed to a verb stem, the action indicates 'you', whether singular, plural, masculine or feminine. This is also true of the pronoun itself, if – as some early grammarians believed – the root was the '*an*' of '*anā*' (I) to which the *tāʾ* was added to form the second person pronoun. Thus the *tannūr* can be interpreted as meaning the vessel of your own light, your ship (*safīna* = *s-f-n*) being a permutation of your soul (*nafs* = *n-f-s*).

---

al-tannūr. See *Fut.*I.493 (Chap. 69), 608 (Chap. 71).

309. See *Fut.*I.493 (Chap. 69).

310. *Tafsīr Ibn Kathīr*, p.36.

The *tannūr* is a sign of prophecy. Just exactly how and where this sign became evident is not clear either from the Qur'anic text or the various commentators who have dealt with this narrative. Some commentators claimed that the sign in question appeared when water began to pour out of the oven in Noah's house. In other texts, it is the combination in the Flood of the burning fire and boiling water that is the sign. Ibn 'Arabī makes it clear in the *Isfār* that the sign was not the conjunction, which was something the astrologers of the time could anticipate based on their knowledge of the heavens. The *tannūr* is something else, falling into the category of apparent miracles. Noah is mocked as a lunatic because he takes this sign as reason for action. But what he possesses to counter their 'scientific' knowledge is unveiling, much like the 'Bearers' of the Qur'an who know it by heart despite being 'illiterate' or non-Arabic speakers.

In a sense, Noah himself is the *tannūr*, for he is a sign never before seen in this world. He is the first of God's messengers. As a Perfect Man he combines the balanced opposites of body (water) and spirit (fire).

Astrological Calculations

The Flood is connected with astrological events and instabilities caused by an immanent conjunction involving Cancer, a water sign governed by the moon, and Leo, a fire sign governed by the Sun. This world was created in the sign of Cancer but God wishes to transfer it to the next world, which is in the more stable sign of Leo. Hence the 'conjunction' mentioned by Ibn 'Arabī seems to herald the passing from a lunar, fluctuating state to a solar, fixed one.

Rising and Falling on the Waves of Pride

There is a connection made in the *Futūḥāt* between the turmoil of Noah's voyage by water, the surge and contrapuntal plunge of the waves, and the egomaniacal claims of tyrants and self-aggrandizers, all based on the root *ṭ-gh-w*. The sea is personified here as an entity that lifts itself to heights as the tyrant does, a bellicose enemy of God's friends who find their salvation in an Ark (*safīna*), made of joined planks. When the water abates, the Ark is said to lower itself (*inkasara*), a word we have already encountered in the particle *bi-*, the *kasra*.[311]

Mount Jūdī[312]

It was said: 'O earth, swallow your waters!' and 'O sky, be gone.' So the water disappeared and the matter was concluded. The [Ark] settled on al-Jūdī. (Q.11:44)

Although legend has it that Noah's Ark came to rest on Armenia's Mount Ararat, the Arabic version gives the name as Jabal Jūdī. There were disputes among the Muslim scholars, from exegetes to geographers, as to exactly where it was located, some saying in the Arabian Peninsula, some in various parts of Mesopotamia.

The fact that both Jūdī and *jūd*, generosity, come from the root *j-w-d* made the association of salvation an easy one to make; indeed existence (*wujūd* – from another root but incorporating *jūd* within it) relies on God's generosity. Ibn ʿArabī says in the *Futūḥāt*'s Chapter on the Secrets of Generosity: 'From generosity issues existence (*ʿan al-jūd ṣadara al-wujūd*). *Jawd* is plentiful rain. It is a permutation (*maqlūb*) of *wajada*.'[313]

S. Hirtenstein has pointed out to me the significance of the letter *wāw* being added to the *jūd* of generosity. The *wāw*, as we shall see when we discuss the six voyages of Moses, is a letter of connection, one associated with the Perfect Human Being who brings together the Manifest and Unmanifest realms of existence.

311. See *Fut.*III.57 (Chap. 315).

312. For background, see Brinner, 'Jūdī'; Reynolds, 'A Reflection on Two Qur'anic Words'.

313. *Fut.*II.179 (Chap. 95).

Men upon the Heart of Noah

In the *Futūḥāt*,[314] mention is made of forty individuals who are 'upon the heart of Noah'. Their attribute is constriction and their supplication is Noah's supplication: *God forgive me and my parents, and him who entereth my house believing, and the believing men and the believing women, and increase not the wrong-doers in aught save ruin* (Q.71:28). Their station is the difficult station of religious (*dīniyya*) jealousy, which is connected to the Name 'Lord'.

The fact that these men are limited to forty brings into discussion the significance of the number forty and connects the men on the heart of Noah to the story of Moses' meeting with God on the mountain, which we will discuss later.[315] These men are devoted to the practice of the forty-day retreat, the *arbaʿīn*, as mentioned in the Prophetic hadith: 'Whoever dedicates himself to God for forty mornings, the springs of wisdom appear from his heart upon his tongue.' As Ibn ʿArabī continues in the *Futūḥāt*,

> he is one of the people of conversation *with* God *from* God. The 'morning' is the manifestation of the entity of the servant as a locus of manifestation, not an entity, for the hidden dimension of his entity is in his locus of manifestation, like the hidden dimension of the night when the morning comes to be.[316]

314. *Fut.*II.10 (Chap. 73).
315. See our Commentary on Moses below.
316. *Fut.*II.44 (Chap. 73).

Abraham: The Voyage of Guidance [Paras. 41–3]

... the son is the inner reality of the father, issuing from him and to him returning.[317]

The Sufi is the son of the Moment.[318]

Like Noah and Joseph, Abraham has an entire sura of the Qur'an named after him, Sura 14. He is mentioned numerous times in the Qur'an in various contexts: his smashing the idols of his father and his discovery of the One God; his immunity to the flames of the fiery furnace; his revivification of the four sacrificial birds, with God's permission; his entreaty for the people of Sodom; his prayer for a righteous son[319] and his near-sacrifice of him on the altar. Through all of these trials, Abraham's being 'rightly guided' is a constant refrain.[320]

The narratives concerning Abraham's request for a righteous son, the announcement of his birth, the dream of his son's sacrifice and Abraham's interpretation of it, and the near-sacrifice itself are found in Q.11:69–73; 15:51–6; 37:99–107; and 51:24–30. Sura 37, however, is the only sura used in this chapter of the *Isfār*, as is also the case in the *Fuṣūṣ* in the chapters on Enoch and Isaac. The material dealing with the near-sacrifice is exceedingly ambiguous. In it, Abraham asks for righteous offspring and receives a son, who is not named. But then, responding to what he believes is God's command in a dream-vision, the ever obedient Khalīl Allāh (Intimate Friend of God) prepares to sacrifice him:

> And he said: Lo! I am going unto my Lord who will guide me. My Lord! Vouchsafe me of the righteous [a son]. So We gave him

317. *Fuṣūṣ*, chapter on Seth (trans. Austin, *Bezels*, p.69).

318. Sufi saying. See *Fut.*II.538ff. (Chap. 238), where one of the definitions of the Moment is: 'The Moment is a file that grinds you down but does not efface you.'

319. The name of this son is never mentioned in the Qur'an, thus sometimes he is taken to be Isaac, sometimes Ishmael/Ismā'īl. Ishmael, in fact, receives little attention in the Qur'an, where the focus is upon Isaac, the subject of the good news (*bushrā*) given to Abraham.

320. For example, Q.16:121; 26:78.

> tidings of a gentle son. And when [his son] was old enough to walk with him, [Abraham] said: O my dear son, I have seen in a dream that I must sacrifice thee. So look, what thinkest thou? He said: O my father! Do that which thou art commanded. Allah willing, thou shalt find me of the steadfast. Then, when they had both surrendered [to Allah], and he had flung him down upon his face, We called unto him: O Abraham! Thou hast already fulfilled the vision. Lo! Thus do We reward the good. Lo! That verily was a clear test. Then We ransomed him with a tremendous victim. (Q.37:99–107)

This passage is followed shortly after by the good news of Isaac: *We gave him the good news of Isaac, a prophet, one of the Righteous* (Q.37:112). Hence the implication is that it is only after Abraham has been tested with Ishmael that he is given his second son Isaac. However, since no name is connected with the sacrifice, the question of which son was intended remained a matter of dispute, especially with the earliest commentators.[321]

The near-sacrifice of Abraham's son, whether Isaac or Ishmael,[322] is rarely treated in the *Futūḥāt*[323] although it is one of the themes in the Isaac chapter of the *Fuṣūs*. While there the emphasis is on the dream and Abraham's failure to do the necessary 'crossing over' or interpretation, the *Isfār* adds another element of interest: the question of bestowal (*wahb*) vs. acquisition (*kasb*), which we will discuss below.[324]

321. See Firestone, *Journey in Holy Lands*, pp. 105ff. By around the 10th century, the interpretation that it was Ishmael began to predominate so that today it is almost universally accepted by Muslim exegetes that he was the intended sacrifice. See Firestone, 'Ishmael'.

322. In the *Fuṣūṣ*, the son in question may appear at first glance to be Isaac given the title of the chapter. But, in the text that follows, there is reference only to his unnamed son. In the *Isfār*, he appears to be Ishmael, following the apparent chronology in Q.37:112 of the announcement of Isaac after the narrative of the sacrifice. But again, as in other writings by Ibn 'Arabī, the sacrificial victim is not specifically named. Austin's bracketed addition in his translation of the *Fuṣūṣ*: '[Isaac said to his father], "O Father, do as you are commanded"', stems, perhaps, from an overhasty desire to resolve the ambiguity. See *Bezels*, chapter on Enoch, p. 87. He is not alone in his reckoning that the son in the *Fuṣūṣ* is Isaac. See also Gilis, *Chatons* I, p. 187 and Affifi's Commentary on *Fuṣūṣ*, p. 70.

323. See *Fut.*I.675 (Chap. 72) in which the son is unnamed. The story that follows is a remarkable example of ransom and substitution based on the example of Abraham and his son.

324. A careful perusal of the Seth chapter in the *Fuṣūṣ* contributes much to the

The 'Ethics of Ambiguity'[325] [Para. 41]

It must be said that in the *Isfār*'s account of the sacrifice, the Shaykh preserves and perhaps even increases the ambiguity already found in the Qur'anic passage. Throughout the passage, the victim/offering is referred to only as 'his son'. The first time either son is mentioned by name is when Isaac is associated with the 'good news' that Abraham receives after the trial of the vision-event and near-sacrifice. The first time Ishmael is mentioned, it is to distinguish him from Isaac as combining acquisition and bestowal as opposed to Isaac's pure bestowal.

Ibn ʿArabī then sets up a series of equivalences in the form of substitutions and oppositions within these substitutions. The first opposition is between what is given as a result of supplication and what is given without supplication. It is because of Abraham's supplication for a son, a created being, that he is commanded to make a sacrifice as expiation. Then the notions of acquisition vs. bestowal are brought in, and the sacrificial victim is said to be acquired from the perspective of supplication and bestowed from the aspect of ransom and its equivalent, substitution, because Abraham did not ask for this. It was a free gift.

The notion of substitution (and ransom, as its more extreme form) is a central one in the story of Abraham's sacrifice in both the *Fuṣūṣ* and the *Isfār*, and finds its place in a number of common themes in the Shaykh's writings. Let us begin with Abraham's dream. In the dream Abraham sees the form of his son being sacrificed and takes the dream at face value instead of making the necessary substitution of the ram, which in the dream appears as a human being. The lesson

---

understanding of Abraham's relationship with his sons in connection with the idea of gifts. Adam's third son, Seth, who is a substitute for the murdered Abel, is an example of pure bestowal.

325. This, of course, is the English translation of Simone de Beauvoir's *Pour une morale de l'ambiguïté* in which Abraham makes an appearance in his Kierkegaardian incarnation as a man who lives under the constant weight of ambiguity, the infinite questioning of actions and uncertainty of choice that is emblematic of the ethical sphere. See De Beavoir, *Ethics of Ambiguity*, p. 133.

here is that in nearly all cases, dreams need to be interpreted. The dreamer must 'cross over' and make the required substitutions, as the Prophet did in the case where he substituted knowledge for milk when he dreamed he was offered and drank his fill of the latter. The next substitution is the substitution of Abraham for his son: 'it was as if he himself had been sacrificed, even though he remained alive' (*Isfār*, para. 41). This is followed in time by the substitution of the ram for the son, which was the original intent of the dream. Then there is the substitution of one son for the other while the latter remains alive. Because the passage contains so many substitutions, so many transmutations and shape-shiftings in form, it appears that the Shaykh also means for us to transpose this story to a metaphysical realm, to ratchet it up a level, so to speak. This is where the puzzling later reference to Isaac's 'dispersal' and 'pulverization' of his father may find some explanation. To access this interpretation we need help from the *Fuṣūṣ*. Oddly enough, this reference to Abraham's sacrifice of his son appears in the Chapter on Enoch (Idrīs) rather than on Isaac, but this is one of the Shaykh's most characteristic traits: to 'scatter' his interpretations throughout his writings, to be found in diverse and unexpected places. In this chapter, Ibn 'Arabī has been speaking about the One and the Many, how ultimately they are nothing but the One, and how adhering to what is logically contradictory is what expresses the ultimate Reality. He illustrates this with the example of numbers, about how they must be affirmed and negated at the same time, in the same way that Creator and creatures are both identical and different. All numbers go back to one as their origin just as all creatures go back to God. All manifestation proceeds from One Source. God is both transcendent Creator and immanent creature. 'Whoever has understood what I have said about the numbers, namely, that to deny them is to affirm them, will know that the transcendent Reality is [at the same time] the relative creature, even though the creature be distinct from the Creator. The Reality is at once the created Creator and the creating creature. All this is One Essence, at once Unique and Many, so consider what it is you see' (*Bezels*, pp. 86–7). It is at this point that Ibn 'Arabī quotes

Q.37:102, the words of the son to the father: 'O Father, do as you are commanded', and then God's words: 'Then We ransomed him with a mighty sacrifice' (Q.37:107). Abraham, his son(s), the ram: all are manifestations of the Formless One, dispersed and scattered in a plethora of forms.

Acquisition vs. Bestowal [Para. 41]

Gifts from God, according to Ibn ʿArabī, are attained either by acquisition or by bestowal. Acquisition requires effort on the part of the servant while God's free gift, symbolized by Isaac, is pure grace. Ishmael represents a combination of the two. He is both bestowal, in answer to Abraham's prayer, and acquisition when ransomed by Abraham's trial. It is only through offering up and 'returning' what had been given that the acquired and the bestowed can be united.

Abraham's guidance is intimately connected with gifts, not only conceptually but also linguistically. The Arabic root *h-d-y* includes both meanings, to guide and to give gifts. *Hidāya*, guidance; reverse the vowels and one gets *hadīya*, gift – and not only gift but offering and even sacrifice. As Ibn ʿArabī confirms: 'Giving gifts is giving from clarity (*bayān*); for that reason, it shares the letters of *al-hudā* [= guidance], because through guidance one gives. The Real's offering to the servant is his soul and the servant's offering to the Real is a return of that soul to Him.'[326] Through the trial of sacrifice, which is essentially Abraham's (and every human being's) offering up his very soul to his Creator, a new level of divine guidance can be reached.[327]

God's Jealousy [Para. 41]

Ibn ʿArabī presents God's extreme testing of Abraham as a result of God's jealousy because of the hitherto barren Abraham's prayer

326. *Fut.*II.180 (Chap. 95).

327. If we may be permitted an 'Ibn Jinnī-ism', by transposing the letters *hā'* and *dāl* and making them emphatic *ḥā'* and *ḍād*, we get *ḍaḥā*, which is the word for ritual sacrifice.

for a righteous son. In presenting Abraham's trial in these terms, Ibn ʿArabī follows such noted Sufi predecessors as al-Qushayrī, who describes the situation as follows:

> Know that it is God's way with his saints that if they find contentment in other than God, heed other than God, or permit other than God to settle in their hearts, that will bring them agitation [of the heart]. He is so jealous for their hearts that He restores them to Himself, empty of all else that has brought them contentment, all else they heeded, and all else they allowed to settle therein. ... This was ... the case with Abraham (peace be upon him). When he took delight in his son Ishmael, God ordered him to sacrifice Ishmael so that he would cast him out of his heart. But 'When they had both surrendered themselves to God and he had laid him prostrate on his forehead' (Q.37:103) and Abraham had purified his inmost being of his attachment to his son, He commanded him to make a substitute sacrifice instead of Ishmael.[328]

What should have been single-minded devotion to God was diverted into a plea for a righteous son. Although Abraham's prayer was answered, it was soon to be a source of trial for him.

The testing of a person's devotion to God is perhaps severest of all when it comes to the natural affection one has for one's human loved ones:

> 'Your possessions and your children are a trial/temptation' (Q.64:15; 8:28) – in other words, We tested you by means of them, whether they will veil you from Us and from what We made a limit for you that you should halt at.[329]

As we will note in the discussion that follows in the paragraphs devoted to Joseph and Moses' final voyage on the subject of God's deception, the notion of God's jealousy is sometimes a difficult one for modern believers to accept in an all-good God. But on an

328. *Principles of Sufism*, trans. von Schlegell, p.264.
329. *Fut.*II.189 (Chap. 108).

ontological level, the situation becomes even more perplexing in that God is the only Being, so of whom is He jealous?

> Jealousy requires affirming the other but in reality there are no others, except the entities of the possible things in respect of their immutability, not in respect of their existence. Jealousy becomes manifest through the immutability of the possible things, and lack of jealousy derives from the existence of the possible things. God is jealous lest the possible things accept existence.[330]

The 'Crossing Over' of Dream Interpretation [Para. 42]

Proper guidance consists of verifying the world of imagination, whether in visionary states or in dreams, since it is in this realm that the realities descend to the individual. He 'crosses over' (*ʿabara*) from the world of sense perception to the world of forms divested of matter, which is apprehended with the inner senses. But the servant is not to halt there among the forms of his imagination; this is not a station that is sought for itself but rather a bridge connecting the world of suprasensible meanings to the material world, and whatever is experienced in the world of the imagination is subject to interpretation (*taʿbīr*) upon crossing back into the world of everyday experience. Thus the proper interpretation of Abraham's dream of sacrificing his son was that Abraham was to sacrifice a ram to his Lord. But Abraham, whose love for his son obscured his vision, took the dream literally and set forth to accomplish what he believed was God's command. In doing so, he did not make the form of his son's sacrifice ascend from the world of imagination to the world of reality by extracting the meaning from the form seen in his dream but caused it to descend by striving to actualize it in 'this world' by materializing it in deed.[331]

330. *Fut.*II.10 (Chap. 73), trans. Chittick, *SPK*, p.388, n.25, slightly modified.

331. We will encounter a similar situation in the narrative of the Sāmirī. See Commentary on Para. 60.

The reason why he somehow 'forgot'[332] what prophets are said to know about the necessity of transforming forms to meanings is that his love for his son temporarily blinded him, much as Jacob's attachment to Joseph and his presumed loss blinded him. Ibn ʿArabī frequently reiterates that often God's tests come by way of temptations through things considered precious in this world – and that, for Ibn ʿArabī, include not only material possessions but familial attachments.[333] On many occasions, including in the *Isfār*'s Paragraph 41, the Shaykh speaks of the singular attachment the father has for the son. 'Our sons are our livers,[334] walking on the earth', he says. 'The child has the same position as the soul.'[335] Thus for Abraham, the sacrifice of his son is more severe than if he had been commanded to sacrifice himself.

Eating from Above and Below [Para. 43]

In a metaphorical description derived from the Qur'an, Ibn ʿArabī speaks of a person's eating '*from above him*' after his having eaten solely '*from below his feet*' (Q.5:66). The Shaykh interprets this verse in a variety of manners. In the *Futūḥāt*, he frequently connects this notion with the difference between the Muslims and the People of the Book since the verse in its entirety reads: *Had they observed the Torah and the Gospel, and what was sent down to them from their Lord, they would have eaten what was above them and what was beneath their feet.* This is often taken to mean that the Jews, Christians and other People of the Book failed to realize the full implications of their Scriptures.[336] Hence perhaps the superiority of Ishmael, the progenitor of the Muslims, is suggested over Isaac, the progenitor of the Jews. Isaac is associated with only one kind of gift, that which is

332. We have seen that Adam was also accused of forgetting. See n.204.

333. 'The greatest temptations are women, wealth, children, and rank (*jāh*).' *Fut.*IV.455 (Chap. 560). The passage goes on to discuss each in turn.

334. According to the Ancients and Medievals, the liver was considered the source of blood.

335. *Fut.*II.615 (Chap. 281).

336. See *Fut.*II.488 (Chap. 206), III.439 (Chap. 371).

bestowed, while Ishmael is associated with two, what is acquired and what is bestowed.

In the *Futūḥāt*'s Chapter 276, bestowed knowledge is the result of God-fearing, and acquired knowledge of hard work.[337] Here Ibn ʿArabī associates the notions of 'from above' and 'below his feet' with how people interpret the Qurʾan. The person who 'eats from below his feet' takes the revelation and interprets it using his own reason. He makes the Book 'lie down' after it has been standing up. Although some rational interpreters may come close to, or hit upon the truth, they do so accidentally and can never reach certainty. Others pass far from the mark; their interpretation is a sort of babble, with no correspondence between words and meanings.

The person who 'eats from above him' stands the Book upright after it has come down to him, declaring his own interpretations invalid in comparison with the incomparability of the text. God then teaches him the meanings, purged of their material substrate. For Ibn ʿArabī, this direct teaching by way of bestowal does not necessarily come to someone who is a follower of a religious law. We know this from the various prophets and saints unconnected with any specific religion.

A connection can also be made between bestowal vs. acquisition and the state (*ḥāl*) vs. the station (*maqām*).[338] The state is given by God and may come to anyone at any time, anywhere. It is transient, riding on the cusp of the moment (*waqt*), even if it sometimes appears to be permanent due to God's continuing creation of similar states, as in His never-ending flow of creation He passes on from task to task (Q.55:29).

> The state is one of the favours of the All-Merciful
> Accorded through an act of solicitude.
> It is not from acquisition or search.[339]

337. See also *Fut.*I.192 (Chap. 27). Here the connection is specifically made between the effort involved in acquiring knowledge (eating beneath one's feet), wayfaring (*sulūk*) and 'donning the sandals' for prayer: '… the one who prays walks in his prayer and in conversation with his Lord, in the verses that save him, waystation by waystation. Every verse is a waystation and a state.'

338. See *Fut.*II, Chaps. 192 and 193.

339. *Fut.*II.384 (Chap. 192).

The station, on the other hand, is the result of earning on the part of those pursuing the spiritual path. It is generally permanent, staying with the disciple as he or she progresses along the way, ceasing only if certain contexts warrant its removal.[340]

> In reality, the station is obtained through works.
> It implies the effort to attain and search.
> It is through the station that the gnostics attain perfection.
> It is the good that is never withdrawn from them,
> Or hidden, or veiled.
> It is constant.[341]

Best of all is the servant who passes beyond state and station, who reaches the 'place' (*makān*), the 'where', where God is said to be with him.[342] This is a particular characteristic of the 'Muhammadians' or 'people of Yathrib'. The individual who reaches this level knows himself by what is bestowed upon him in every moment. (And 'he who knows himself knows his Lord'.) But this is a 'difficult' knowledge: 'One cannot know what is in the knowledge of God, nor can one know his own eternally determined predisposition to receive, for to be, at each instant, aware of one's [eternal] predisposition is one of the most difficult kinds of knowledge.'[343] When the servant knows what his Lord knows about him in his latent state of pure possibility, he knows that he will receive only what he is predisposed to receive, whether he asks for specific or general gifts and whether he expresses his request by word or by state.[344]

340. Ibn 'Arabī gives the example of the state of scrupulousness (*wara'*), which applies only in cases where something is either forbidden or of a dubious nature, and the stations of repentance and legal prescription which cease with death. See *Fut.*II.385 (Chap. 192).

341. *Fut.*II.385 (Chap. 193).

342. *Fut.*II.386 (Chap. 194).

343. *Fuṣūṣ*, chapter on Seth (trans. Austin, *Bezels*, p.62).

344. See *Isfār*, Para. 43: '... the divine affairs never descend save in accordance with the preparedness and the locus.'

Subsistence vs. 'Pulverization' [Para. 43]

When the human being 'passes over' the bridge of imagination to the world of realities, he sees things as they are and is given pure bestowal unmixed with any acquisition. At this level, he begins to 'eat from above', and comes to know the true interpretation of the Noble Qur'an, his dream visions and indeed everything he contemplates in any of the realms of existence. He has access to knowledge that is beyond that acquired by his own efforts, bestowed by divine inspiration. This bestowal gives him subsistence (*baqā'*) in God, hence God becomes his faculties of perception. Pulverization (*saḥq/ isḥāq*), on the other hand, implies dispersal and distance. The reader who is acquainted with the narratives of the Qur'an in all likelihood will recall at this point a similar instance of pulverization that went under a different, albeit also rhyming, word '*daqq*'. In the story of Moses, which is not recounted in the *Isfār*, Moses asks for a vision of God and is told he will not see Him. God shows Himself to the mountain, however, and the mountain is reduced to dust.

Beyond appreciating the clever play on words between *isḥāq* as Isaac and *isḥāq* as pulverization, one could say that Isaac 'pulverizes' his father, because through God's promise: 'I will make thy seed as the dust of the earth' (Gen. 13 :16), Abraham will become the Father of countless generations.[345] In this sense, as Ibn 'Arabī says at the end of this chapter: 'The son is from the world of dispersal.'[346]

But when transferred to the spiritual level the matter becomes more complicated, and we will find that the Shaykh's words remain obscure without reference to a number of passages in the *Futūḥāt*, along with some help from Ibn 'Arabī's predecessor, al-Qushayrī. First of all, suggested here by the combination of the words *isḥāq* (pulverizing)

345. 'And [H]e brought him forth abroad, and said, Look now towards heaven, and tell the stars, if thou be able to number them: and [H]e said unto him, So shall thy seed be' (Gen. 15: 5). This scattering of stars calls to mind the descent of the Qur'an as *nujūman*, in fragmentary or 'star-like' form. See n. 124.

346. *Isfār*, Para. 43.

and *maḥq* (effacement) is the saying of Abū ʿAlī al-Daqqāq[347] as found in the chapter on the Moment (*waqt*) in al-Qushayrī's *Risāla*, which Ibn ʿArabī echoes in his own chapter on the Moment in the *Futūḥāt* when giving certain well-known definitions of the Sufis: 'The Moment is like a file: it pulverizes you, but does not efface you completely.'[348] Duality rules out your being completely annihilated in the Divine Presence. In addition, pulverization is associated with dispersal and distance linguistically, since the roots *s-ḥ-q* and *b-ʿ-d* can be synonymous. A person who is 'pulverized' like dust filings sees these particles as discrete rather than a unity.

Contemplation, on the other hand, is connected with annihilation, hence the title of one of the Shaykh's treatises, 'Annihilation in Contemplation' (*K. al-Fanāʾ fī al-mushāhada*).[349] When one contemplates the Reality, light floods the soul and the ego disappears. As al-Junayd says: 'God's existence appears when you lose yours.'[350]

The chapters in the *Futūḥāt* on Gathering and Dispersal[351] shed some light on this difficult section of the *Isfār*. Again it is Abū ʿAlī al-Daqqāq who presides over this discussion in both Qushayrī's *Risāla* and Ibn ʿArabī's *Futūḥāt*. He defines the two opposing terms as follows: 'Separation is something that is attributed to you; gathering, on the other hand, is something that is taken from you.'[352] Qushayrī explains that whatever you acquire with your own effort is taken from you, while whatever God bestows upon you subsists. As Ibn ʿArabī writes, quoting the Qurʾan: *What is with you runs out, while what is with Allah subsists* (Q.16:96). As long as a person sees his

347. Jurist, Qurʾan commentator, belletrist and Sufi, fl. 10th and 11th century. Qushayrī was a devoted student of al-Daqqāq, and ʿAṭṭār mentions that he was well-known for his chanting of nostalgic laments. See La-Shayʾ, 'Abū ʿAlī al-Daqqāq', p.456.

348. *Risāla*, trans. Knysh, p.76. The words here are *yasḥaq* and *yamḥaq*, the same as in the *Isfār*. See also *Fut.*II.539 (Chap. 238).

349. See p.262.

350. *Risāla*, p.98.

351. Chaps. 222 and 223. Chittick has translated Chap. 222 in *Meccan Revelations*, pp.162–88.

352. *Risāla*, trans. Knysh, p.87. I have replaced Knysh's 'unification' with 'gathering.'

deeds as his own deeds, whether obedient or otherwise, he is in a state of separation and distance. But when the person sees his deeds as God's deeds, he is in a state of unification and closeness to God.

There is also a hint of polemics in the notion of Isaac being associated with pulverizing and scattering, in that this progenitor of the Children of Israel bequeaths to his offspring the fate of constant dispersal and migration. Moses' remarks to the Sāmirī in the later chapter on his Voyage of Anger and Return, that he has sown seeds of dissent among the *Banī Isrāʾīl* (Children of Israel), further confirms the notion of separation and disharmony in the community of Moses. It is on a critical note that this section ends, laying the cause of the Jews' perpetual humilation on their failure to reflect on the true nature of God's attributes.

Lot: The Voyage of Approach and No Turning Back [Paras. 44–5]

The story of Lot is recounted numerous times in the Qurʾan as an exemplary tale of the destruction of people who engage in practices displeasing to God and the grace that comes to righteous believers.[353]

Issues, such as the power of concentrated will, which concern Ibn ʿArabī in the *Fuṣūṣ*'s chapter on Lot, are absent here, at least explicitly. Instead, the issue here is certainty, although there is of course an inherent connection between power and certainty, which we will turn to later.

As we have mentioned earlier, there are two linguistic features that are of interest to Ibn ʿArabī when he discusses Lot's story in the *Isfār*. The first is Lot's name, Lūṭ in Arabic, which he says is derived from *lāṭa, yalūṭu*, to cling, adhere or stick to something. Lot clings to the Divine Presence but finds no support from his people, who are immersed in wickedness. His regret at being defenceless

353. Q.7:80; 11:70–83; 15:57–77; 21:74; 26:160–74; 27:54–8; 29:26; 28–34; 37:133–8; and 54:33–9.

against them – *If only I had some power over you, or had recourse to some firm support* (Q.11:80) – is the point of departure in the *Fuṣūṣ* for the discussion of humankind's inherent weakness.[354] It is a remark that occasions a response from Muhammad: 'God have mercy on my brother Lot, who sought refuge in a strong support.'[355]

When Lot flees from his errant people's imminent destruction, it is to meet Abraham in 'Yaqīn', in certainty, a station that Abraham has reached before him: *Thus did We show Abraham the kingdom of the heavens and the earth that he might be of those possessing certainty* (Q.6:75) – as Ibn ʿArabī explains: 'the eye of certainty (*ʿayn al-yaqīn*), because it is from vision and contemplation'.[356]

The chapter concludes with a startlingly beautiful poem that seems to weave in several strands of interpretation that were found in previous chapters: the human being's inseparability from God – likened to a shadow – in life or in death; and the sameness of the voyage of ascent and the voyage of descent, guidance and erring.

Certainty

In the *Futūḥāt*, Ibn ʿArabī has three chapters dealing with certainty.[357] It is perhaps here that the interplay between issues of power/incapacity and certainty/doubt can best be seen. Ibn ʿArabī defines certainty as: 'everything that is made firm and settled and cannot be shaken by anything, be it a Real or a creature'.[358] There is little that is certain in the natural world, says the Shaykh, for nothing remains

354. See *Fuṣūṣ*, chapter on Lot (trans. Austin, *Bezels*, pp.157–8).

355. Muslim, *al-lim*, *īmān* I.280. See *Fut.*IV.54 (Chap. 440) where this hadith is again quoted. At issue is the notion of *himma*, or effective spiritual power, which the highest of individuals do not make use of, even if they have it.

356. *Fut.*III.340 (Chap. 367). See also *Fut.*I.206 (Chap. 31). Ibn ʿArabī appears to take this term, *ʿayn al-yaqīn*, from al-Tustarī, who refers to it in his *Tafsīr* (p.81): '... the light of certainty unveils the knowledge of the eye of certainty, and this is the attainment of God, Exalted is He. For this certainty, by virtue of the light of certainty that leads to the eye of certainty, is not something that is brought into being, nor is it something that is created; rather it is a light from the light of the essence of God ...'.

357. Chaps. 122, 123 and 269.

358. *Fut.*II.571 (Chap. 269).

the same for two instants, God continually creating the world afresh, 'every day upon some task'. In addition,

> certainty has in it a whiff of resistance to the divine force. ... If [certainty] comes from God without any action on the part of the servant, the servant accepts it out of courtesy with God and does not reject it from God when God wants this servant to become a locus for the existence of this certainty. Its property in this locus is attachment to God in pushing away harm from this servant.[359]

Thus the gnostic does not seek certainty of his own free will, but empties himself and awaits the coming of certainty that is indicated in God's words: *Worship your Lord until certainty comes to you* (Q.15:99).

The word *yaqīn* is also of linguistic interest to Ibn ʿArabī in the *Isfār* for it not only means the quality of certainty but is also the name of the town to which Lot flees – or as the Qurʾan puts it, 'journeys by night' – to avoid the fate of Sodom's sinful inhabitants. Such a place really does exist.[360] It is the site of a mosque that Ibn ʿArabī calls 'the Masjid of al-Yaqīn' and 'the Masjid of Abraham the Khalīl (Intimate Friend)'.[361] Ibn ʿArabī visited it on his way to Mecca. According to Ibn ʿArabī, it was at this place that the angels met Abraham, gave him the good news about the impending advent of a righteous son and informed him that they were on their way to destroy Lot's people.[362] It is also the town to which he returns in order to meet Abraham, which is located near enough to his former

359. *Fut.*II.205 (Chap. 123).

360. The mosque, also known today as Nabi Yaqīn, is located two kilometres south of the village of Bani Naʿīm, itself five kilometres southeast of Hebron. It was built in 963 and was visited by such noted travellers as Shams al-Dīn al-Muqaddasī (b. 946), who visited it shortly after it was constructed, and Ibn Battuta, who travelled there in 1326. The village mosque in Bani Naʿīm supposedly houses the tomb of the Prophet Lot. See abrahampath.org/path/hebronhebron-sites/nebi-yaqin/ which also shows a contemporary photograph of the mosque. See also 'Description of Syria and Palestine by Mukaddasi', in *The Library of the Palestine Pilgrims' Text Society*, vol. III, p. 52: 'It is related that when Abraham first saw from here, afar off, the Cities of Lot, he stood as one rooted, saying, "Verily I now bear witness, for the word of the Lord is The Truth" (al-Yakin).'

361. See *Fut.*II.205 (Chap. 122).

362. *K. al-Yaqīn*, p. 65.

town that he can hear the cries of his people when they meet their deaths in a downpour of brimstone on the following morning, God, in effect, having turned the place upside down (see Q.15:74). When Lot sees this from his refuge at al-Yaqīn, he prostrates himself and says: 'I bear witness that this is certainty.'[363] Ibn 'Arabī composed a short treatise on the very spot of this prostration, *Kitāb al-Yaqīn*.

In *K. al-Yaqīn* we find two more suggestive word derivations that are relevant to the story of Lot. *Yaqīn*, he says, is derived from *yaqn al-ma'*, the standing of water in a ditch, and *yaqn*, which is the wood that a navigator uses to steer a ship – in other words, a kind of rudder.[364] Hence certainty bestows a settling of knowledge in the heart and provides a guiding principle for one's actions. Belief, which is subject to the buffeting winds of doubt, is replaced by firm knowledge that cannot be shaken. Knowledge – and by this Ibn 'Arabī means the knowledge (*'ilm*) that perceives things as they really are in themselves, not ordinary speculative knowledge – 'must rely on certainty, for certainty is the spirit of knowledge and peace of mind (*ṭuma'nīna*) is its life'.[365]

The chapter heading is also of more than a little interest, for it combines two words *iqbāl* (approach) and *iltifāt* (turning back), movements that are connected with certainty. The first, 'approach', suggests a movement towards certainty that with the arrival of God's overwhelming punishment became certainty in God's words and deeds.

Turning back, which is what Lot's wife does, suggests the hesitation that accompanies doubt. In the *Isfār*, Ibn 'Arabī makes this wife the personification of 'the soul that commands to evil'. We will meet this soul again in the chapter of Joseph.

'Crossing over' in Qur'an Interpretation

In the *Isfār*'s previous chapter, on Abraham, we discussed the method of 'crossing over' from form to meaning as applied to dreams. It is in

363. Ibid.
364. Ibid. p.46.
365. Ibid. p.54.

this chapter on Lot that Ibn ʿArabī gives the principles that guide his interpretation of God's signs in the Qur'an.

Ibn ʿArabī's method of Qur'an interpretation is based on the correspondence between external form and inner meaning that is not determined by human devising but by God's imposition. As he states in the *Futūḥāt*:

> Since we know that God … has joined a designated spirit to every sensible form, we interpret the Lawgiver's speech in its internal dimension according to the determination that coincides with the external one, step by step, because the external dimension includes its sensible form. The divine suprasensible spirit in that form is what we call 'crossing over (*iʿtibār*) in the internal dimension', from 'crossing over the *wadī*', when you go over it. It is the Most High's saying: 'So "cross over" (*fa-ʿtabirū*)[366] O ye who have eyes!' (Q.59:2); that is, pass over the forms you see with your eyes to the meanings and spirits in your interior dimension … then you will perceive them with your insights. So He commanded and encouraged 'crossing over'.
>
> The religious scholars, especially the people who are fixated on the external dimension, are inattentive to this matter. They have no 'crossings-over' except astonishment. There is no difference between their intellects and those of small boys! They do not 'cross over' at all from these external forms, as God has commanded them to do![367]

As in the voyage of Abraham that preceded Lot's in the *Isfār*, we are not meant to stop with the externalities of the Qur'an but to use its dictates and stories to 'cross over' to the inner significance. The stories themselves merely serve as bridges to knowledge of the self and signposts along the path to God to point out the way.

366. Sometimes translated as: 'take warning' (Yusuf Ali, Sahih International), 'learn a lesson' (Pickthall) or 'take heed' (Arberry).

367. *Fut.*I.551 (Chap. 70).

Jacob and Joseph: The Voyage of Ruse and Trial [Paras. 46–9]

The Qur'an calls Sura 12, the sura devoted exclusively to Joseph's narrative, the *most beautiful of stories* (Q.12:3), and Ibn ʿArabī's section detailing Joseph's voyage reflects this concern. Joseph's successive temptations and trials are due to his beauty and the nobility and high rank it occupies, as well as the tenderness and appeal of his youth and the mercy that naturally accompanies it.

The story of Joseph, the only complete narrative in the Qur'an, is one so well known that it hardly needs retelling. And true to form, Ibn ʿArabī will not retell it in a conventional way, as he prefers to concentrate on a few aspects, giving them a novel interpretation.

Unlike his other treatments of Joseph in the *Fuṣūṣ* and *Futūḥāt*, here Ibn ʿArabī presents an allegory of the soul. Dream interpretation, which is the main concern of the Joseph chapter in the *Fuṣūṣ*, is only briefly mentioned. Imagination and imaginalization, the focus of the Joseph section in the *Futūḥāt*'s Chapter 167, is not alluded to, nor is the question of why Joseph did not immediately accept the king's command to leave his prison, choosing instead to await his vindication by the women of the court – which is the subject that perplexes Ibn ʿArabī during his mystical visit to Joseph in the third heaven.[368]

One common element in all narratives having to do with Joseph, however, is beauty. In Islamic tradition, Joseph is associated with Venus, the planet of love and beauty. A Prophetic hadith states that Joseph and his mother were given half the beauty of the world.[369] It is a predominantly feminine beauty he has, the beauty of a beardless youth – a beauty that proves irresistible to Potiphar's wife, named Zulaykha in legends. Her love for Joseph is such that when she cuts herself every drop of blood that falls to the ground cries out: 'Joseph! Joseph!'[370] In the Qur'an, the 'woman' is commanded by her soul

368. *Fut.*III.347 (Chap. 367). See also *Fut.*IV.181 (Chap. 537).

369. Cited in Bernstein, *Stories of Joseph*, p. 148.

370. *Fut.*II.337 (Chap. 178).

to evil. In the *Isfār*, she represents the Universal Soul who tempts Joseph with the knowledge she contains.

Ibn ʿArabī points out here, as in other places, that normally beauty elicits mercy and tenderness. The young child and the woman inspire feelings of kindness and mercy.

> 'Child' (*ṭifl*) is taken from '*ṭafal*' [= tender, soft], which is the dew that descends from the sky in the early morning and evening. It is weaker than the water that descends from the heavens. The child to the grown person is like the drizzle to the downpour … and other kinds of descending rain, since it has frailty – and the frail person is always the object of mercy … .[371]
>
> Do you not see how the child acts on the older person in a special way, so that the older person comes down from his position of superiority, plays and chatters with him, and opens his mind to him. Thus, he is under the child's influence without realizing it. Furthermore, the child preoccupies him with its rearing and protection, the supervision of his interests and the ensuring that nothing might cause it anxiety. All this demonstrates the action of the younger on the older by virtue of the power of his [spiritual] station, since the child's contact with his Lord is fairly recent, being a new creature. The older person, on the other hand, is more distant from that contact. One who is closer to God exerts power over one who is further from Him, just as the confidants of a king wield power over those further removed from his presence. The Apostle of God would expose himself to the rain, uncovering his head to it, saying that the rain had come fresh from his Lord. Consider, then, how majestic, sublime, and clear is our Prophet's knowledge of God. Even so, the rain had power over the best of humanity by virtue of its proximity to its Lord, like a divine emissary summoning him in his essence, in a silent way. He exposed himself to it so that he might receive what it had brought him from its Lord to him. Indeed, he would not have exposed himself to it but for the divine benefit implicit in its contact with him. This, then, is the message of water from which God created every living thing;[372] so understand.[373]

371. *Fut.*I.536 (Chap. 69).

372. Note that this is from Q.21:30, not cited by Austin.

373. *Fuṣuṣ*, trans. Austin, *Bezels*, p.252. Note that here the subjects of these remarks are

> Everything that is close to generation is closer in signification, greater in sanctity, and more abounding in the appeal to mercy than the old, the one who is far from this station.[374]

It is only because God removed these natural feelings of mercy and solicitude from the hearts of Joseph's brothers that they felt no qualms about casting him into the pit.

Joseph's voyage in the *Isfār* is the story of the soul's journey in essential servanthood. It is the quality of servanthood, rather than any external appearance, that makes a person truly beautiful because in this state of lowliness, dependence (upon God) and contingency the human being displays himself as he truly is. God confers the specific beauty of lordship only on servants who make no claims of exaltedness or power on their own part;[375] it is thus an accidental beauty and nobility that can be taken away at any moment, as was the case with Joseph. This worldly beauty and high station are more of a test than a boon – in their wake comes the trial of humility and humiliation. Herein lies the Divine Hidden Ruse, or Deception.[376] What appears to be a God-bestowed favour turns out to be the source of prolonged testing. Joseph, the darling of his father, is sold into slavery by his brothers, who represent the soul commanding to evil (*al-nafs al-ammāra* [*bi-l-sū'*])[377] and the soul that blames (*al-nafs al-lawwāma*).[378] In Joseph's servanthood there is no nobility (*ʿizz*) or rest – one thinks here of the soul at rest (*al-nafs al-muṭma'inna*).[379] The Qur'an states that: *The [brothers] sold him for a miserable price, for a few dirhams counted out: in such low estimation did they hold him!* (Q.12:20). But it is God who buys the soul of the believer for a low

---

the children slain by Pharaoh in his attempts to murder Moses.

374. *Fut.*II.190 (Chap. 108).

375. Raising oneself to the level of Lordship calls for a decisive response on the part of the Almighty. See, for example, *Fut.*IV, Chaps. 402 and 429.

376. The notion of the hidden Divine Ruse will be discussed further in connection with the final voyage of Moses.

377. See Q.12:53: '… indeed the soul is an enjoiner of evil'.

378. See Q.75:2: 'I call to witness the blaming soul.'

379. See Q.89:27: 'O [thou] soul, in [complete] rest and satisfaction!'

price, the price of temporal accidents. The relevant Qur'anic quotation is: *Allah hath purchased of the believers their persons and their goods* (Q.9:111). In exchange, God gives sovereignty to obey or disobey, to do right and do wrong. Despite being stripped of his former station, Joseph remains good and beautiful in his essential servanthood, which is true 'divine' nobility.

Once in the city, Joseph is turned over to Zulaykha; in other words, the believer's individual soul encounters the Universal Soul. She succumbs to his beauty and offers herself to him, commanding him and tempting him to take the divine realities she possesses. But taking these divine realities without the divine command would be a claim of independence, an attribute belonging exclusively to God. Joseph 'receives the sign of his servanthood' and desists. In many commentaries, it is the face of his father that appears to him, countermanding the temptations of Zulaykha.[380] The interpretation of Jacob as intellect fits in well with this vision. It is the role of intellect to tame the soul's desires and to combat the temptations that beset it. Despite this, however, Zulyakha/Universal Soul imprisons Joseph/soul in a body. He beseeches the Lord with his servanthood. The Universal Soul acknowledges that it was she who sought him. At this, the soul is rewarded with masterhood.

The women of the court, who cut their hands when they see Joseph's beauty, here represent the particular souls who see the believer's soul and say it is an angel, purified of natural desires. Hence Joseph is associated with safeguarding his chastity, his steadfast innocence and veracity, and his guardianship of the treasuries of the king (see Q.12:55).

Joseph's father, Jacob, represents the intellect in this interpretation. Ibn 'Arabī frequently notes that intellect restricts. This is the opposite of love: 'One of the attributes of love is straying and bewilderment, and bewilderment negates the intellect, for the intellect gathers you together while bewilderment disperses you. The brothers of Joseph said to Jacob: "Truly thou art in thine old

380. See Bernstein, *Stories of Joseph*, p. 17.

wandering mind" (Q.12:95), meaning his bewilderment in love of Joseph.'[381]

Jacob is also associated in the *Isfār* and elsewhere with grief and patience.[382] It is clear that he both exemplifies the Qur'anic dictum *Your possessions and your children are a trial/temptation* (Q.64:15; 8:28), and justifies the ascription of the title of this voyage, the voyage of ruse and trial, to him. When Jacob, the intellect, is cut off from Joseph, the soul, he experiences the pain of separation, and because of his incessant weeping he loses his sight. Intellect without Soul is blind. Grief is a fire producing corporeal whiteness and spiritual light. Sightless without Joseph, and suffering in his homeland from the drought of his loss, he hears of his son's prosperity in the city to which he has been transported. He inhales the scent of the shirt imbued with Joseph's form, which Joseph has sent him, and he begins his voyage to him in nobility, rather than humility. Reunited with his son, however, he prostrates himself humbly before him. Intellect prostrates itself before Soul and accepts Soul as its teacher. Intellect's essence subsists in the Soul and Soul makes Intellect joyful.

The cosmological relationship of Soul to Intellect is one of emanation. In Qur'anic terms, the Intellect is the Pen and the Soul the Tablet the Pen inscribes. Microcosmic human beings mirror this macrocosmic relationship. The soul has both a passive, receptive, feminine face turned to what is above it, and an active, emanative, masculine one, turned to what is below. As a former of images, the soul provides embodiment to spiritual realities. Dream interpretation derives from the world of imagination, a liminal (*barzakhī*) world between intellect and sense, taking from both. Joseph was able to rebuff the woman because of the domination of the female aspect in his soul. This is because the relationship of two female entities is not dominated by the mutual love and mercy characterizing the female/male relationship. Were the masculine element [intellect] to dominate Joseph's soul, he could not have resisted.

381. *Fut.*II.338 (Chap. 178).
382. See *Fut.*IV.156 (Chap. 515).

Relative to this discussion, Ibn ʿArabī provides a supplemental disquisition on tenderness for women, and men who look like women. It is a theme that receives a more extensive treatment in Chapter 108 of the *Futuḥāt*: On knowledge of temptation (*fitna*) and appetite (*shahwa*); and the companionship of young men (*aḥdāth*) and women. This chapter provides a fine supplement to the *Isfār*'s remarks about Joseph since it reiterates the notions of beauty, tenderness and inclination connected with all things that are new and/or because their soft, smooth and fresh appearance awaken feelings of strong attraction. While the word Ibn ʿArabī uses in the *Isfār* for young man is *ghulām*, in the *Futūḥāt*'s Chapter 108 the word is *ḥadath*, which allows him to play on the various meanings associated with this root: novelty, Prophetic tradition (*ḥadīth*), temporal creation, conversation, events (usually of an unfortunate kind), first rains, ritual impurity and young man.

In addition, it mentions another facet of temptation that applies not only to the Joseph story but to the inherent trials occasioned by God's appointment of individuals to be His vicegerents, whether they be prophets, messengers or God's special friends. The irony of the matter is that it is only the complete servant, the lowest of the low, who is assigned to represent the source of all highness, power and perfection. When God becomes the sight, hearing and all the faculties of such an individual, there is a temptation that he will forget his essential status of servanthood. Furthermore, it may escape his attention that God Himself descends to the level of the most abject of His servants, the broken-hearted, the sick and the hungry.

The Six Voyages of Moses (Paras. 50–70)

Only the prophet Moses has more than one voyage assigned to him. With six prophets preceding him: Adam, Idrīs, Noah, Abraham, Lot and Joseph/Jacob (son and father considered as one unit), he himself has six voyages. These are: the Voyage of the Divine Appointed Time, the Voyage of Satisfaction, the Voyage of Anger and Return, the Voyage of Striving for One's Household, the Voyage of Fear and the Voyage of Precaution. Although the Prologue mentions Moses' voyage in the company of Khiḍr, a voyage in which he is instructed in patience and courtesy, this voyage, oddly enough, does not form part of the *Isfār*'s six-part Moses cycle.

It is not immediately clear why Moses has received much more attention than any of the other prophets,[383] or why the number six is associated with him. Numbers in Ibn ʿArabī's works are not assigned arbitrarily, for 'number is the secret of secrets of God with respect to existence'.[384] Six was a significant number for Ibn ʿArabī,[385] so much so that his *Futūḥāt* is divided into six parts, based on the principle Attributes of God: Knowing, Willing, Powerful, Speaking, Hearing and Seeing. Although in reality there are seven Essential Attributes, the supreme Attribute 'Living' underlies the other six and embraces all.[386] The first part of *Kitāb al-Isrā'* also contains six chapters, the sixth corresponding to the Prophet Muhammad's *isrā'*, 'perhaps an allusion to the six directions of physical space and, therefore, the special nature of this horizontal journey *in the world*'.[387] Thus it is worthwhile to attempt an exploration of why Moses has six voyages.

Six stands out first of all for the six days of creation: *He created the heavens and the earth in six days* (Q.10:3). Furthermore, it is on the sixth day that Adam is created. Thus six is the number of the microcosmic Human Form.[388] There are six genera: angels, jinn, minerals, plants, animals and human beings, in that order.[389] Hence the human

383. The chapter devoted to Moses in the *Fuṣūṣ* is also the longest in the book.

384. *Fut.*I.81 (Chap. 2).

385. In his paper and podcast 'The Mystic's Kaʿba', Hirtenstein alludes to a little-known treatise of the Shaykh's titled 'On the Nature of the Six Faces of the Heart', and also points out that in his best-known poem from the *Tarjumān al-ashwāq* there are six forms the poet's heart has become capable of assuming: 'My heart has become capable of every form: it is a pasture for gazelles and a convent for Christian monks, and a temple for idols and the pilgrim's Kaʿba and the tables of the Tora and the book of the Koran' (trans. Nicholson).

386. See also *Fut.*I.106 (Chap. 5), II.493 (Chap. 208); and Hirtenstein, *Unlimited Mercifier*, pp. 215–16.

387. Beneito, 'Ark of Creation', p. 36, n. 57. Author's italics.

388. See *Fut.*I.645 (Chap. 71).

389. Occasionally, angels and jinn are combined and the Real is made the top level. See

being is the sixth and last genus – last in order to serve creation as its vicegerent.[390] In most *mi'rāj* accounts, Moses is the presiding prophet of the sixth heaven, corresponding to the planet Jupiter.[391] Delving further, we find also a description of the merits of the number six in the section devoted to the Divine Name 'the Last'.[392] Six, says Ibn 'Arabī, is the first perfect number and the root of every perfect number.[393] It can be divided into halves, thirds and sixths.[394] Every hexad thus shares in this perfection. The six-sided shape is the 'most excellent and firmest of shapes' because it most resembles the circle; like it, it leaves no room for the void.[395] Ibn 'Arabī gives as an example the bee's six-sided house which it fills with honey as the cosmos is completely filled with God's mercy.[396] As P. Beneito points out, the human being has six directions: right, left, front, back, up and down, with six parts of his body corresponding to them: strong side, weak side, face, back of the head, head and feet, respectively.[397] And, as mentioned earlier, Satan can approach from only four of these directions.[398] Unlike other angels, he cannot move along a vertical axis. It may be that Moses' six voyages include the six directions. There are six faculties of human perception: the five senses and reason.[399] The Prophet Muhammad was given six things that no one else was given before him[400] and by encompassing the six directions his mission was

---

*Fut.*I.57 (Chap. 2).

390. See *Fut.*I.137 (Chap. 10).

391. In examining the *mi'rāj* account of the Muhammadan follower and the philosopher in the *Fut.*, Chap. 167, we find another strange connection of Moses with Noah, since it is in the sixth heaven that the follower learns of the non-transmutation of substance, something that Noah learns in the sign of the *tannūr*.

392. *Fut.*II.431ff. (Chap. 198, Section 14).

393. See also *Fut.*II.469 (Chap. 198, section 38).

394. *Fut.*I.55 (Chap. 2).

395. *Fut.*II.433 (Chap. 198, section 14). See also *Fut.*III.120 (Chap. 332).

396. *Fut.*II.433. See also *Fut.*III.142 (Chap. 337).

397. See *Fut.*I.123–4 (Chap. 7), III.230 (Chap. 351).

398. See *Fut.*II.493 (Chap. 208). The vulnerable directions are: from before, from behind, from the right and from the left.

399. See *Fut.*I.213 (Chap. 34).

400. See *Fut.*I.144ff. (Chap. 12). See also *Fut.*III.142 (Chap. 337).

made universal.[401] Among the letters, *wāw* is given the level of six – it is equal to the number six in numerology/gematria, and translates as 'and'. Thus it is a connecting particle and joins the divine to the human. As a letter it is related to the *hā'*, joining it to form the word '*huwa*' (He/he); it is concealed in the command '*Kun*' (God's existence-giving Word 'Be!'). There are six so-called 'holy' letters that do not connect with what comes after them, although the other letters connect to them: *alif, dāl, dhāl, rā', zā'* and *wāw*. They connect to 'the six high spheres of the apogee' from which the six directions come into existence.[402] There are six 'small letters' – movements – that allow the pronunciation of words. For the declined letters: elevation (*raf'*), establishment (*naṣb*), lowering (*khafḍ*) and opening (*fatḥ*); for the stable letters: breaking (*kasr*) and contraction (*ḍamm*).[403] The sum of the numbers of letters corresponding to the Divine Presence (three letters) and the Human Presence (three letters) equals six. There are six daily ritual prayers (sometimes called 'presences' by Ibn 'Arabī) in Islam: the five mandatory prayers and the supererogatory *witr* prayer.[404] There are six metals named by the alchemists: gold, silver, copper, tin, lead and iron. Although not overtly mentioned by Ibn 'Arabī, Solomon's Seal (= Shield/Star of David) is a six-pointed star, which in gnostic symbolism signifies the uniting of the microcosm and the macrocosm, or the Human Being and the Divine.[405] In a sense, Moses brings to perfection the qualities of the human vicegerent in the time before the Prophet Muhammad.

401. See *Fut.*III.141 (Chap. 337), 350 (Chap. 367).

402. 'Knowledge of these six letters is a great sea whose bottom cannot be reached. Only God knows their reality; they are the "keys of the Unseen"' (*Fut.*I.84).

403. See ibid. (Chap. 2).

404. See *Fut.*II.43 (Chap. 73).

405. A wealth of material on this symbol can be found in Rozensweig's *Star of Redemption*.

The Voyages of Moses: I. The Voyage of the Divine Appointment of Moses [Paras. 50–4]

This chapter begins the Moses cycle with a Moses who is content to serve God without any desire of his own, maintaining his servanthood, not seeking any independent movement (*jāmid* – a word most often associated with 'inanimate' rocks, metals and ice). What awakens the desire to 'hasten' (*'ajal*) – a word that becomes central in this cycle and soon comes to include two words, one unrelated in meaning but of the same root: *'ijl* (calf), and the near-homophone *ajl*, fixed time, fate, destiny – is God's making an appointment to meet him. Hence Moses passes from a state of spiritual sobriety to a state of intoxicated desire to see his Lord.[406] The voyage is made in haste from the people in order to give God pleasure (a theme continuing in the next chapter). So from a state of such fixity that Ibn 'Arabī gives it the same term that is used for inanimate objects such as rocks, Moses springs into action, hurrying to keep his appointment with the Lord, the initial 'fixed term' of thirty days.

The 'fixed term' (*ajl*) in Islamic thought is generally associated with the limits of life, culminating in the inevitability of death: *He it is created you from clay, and then decreed a stated term. And there is in His presence another determined term; yet ye doubt within yourselves!* (Q.6:2); *It is He who doth take your souls by night, and hath knowledge of all that ye have done by day. By day doth He raise you up again that a term appointed be fulfilled. In the end unto Him will be your return; then will He show you the truth of all that ye did* (Q.6:60). While some hastening is praiseworthy and eminently courteous, as in carrying out God's commands,[407] not all hastening is good, as we shall see in

406. In *Fut.*III.116 (Chap. 331) this desire results in a breach of courtesy in that Moses asks his Lord for a vision of Him, something that would have been granted had he not asked, and is refused. In his state of desire to encounter his Lord he is described as 'intoxicated'. His repentance restored him to God's favour. See Q.7:143.

407. See *Fut.*IV.472 (Chap. 560): 'Guard against hastening (*'ajala*) except in the homelands that the Messenger of God – peace and blessings upon him – commanded you to hasten and be quick in, such as performing the ritual prayer in the first part of its appointed time, honouring the guest, preparing the dead [for burial] and the virgin [for marriage] when she

more than one of the Moses voyages. For example, in most cases, the span of a person's life is not known in advance, and hastening to encounter God face-to-face – in other words, suicide – is prohibited: 'The servant is commanded to remain still, under the courses of fate and what God brings him in the nighttime and the daytime. He says in censuring someone who hastens to his fate: "My servant has hastened to Me by his own doing; I have forbidden him Paradise."'[408] Hastening God's decrees in general is discouraged: *[Inevitable] cometh [to pass] the Command of Allah. Seek ye not then to hasten it* (Q.16:1). *The human being is a creature of haste: soon [enough] will I show you My Signs; then ye will not ask Me to hasten them!* (Q.21:37). *No people can hasten their term, nor can they delay [it]* (Q.23:43). As we have noted earlier, Muhammad himself was urged not to hasten to recite the Qur'an to his community (see Q.20:114) but to reveal it in stages.

As Ibn 'Arabī notes in the *Isfār*, the fixed term God appointed for Moses was originally specified as thirty nights – an approximate lunar month – but God kept the true number of forty hidden so as not to alarm Moses presumably of his impending 'death' and 'decomposition' – which can also be read as his spiritual transformation from *fanā'* (annihilation) to the annihilation of annihilation (*fanā' fī al-fanā'*) in *baqā'* (subsistence).[409] The medieval macrocosm and microcosm were made up of numerous tetralogies: fours, forties and so forth.[410] 'Four is the number of encompassment[411] because

reaches puberty, and every deed that is for the sake of the next world. Being quick in [such actions] is better than being slow. Apply procrastination and slowness to the things of this world. The things of this world that you miss you will not regret, indeed you will rejoice in missing them. But the things of the next world that you miss you will regret.'

408. *Ḥadīth qudsī*. See Hirtenstein and Notcutt, *Divine Sayings*, p. 59. It appears in Muslim, *Ṣaḥīḥ*. *Fut*.II.294 (Chap. 175). See also *Fut*.I.534–5 (Chap. 69).

409. See *Fut*.II, Chaps. 220 and 221, and Ibn 'Arabī's *K. al-Fanā' fī al-mushāhada*.

410. S. Hirtenstein notes the importance that the number four has for Ibn 'Arabī in his Introduction to *Four Pillars* (p. 24) and connects it to the Prophet's *isrā'*: 'In the *Ḥilyat al-abdāl* the four pillars or exterior principles are the prerequisites for spiritual ascension. The pillars correspond, then, in a certain sense, to the *isrā'*, the overland nocturnal journey from Mecca to Jerusalem accomplished by the Prophet prior to his ascension into heaven (*mi'rāj*), an Abrahamic spiritual journey from the 'place of Ishmael' to the 'place of Isaac', a purification process that takes place beyond the four exterior dimensions.'

411. 1 + 2 + 3 + 4 = 10.

it brings together the simple elements.'[412] The human being, says Ibn ʿArabī, is not directly composed of the simple four elements but of composite qualities or temperaments: black bile (cold and dry), yellow bile (hot and dry), phlegm (cold and wet) and blood (hot and wet). All of these composites and the elements they are composed of must dissolve in the forty-day ordeal of retreat, the *arbaʿīn*, until the servant becomes a totality, an 'all': all-ear, all-heart and finally all-tongue of God. It is a terrifying process as Ibn ʿArabī presents it in *Risālat al-Anwār* (*Journey to the Lord of Power*) and the account of his own spiritual *miʿrāj* in the *Futūḥāt*.[413]

> This *isrā'* [in God] dissolves their composite nature (*ḥalla tarkībahum*).[414] He informs them through this *isrā'* of everything that corresponds to them in each world by making them pass over the various kinds of composite and simple worlds. With each world [the servant] abandons everything in his essence that corresponds to it. The form of his abandoning it with [each world] is that God sends down a veil between him and what he abandons of it in that kind of world, so he does not witness [what he abandoned] while the witnessing of what remains subsists with him, until he subsists with the Divine Secret, which is the Specific Face that is from God to him. When he remains alone, the veil of covering is raised from him and he remains with the Most High, just as everything in him remained with what corresponded to it. In this *isrā'* the servant remains He and not-He. Since [the servant] remains He/not-He, He makes him voyage with respect to Him, not with respect to not-Him in a subtle, suprasensible *isrā'*, because in [his] root he is upon the form of the cosmos while in his form he is upon the form of the Most High.[415]

412. *Fut.*I.80 (Chap. 2).

413. See *Fut.*III.335 (Chap. 367) in which the Shaykh is divested of his elemental body, element by element.

414. Ibn ʿArabī calls this *miʿrāj al-taḥlīl* in *R. al-Anwār*. See also the English trans. by Harris, *Journey to the Lord of Power*.

415. *Fut.*III.343 (Chap. 367).

The Siwāk

After the initial thirty days of retreat, Moses uses the *siwāk*, a kind of toothpick.[416] Its use is considered an observance of courtesy, *adab*,[417] a quality that Moses is cautious to observe, thinking it will be pleasing to God. In the interpretation of Ibn Kathīr cited below, however, the action – here connected with the eating of a plant – has the opposite effect on the Almighty:

> Allah instructed him to purify himself by fasting for thirty days, after which he was to go to Mount Sinai, where he would be given the law by which he would govern his people. The ancients said that after Moses fasted thirty days, he hated to speak to his Lord because of the odour of his mouth. He ate a plant of the earth and then his Lord said to him: 'Why did you break your fast?' Moses said: 'O my Lord, I disliked to speak to You with my mouth not having a pleasant smell.' Allah said: 'Do you not know, Moses, the odour of the faster's mouth is more fragrant to Me than the rose. Go back and fast ten days; then come back to Me.' Moses did what Allah commanded.[418]

But *siwāk* does not only refer to the stick for cleaning the teeth. Ibn ʿArabī says:

> The *siwāk* is everything by which one purifies the tongue of the heart, including Qur'anic *dhikr*, which is the most complete purification, and everything that pleases God. For divine sweet fragrances emanate from someone who has these attributes that the people of the scents among the unveiled ones can smell. The Messenger of God – peace and blessings upon him – said concerning the *siwāk*: 'It purifies the mouth and pleases the Lord.' The *siwāk* lifts the veils that are between God and His servant so that he contemplates Him, for it contains two great attributes: purification and pleasing God.

416. See Wensinck, 'Miswāk'. The *miswāk* is the same as the *siwāk*.

417. See *Fut.*I.468 (Chap. 69), where use of the *siwāk* is specifically included under the rubric of *adab*, along with dressing in good clothing for the congregational prayer on Friday. See also *Fut.*IV.473 (Chap. 560).

418. Trans. Geme'ah, *Stories of the Prophets*, p.125.

> The [following] hadith points to this meaning in his – peace and blessings upon him – saying: 'One prayer with the *siwāk* is better than seventy without the *siwāk*.' In the *siwāk* is an indication for the ones who pray through their Lord not through themselves, because it has come [in a Prophetic tradition] that 'God has seventy veils.' So relate what I have mentioned to you to these reports and you will see wonders.[419]

It should be noted that there is a wonderful play on words here, in that *siwāk(a)* means also 'other than you'. The Shaykh combines two hadith that mention the number seventy and suggests that by using the *siwāk*/praying in God's company the veils between servant and Lord are removed and their likeness or equivalence is made manifest.

During the thirty-night tryst, which is quite beyond ordinary concepts of retreat, endured in stillness and silence,[420] Moses is made 'all-ear' in order to listen to God's voice, and 'all-tongue' so as to transmit the full Word. He is given the capacity to engage in face-to-face/mouth-to-mouth unmediated conversation with God and to witness His Self-Disclosure: *And Allah spoke directly to Moses* (Q.4:164). It is very possible that this meeting will involve a move from being one of the *ahl al-bā'* to one of the *ahl al-lām*.[421] God subsists in him as the only agent of his hearing, sight and all his other faculties. His encounter with his Lord will strip him from himself – he will proceed from *fanā'* to *baqā'* and there will be no more Moses.

But this is a situation of the utmost danger, which is why an additional ten-day period is required to strip Moses of the attributes of glory and holiness, which rival those of his Lord and prevent him from entering into the Divine Presence. He must be returned to his essential servanthood.

419. *Fut.*I.468 (Chap. 69). See also *Fut.*I.653ff. (Chap. 71).

420. See *Fut.*II, Chaps. 78 and 79 on *Khalwa*/Abandoning *Khalwa*.

421. See Hirtenstein, *Four Pillars*, p. 19, and n. 209 of this Commentary. See also *Fut.*I.112 (Chap. 5).

The Number Forty

As for the number forty, it is not an insignificant one in religious history and consciousness. An ancient system of time reckoning, quite evident in the Hebrew Bible, was based on forty-day cycles. Among numerous references to this number, we may single out the fact that it is the number of the days and nights of the Flood; the period of purification from childbirth (of male infants – female infants required a doubling of this number);[422] the number of days/nights Elijah fasted;[423] and the number of days Jonah warned the people of Nineveh.[424] Christianity adopted the fondness for the number forty: thus it is the number of days Jesus was tempted in the wilderness,[425] the days of Lent and the period between Easter and Ascension.[426] In letter-based numerology (*jafr/gematria*) it is equivalent to the letter *mīm* (Arabic)/*mem* (Hebrew)[427] with all its manifold symbolism.[428] As M. Chodkiewicz writes in his study of the 'endless voyage', 'it is frequently associated with the period that precedes the infusion of the spirit into the body, or, on the other hand, with the length of time after which the spirit is separated from the body.'[429]

Ibn 'Arabī has a number of interesting references to the number forty, some of which have to do either directly or indirectly with Moses.

> The reality of the station of the appointed time (*mīqāt*) of Moses is the forty nights of these forty [men who are upon the heart of Noah]. For the nighttime belongs to what is hidden and the daytime

422. Lev. 12:2–5.

423. 1 Kgs 19:8.

424. Jonah 3:4.

425. Matt. 4:2; Mark 1:13; Luke 4:2.

426. Acts 1:3.

427. Associated, incidentally, with 'water' (Arabic *ma'*/Hebrew *mayim*), which is appropriate for the unleashing of the waters of the Flood.

428. For the special status of the *mīm* for Ibn 'Arabī, see *K. al-Mīm wa al-wāw wa al-nūn*, trans. Gilis *Le Livre du mīm*. See also Chodkiewicz's remarks in 'Endless Voyage', p.79, n.16: 'In Islam, the number 40, which is the value of the letter *mīm*, is endowed with substantial symbolic importance.'

429. Ibid.

belongs to what is manifest. *And he completed the whole time appointed by his Lord of forty nights* (Q.7:142).[430]

In Chapter 73 of the *Futūḥāt*, Ibn ʿArabī's discussion about the seven Substitutes (*abdāl*) who are 'upon the foot' of one of the major prophets is subsequently given a more detailed elaboration about those followers who are 'upon the heart' of a given prophet, now given a precise number.[431] The men 'upon the heart' of Moses number forty, which corresponds with the station of Moses' 'appointed time' (*mīqāt*) – the forty nights Moses consecrated to the Lord as mentioned in the Qur'an: *And he completed the whole time appointed by his Lord of forty nights* (Q.7:142). Nights, not days, for nighttime is associated with the Unseen, daytime with what is manifest. Forty, not thirty, because as we have seen the number forty has certain spiritual and transformational qualities in many traditions. In the *Futūḥāt*, these forty men are associated with a specific retreat known as the '*arbaʿīn*' (= forty), and in both the *Futūḥāt* and *Isfār* Ibn ʿArabī quotes the Prophetic hadith: 'He who devotes himself exclusively to God for forty mornings, the founts of wisdom will spring from his heart [and] upon his tongue.' Silent devotion to God, or *dhikr nafsī*,[432] is a prerequisite to wise speech.

Deputizing Aaron

The chapter ends with a caution that one who ascends the mountain to meet with his Lord face-to-face should leave behind him someone to watch over his people, as Moses left his brother Aaron as a substitute in his absence. M. Chodkiewicz has an insightful interpretation

430. *Fut.*II.10 (Chap. 73).

431. It should be noted that the *abdāl* of the prophets are seven: Those 'upon the foot' of Abraham, Moses, Aaron, Idrīs, Joseph, Jesus and Adam, while those 'upon the heart' of a given individual coincide only in the case of Adam, Moses and Abraham. The individuals in the latter case are: Adam, Noah, Moses, Abraham, Gabriel, Michael, Israfil (the angel who blows the trumpet on the Day of Resurrection) and David. For being 'on the foot' and 'on the heart' of a given individual, see *Fut.*IV.77 (Chap. 463).

432. *Fut.*II.152 (Chap. 78).

of this: 'For, like Moses on Mount Sinai, he will collapse, struck down (*ṣāʿiqan*) by the power of the theophany: his 'people' – his own human nature – who have remained at the foot of the mountain, must remain under the guard of Divine Law.'[433]

The Voyages of Moses: II. The Voyage of Good Pleasure [Paras. 55–7]

This voyage is once again connected not only to good pleasure, previously alluded to in the first voyage, but also continues the theme of hastening (*ʿajl*). In this case, Moses hastens to meet the Lord so that He will be satisfied. Haste in carrying out righteous deeds is enjoined in the Qur'an (for example, Q.3:114), and the classic example is Abraham's hastening to serve his angelic guests (Q.11:69). This kind of hastening evokes God's good pleasure and does not violate the rules of courtesy.

Servant and Lord share in good pleasure, although in different ways. Engaging in the one activity the utterly and essentially destitute servant was created for, namely to worship God, will never come close to being adequate, while the gifts of God, who is rich beyond measure, to His creatures are perpetual and infinitely abundant. It is clear that any attribute the Divine and the human share can only be seen in terms of correspondence rather than identity. Nonetheless, Lord and servant meet in the mutual waystations of good pleasure, as existence-giving descends and adoration ascends in the divine/human tryst.

Mutual satisfaction and good pleasure, however, should not be emphasized to the exclusion of a hint of discord that darkens this passage. In the first place, there appears to be a note of criticism in the last part of the Lord's question to Moses: *What made you hasten from your people, O Moses?* (Q.20:83; our emphasis) as if to imply that Moses' place was with his people, whom he had left without guidance.[434] And Moses' first response, before claiming that his aim was

433. 'Endless Voyage', p.80.

434. In addition, there does not seem to be much point in hurrying to meet a God who is ever-present and 'closer than the jugular vein'.

God's good pleasure, was that: *they are close on my footsteps* (Q.20:83). It is not clear who 'they' are, and this ambiguity creates a divergence in the interpretation of this verse. If 'they' are Pharaoh's army, then Moses' voyage is one of flight, as we shall consider in his Voyage of Fear. If 'they' are Moses' own people, as they seem to be in this particular interpretation, he mistakenly believes that they so firmly adhere to his example that they are quite safe being left without his counsel. Indeed it is during this voyage that God informs Moses that He has placed a test before his people and that they have failed it. They are not, in fact, following Moses but worshipping a statue of a calf. All of this forms part of God's hidden ruse, to which we have alluded before and to which we will return again in the final chapter. It is God who has unveiled to the Sāmirī[435] just enough of the Bearers of the Throne that he falls into error as to what he has seen and proceeds to mislead the others. Moses does not descend the mountain to return to his people in a state of unadulterated bliss. The saga continues into the next chapter.

The Voyages of Moses: III. The Voyage of Anger and Return [Paras. 58–60]

> My heart is the Sāmirī of the Moment: as often as it sees the footprints it sees the golden one that was turned to gold.[436]

Ibn 'Arabī frequently uses the contrasting attributes of good pleasure and anger, most often in connection with the Prophet and God. God's mercy precedes His wrath. The voyage of good pleasure thus precedes the voyage of anger. Anger is followed by turning in repentance, which occasions once again good pleasure.

435. The Sāmirī, or 'Samaritan', is found in Q.22:85, 87 and 95 as the appellation of the man who tempted the Israelites into the sin of worshipping a Golden Calf that lowed. Scholars have put forth various theories as to who this character might be and what he is doing in the text, including the plausible theory that the story in I Kings 12:28 of Jeroboam and his talking calf may have been conflated with the story of the sin of the Israelites. See Heller, 'al-Sāmirī'.

436. Ibn 'Arabī, *Tarjumān*, trans. Nicholson, p. 112. I have changed his translation of *waqt* as 'time' to 'Moment' in keeping with the other references to this term throughout the text.

Moses' third voyage begins with the Qur'anic verse: *And when Moses returned to his people, angry and grieved* (Q.7:150). Although Ibn 'Arabī does not finish the verse, the concluding words are: *He said: 'Evil it is that ye have done in my place in my absence: Did ye make haste to bring on the judgement of your Lord?* The context is Moses' return from his encounter with God on the mountain, when he discovers that in his absence the people have tired of waiting for him and have 'hastened' to fashion a Golden Calf – the words meaning 'haste' and 'calf', we repeat, are written exactly the same.

This section works in tandem with the preceding one by continuing the themes of delay and haste and by resuming the story of the Sāmirī who incites Moses' people to idol worship based on his own false interpretation (*ta'wīl*) of what he sees. Since Moses is late in returning, having prolonged his retreat and fast for an additional ten days, his people become impatient: 'Humankind is born hasty.'

Although the Sāmirī has joined in the general impatience with Moses' delay on the mountain, taking it upon himself to fashion the animal form, Moses himself is guilty of a kind of rashness in presuming that his brother and deputy Aaron has played a role in encouraging this sacrilegious act. He treats Aaron harshly but later repents when Aaron enjoins him to mercy.[437] The story of Moses' pulling Aaron's beard is in the Qur'an as well as in Ibn Kathīr:

> On his return Moses saw his people singing and dancing around the calf statue. Furious at their paganistic ritual, he flung down the Tablet of the Law he was carrying for them. He tugged Aaron's beard and his hair, crying: 'What held you back when you saw them going astray? Why did you not fight this corruption?'

437. The same story is told in the *Fuṣuṣ*, chapter on Aaron (trans. Austin, *Bezels*, pp. 243–4) with a bit of a twist: Moses is said to have realized more than Aaron what the people were really worshipping: 'being aware that God has ordained that none might be worshipped save Him alone, and that what God ordains surely happens. His rebuke to his brother was because of his [impulsive] rejection of the affair, as also his lack of adequacy [to the occasion]. The gnostic is the one who sees God in everything, indeed, sees Him as the essence of everything.' Ibn 'Arabī's conclusion, anathema to his critics, is that God is inescapably worshipped in every form, even the form of idols.

> Aaron replied: 'O son of my mother, let go of my beard! The fold considered me weak and were about to kill me. So make not the enemies rejoice over me, nor put me among the people who are wrong-doers.'[438]

The Sāmirī, as we have said, saw one of the four Bearers of the Throne[439] who appeared in the form of a bull[440] and he took the part for the whole, believing it to be Moses' God. He also had observed that

> it is a particular characteristic of the spirits that everything on which they descend becomes alive, and life begins to pervade it. Thus did al-Sāmirī arrogate [to himself] some of the influence of the messenger Gabriel, who is a spirit. When he realized that it was Gabriel, and knowing that all he touched would come alive, al-Sāmirī snatched some of it [the dust from the footprint], either with his hand or with his fingertips. Then he transferred it to the [golden] calf, so that it lowed … .[441]

Life-giving is also attributed to Jesus, Abraham, Khiḍr and even Abū Yazīd who brought an ant back to life by breathing on it. In effect, it is only through God's permission that such acts are effective. The Sāmirī, then, who is little better than a magician, is thus given the power to make a statue speak, which is a characteristic of a living thing, all because of the power inherent in the life-giving Spirit.

D. Gril has made a fascinating observation with respect to the Sāmirī. The Sāmirī, he says, 'has followed the path that is the inverse of proper interpretation'.[442] Having been privy to a vision

438. Ibn Kathīr, trans. Geme'ah, *Stories of the Prophets*, p. 127.

439. In this world there are four; in the next there will be eight. See *Fut.*I.147–8 (Chap. 13).

440. 'It was said that one has the form of a man, the second of a lion, the third of an eagle, and the fourth of a bull' (*Fut.*I.148, Chap. 13).

441. *Fuṣūṣ*, chapter on Jesus (trans. Austin, *Bezels*, p. 175) with slight amendment. See also *Fut.*I.237 (Chap. 40).

442. Introduction, *Dévoilement*, p. xxiv.

of the Bearers of the Throne – a 'theophany in forms' – he should have 'crossed over' from these forms to the world of the intelligibles and the Divine Presence. Instead he went the other way, descending into matter by fashioning a calf out of the melted jewellery of Moses' folk. In this he is not so very different from Abraham, who sought to make the dream image of his sacrificed son a material reality.

The Voyages of Moses: IV. The Voyage of Striving for One's Household [Paras. 61–3]

The Danish philosopher Soren Kierkegaard has formulated the general principle of this chapter very succinctly, drawing upon a common etymological root in Danish: 'The nourishment is in the need.'[443]

The narrative of Moses' striving[444] for the sake of his family and finding God at the source of his need is found dispersed in Q.19:52; 20:10–16; 27:7–8; and 28:29–30. It is similar to the biblical story of Moses' encounter with the Voice of God that comes from the Burning Bush.[445] A brief recounting of it comes at the end of the chapter on Moses in the *Fuṣūṣ* and it is also found numerous times in the *Futūḥāt*.[446] Ibn 'Arabī recounts there:

> As for Moses, he was exerting himself fully in seeking fire for his people. It is this that brought him out striving for his family, as he was commanded to do. The prophets are the most severe of all people in making demands upon themselves to undertake the commands of the Real. So there was nothing in Moses' soul save that for which he had come. When he saw his need – the fire that was shining from the tree 'from the right side of al-Ṭūr' (Q.19:52) – God called to him from his need itself as was appropriate to the

443. *Journals and Papers*.

444. The word *sa'y* means in addition to 'striving' and 'endeavour': 'walking' or 'moving towards', 'pursuing' and even 'running towards'. It is also the term used for the walk between the two hills of al-Ṣafā and al-Marwa, which pilgrims perform seven times in succession during the Pilgrimage.

445. Ibn 'Arabī also claims to have experienced this station when he found water once in the desert. See *Fut*.I.609 (Chap. 71).

446. For example, *Fut*.II.277 (Chap. 167).

moment: 'I am thy Lord, so put off thy two shoes; thou art in the holy riverbed Ṭuwā. I myself have chosen thee, so listen to what is revealed.' He did not say, 'to what I reveal.' 'Verily I am God' (Q.20:12–14).

He made Moses firm through the first address, which was the calling, for he had come to borrow a firebrand or to find guidance at the fire. That is Moses' words, 'I may bring you news from it' (Q.28:29), that is, someone who would lead him to his need. Thus he was expecting the call. He had prepared his hearing and his eyesight – [his eyesight] for the vision of the fire, and his hearing for someone who would lead him to his need. Hence, when the call came to him with something appropriate, he did not deny it and he remained firm.

When Moses came to know that the caller was his Lord, while he was already secure in his firmness, and when the call came to him from outside, not from himself, he remained firm in order to give courtesy its full due while he was listening. After all, every sort of self-disclosure has a ruling property, and the ruling property of the call of this self-disclosure is to be prepared for listening to what it brings. So he was not thunderstruck,[447] and he did not become absent from witnessing, for this was an address that underwent binding for the sake of what is heard by the ears, and it was a differentiated address.

That which keeps human beings firm in their sensation and in witnessing sensory objects is their heart that governs their body. But this divine speech to Moses had no face turned toward the heart, so here the heart had nothing but what it received from its hearing, eyesight, and faculties according to habit. Thus, for Moses this state did not transgress its ruling property.[448]

447. Ibn 'Arabī concludes this passage by contrasting it with Muhammad's experience: 'As for the situation of Muhammad, that was a descent on the heart and an undifferentiated address "like a chain across pebbles". So turn your attention to this simile. The heart was occupied with what descended upon it so as to receive it, so it became absent from the governing of its body. This is called "swooning" and "being thunderstruck". The same is true of the angels.'

448. *Fut.*III.215 (Chap. 350), trans. Chittick, *SDG*, p.111, with slight modification.

An additional exegesis is given in *Futūḥāt* Chapter 332:

> God the Most High said in the case of Moses – upon him be peace – informing us: 'And We called him from the right side of al-Ṭūr' (Q.19:52). He made the call from al-Ṭūr because of his inclination (*inḥināʾ*), since [Moses] went out to seek fire for his family due to the loving affection (*ḥunūww*) he had for them. It is what inclination for the one who was created from curvature (*inḥināʾ*) – namely his wife – gave him, because she was basically created from the rib, and the rib is curved. The curvature in the ribs is because of the straightness (*istiqāma*) of the configuration and the preservation of what it inclines to/attaches to/curves toward from the internal organs, in order to embrace with its curvature everything that they contain. ... The Self-Disclosure to Moses happened in the very form of his need. He saw a fire, because it was the object of his quest and he was seeking it. His Lord called him from it but [Moses] did not know that because of his occupation with what he went [searching] for. ...
>
> Like the fire of Moses, he saw it, his very need
> It is the Divinity, but he did not know it.[449]

Thus the voyager is bidden to seek God wherever he most has need: if he is hungry He is the food, if he is thirsty He is the water, if he is ill He is the remedy, if he is homeless He is the shelter; for as Moses discovered, wherever this place is, there God is. 'God revealed to Moses, "O Moses, place none other than Me in the place of your need and ask Me even for the salt you put in your dough."'[450]

In his extensive account of the viziers of the apocalyptic Mahdi in the *Futūḥāt*, Ibn ʿArabī gives one of their qualifications as striving to the utmost of their ability to fulfil the needs of humankind, and he recounts the story of Moses going out in search of fire for his family. It is particularly notable that he uses the word '*asfara*' (unveil) here to describe what Moses is granted as a result of his striving: 'The outcome of that quest was unveiled to him from the speech of his Lord. For

449. *Fut.*III.119 (Chap. 332).
450. *Fut.*II.264 (Chap. 162).

God the Most High spoke to him in his very need itself, which was fire in form, and no thought of that thing had come to him.'[451]

Sense Perception

Ibn ʿArabī's notion of sense perception differs from that of certain of his contemporaries in that he regards it as stemming from a unity rather than from the distinct faculties in themselves. In the *Futūḥāt*[452] he explains that God puts together the perceptions and what perceives them in a way that is customary but which can be broken. Thus although we habitually see through our eyes and hear through our ears, God sometimes causes a person to see through his ears, hear through his eyes and so forth. There is a suggestion in the passage relating to Moses and the fire that this may have been one of these cases since he hears a voice but sees a fire. It also may be the case that God bestows upon a single sense faculty the ability to attain complete knowledge of reality.[453]

In his short and suggestive treatment of this theme, Ibn ʿArabī gives yet another instance of the interplay of unity and diversity. He expands upon this notion in the poem that follows, which alludes to the oneness of essence and manyness of properties. He goes on to say that although God's Essence is unknowable, His exalted qualities unfathomable, God has deposited signs within creation that enable His creatures to know Him to a certain degree.

People of the House

Speaking of the good that comes in exerting oneself for others, especially one's family, leads the Shaykh to mention a specific family – the family of the Prophet Muhammad. As Ibn ʿArabī notes here

451. *Fut.*III.336 (Chap. 365). It is interesting to note that the passage continues with the story of Moses' fleeing from his enemies, which will be dealt with in the next chapter of the *Isfār*.

452. *Fut.*I.213 (Chap. 34).

453. *Fut.*I.218 (Chap. 35).

and on several occasions in the *Futūḥāt*, the People of Muhammad's House, the *Ahl al-Bayt*, have a very special status in Islam. In the *Futūḥāt*'s Chapter 29 on Salmān the Persian and the *Ahl al-Bayt*, the Shaykh uses the same verse he quotes in the *Isfār*: *And Allah only wishes to remove all abomination from you, ye members of the Family, and to make you pure and spotless* (Q.33:33) and discusses it in much the same way. Also in the verse that we have encountered before: *That Allah may forgive thee of thy sin that which is past and that which is to come* (Q.48:2) the purification and safeguarding from sin is once again emphasized.

One of the divine hidden ruses mentioned by the Shaykh in the *Futūḥāt* involves the Prophet's family; some people express love for God and His Messenger while hating or criticizing those belonging to Muhammad's House.[454] It is a test for the Muslims to put up with anything they might judge to be ill-conduct on the part of Muhammad's extended family, bearing it with patience and acceptance.[455] And who are these members of Muhammad's extended family? The *Isfār* tells us, citing the Prophetic hadith, that they are the 'People of the Qur'an, the People of God and His elite.'[456] Ibn ʿArabī thanks God that he is one of their number. And what is the least of its requirements? That one carry the words of the Qur'an in his breast and assume and realize its character traits. Hence we are back again at the example of Abū Yazīd who did not die until he had 'memorized' the Qur'an, to which the Shaykh now adds the story of Abū al-ʿAbbās al-Khashshāb and the disciple recounted in *Isfār* Paragraph 63. All of this serves to emphasize the superiority of those who have embodied ethical and spiritual virtues over those who merely parrot them by rote or examine them with the inadequate though sometimes overly self-satisfied instruments of rational speculation.

454. *Fut.*I.198 (Chap. 29).

455. See also *Fut.*IV.448–9 (Chap. 560), where the recipient of the Shaykh's advice is cautioned not to fight with the people of the *dhikr* of *tawḥīd* – There is no god but Allah – even if they are guilty of immense sins. As long as they are not guilty of associating others with God, God meets their sins with forgiveness.

456. *Isfār*, Para. 63.

> [T]he exoteric scholars have preferred this world to the next and the side of creation to the side of the Real. They have become accustomed to taking knowledge from books and from the mouths of men of their own kind. They think they are of the Folk of Allah because of that which they know and by which they surpass the common people. All of this has veiled them from knowing that God has servants whom He has undertaken to teach, in their inmost mystery, what He has sent down in His Books and upon the tongues of His messengers.[457]

The upshot of this section, therefore, is that it is possible for anyone to belong to the family of the Prophet, not just those who claim blood relationship, as long as they embody the Prophetic character traits and become living exemplars of the Qur'an. It is to point out this fact that the Shaykh dedicated a chapter of the *Futūḥāt* to Salmān the Persian, who was not related to the Prophet by birth but became so by adoption due to his fine qualities.

The Voyages of Moses: V. The Voyage of Fear[458] [Paras. 64–7]

> Then, when he was sought [for the crime he had committed], he left [that place] in flight, outwardly afraid, while inwardly seeking deliverance, since all motivation springs from love, the observer being diverted from this by its other less important causes.[459]

The context of this chapter of the *Isfār* is Moses' flight from Pharaoh to his Lord, as narrated in the Qur'an, Suras 26 and 28. Ibn 'Arabī,

457. *Fut.*I.279 (Chap. 54), trans. Chittick, *SPK*, p.248. The entire section (pp.246–50) merits close reading.

458. Ibn 'Arabī remarks in Chap. 82 (*Fut.*II.155), discussed below: 'We have mentioned this Musawī flight in *K. al-Isfār 'an natā'ij al-asfār*. He writes that he has called Moses' flight *safar al-ṭalab*, a term that can bear contradictory meanings. Although the more common meaning has to do with seeking, it can also mean distancing. For this latter meaning, see Lane, *Lexicon*, vol. 1, p.164: 'He, or it, ... was, or became, distant, or remote.' (I thank Stephen Hirtenstein for this reference.) It is possible that Ibn 'Arabī, in his characteristic way, intended to convey both meanings at once, perfectly conveying the sense of the Prophet's words: 'I seek refuge in Thee from Thee.'

459. *Fuṣūṣ*, chapter on Moses (trans. Austin, *Bezels*, p.257).

both here and in the *Futūḥāt*, connects fear[460] with a special kind of hastening – flight – and joins it as well to faith, and ultimately to unveiling what is concealed and prophecy.[461]

Flight is a specific kind of voyaging, one propelled in most instances by fear and avoidance. Ibn ʿArabī devotes several chapters in the *Futuḥāt* to this seemingly negative sort of travel. In addition to Moses' fifth voyage, the *Isfār*'s mention in the Prologue of Jonah's voyage, though not one of the elaborated texts, is also a flight. Lot's departure from Sodom may also be considered a flight. In fact, Ibn ʿArabī most often gives fleeing a positive value. In the *Futūḥāt*, he gives the Prophet Muhammad's pre-Revelation retreats from society and seclusion in a cave on Mount Ḥirāʾ as an example of commendable flight: 'He fled to his Lord until the Real came upon him suddenly. Then God sent him as a rightly guided messenger to His servants.'[462] It is similarly due to Moses' flight that he is appointed vicegerent. As in the story of Adam, what on the surface appears to be something negative has positive repercussions.

Moses' fears are listed in *Futūḥāt*, Chapter 16.[463] First there is his natural fear of serpents when he sees the magicians' snakes gliding and when his own staff turns into a serpent. His second fear was for his community, that they might be misled and not be able to distinguish between imagination and reality, or between what is from God and what is not. He feared that he would be considered a common magician, but the fear he evinced upon seeing the snakes was convincing for Pharaoh's magicians and the eyewitnesses, since a magician would not be afraid of his own optical illusion. Sura 26 describes Moses' fear numerous times. He fears that the people to whom God wishes to send him do not fear God (Q.26:11) and that they will accuse him of falsehood (Q.26:12), that he will feel

460. The word he uses here is *khawf*, as opposed to another word frequently given the same translation: *taqwā*, which has more of a specific meaning suggesting 'God-fearing'.

461. See *Fut.*II.184 (Chap. 100: On the Station of Fear).

462. *Fut.*II.22 (Chap. 73).

463. See also *Fut.*I.235 (Chap. 40), which also discusses Moses' fear in connection with the serpents.

constrained in heart and halting in speech (Q.26:13) and finally, that he will be punished for the crime he committed (Q.26:14): slaying the Egyptian.[464] When Moses fulfils his mission and speaks to Pharaoh, Pharaoh accuses him not only of smiting the Egyptian but also of ingratitude, since Moses had been adopted as Pharaoh's son. It is at this point that Moses pronounces the speech given at the beginning of this chapter of the *Isfār*: *So I fled from you when I feared you; and My Lord bestowed upon me a command and made me one of His Messengers* (Q.26:21).[465] Thus the implication is that it was because of Moses' fear and flight that he was made a legislating prophet, although he himself was unaware of the real source of his flight at the time, assigning it to Pharaoh rather than to God.[466]

Unstated but certainly suggested is the Prophet Muhammad's *hijra* (emigration) from Mecca, where he was in imminent danger, to Medina, which resulted in his final victory. This is confirmed in Chapter 82 of the *Futūḥāt* (On Flight): 'Fleeing resulted in (*antaja*)[467] Moses' mission and rule, for he became a vicegerent and a messenger; the messenger does not become a ruler until he is a vicegerent.'[468]

Chapter 82 contributes much to the understanding of this voyage of Moses by pointing out the relevance of the prepositions 'from' (*min*) and 'to' (*ilā*), which set the course of flight. 'From' and 'to' are extremes marking the beginning and end. There appear to be two distinctly opposite kinds of flight, determined by the two prepositions: a flight 'from' something specific that mentions no specific

464. The *Fuṣūṣ* quite remarkably attributes the slaying of the Egyptian to God's inspiration: 'The first test was his killing of the Egyptian, which was inspired in him by God and deposited in his inmost heart, although he himself did not know it. He did not really have any interest in killing him, although he did not hesitate when God's command came to him. That is because the prophet is inwardly protected, being unaware of something until God informs him of it.' (*Fuṣūṣ*, chapter on Moses, trans. Austin, *Bezels*, p.256.)

465. See also *Fut.*IV.183ff. (Chap. 539: On knowledge of the state of the Pole whose station is: 'Therefore flee unto Allah; lo! I am a plain warner unto you from Him. And set not any other god along with Allah; lo! I am a plain warner unto you from Him', Q.51:50–1.)

466. See *Fut.*III.264 (Chap. 358).

467. The Arabic is *antaja*, from the same root as *natā'ij* (results), which figures in the title of the book: *al-Isfār 'an natā'ij al-asfār*.

468. *Fut.*II.155 (Chap. 82).

'to' and a flight 'to' something specific that has no designated 'from'. Although Moses' flight had a designated 'from' in the form of Pharaoh, it had no designated 'to' other than a general salvation (*najāh*). The flight that has a designated 'to' may be the flight to God, which is enjoined by God in the Qur'an: *Flee to Allah* (Q.51:50). 'We may flee "*to* Him, *from* Him", such as his saying: "I seek refuge with Thee from Thee!" and we may flee "*to* Him" *from* a certain being from among the beings; or from a certain attribute from among the attributes – whether divine or not divine – or an attribute of an act or something other than an attribute of an act.'[469] In Chapter 539 of the *Futūḥāt*, Ibn ʿArabī puts the situation in stark terms: 'the Mūsawī flees *from* and the Muhammadī flees *to*, from God the Most High's command to him to flee.'[470]

'Flee to Allah', the Qur'an tells us, to the all-encompassing Name. It was a specific Name, however, that demanded of Moses, as it demands of us, to flee to Him: 'it is the Name "the Bestower" (*al-Wahhāb*), which He gives as a special favour. That bestowal made [Moses] a messenger necessarily.'[471] It was of no importance that Moses' flight was 'from' Pharaoh, a mere creature, although Ibn ʿArabī points out that (in contradistinction to earlier communities) the Muhammadian community has been freed of this necessity to fear any created thing. That specific flight, in any case, was cut off by Pharaoh's drowning. Of greater importance is the fact that Moses did not mention 'to' what he was fleeing. He was thus recompensed with *ḥukm* – temporal authority of all kinds: imamate, messengerhood, vicegerency – which is also cut off, unlike sainthood. On the other hand, the flight associated with Muhammad is a flight <u>to</u> God: 'the flight *to* God gives what subsists along with God's subsistence. It is not specifically designated, but the designation is *to* God, whether the flight is or is not *from* God; the consideration here is *to* whom one flees, while in the case of Moses it was *from* whom he fled.'[472]

469. Ibid.
470. *Fut.*IV.183 (Chap. 539).
471. Ibid.
472. *Fut.*II.155 (Chap. 82).

> If you want to know concerning your flight whether you are Musawī or Muhammadī, then contemplate the beginning of the goal which is the particle 'from' and [contemplate] the end of the goal which is the particle 'to', for the Prophet Muhammad says: 'Flee then to Allah. I am from Him a Warner to you' (Q.51:50). And he said in his seeking refuge: 'I seek refuge with You.' So this is his command and his supplication. And He said about Moses by way of informing us: 'I fled from you when I feared you' (Q.26:21). And He said to the Muhammadī: 'Be ye not afraid of them, but fear Me' (Q.3:175). The governing principle with the Muhammadī is the end of the goal while with the Musawī it is the beginning of the goal.[473]

The Muhammadian community has been enjoined to flee to Allah, a Being who has no 'where', hence the flight of the Muhammadians is shrouded in unknowing:

> No one who flees to Him knows, when He meets him and takes his hand, where He is taking him. For God is swifter to meet the one who flees to Him than the one who flees to Him [is to meet God]. He says – and He is the Truthful, the Most High: 'Whoever comes to Me hastening, I come to him rushing',[474] hence He describes Himself as meeting His servant when he comes to Him by doubling the way he comes to Him at the time. The coming of the one who flees is more forceful than rushing, so the Real's coming to him will be more forceful than that.[475]

In the *Futuḥāt*'s Chapter 100, which is specifically dedicated to the station of fear, the servant is said to fear both the veil and the lifting of the veil. He fears the veil because the veil is ignorance of God, but he fears the lifting of the veil because in it lies his annihilation as an ego, ironically not for egotistical reasons but because it takes a certain separation between servant and Lord to enjoy the Lord's company.[476] Hence the station of fear is a station of indeterminate

473. *Fut.*IV.431 (Chap. 559).
474. Prophetic hadith.
475. *Fut.*II.155 (Chap. 82).
476. *Fut.*II.184 (Chap. 100).

'bewilderment and halting'.[477] If it is a station, it is intimately linked with the Divinity; if it is a state, it is fear of any number of individuals or secondary causes.

In the chapter that follows, the Shaykh reassures the disciple that contemplating the glories of God's Face will allow him to subsume his light in the Light of God's glory. 'No entity of theirs has gone, but no entity of theirs is manifest. So they are seen and not seen, because they are behind the veil of the Most Magnificent Light.'[478] This brings to mind the many accounts of Moses' face shining like a sun when he descended from his appointed tryst with his Lord.[479] But whether this station frees one from the danger of the Divine Ruse, which we will discuss in the next section, the Shaykh, out of precaution, is not prepared to discuss.

The Janus-Faced Hypocrite and the Jeroboa's Tunnel [Para. 67]

Surely the hour is coming – I am about to make it manifest[480]
Verily the hour is coming; My design is to keep it hidden.[481]

Words derived from the root *kh-f-y*, which means both to reveal and conceal, are one of those oddities of the Arabic language that are called *'aḍdād*, homonyms which have multiple and contrary meanings, or to give them their English technical terms, autoantonyms, self-antonyms, contronyms, antagonyms and Janus-words.[482] The question of *'aḍdād* was repeatedly studied by the Arab lexicographers because its irrationality was hard to fathom. After all, Arabic was supposed to be a language of unparalleled logic and harmony, and such features were embarrassing and difficult to explain. In particular, it was hard for anyone who believed in the divine

477. Ibid.

478. *Fut.*II.185 (Chap. 101).

479. See, for example, *Fut.*IV.50 (Chap. 438).

480. Q.20:15, trans. Shakir; our emphasis.

481. Q.20:15, trans. Yusuf Ali; our emphasis.

482. A few examples in English are: adumbrate, cleave, dust, fast, trim and weather. For more, see www.answerbag.com/q_view/13312, and the extensive list in http://en.wikipedia.org/wiki/List_of_auto-antonyms_in_English, both accessed May 2014.

imposition of language to understand why God would have assigned opposite meanings to the same word. Ibn al-Anbārī (d. 939/40) in his *Kitāb al-ʿAḍdād* examines this question perhaps more than anyone. He attributes this feature to the mixed character of classical Arabic with its variety of dialects and accretions from foreign tongues.[483]

All well and good. Ibn ʿArabī's fascination with the Arabic language knew no bounds and his bringing up this example of *ʿaḍdād* is a case in point. But one wonders what this strange paragraph with its talk about hypocrites and jeroboas has to do with anything, although we do recall that revealing and concealing plays a large role in this text.[484] The key to understanding this paragraph, however, comes in the Janus-faced verb *khafiya*, and its connection to Moses' previous voyage, the Voyage of Striving for One's Household. It turns out that in the Qur'anic passage that narrates Moses' search for fire, which culminated in the voice from the Burning Bush, God addresses Moses with the ambiguous verse that heads our commentary on this paragraph. Since the verses that precede this verse provide resonance, we cite them as well:

1. *Ṭa-Ha.*[485]
2. *We have not sent down the Qur'an to you so that you should feel distress,*
3. *But only as a reminder to those who fear Allah,*
4. *A revelation from Him Who created the earth and the high heavens.*
5. *Allah the All-Merciful is established on the Throne.*
6. *To Him belongs what is in the heavens and on earth, and all between them, and all beneath the soil.*
7. *If thou pronounce the word aloud, (it is no matter): for verily He knoweth what is secret and what is yet more hidden.*
8. *Allah. There is no god but He! To Him belong the most Beautiful Names.*

483. Rabin, *Ancient West-Arabian*, p. 19.

484. Ibn ʿArabī also uses this example in Chap. 68 of the *Futūḥāt* in connection with the practice of wiping over one's shoes in ablution. There the root *kh-f-y* is made to resemble the root *kh-f-f*, which gives *khuff* = shoe. 'We say that shoes (*khuff*) are called *khuff* from "hiddenness" (*khafāʾ*) because they veil the foot in an absolute fashion.' He then remarks that this is a 'marvellous secret' and gives the Imrū al-Qays verse about the jeroboas (*Fut.*I.347).

485. The opening line, from which this sura takes its name, consists of two of the isolated letters opening some suras whose meaning is concealed, known only to God.

9. *Has the story of Moses reached thee?*
10. *Behold, he saw a fire: So he said to his family, 'Tarry ye; I perceive a fire; perhaps I can bring you some burning brand therefrom, or find some guidance at the fire.'*
11. *But when he came to the fire, a voice was heard: 'O Moses!'*
12. *'Verily I am thy Lord! Therefore put off thy shoes: thou art in the sacred valley Ṭuwā.'*
13. *'I have chosen thee: listen, then, to the inspiration.'*
14. *'Verily, I am Allah. There is no god but I: So serve thou Me, and establish regular prayer for celebrating My praise.'*
15. *'Verily the Hour is coming. My design is to keep it hidden/is to make it manifest, for every soul to receive its reward by the measure of its endeavour.'*[486] (Q.20:1–15)[487]

Thus the passage is another somewhat obscure reference to apocalyptic times that we have had hints to previously: the question of knowledge vs. practice and the talking *gharqad* bush of Paragraph 8, the 'sign of the *tannūr*' and 'unveiled leg' of Paragraph 40. The

486. Arabic: *saʿy*, the same root as we find in the title of the previous voyage.

487. This translation is by Yusuf Ali. Note below some of the variations in translating this problematic verse. Is God concealing or revealing? (The emphases are mine):

George Sale (1734): Verily the hour cometh: I will surely manifest the same, that every soul may receive its reward for that which it hath deliberately done.

Edward Henry Palmer (1880): Verily, the hour is coming, I almost make it appear, that every soul may be recompensed for its efforts.

Yusuf Ali (1938): Verily the Hour is coming – My design is to keep it hidden – for every soul to receive its reward by the measure of its Endeavour.

Muhammad Shakir: Surely the hour is coming – I am about to make it manifest – so that every soul may be rewarded as it strives.

M. M. Pickthall (1930): Lo! the Hour is surely coming. But I will to keep it hidden, that every soul may be rewarded for that which it striveth (to achieve).

Mohsin Khan: Verily, the Hour is coming – and I am almost hiding it from Myself – that every person may be rewarded for that which he strives.

Muhammad Asad: Behold, [although] I have willed to keep it hidden, the Last Hour is bound to come, so that every human being may be recompensed in accordance with what he strove for [in life].

Amutal Rahman Omar: Surely, the Hour (of Resurrection) is bound to come. I am about to unveil it, so that every soul may be rewarded in accordance with its endeavour.

A. J. Arberry (1955): The Hour is coming; I would conceal it that every soul may be recompensed for its labours.

ambiguity of this verse is particularly well-suited to the Shaykh's general theme of veiling/unveiling, manifesting/concealing. The signs of the Hour, he suggests, are both hidden and apparent, and for those able to read the signs in this last third of the night, there are ample opportunities to reap spiritual knowledge and gain salvation.

A brilliant play on words brings together two species known for their devious concealment. The jeroboa hiding in its hole (*nāfiqā'*) believes it is safe by having an escape route through the second door, just as the Janus-faced hypocrite (*munāfiq*) with his assurances of faith, readily discarded in other company, believes he is safe from human and divine opprobrium by his clever subterfuge. In the end, however, God turns out to be the ultimate Trickster, Master of the Divine Hidden Ruse, as we shall see in the following section.[488]

The Voyages of Moses: VI. The Voyage of Caution [Paras. 68–70]

Voyages are accomplished inwardly, and the most hazardous ones, needless to say, are made without moving from the spot.[489]

The brief poem that initiates the final voyage is only implicitly connected with Moses, whose name does not appear either in the two-line verse or indeed in the chapter at all. The speaker of the lines referring to the night journey with his family, the world of creation and command, and God's decree of death to the 'enemy of religion' by drowning, could be anyone: Moses, Ibn 'Arabī, or even the present reader. While Pharaoh is clearly the absent individual alluded to in the initial poem and opening line of the chapter, the

488. Ibn 'Arabī uses the example of the two exits in a number of startlingly different ways. For example, he compares the two exits of impure excretions – urine and faeces – to the hypocrite and the doubter. See *Fut.*I.354 (Chap. 68). Again in Chap. 70 (*Fut.*I.587) he uses the jeroboa's tunnel as a vivid metaphor, focusing here on the root *n-f-q*, which gives, as we have seen, the meanings of tunnel (*nafaq*), hypocrite (*munāfiq*) and now 'to spend' (*nafaqa*) as related to the two aspects of giving and taking, expressed by the two hands of Creator and creature, as well as the recourse to two (or more) meanings of ambiguous terms.

489. Miller, *The Colossus of Maroussi*, p.85.

address that follows gradually takes the form of a warning to every voyager to be God-wary.

In the *Futūḥāt*, Ibn ʿArabī has explicitly connected caution to both unveiling (*sufūr*) and voyaging (*safar*) in the opening poem of his Chapter 174: On Knowledge of the Station of the Voyage and Its Secrets. He writes:

> Unveiling (*sufūr*) is a sign of fear (*khawf*) and caution (*ḥadhar*).
> This is the custom when conveying the news.
> For if you see that the maiden of the tribe has removed her veil
> (*safarat*),
> Let your ransom from this be upon caution.[490]

As noted previously, Ibn ʿArabī gives the same example early on in the *Isfār* both to connect unveiling to voyaging through the Arabic linguistic root *s-f-r* and to suggest the dangers inherent in both external and internal 'voyaging'. It is of vital importance to know how to read the signs correctly, thus fear and caution are the attributes of this station.

In the lines that follow those we have quoted above, the Shaykh takes up notions that appear to have little to do with voyaging, yet when considering the extended meaning of *safar* as reflection on both the cosmos and the Qurʾan, the disparate pieces begin to fall into place.

> For that reason we claim that the possible things among the
> forms (*ṣuwar*)
> In their roots have no concrete reality.
> Do not profess any doctrine of insubstantiation (*ḥulūl*),
> For these forms have no existence,
> Although they may be engendered (*takwīn*) in the *sūras* (*suwar*).

What is particularly notable here in connection with the *Isfār* is the juxtaposition of forms and (Qurʾanic) suras. Both may be taken as signs (*āyāt*) of God, the first visible to the eye and the second gleaned

490. *Fut.*II.293.

from Revelation. Both are paths available to all, regardless of intellectual capacity or acuity, but what will be learned from them depends on the spiritual insight and unveiling of the individual seeker.

Predestination [Para. 68]

Although only briefly alluded to in this final chapter, the 'secret of predestination' (*qadar*) is a topic that stimulated Ibn 'Arabī's interest in many of his works.[491] It is a delicate topic, for it brings into question notions of free will and individual responsibility. The *Isfār*'s chapters on Adam's voyage and Moses' voyage for the sake of his household have already touched upon this issue, and the *Futūḥāt* discusses it in more detail. The crux of the matter is this, as Ibn 'Arabī cites as his proof text: *None of us there is, but has a known station* (Q.37:164). This station is known only to God, for He alone knows the preparedness and capacity of every fixed entity. Prophets and messengers are safeguarded from sin; this is their station, their *'iṣma*, or sinlessness, despite the appearance of their actions. Saints, or friends of God – those individuals included in the People of the (Prophet's) House – also have a measure of protection, their *ḥifẓ*, although it is not as extensive as that of the prophets and messengers since they are not charged with the promulgation of God's message.[492] Certain individuals belonging to categories covered in Q.33:35[493] are also predeterminately forgiven their sins.[494] Unless individuals are informed of their

491. See, for example, *Fuṣūṣ*, chapter on Ezra.

492. See *Fut.*I.515 (Chap. 69).

493. 'Lo! Men who surrender unto Allah and women who surrender, and men who believe and women who believe, and men who obey and women who obey, and men who speak the truth and women who speak the truth, and men who persevere and women who persevere, and men who are humble and women who are humble, and men who give alms and women who give alms, and men who fast and women who fast, and men who guard their modesty and women who guard [their modesty], and men who remember Allah much and women who remember. Allah hath prepared for them forgiveness and a magnificent reward' (Q.33:35).

494. 'God has prepared for them forgiveness before the predestined sin has been committed, out of solicitude towards them. This indicates that they are among the "servants whom sin does not harm". It has come in the *Ṣaḥīḥ* from a divine report: "Do what you will,

known station by God, the secret of their predestination remains unknown and they cannot be certain to be free of myriad temptations and trials as they voyage in the 'world of creation and command'.

The question then arises: if a person's station is known and fixed for all eternity, what good is the law? If I am predestined to commit disobedient acts, then where is my free will? Paradoxically, however, as Ibn 'Arabī explains, the known station of 'the two weighty ones' – humankind and jinn – is its very unknowability until the very end of their lives. Alone among God's creatures, these two groups only arrive at their known station when they cease travelling in the world of creation and command, that is, when they take their final breath. Their entire lives consist of the voyage of ascent – by following God's commands – or the voyage of descent – by following their own desires and yielding to temptation.[495]

Temptation and Trial [Para. 69]

Temptation comes in many forms, as Ibn 'Arabī points out in many places in his writings. One of the greatest temptations is the knowledge that one is created upon the form of the Real. While on the one hand, seekers are exhorted to know themselves as a way of knowing their Lord, the trial is then to not wax proud in this knowledge but to remain at the root of servanthood, in imitation of the Prophet Muhammad, rather than to claim lordliness, in imitation of Pharaoh.

One must also be scrupulous in courtesy towards the Divine Reality. This consists in attributing to Him only what He has revealed about Himself, aware that any claims on the part of the intellect are essentially false, since intellect cannot know Him in any way. If what God claims in His Revelation entails what appears contradictory or

for I have forgiven you." Such sins are not committed by such as these save by the determined predestination, not sacrilegiously. Abū Yazīd was asked, "Does a knower transgress?" He replied: "The command of Allah is a decree determined" (Q.33:38). The knowers, the people of [God's] solicitude, may transgress/disobey in accordance with what has been determined in order to execute the precedent decree.' *Fut.*II.23 (Chap. 73).

495. See *Fut.*I.259 (Chap. 47).

impossible to the intellect, the intellect's tools must be set aside. The intellect's tool is logic, and the Aristotelian logic that Ibn ʿArabī's contemporaries among the philosophers favoured champions three principles, all of which are demolished by Ibn ʿArabī. First is the law of identity: if you have A then you have A. Second is the law of the excluded middle: for any statement, either that statement is true or its negation is true. Third is the law of noncontradiction: contrary statements cannot both be true.[496] As we have seen in this text, these rational laws do not apply when speaking about the ultimate Reality in which paradox reigns. And we have observed throughout the *Isfār* the Shaykh's criticism of those who interpret Scripture based on intellect as opposed to divine informing.

Another form of temptation and trial comes to those who have been given charismata of various sorts; these rare gifts are a major sign of God's hidden ruse. The sober among God's folk do not exhibit them unless a divine command comes to them to do so. We are reminded of the Sāmirī in the previous chapters, who formed a calf and induced it to low – certainly an exhibit of magical powers. Contrast this to Moses' turning his rod into a snake – by God's command.

Perhaps the most puzzling sort of temptation that calls for precaution is the temptation to feel secure in God's favour, that the place one must be most wary is precisely that place where one feels safe, and that one must be most cautious of precisely the One to whom one goes for recourse.

Above all, one must beware of God's hidden ruse. That Moses is well aware of God's hidden ruse is evident in his saying in the wake of the incident of the calf: *It is but Thy trial. Thou sendest whom Thou wilt astray* (Q.7:155), in other words, *You make perplexed – 'and Thou guidest whom Thou wilt'* (Q.7:155).[497] Moses is no stranger to

496. 'The stubborn person [who denies the law of noncontradiction] should be subjected to burning, since [to him] fire and not-fire are the same; and he should suffer the pain of beating, since [to him] pain and not-pain are the same; and he should be denied food and drink, since [to him] eating and drinking and abstention from them are the same' (Avicenna, *The Metaphysics of The Healing*, commenting on Aristotle's *Topics*).

497. *Fut.*II.189 (Chap. 108). See also *Fut.*II.159 (Chap. 85).

trial: 'God tempted him many times, testing him in many situations, so that patience with God's trials might be realized in him.'[498] One must beware of the Divine Ruse more when things are going well and one is feeling particularly blessed than when one is undergoing severe trials: 'So take caution for yourself, for the temptation through expansiveness (*ittisāʿ*) is greater than the temptation through constraint (*ḥaraj*) and narrowness.'[499]

Caution Against Relying upon Thought and Reflection [Para. 69]

As if to come full circle,[500] this final voyage of the *Isfār* expresses the caution one must take with respect to relying upon one's intellect rather than upon God's Revelation. Although there is a use for proper reflection when it is kept within bounds, allowing one's reason to roam in areas where it can never ascertain the truth of its own accord is a dangerous enterprise. Speculation on the nature of God's Essence is expressly forbidden and at best one must limit one's search for knowledge to God's signs, in the cosmos and in oneself.

The way of the intellect is the way of the philosopher, who shares the category of voyaging <u>in</u> God with the messengers, prophets and saints.[501] Chapter 190 of the *Futūḥāt*, which we have discussed above, describes the stages of the voyage of reflective thought (*fikr*).[502] The highest point reflective thought is able to reach of its own accord appears to be knowledge that God has sent messengers and that there is proof for their veracity. At this point, the philosopher

498. *Fuṣūṣ*, chapter on Moses (trans. Austin, *Bezels*, p.256).

499. *Fut.*II.189 (Chap. 108).

500. The *Isfār* ends where in a sense it begins, with references in the opening poem to setting out on a Night Journey and to the drowning of the uncautious voyager in the sea of his own erroneous reflections. Further insight regarding Pharaoh, the egomaniacal arch-rationalist, versus Moses, the man of inspired vision, may be drawn from a careful perusal of the verbal exchange between the two in the Moses chapter in the *Fuṣūṣ*. See also *Fut.*III.90 (Chap. 324), where the discussion focuses on Pharaoh's presumptuous seeking to know the Essence of God. For Pharaoh's complex role in the writings of Ibn ʿArabī, see Gril, 'Le personage coranique'.

501. See *Isfār*, Para. 7.

502. See section on *safar*, pp.156–9.

acknowledges that he is among those to whom the Messenger has been sent and he enters the higher path of voyaging as a believer.[503]

There is nothing inherently wrong with the voyage of reflective thought; the Shaykh himself admits to his own wayfaring along that path, mounted upon the Burāq of his *fikr.* Moreover, the Qur'an is full of directives to the signs visible in the cosmos for 'those who reflect'[504] and draw lessons. But there are two primary dangers in this mode of 'travel', which, as we have seen, Ibn 'Arabī has likened to a sea voyage.[505] The first danger is that there is no guide available for the philosopher until he reaches that transformative moment when he recognizes the truth of the Messenger. In fact, until that point, he tends to disparage the believers in their reliance on, and imitation of their guide. He may stray from the course at any juncture, or like Pharaoh in the poem that begins the *Isfār*'s chapter on caution, he may drown in the gloomy seas of his own erroneous opinions.

The second danger is that the way of the philosopher is only one way among others, and it simply does not lead all the way to the knowledge he seeks.

The speculative thinker is restricted by the authority of his thought (*fikr*), but thought has only its own specific playing field among the playing fields in which to roam. Every faculty in the human being has a playing field in which it roams that it should not overstep. Whenever it oversteps its field, it falls into error and mistake and is described as having deviated from its straight path.[506]

What the philosopher learns on his progression through the realms of scientific investigation is very different from what the believer learns. The rather pitiful picture Ibn 'Arabī paints of the philosopher in the *Futūḥāt*'s chapter on the Alchemy of Happiness vividly demonstrates this path's deficiency. The speculative philosopher

503. See *Fut.*II.270ff. (Chap. 167), 'The Alchemy of Happiness', in which the spiritual *mi'rāj* of a philosopher and a believer is beautifully differentiated. See also Hirtenstein, 'The Brotherhood of Milk'.

504. For example, Q.13:3; 30:21.

505. See *Isfār*, Para. 7 and Commentary, pp. 145–7.

506. *Fut.*II.281 (Chap. 167). Both the speculative thinker and Pharaoh are described as overstepping their bounds.

has learned none of the esoteric truths on his philosophical *miʿrāj* and must wait, dejected, outside the heavenly Visited House for his companion, the believer, to complete his celestial ascent and return to him. He cannot even confess his faith at this point but must return to the beginning of the path where, as a believer, he will have to make the ascent again.

CONCLUSION

In the end, which has no end, we keep voyaging through this life, pausing only to contemplate the signs in the horizon and in ourselves, reaping whatever knowledge is in keeping with our preparedness and our receptivity. When one voyages in the company of the Shaykh al-Akbar one must be ready to wander in myriad directions, pausing to observe the various signposts and waymarks, learning lessons from the individuals one encounters, occasionally taking off after a mirage only to be returned to the path through God's grace and solicitude. Guiding vision most often comes to us in momentary flashes, cautionary advice in fragmentary phrases. But whatever the voyage, whether from, in or to, it is never without its with, and He is the best Companion.

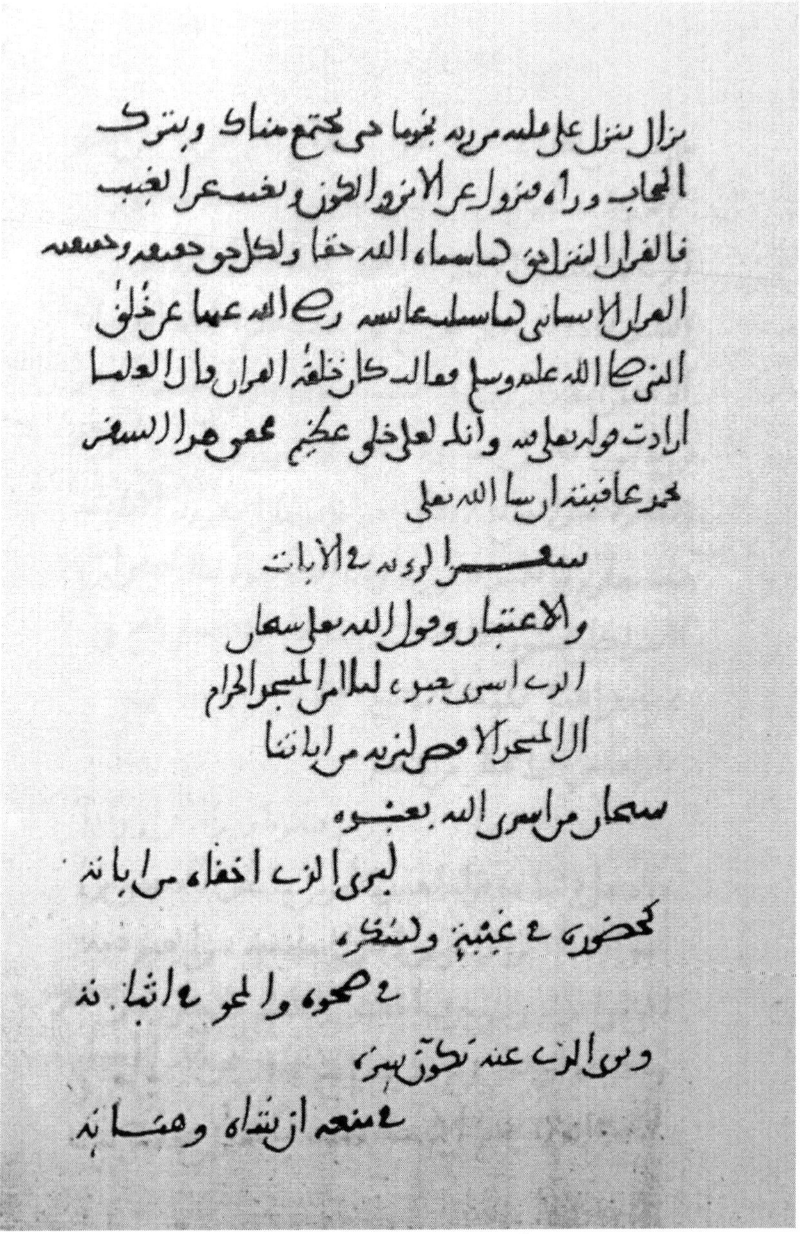
يزال ينزل على قلبه مريده بنجومها حتى يجتمع هناك ويترك
الحجاب وراءه فيزول عن الاين والكون ويحضر عن الغيب
فالقرآن المنزل حق كما اسماء الله حقا ولكل حق حقيقة وحقيقة
القرآن الانساني كما سئلت عائشة رضي الله عنها عن خلق
النبي صلى الله عليه وسلم فقالت كان خلقه القرآن وقال العلماء
ارادت قوله تعالى وانك لعلى خلق عظيم فحق هذا السفر
نحو عافيته ان شاء الله تعالى
شعر اورده في الآيات
والاعتبار وقول الله تعالى سبحان
الذي اسرى بعبده ليلا من المسجد الحرام
الى المسجد الاقصى لنريه من آياتنا
سبحان من اسرى الله بعبده
ليري الذي اخفاه من آياته
لحضوره في غيبة وبسكره
في صحوه والمحو في اثباته
وبين الذي عنه تكون بسره
في منعه ان شاه وهباته

Folio 20b from the holograph, MS. Yusuf Ağa 4859, undated.

BIBLIOGRAPHY

The following abbreviations are used:

EI = *Encyclopaedia of Islam*, 1st edn. M. T. Houtsma (ed.). Leiden: E. J. Brill and Luzac, 1913–38.
EI2 = *Encyclopaedia of Islam*, 2nd edn. P. Bearman, Th. Bianquis, C. E. Bosworth, E. van Donzel and W. P. Heinrichs (eds.). Leiden: Brill, 1991–2004.
EI3 = *Encyclopaedia of Islam*, 3rd edn. G. Krämer, D. Matringe, J. Nawas and E. Rowson (eds.). Brill Online, 2009–.
EQ = *Encyclopaedia of the Qur'ān*. Jane Dammen McAuliffe (ed.). Leiden: Brill, 2010.
JAOS = *Journal of the American Oriental Society.*
JMIAS = *Journal of the Muhyiddin Ibn 'Arabi Society.*

abrahampath.org/path/hebronhebron-sites/nebi-yaqin/accessed 20/4/2015.

Abrahamov, Binyamin. 'Acquisition', *EI3*.

—— *Ibn al-'Arabī and the Sufis.* Oxford: Anqa Publishing, 2014.

Abū Dāwūd. *al-Sunan*. A. S. 'Alī (ed.). Cairo: Muṣṭafā al-Bābī al-Ḥalabī, 1952.

Addas, Claude. 'Abū Madyan and Ibn 'Arabī'. In *Muhyiddin Ibn 'Arabi: A Commemorative Volume*, S. Hirtenstein and M. Tiernan (eds.). Shaftesbury: Element, 1993, pp. 163–80.

—— *Quest for the Red Sulphur.* Peter Kingsley (trans.). Cambridge: Islamic Texts Society, 1993.

Affifi, A. E. 'The Works of Ibn 'Arabī in the Light of a Memorandum Drawn up by Him (*Fihris al-mu'allafāt*)'. *Bulletin of the Faculty of Arts, Alexandria University*, 8 (1955), pp. 109–17 and 193–207.

—— (ed.). *Fuṣūṣ al-ḥikam.* Teheran: Intishārāt al-Zahrā, n.d.

Algar, Hamid (trans.). Najm al-Dīn Rāzī's *The Path of God's Bondsmen from Origin to Return.* North Haledon, NJ: Islamic Publications International, 1980.

Ali, Abdullah Yusuf (trans.). *The Holy Qur'ān: Arabic Text with an English Translation and Commentary.* Lahore: Muhammad Ashraf, 1937–38.

Altmann, Alexander. 'The Delphic Maxim in Medieval Islam and Judaism'. In *Biblical and Other Studies*, A. Altmann (ed.). Cambridge, MA: Harvard University Press, 1963, pp. 196–232.

Amir-Moezzi, Mohammad Ali (ed.). *Le Voyage initiatique en Terre d'Islam*. Leuven and Paris: Peeters, 1996.

Āmulī, Ḥaydar. *Inner Secrets of the Path*. Asadullah D. Yate (trans.). Shaftesbury: Element, 1991.

al-Ansārī al-Harawī, Abū Ismāʿīl ʿAbdallāh. *Manāzil al-sāʾirīn*. Beirut: Muʾassasat al-Balagh lil-Ṭibaʾah wa-al-Nashr wa-al-Tawziʾ, 2004.

Arberry, A. J. *The Koran Interpreted*. London: Allen & Unwin, 1955.

Austin, R. W. J. (trans.). *The Bezels of Wisdom*. Trans. of *Fuṣūṣ al-ḥikam*. New York: Paulist Press, 1980.

—— *Sufis of Andalusia*. Partial trans. of *Rūḥ al quds* and *al-Durra al-fākhira*. London: Allen & Unwin, 1971.

Avicenna. *The Metaphysics of The Healing: A Parallel English–Arabic Text*. Michael E. Marmura (ed. and trans.). Provo, UT: Brigham Young University Press, 2005, p. 43.

Bashier, S. H. *Ibn al-ʿArabi's Barzakh: The Concept of the Limit and the Relationship between God and the World*. Albany, NY: SUNY Press, 2004.

Bayrak al-Jerrahi, Tosun, and Rabia Terri Harris al-Jerrahi (trans.). 'al-Istilāḥāt al-Ṣūfiyya'. In *What the Seeker Needs*. Putney, VT: Threshold, 1992.

Beneito, Pablo. 'The Ark of Creation', *JMIAS*, 40 (2006), pp. 21–57.

—— 'Past and Future of Knowledge: The Time of Gnosis in Ibn ʿArabī's Writings'. MIAS podcast, originally presented at TURKKAD International Ibn Arabi Symposium, Istanbul, May 2008. www.ibnarabisociety.org/podcasts

—— 'The Time of Deeds and the Time of Spiritual Knowledge: The Past and Future of Gnosis and Sainthood in Ibn ʿArabī's *K. al-Isfār*', *JMIAS*, 50 (2011), pp. 35–44.

Beneito, Pablo, and Stephen Hirtenstein. 'Ibn ʿArabī's Treatise on the Knowledge of the Night of Power and Its Timing', *JMIAS*, 27 (2000), pp. 1–19.

—— *The Seven Days of the Heart*. English translation of *Awrād al-usbūʿ*. Oxford: Anqa Publishing, 2008.

Bernstein, M. S. *Stories of Joseph: Narrative Migrations between Judaism and Islam*. Detroit: Wayne State University Press, 2006.

Brinner, William M. (trans.). *The History of al-Ṭabarī: Prophets and Patriarchs*. Albany, NY: SUNY Press, 1987.

—— 'Jūdī', *EQ*, vol. 3, pp. 68–9.
—— (trans.). al-Tha'labī, *'Arā'is al-majālis fī qiṣaṣ al-anbiyā' or: Lives of the Prophets*. Leiden: Brill, 2002.
al-Bukhārī. *al-Ṣaḥīḥ*. [Egypt]: Dār Maṭābi' al-Sha'b, 1958/9.
Burckhardt, Titus. *Mystical Astrology According to Ibn 'Arabi*. Translated from French by Bulent Rauf. Louisville, KY: Fons Vitae, 2001.
Burton, M., and R. Burton. *International Wildlife Encyclopedia*. Tarrytown, NY: Marshall Cavendish, 2002.
Cahen, Cl. 'Kasb', *EI2*, vol. IV, pp. 690–2.
Chittick, W. C. 'Ibn Arabi'. In *The Stanford Encyclopedia of Philosophy* (Fall 2008 Edition), Edward N. Zalta (ed.). http://plato.stanford.edu/archives/fall2008/entries/ibn-arabi
—— *The Self-Disclosure of God: Principles of Ibn al-Arabi's Cosmology*. Albany, NY: SUNY Press, 1998.
—— *The Sufi Path of Knowledge: Ibn al-Arabi's Metaphysics of Imagination*. Albany, NY: SUNY Press, 1989.
—— 'Two Chapters from the *Futūḥāt al-Makkiyya*'. In *Muhyiddin Ibn 'Arabi: A Commemorative Volume*, S. Hirtenstein and M. Tiernan (eds.). Shaftesbury: Element, 1993, pp. 90–123.
—— and J. W. Morris (eds.). *The Meccan Revelations*, vol. I. New York: Pir Publications, 2002.
Chodkiewicz, Michel. 'The Endless Voyage'. In *The Journey of the Heart*, J. Mercer (ed.). Oxford: Muhyiddin Ibn 'Arabi Society, 1996, pp. 71–84.
—— (ed.) *Les Illuminations de la Mecque*. Paris: Albin Michel, 1997.
—— *An Ocean Without Shore: Ibn Arabī, the Book and the Law*. David Streight (trans.). Albany, NY: SUNY Press, 1993.
—— *Seal of the Saints: Prophethood and Sainthood in the Doctrine of Ibn 'Arabī*. L. Sherrard (trans.). Cambridge: Islamic Texts Society, 1993.
Colby, Frederick S. (trans.). *The Subtleties of the Ascension: Early Mystical Sayings on Muḥammad's Heavenly Journey: Abū 'Abd al-Raḥmān al-Sulamī*. Louisville, KY: Fons Vitae, 2006.
Collins, J. J. 'The Sage in Apocalyptic and Pseudepigraphic Literature'. In *The Sage in Israel and the Ancient Near East*, John G. Gammie and Leo G. Perdue (eds.). Winona Lake, IN: Eisenbrauns, 1992, pp. 343–54.
Cook, D. *Studies in Muslim Apocalyptic*. Princeton: Darwin Press, 2002.
Corbin, Henry. *Creative Imagination in the Sufism of Ibn 'Arabī*. Princeton: Princeton University Press, 1969.

—— *The Voyage and the Messenger: Iran and Philosophy*. Berkeley: North Atlantic Books, 1998.

Cornell, Vincent. *The Way of Abū Madyan*. Cambridge: Islamic Texts Society, 1996.

De Beavoir, Simone. *The Ethics of Ambiguity*. Bernard Frechtman (trans.). New York: Citadel, 2000.

Doufikar-Aerts, Faustina. *Alexander Magnus Arabicus: A Survey of the Alexander Tradition through Seven Centuries: from Pseudo-Callisthenes to Ṣūrī* (Mediaevalia Groningana New Series 13). Paris-Louvain-Walpole, MA: Peeters, 2010.

Edinger, Edward F. *The Mysterium Lectures: A Journey Through C. G. Jung's Mysterium Coniunctionis*. Toronto: Inner City Books, 1995.

Elmore, Gerald. 'The Flight of the Fabulous Gryphon'. In *Journey of the Heart*, J. Mercer (ed.). Oxford: Muhyiddin Ibn 'Arabi Society, 1996, pp. 85–111.

—— 'Ibn al-'Arabī's Testament on the Mantle of Initiation (*al-Khirqah*)', *JMIAS*, 26 (1999), pp. 1–26.

—— *Islamic Sainthood in the Fullness of Time: Ibn 'Arabī's Book of the Fabulous Gryphon*. Leiden: Brill, 1998.

—— 'Some Recent Editions of Books by Ibn al-'Arabī published in the Arab World', *Arabica*, 51.3 (2004), pp. 360–80.

Encyclopaedia Islamica. Wilferd Madelung and Farhad Daftary (eds.). Brill Online, 2010–.

Encyclopaedia Judaica, vol. 17, pp. 718–40. Michael Berenbaum and Fred Skolnik (eds.). Detroit: Macmillan, 2007.

Fenton, Paul, and Maurice Gloton (trans. with introduction and notes). *Inshā' al-dawā'ir*. English translation as 'Description of the Encompassing Circles'. In *Muhyiddin Ibn 'Arabi: A Commemorative Volume*, S. Hirtenstein and M. Tiernan (eds.). Shaftesbury: Element, 1993, pp. 12–43. French translation as *La Production des cercles*. Paris: Éditions de l'Éclat, 1996.

Firestone, Reuven. 'Ishmael', *EQ*, vol. 2, p. 563.

—— *Journeys in Holy Lands: The Evolution of the Abraham–Ishmael Legends in Islamic Exegesis*. Albany, NY: SUNY Press, 1990.

Fox, Everett. *The Five Books of Moses*. New York: Schocken Books, 1995.

Frank, Richard. 'Moral Obligation in Classical Muslim Theology', *Journal of Religious Ethics* 11 (1983), pp. 203–23.

—— *Philosophy, Theology and Mysticism in Medieval Islam: Texts and Studies on the Development and History of Kalām*, vol. I. Aldershot: Ashgate, 2006.

—— 'The Structure of Created Causality According to al-Ash'arī', *Studia Islamica*, 25 (1966), pp. 13–75.

Frye, Northrop. *The Great Code: The Bible and Literature*. San Diego: Harcourt Brace, 1982.

Gardet, Louis, and M. Anawati. *Introduction à la théologie musulmane*. Paris, 1948.

Gardet, L. 'Kasb', *EI2*, vol. IV, pp. 692–4.

Geme'ah, Muḥammad Mustafa (trans.). *Stories of the Prophets*. English translation of Ibn Kathīr's *Qiṣaṣ al-anbiyā'*. Riyadh: Darussalam, n.d.

Gilis, Charles-André (trans.). *Les Chatons de la sagesse*, 2 vols. French translation of *Fuṣūṣ al-ḥikam*. Paris: al-Bouraq, 1999.

—— *Études complémentaires sur la califat*. Paris: Éditions al-Bustane, 1995.

—— (trans.) *Le Livre du Mīm, du wāw et du nūn*. French translation of *K. al-Mīm wa-l-Wāw wa-l-Nūn*. Beirut: al-Bouraq, 2002.

—— *René Guenon et l'avènement du troisième Sceau*. Paris: Éditions traditionnelles, 1991.

Gordon, Matthew S. 'Journey', *EI3*.

Graves, Robert. *The White Goddess*. New York: Farrar, Straus and Giroux, 1966.

Gril, Denis. '*Adab* and Revelation or One of the Foundations of the Hermeneutics of Ibn 'Arabi'. In *Muhyiddin Ibn 'Arabi: A Commemorative Volume*, S. Hirtenstein and M. Tiernan (eds.). Shaftesbury: Element, 1993, pp. 228–63.

—— 'De la Proximité'. In *Les Illuminations de La Mecque*, M. Chodkiewicz *et al.* (eds.). Paris: Sindbad, 1988, pp. 332–47.

—— *Les Dévoilement des effets du voyage*. Edn. and French trans. of *al-Isfār 'an natā'ij al-asfār*. Paris: Éditions de l'Éclat, 1994.

—— 'Le personage coranique de Pharaon d'après l'interprétation d'Ibn 'Arabi', *Annales Islamologiques*, 14 (1978), pp. 37–57.

—— 'The Journey through the Circles of Inner Being according to Ibn 'Arabī's *Mawāqi'al-nujūm*', *JMIAS*, 40 (2006), pp. 1–20.

Guenon, René. *The Great Triad*. Hillsdale, NY: Sophia Perennis, 2001.

—— 'Hermes', *Studies in Comparative Religion*, 1.2 (Spring 1967), pp. 79–83.

al-Ḥabashī, 'Abdallāh Badr. 'The *Kitāb al-inbāh 'alā tarīq Allāh* of 'Abdallah Badr al-Habashi: An Account of the Spiritual Teaching of Muhyiddin Ibn 'Arabi'. D. Gril (French intro. and trans). K. Holding (English trans.). *JMIAS*, 15 (1994), pp. 10–36.

al-Ḥakīm, Su'ād (ed.). *Al-Isrā' ilā maqām al-asrā, aw K. al-Mi'rāj*. Beirut: Dandara, 1988.

—— *al-Muʿjam al-Ṣūfī*. Beirut: Dandara, 1981.

Harris, Rabia Terri (trans.). *Journey to the Lord of Power*. Trans. of *R. al-Anwār*. Rochester, VT: Inner Traditions, 1981.

Heer, Nicholas. 'A Sufi Psychological Treatise', *The Muslim World*, LI (1961); No. 1, pp. 25–36; No. 2, pp. 83–91; No. 3, pp. 163–72; No. 4, pp. 244–58. (Trans. of al-Tirmidhī's *Bayān al-farq*.)

Heer, Nicholas, and Kenneth L. Honerkamp. *Three Early Sufi Texts*. Louisville, KY: Fons Vitae, 2003.

Heller, B. 'al-Sāmirī', *EI2*, vol. VIII, p. 1046.

Hirtenstein, Stephen. 'The Brotherhood of Milk: Perspectives of Knowledge in the Adamic Clay', *JMIAS*, 33 (2003), pp. 1–21.

—— (ed. and trans.). *The Four Pillars of Spiritual Transformation*. Edn. and trans. of *Ḥilyat al-abdāl*. Oxford: Anqa Publishing, 2009.

—— 'The Land of the Olive: Between East and West', *JMIAS*, 40 (2006), pp. 67–88.

—— 'The Mystic's Kaʿba: The Wisdom of the Heart According to Ibn ʿArabī', *JMIAS*, 48 (2010), pp. 19–43. Also available as a podcast on the Muhyiddin Ibn ʿArabi Society website, accessed 4 October 2014.

—— *The Unlimited Mercifier: The Spiritual Life and Thought of Ibn ʿArabī*. Oxford: Anqa Publishing, 1999.

—— and M. Notcutt (trans.). *Divine Sayings: 101 Hadith Qudsi: The Mishkāt al-Anwār of Ibn ʿArabī*. Oxford: Anqa Publishing, 2004.

—— and M. Tiernan (eds.). *Muhyiddin Ibn ʿArabi: A Commemorative Volume*. Shaftesbury: Element, 1993.

Ibn al-Anbārī, Muḥammad b. al-Qāsim. *Kitāb al-Aḍdād fī al-lugha*. Cairo: al-Maṭbah al-Ḥusayniyya al-Miṣriyya, 1907.

Ibn ʿArabī, Muḥyī al-Dīn. *K. al-ʿAbādila*. ʿA. A. ʿAṭā (ed.). Cairo: Maktabat al-Qāhira, 1969.

—— *R. al-Anwār*. In *Rasāʾil Ibn ʿArabī*. Hyderabad, 1948.

—— *Awrād al-usbūʿ*. P. Beneito and S. Hirtenstein (English trans.), *The Seven Days of the Heart*. Oxford: Anqa Publishing, 2008.

—— *Ayyām al-shaʾn*. In *Rasāʾil Ibn ʿArabī*. Hyderabad, 1948.

—— *K. al-Fanāʾ fī al-mushāhada*. M. Vâlsan (French trans.), *Le livre de l'extinction dans la contemplation*. Paris: Éditions de l'Oeuvre, 1984. S. Hirtenstein and L. Shamash (English trans.), 'The Book of Annihilation in the Contemplation', *JMIAS*, 9 (1991), pp. 1–17.

—— *Fihris al-muʾallafāt*. A. Affīfī, 'The Works of Ibn ʿArabī in the Light of a Memorandum Drawn up by Him' (partial trans.), *Bulletin of the Faculty of Arts, Alexandria University*, 8 (1955), pp. 109–17 and 193–207.

—— *Fuṣūṣ al-ḥikam*. R. W. J. Austin (English trans.), *Bezels of Wisdom*. New York: Paulist Press, 1980. C-A. Gilis (French trans.), *Les Chatons de la sagesse*. Paris: al-Bouraq, 1999.

—— *al-Futūḥāt al-Makkiyya*. 4 vols. Repr. Beirut: Dār Ṣādir, n.d.

—— *Ḥilyat al-abdāl*. In *Rasā'il Ibn 'Arabī*. Hyderabad, 1948. S. Hirtenstein (English edn. and trans.), *The Four Pillars of Spiritual Transformation*. Oxford: Anqa Publishing, 2009.

—— *Inshā' al-dawā'ir*. Paul Fenton and Maurice Gloton (English trans.), 'Description of the Encompassing Circles'. In *Muhyiddin Ibn 'Arabi: A Commemorative Volume* (S. Hirtenstein and M. Tiernan (eds.). Shaftesbury: Element, 1993, pp. 12–43, and (edn. and French trans.), *La Production des cercles*. Paris: Éditions de l'Éclat, 1996.

—— *al-Isfār 'an natā'ij al-asfār*. D. Gril (French trans.), *Les Dévoilement des effets du voyage*. Paris: Éditions de l'Éclat, 1994. C. Varona Nervion (Spanish trans.), *El splendor de los frutos del viaje*. Madrid: Siruela, 2008. A. A. Shahi (Urdu trans.), *Ruhani Asfar aur un ke samaraat*. Pakistan: Ibn al-Arabi Foundation, 2010.

—— *al-Istilāḥāt al-Ṣūfiyya*. T. Bayrak and R. T. Harris (trans.). In *What the Seeker Needs*. Putney, VT: Threshold, 1992.

—— *al-Ittiḥād al-kawnī*. D. Gril (edn. and French trans.), *Le Livre de l'Arbre et des Quatre Oiseaux*. Paris: Les Deux Océans, 1984. A. Jaffray (English trans.), *The Universal Tree and the Four Birds*. Oxford: Anqa Publishing, 2007.

—— *al-Mashāhid al-qudsiyya*. P. Beneito and S. al-Ḥakīm (ed. and Spanish trans.), *Las Contemplaciones de los Misterios*. Madrid: Editora Regional de Murcia, 1994. S. Ruspoli (edn. and French trans.), *Le Livre des contemplations divines*. Paris: Sindbad, 1999. C. Twinch and P. Beneito (English trans.), *Contemplation of the Holy Mysteries*. Oxford: Anqa Publishing, 2001.

—— *Mawāqi' al-nujūm wa-maṭāli' ahillat al-asrār wa-l-'ulūm*. M. Badr al-Dīn al-Na'sānī (ed.). Cairo: Maktaba Muḥammad 'Alī Ṣabīḥ, 1965.

—— *K. al-Mīm wa-l-Wāw wa-l-Nūn*. In *Rasā'il Ibn 'Arabī*. Hyderabad, 1948. C-A. Gilis (French trans.), *Le Livre du Mīm, du wāw et du nūn*. Beirut: al-Bouraq, 2002.

—— *Mishkāt al-anwār*. S. Hirtenstein and M. Notcutt (trans.), *Divine Sayings: 101 Hadith Qudsi*. Oxford: Anqa Publishing, 2004.

—— *Rasā'il Ibn 'Arabī*. Hyderabad, 1948.

—— *Rasā'il Ibn al-'Arabī*, vol. 2. Damascus: Dār al-Ṣadakā li-l-Thaqāfa wa-l-Nashr, 1998, pp. 95–142.

—— *Tarjumān al-ashwāq*. R. A. Nicholson (ed. and trans.). London: Royal Asiatic Society, 1911.
—— *'Uqlat al-mustawfiz*. H. Nyberg (ed.). In *Kleinere Schriften des Ibn al-'Arabī*. Leiden: Brill, 1919.
—— *K. al-Yaqīn*. In *Rasā'il Ibn 'Arabī*, vol. 4, Sa'īd 'Abd al-Fattāḥ (ed.). Beirut: al-Intishār al-'Arabī, 2004.
Ibn Ḥanbal, Aḥmad. *al-Musnad*. Beirut: Dār Ṣādir, n.d.
Ibn Janāh, Abū al-Walīd Marwān. *Sefer ha-riqmah*, Michael Wilensky (ed.). Berlin: ha-Aqademyah, 1928–30.
Ibn Jinnī. *al-Khaṣā'iṣ fī 'ilm uṣūl al-'Arabiyya*. M. A. Najjār (ed.). Cairo: 1952.
Ibn Kathīr, Ismā'īl ibn 'Umar. *Qiṣaṣ al-anbiyā'*. Cairo: Dār al-Kutub al-Hadītha, 1968. Muḥammad Mustafa Geme'ah (English trans.), *Stories of the Prophets*. Riyadh: Darussalam, n.d.
—— *Tafsīr Ibn Kathīr*. Muhammad Saed Abdul-Rahman (trans.). 2nd edn., vol. 1. London: MSA Publication, 2009.
Ibn Majā. *al-Sunan*. M. F. 'Abd al-Bāqī (ed.). Cairo: Dār Iḥyā' al-Kutub al-'Arabiyya, 1952.
Ibn Taymiyya. *al-Istighātha fī radd 'alā al-Bakrī*. 'Abd Allah b. Dujayn al-Suhaylī (ed.). 2 vols. Riyadh: Dār al-Watan, 1997.
Jaffray, Angela. 'Ibn 'Arabī on *Himmah*: The Spiritual Power of the Strong-Souled Individual'. MIAS podcast. www.ibnarabisociety.org/podcasts.
—— (trans.) *The Universal Tree and the Four Birds*. English trans. of *al-Ittiḥād al-kawnī*. Oxford: Anqa Publishing, 2007.
Jung, C. G. 'The Practice of Psychotherapy: Essays on the Psychology of the Transference and Other Subjects'. In *Collected Works of C. G. Jung*, vol. 16. G. Adler and R. F. C. Hull (trans.). Princeton: Princeton University Press, 1985.
Khalilieh, H. S. *Islamic Maritime Law: An Introduction*. Leiden: Brill, 1998.
Khan, Pasha M. 'Nothing but Animals', *JMIAS*, 43 (2008), pp. 21–50.
Kierkegaard, Soren. *Journals and Papers*, I, p. 340. H. V. and E. H. Hong (eds. and trans.). 7 vols. Princeton: Princeton University Press, 1967–78.
Kindermann, H. 'Rabī'a and Muḍar', *EI2*, vol. VIII, pp. 352–4.
al-Kisā'ī, Muḥammad b. 'Abd Allāh. *Qiṣaṣ al-anbiyā'*. W. M. Thackston, Jr (trans.), *The Tales of the Prophets*. Boston: Hall, 1978.
Knysh, Alexander. *Ibn 'Arabī in the Later Islamic Tradition: The Making of a Polemical Image*. Albany, NY: SUNY Press, 1999.

—— '"Orthodoxy" and "Heresy" in Medieval Islam: An Essay in Reassessment', *The Muslim World*, 83 (1993), pp. 48–67.

—— (trans.) *al-Qushayrī's Epistle on Sufism: al-Risala al-qushayriyya fi 'ilm al-tasawwuf.* Reading: Garnet Publishing, 2007.

Kraus, Paul. *Jābir ibn Ḥayyān: Contribution à l'histoire des idées scientifiques dans l'Islam: Jābir et la science grecque.* Paris: Les Belles Lettres, 1986.

al-Kulaynī, Muḥammad b. Ya'qūb, *K. al-Kāfī*, vols. 1–8. M. Sarwar (trans.). The Islamic Seminary, INCNY. www.holybooks.com/wp-content/uploads/Al-Kafi.pdf

Lane, Edward William. *An Arabic–English Lexicon.* 8 vols. Beirut: Librairie du Liban, 1968.

La-Shay', Hussein. 'Abū 'Alī al-Daqqāq'. In *Encyclopaedia Islamica.* Wilferd Madelung and Farhad Daftary (eds. in chief). Brill, 2010, vol. 1, pp. 456–7.

Lory, Pierre. *Les commentaires ésotériques du Coran d'après 'Abd ar-Razzāq al-Qāshānī.* Paris, 1980 (= Tafsīr Ibn al-'Arabī).

Mālik ibn Anas. *Muwaṭṭā'.* www.sunnah.com/malik.

Martelli, Matteo. 'Divine Water in the Alchemical Writings of Pseudo-Democritus'. *Ambix*, vol. 56, no. 1 (March 2009), pp. 5–22.

Martin, Erica. 'Noah in the Qur'an'. In *Noah and His Book(s).* Michael E. Stone, Aryeh Amihay and Vered Hillel (eds.). Atlanta: Society of Biblical Literature, 2010, pp. 253–75.

Massignon, Louis. 'Huwa Huwa', *EI2*, vol. III, p. 642.

Melchert, Christopher. 'Asceticism', *EI3.*

—— 'The Piety of the Hadith Folk', *International Journal of Middle East Studies*, 34, no. 3 (Aug. 2002), pp. 425–39.

Mercer, John (ed.). *The Journey of the Heart.* Oxford: Muhyiddin Ibn 'Arabi Society, 1996.

Merton, Thomas. *Conjectures of a Guilty Bystander.* Garden City, NY: Image, 1966.

Miller, Henry. *The Colossus of Maroussi.* New York: New Directions, 1958.

Morris, James W. 'He Moves You Through the Land and the Sea'. In *The Journey of the Heart.* J. Mercer (ed.). Oxford: Muhyiddin Ibn 'Arabi Society, 1996, pp. 41–69.

—— 'Ibn 'Arabī's "Esotericism": The Problem of Spiritual Authority'. *Studia Islamica*, LXXI (1990), pp. 37–64.

—— 'Ibn 'Arabī's Rhetoric of Realisation: Keys to Reading and "Translating" the Meccan Illuminations'. Part I, *JMIAS*, 33 (2003), pp. 54–99;

Part II, *JMIAS*, 34 (2003), pp. 103–45.
—— *The Reflective Heart: Discovering Spiritual Intelligence in Ibn 'Arabī's Meccan Illuminations*. Louisville, KY: Fons Vitae, 2005.
—— Review of D. Gril's edn. and trans. of *K. al-Isfār*, *JMIAS*, 17 (1995), pp. 103–5.
—— 'The Spiritual Ascension of Ibn 'Arabī and the Mi'raj', Part I, *JAOS*, 107, no. 4 (1987), pp. 629–52; Part II, *JAOS*, 108, no. 1 (1988): pp. 63–77.
Mourad, S. A. *Early Islam between Myth and History: al-Hasan al-Basri (d.110 H/728 CE) and the Formation of His Legacy in Classical Islamic Scholarship*. Leiden: Brill, 2006.
Mullā Ṣadrā. *al-Ḥikma al-muta'āliya fī al-asfār al-'aqliyya al-arba'a (The Transcendent Wisdom Concerning the Four Journeys of the Intellect)*. 9 vols. R. Lutfi *et al.* (eds.). Tehran and Qom: Shirkat Dār al-Ma'ārif al-Islāmiyyah, *c.*1958–69.
al-Muqaddasī, Shams al-Dīn. 'Description of Syria, Including Palestine', (trans. Guy Le Strange). In *The Library of the Palestine Pilgrims' Text Society*, vol. III. London, 1896, pp. iii–103.
Muslim. *Al-Ṣaḥīḥ*. Cairo: Maṭba'a Muḥammad 'Alī Ṣabīḥ, 1915–16.
Neher, André. *L'Existence juive*. Paris: Seuil, 1962.
Netton, Ian R. 'Riḥla', *EI2* Online, 2010.
Nicholson, R. A. (trans.). *The Tarjumān al-ashwāq*. London: Theosophical Publishing House, 1911, repr. 1978.
Nooteboom, Cees. *Nomad's Hotel: Travels in Time and Space*. Orlando, FL: Houghton Mifflin (Mariner), 2009.
Nyberg, H. S. *Kleinere Schriften des Ibn al-'Arabī*. Leiden: Brill, 1919.
Online Qur'an Project. www.al-quran.info
Orlov, Andrei A. *The Enoch-Metatron Tradition*. Tübingen: Mohr Siebeck, 2005.
Ouaknin, Marc-Alain. *Zeugma*. Paris: Seuil, 2008.
Peters, R. 'Safar', *EI2*, vol. VIII, p. 764.
Pickthall, M. M. (trans.). *The Meaning of the Glorious Qur'an*. New York: Knopf, 1930.
Polish, Daniel F. *Talking about God: Exploring the Meaning of Religious Life with Kierkegaard, Buber, Tillich, and Heschel*. Woodstock, VT: Skylight Paths, 2007.
al-Qushayrī, Abū al-Qāsim. *Al-Risāla*. A. Knysh (trans.), *al-Qushayrī's Epistle on Sufism*. Reading: Garnet Publishing, 2007. B. von Schlegell, *Principles of Sufism* (partial trans.). Berkeley: Mizan, 1990.

Rabin, Chaim. *Ancient West-Arabian*. London: Taylor's Foreign Press, 1951.
Rāzī, Najm al-Dīn. *Mirṣād al-ʿibād min al-mabdāʾ ilā al-maʿād*. H. Algar (trans.), *The Path of God's Bondsmen from Origin to Return*. North Haledon, NJ: Islamic Publications International, 1980.
Reynolds, Gabriel Said. 'A Reflection on Two Qur'anic Words (*Iblīs* and *Jūdī*), with Attention to the Theories of A. Mingana', *JAOS*, 124.4 (2004), pp. 675–89.
Rippin, Andrew. 'Tafsīr', *EI2*, vol. X, pp. 83–8.
Rizvi, Sajjad. 'Mulla Sadra'. In *The Stanford University Encyclopedia of Philosophy*. Summer 2009 Edition. Edward N. Zalta (ed.). http://plato.stanford.edu/archives/sum2009/entries/mulla-sadra
Rozensweig, Franz. *Star of Redemption*. William W. Hallo (trans.). Notre Dame, IN: University of Notre Dame Press, 1985.
Sahih International. *The Qur'ān: Arabic Text with Corresponding English Meanings*. Jeddah: Dar Abul Qasim, 1997.
Sands, Kristin Zahra. *Sufi Commentaries on the Qur'an in Classical Islam*. Oxford and New York: Routledge, 2006.
al-Sarrāj, Abū Naṣr. *K. al-Lumaʿ fī al-taṣawwuf*. R.A. Nicholson (ed.). London: Luzac, 1914.
Schwartz, M. '"Acquisition" (*kasb*) in Early Islam'. In *Islamic Philosophy and the Classical Tradition*, S. M. Stern and A. Hourani (eds.). Columbia, SC: University of South Carolina Press, 1972, pp. 355–87.
Sells, Michael. *Early Islamic Mysticism*. New York: Paulist Press, 1996.
von Schlegell, Barbara. *Principles of Sufism*. Trans. of al-Qushayrī's *Risāla*. Berkeley: Mizan, 1990.
Scholem, Gershom. *Alchemy and Kabbalah*. Putnam, CT: Spring Publications, 2006.
Schrieke, B., and J. Horovitz. 'Miʿrādj', *EI2*, vol. VII, pp. 97–100.
Shahi, Abrar Ahmad. *Ruhani Asfar aur un ke samaraat*. Urdu trans. of *K. al-Isfār ʿan natāʾij al-asfār*. Pakistan: Ibn al-ʿArabi Foundation, 2010. Repr. 2012.
Shamash, Layla. 'People of the Night'. In *Prayer and Contemplation*, S. Hirtenstein (ed.). Oxford: Muhyiddin Ibn ʿArabi Society, 1993, pp. 42–52.
Smith, Jane Idleman, and Yvonne Yazbeck Haddad. *The Islamic Understanding of Death and Resurrection*. Oxford: Oxford University Press, 2002.
Stern, S. M., and A. Hourani (eds.). *Islamic Philosophy and the Classical Tradition*. Columbia, SC: University of South Carolina Press, 1972.

al-Suyūṭī, Jalāl al-Dīn. *al-Itqān fī ʿulūm al-Qurʾān*, vol. 1. Beirut: al-Maktaba al-Thaqafiyya, 1973.

—— *The Perfect Guide to the Sciences of the Qurʾan: Al-Itqan fi ʿUlum al-Qurʾan*, vol. 1. H. Algar (trans.). Reading: Garnet Publishing, 2011.

al-Ṭabarī, Abū Jaʿfar Muḥammad. *The History of al-Ṭabarī: Prophets and Patriarchs*. W. Brinner (trans.). Albany, NY: SUNY Press, 1987.

—— *Jāmiʿ al-bayān ʿan taʾwīl āy al-Qurʾān*. Beirut: Dār Iḥyāʾ al-Turāth al-ʿArabī, 2011.

al-Thaʿlabī, Abū Isḥāq. *ʿArāʾis al-majālis fī qiṣaṣ al-anbiyāʾ*. W. Brinner (trans.). Leiden: Brill, 2002.

Thackston, Wheeler M. (trans.). Muḥammad b. ʿAbd Allāh al-Kisāʾī, *Tales of the Prophets (Qiṣaṣ al-anbiyāʾ)*. Boston: Hall, 1978.

al-Tirmidhī. *Bayān al-farq bayn al-ṣadr wa al-fuʾād wa al-lubb*. Cairo, 1958. N. Heer (English trans.), 'A Sufi Psychological Treatise', *The Muslim World*, LI (1961), nos. 1–4; N. Heer and K. Honerkamp, *Three Early Sufi Texts*. Louisville, KY: Fons Vitae, 2003.

—— *Al-Jāmiʿ al-ṣaḥīḥ, wa-huwa sunan al-Tirmidhī*. A. M. Shākir (ed.). Cairo: al-Maktaba al-Islāmiyya, 1938.

—— Jāmiʿ: *K. tafsīr al-Qurʾān*. www.sunnah.com

Toorawa, Shawkat M. 'Trips and Voyages'. *EI2*, online version. *EI2*, print version, vol. V, p. 372.

Tottoli, Robert. *Biblical Prophets in the Qurʾan and Muslim Literature*. Richmond, Surrey: Curzon Press, 2002.

al-Tustarī, Sahl b. ʿAbd Allāh. *Tafsīr*. Annabel Keeler and Ali Keeler (trans.). www.altafsir.com/al-Tustari.asp

Twinch, Cecilia, and Pablo Beneito. *Contemplation of the Holy Mysteries*. Oxford: Anqa Publishing, 2001.

Vâlsan, Michel. 'L'Investiture du Cheikh al-Akbar au Centre Suprême', *Études Traditionelles*, 311 (Oct.–Nov. 1953), pp. 300–11.

VanderKam, James C. *Enoch: A Man for All Generations*. Columbia, SC: University of South Carolina Press, 2008.

—— *Enoch and the Growth of an Apocalyptic Tradition*. Washington, DC: Catholic Biblical Association of America, 1984.

Varona Nervion, C. *El splendor de los frutos del viaje*, Madrid: Siruela, 2008.

Wensinck, A. J. 'Miswāk', *EI2*, vol. VII, p. 187.

Wensinck, A. J., J. P. Mensing and J. Brugman. *Concordance et indices de la tradition musulmane*. Leiden: Brill, 1936–69.

Wilson, Peter Lamborn. *The Caravan of Summer.* www.hermetic.com/bey/caravan.html

Wolfson, Harry Austryn. *The Philosophy of the Kalam.* Cambridge, MA: Harvard University Press, 1976.

Yahia, Osman. *Histoire et classification de l'oeuvre d'Ibn 'Arabī: Étude critique.* Damascus: Institut Francais de Damas, 1964.

Yousef, Mohamed Haj. *Ibn 'Arabī: Time and Cosmology.* Oxford: Routledge, 2008.

Zornberg, Avivah Gottlieb. *The Murmuring Deep: Reflections on the Biblical Unconscious.* New York: Schocken Books, 2009.

INDEX OF QUR'ANIC VERSES

2:14 Verily, we did but mock 122
2:15 [Allah Himself] doth mock them ... 122
2:28 ye were without life, and He gave you life ... to Him will ye return. 149
2:29 It is He Who hath created for you all things that are on earth ... 42
2:30 Lo! I am about to place a vicegerent in the earth. 210
2:38 We said: Go down, all of you, from hence. 71, 210
2:74 Thenceforth were your hearts hardened: They became like a rock ... 152
2:156 To Allah We belong, and to Him is our return. 142
2:184 As for one among you who is ill or upon a voyage ... 161
2:197 So make provision ... for the best provision is godfearing. 76, 146
2:210 [Wait they for naught else than that Allah should come unto them] in the shadows of the clouds ...? 50
2:248 A Sign of his authority is that there shall come to you ... 38, 173, 225
2:260 My Lord, show me how You give life to the dead ... 97
2:282 And if two men be not at hand, then a man and two women ... 74
2:286 Allah tasketh not a soul beyond its scope. 108
3:7 He it is Who has sent down to thee the Book ... 45
3:7 But those in whose hearts is deviation follow the part that is ambiguous ... 20
3:30 Allah biddeth you be cautious of Him. 124
3:45 Behold! the angels said: 'O Mary! Allah giveth thee glad tidings ... 38
3:55 Allah said: 'O Jesus! I will take thee and raise thee to Myself ...' 38
3:114 They believe in Allah and the Last Day ... They are in the ranks of the righteous. 268
3:137 Travel through the earth ... the end of those who rejected Truth. 24
3:175 Fear them not; fear Me, if ye are believers. 118, 281
4:56 As often as their skins are consumed ... that they may taste the torment. 44
4:58 Allah doth command you to render back your Trusts ... 76
4:71 [O ye who believe!] Take your precautions ... 123
4:158 Nay, Allah raised him up unto Himself; and Allah is ... Wise. 38
4:161 That they took usury, though they were forbidden 76
4:164 to Moses Allah spoke direct. 265
4:171 Say not 'Trinity' ... Far exalted is He above having a son. 38, 76
5:20 seated upon the Throne 144
5:66 If only they had stood fast by the Law, the Gospel ... 94, 242
5:117 what Thou didst command me to say, to wit, worship Allah ... 76
5:119 Allah is satisfied with them and they are satisfied with Him. 109
6:2 He it is created you from clay, and hath decreed a term ... 104, 105, 261
6:14 Say: Nay! but I am commanded to be the first of those who bow ... 76
6:35 And if their turning away is distressful for thee, then if thou canst seek a burrow ... 122
6:35 If Allah willed, He could have brought them all ... to guidance. 122
6:56 Say: I am forbidden to worship those ... whom ye call upon. 76
6:59 He knoweth whatever there is on the earth and in the sea. 41
6:60 It is He who doth take your souls by night ... 261
6:63 Who is it that delivereth you from the dark recesses of land and sea ... 41
6:71 Say: [Allah]'s guidance is the [only] guidance ... 76

6:75 Thus did We show Abraham the kingdom ... certainty. 84, 248
6:96 the determination of the All-Mighty, All-Knowing 90
6:97 It is He who maketh the stars for you, so that you might be guided ... 41, 146
7:3 Little it is ye remember of admonition. 73
7:17 Then we will come to them from before them and ... their left. 154
7:23 Our Lord, we have wronged ourselves. 73
7:26 O Children of Adam! We have revealed unto you raiment ... 76
7:29 Say: My Lord hath commanded justice ... 76
7:29 This is how you have been created, and this is the way ... return. 150
7:54 His, verily, is all creation and command. ... 42, 122
7:80 We also [sent] Lot. He said to his people: Do ye commit lewdness ... 247
7:142 And We did appoint for Moses thiry nights ... 104, 267
7:143 And when Moses came to Our appointment ... 37, 38, 103
7:143 Moses fell down in a swoon. When he recovered ... the first to believe. 261
7:150 And when Moses returned to his people, angry and grieved ... 111, 270
7:150 he cast down the tablets and seized his brother by the head ... 113
7:151 He said: My Lord! Have mercy on me and on my brother ... 113
7:154 in the writing thereon was guidance and Mercy 113
7:155 And Moses chose seventy of his people for Our place of meeting... 112
7:155 It is but Thy trial. ... Thou guidest whom Thou wilt. 289
7:185 Have they not considered ... their term draweth near? 84
8:17 Thou threwest not when thou threwest, but Allah threw. 161, 167, 196
8:28 Your possessions and your children are a trial/temptation 240, 256
9:2 Wander throughout the land for four months ... 164–5
9:31 They take their priests and their anchorites to be their lords ... 76
9:111 Allah hath purchased of the believers their persons and their goods. 255
9:112 Those that turn to Allah in repentance ... limit set by Allah. 164, 165
9:118 Then turned He unto them that they might turn [repentant to Him]. 150
10:3 Verily your Lord ... regulating and governing all things. 42, 258
10:5 He made for [the moon] its mansions. 36
10:6 Verily, in the alternation of the night and the day ... who fear Him. 84
10:22 It is He who makes you go by land and by sea. 41, 146
10:23 Then comes a stormy wind and the waves come to them ... 145
10:32 After the truth what is there save error? 82
10:104 Say: O ye men! If ye are in doubt as to my religion ... 76
11:17 Is he [to be counted equal with them] who relieth on a clear proof ... 110
11:37 Build the ark under Our eyes and by Our inspiration. 87
11:40 two of every kind 88
11:41 Embark therein! In the name of Allah be its course and its mooring. ... 88
11:42 [And it sailed with them] amid waves like mountains. 86
11:42 O my son! Come ride with us 86
11:43 and he was among those who drowned 86
11:43 I shall betake me to some mountain that will save me from the water. 86
11:43 This day there is none that saveth ... He hath had mercy. 86
11:44 Then the word went forth: ... those who do wrong! 86, 87, 233
11:44 it was said 'banished'... and it was said: 'O earth, swallow your water.' 90
11:46 O my Lord, my son is of my family ... among the ignorant.' 222
11:55 He is upon a straight path. 45
11:69 There came Our messengers to Abraham with glad tidings. ... 268
11:80–1 If only I had some power over you, or ... firm support. 96, 248

11:81 So travel with thy people in a part of the night ... 37, 96–7
11:112 Therefore stand firm as thou art commanded. 76
11:120 And all that We relate unto thee of the story of the messengers ... 98
11:123 To Him all affairs shall be returned ... He is upon a straight path. 45, 149
12:3 most beautiful of stories 252
12:20 for a low price ... in such low estimation did they hold him! 99, 100, 254
12:21 Receive him honourably. 100
12:24 he desired her 100
12:24 That We might ward off from him evil and lewdness. 101
12:31 This is not a human being. This is no other than some noble angel!' 100
12:32 He proved continent, but if he does not do ... shall be imprisoned. 100
12:40 He hath commanded that ye worship none but Him ... understand not. 76
12:53 Nor do I absolve my own self: indeed the soul is an enjoiner of evil ... 87, 97, 254
12:55 [Joseph] said: Set me over the storehouses of the land ... 255
12:62 And [Joseph] told his servants to put their stock-in-trade ... back. 163
12:70 At length when he had furnished them ... brother's saddle-bag. 163
12:75 The penalty should be that he in whose saddle-bag it is found ... 163
12:84 And his eyes were whitened with sorrow. 100
12:95 Truly thou art in thine old wandering mind. 255–6
12:100 This is the interpretation of my dream of old. 102
12:101 O my Lord! Thou hast given me [something] of sovereignty. 101
12:101 Thou hast taught me ... of the interpretation of dreams. 102
13:2 each runneth unto an appointed term. 56
13:3 Behold, verily in these things there are signs for those who consider! 291
13:36 Say: I am commanded to worship Allah, and not to join partners ... 76
14:5 'Bring out thy people from the depths of darkness into light ... 41
15:12 Even so do we let it creep into the hearts of the sinners. 14
15:65 Then travel by night with thy household ... ye are ordered. 168
15:74 And We turned [the cities] upside down, and rained down ... 250
15:87 We have given you [Muhammad] ... and the Tremendous Qur'an. 60, 61
15:99 Worship your Lord until certainty comes to you. 249
16:1 [Inevitable] ... the Command of Allah. Seek ye not then to hasten it. 262
16:12 And the stars are made subservient by His command. 82
16:50 They fear their Lord above them, and do what they are commanded. 119
16:69 Then to eat of all the produce and find with skill ... paths of its Lord. 14
16:90 Allah commands justice, the doing of good ... 76
16:96 What is with you runs out, while what is with Allah subsists. 246
16:121 He showed his gratitude for the favours of Allah ... Straight Way. 235
17:1 Glorified be He who made His servant voyage by night ... 36, 62, 70, 98, 138, 191, 192, 197
17:44 There is not a thing but celebrates His praise ... 192
17:70 We have honoured the sons of Adam; provided them with transport ... 41
17:105–6 We sent down the [Qur'an] in Truth ... 58
18:29 We have prepared for disbelievers Fire. Its Canopy encloseth them. 50
18:65 taught knowledge from His Presence 38
18:94 They said: O Dhū al-Qarnayn! Gog and Magog do great mischief ... 39
19:52 And we called him from the right side of al-Tur ... converse. 272, 274
19:56–7 And make mention in the Book of Idrīs. ... high position. 36, 80, 214
20:1–15 Ṭa-Ha... 283–4
20:5 The All-Merciful, who sits on the Throne. 35, 42, 174

20:7 He knows the secret and the more hidden. 103–4
20:10 I see a fire afar off. Peradventure I may bring you a brand ... 115, 272
20:12–14 Verily I am thy Lord! therefore put off thy shoes... 155, 273
20:15 Verily the hour is coming; I am about to remove that which conceals ... 282
20:39 Throw [the child] into the chest, and throw [the chest] into the river... 38, 225
20:53 He Who has, made for you the earth like a carpet spread out ... 14
20:74 Verily he who comes to his Lord as a sinner, for him is Hell ... 171
20:77 We revealed to Moses that he should journey by night ... 168
20:83 What hath made thee hasten from thy folk, O Moses? 104, 108, 110, 268
20:84 I hastened to Thee that Thou mightest be well pleased. 104, 108, 110
20:84 They are close upon my track 110, 269
20:85 Lo! We have tried thy folk in thine absence 110
20:85 and al-Sāmirī hath misled them 110
20:88 This is your God and the God of Moses 110, 111, 112
20:88 but he forgot 111
20:89 it returneth no saying unto them and possesseth ... hurt nor use. 111
20:90 Your Lord is the All-Merciful, so follow me and obey my order. 111, 112
20:90 O my people! Ye are but being seduced by him. 112
20:91 They said: We shall by no means cease to be devoted ... 112
20:94 and he said: Son of my mother! Clutch not my beard nor my head ... 113
20:95 And what hast thou to say, O Sāmirī? 113
20:96 and then threw it 113
20:111 Faces shall be humbled before the Living, the Subsisting. 116
20:114 And hasten not with the Qur'an ... perfected unto thee. 60, 188, 262
20:115 [And verily We made a covenant of old with Adam, but] he forgot. 74
20:121 And Adam disobeyed his Lord.' 73
21:30 Have not those who disbelieve ... Will they not then believe? 53, 253
21:32 And We have made the heavens as a canopy well guarded. 182
21:33 They float, each in an orbit. 55
21:35 We try you with evil and with good, as an ordeal. 72
21:37 The human being is a creature of haste: ... not ask Me to hasten them! 262
21:74 And to Lot, too, We gave Judgment and Knowledge ... 247
21:85–6 And [remember] Ishmael, Idris, and Dhū al-Kifl ... 214
21:101 kindness hath gone before 110
21:103 The supreme terror will not grieve them ... 46
22:27 They will come to thee on foot and on every kind of camel ... 194
22:31 Whoever associates partners with Allah ... him to a place far off. 94
22:46 Do they not travel through the land...? 158
22:46 [For indeed it is not the eyes that grow blind,] but it is the hearts ... 69
23:27 [T]ake thou on board pairs of every species, male and female. 14
23:43 No people can hasten their term, nor can they delay [it]. 262
23:88 in whose hand is sovereignty of all things. 84
24:2 In the matter of God's religion, let no pity for them seize you. 181
24:35 Allah is the light of the heavens and the earth. 183
24:37 who fear a day when hearts and eyes will be overturned 119
24:37 whom neither traffic nor merchandise can divert ... 119
24:44 Allah alternates the night and the day. ... 84
25:1 Blessed is He who sent down the criterion to His servant ... 59
25:32 Those who reject Faith say: Why is not the Qur'an revealed to him all at once? ... 58, 136
26:11 The people of the Pharaoh: will they not fear Allah. 278
26:12 O my Lord! I do fear that they will charge me with falsehood. 278

26:13 My breast will be straitened. And my speech may not go [smoothly]. 279
26:14 And they have a charge of crime against me ... 279
26:21 I fled from you ... made me one of His Messengers. 37, 118, 279, 281
26:53 We revealed to Moses that he should journey by night ... 123, 168
26:57 And lo! We are all amply warned. 123
26:78 it is He Who guides me 235
26:192–4 And lo! It is a revelation of the Lord of the Worlds ... 39
26:200 Thus have We caused it to enter the hearts of the sinners. 14
27:50 So they plotted a plot; and We plotted a plot, while they perceived not. 122
27:52 Now such were their houses, in utter ruin ... 94
27:91 For me, I have been commanded to serve the Lord ... 76
28:21 So he departed from thence, fearing, vigilant. 118
28:29 I may bring you news from it 273
28:32 Move thy hand into thy bosom, and it will come forth white ... 14
29:15 But We saved him and the companions of the Ark ... 224
29:20 Travel through the earth and see how Allah did originate creation ... 158
29:26 But Lot had faith in Him ... He is Exalted in Might, and Wise. 247
29:67 Have they not seen that We have appointed a sanctuary immune... 70
30:7 They know a manifest side of the life of this world ... 178
30:21 Verily in that are Signs for those who reflect. 291
30:40 some We caused the earth to swallow up; and some We drowned. 41
30:42 Travel through the earth and see what was the end ... 13, 158
31:31 Hast thou not seen how the ships glide on the sea by Allah's grace... 41
33:4 And Allah speaks the truth and He guides on the Path. 57, 71, 98, 114, 127, 171
33:33 Allah's wish is but to remove uncleanness far from you... 116, 276
33:35 Lo! Men who surrender unto Allah and women who surrender ... 287
33:38 The command of Allah is a decree determined. 288
34:19 But they said: 'Our Lord! Place longer distances ... 41
35:10 To Him ascends the Good Word. He exalts every righteous deed. 39, 60
35:28 Those truly fear Allah, among His servants, who have knowledge. 119
35:35 It is He who, out of His bounty, has settled us in an abode ... 174
36:38 the determination of the All-Mighty, All-Knowing 90
36:39 And for the moon We have appointed mansions/waystations ... 42, 150, 151
36:40 They float, each in an orbit. 55
36:83 sovereignty of all things 84
37:21 This is the Day of Separation, which ye used to deny. 50
37:99 Lo! I am going unto my Lord. He will guide me. 91
37:100 My Lord! Grant me a righteous [son]. 91, 95
37:102 O Father, do as you are commanded. 239
37:103 When they had both surrendered themselves to God ... 240
37:107 Then We ransomed him with a mighty sacrifice. 239
37:112 And We gave him the good news of Isaac, a prophet ... 92, 236
37:164 None of us there is, but has a known station. 123, 287
37:180 Glory be to your Lord, the Lord of might ... 177, 193
38:3 Thus does Allah set forth ... their lessons by similitudes. 139
39:11 Say: Verily, I am commanded to serve Allah with sincere devotion. 76
39:20 [B]eneath them flow rivers: [such is] the Promise of Allah. ... 14
40:35 Thus doth Allah seal over every self-aggrandizing, tyrannical heart.' 67
40:66 I have been forbidden to invoke those whom ye invoke besides Allah ... 76
41:5 between Us and thee is a screen 54
41:9–10 Is it that ye deny Him Who created the earth? ... 36, 53

41:10 He measured in it its kinds of sustenance.'55
41:11–12 Then He sat upon upon the heaven ... 42, 53, 54, 55, 56, 57, 81, 90, 155, 158, 217
41:31 There ye will have [all] that your souls desire. 75
41:42 No falsehood can approach it from before or behind it ... 123
41:53 We shall show them Our signs on the horizons and within themselves... 8, 68, 206
41:54 Are they still in doubt about the meeting with their Lord? ... 143
42:11 Nothing is as His likeness, and He is the All-Hearing, the All-Seeing. 45, 124, 177, 185, 194, 202, 223
42:15 call [them to the Faith], and stand steadfast as thou art commanded ... 76
42:32–3 And of His Signs are the ships like banners on the sea. ... 41
42:53 Do not all things reach Allah at last? 120
43:32 And We raised some of them above others in degree ... 82
43:84 It is He Who is Allah in heaven and Allah on earth ... 144
44:3 We have sent it down in a blessed night ... 35, 58, 188
44:4 In which every wise command is made clear. 188
44:49 Taste! Lo! Thou wast forsooth the mighty, the noble. 67
45:13 And He hath submitted unto you whatsoever ... the earth. 82
47:10 Do they not travel through the earth ... 138, 139
47:38 And if ye turn away, He will exchange you for some other folk ... 120
48:2 That Allah may forgive ... which is past and that which is to come. 211, 276
50:16 closer to [the human being] than his jugular vein 143, 144, 194, 268
50:29 The word that cometh from Me cannot be changed. 50
51:7 By the heavens possessing orbits 158
51:21 And in yourselves. Can ye then not see? 68
51:50–1 Therefore flee unto Allah; lo! I am a plain warner ... 279, 280, 281
51:56 I did not create jinn and human beings except to worship [Me]. 196–7
53:9–11 distance of two bows' lengths or nearer. ... 36, 68, 69, 208
53:14 near the Lote tree of the Limit. 52
54:14 She floats under Our eyes, a recompense ... 87
54:34–5 We sent against them a violent tornado ... 97
55:29 Whosoever is in the heavens and the earth is in request of Him. ... 53, 243
56:62 and truly you have known the original creation 150
57:4 with you wheresover ye may be. 143, 174, 205
57:4 He it is Who created the heavens and the earth in Six Days ... 42
57:13 a wall will be put up betwixt them, with a gate therein. ... 71
57:21 Such is the bounty of Allah ... 49
58:8 Seest thou not those who were forbidden secret counsels ...? 76
59:2 So 'cross over' O ye who have eyes. 251
59:21 If We had caused this Qur'an to descend upon a mountain ... 107
59:22 Knower of the Unseen and the Witnessed, the All-Merciful, the All-Compassionate 124
59:23 He is Allah, than whom there is no other god ... 124, 202
59:24 the Creator, the Shaper out of naught, the Fashioner 124
59:24 the Wise 124
60:9 Allah only forbids you, with regard to those who fight you for Faith ... 76
62:2 It is He who has raised up ... a Messenger from among them. 189
62:4 Such is the bounty of Allah ..., and Allah is of infinite bounty. 49
64:15 Your possessions and your children are a trial/temptation 240, 256
64:16 Keep your duty to Allah as best you can. 108

65:7 Allah asketh naught of any soul save that which He hath given it. 108
65:12 Allah is He who created seven heavens and of the earth ... 186
66:5 It may be, if he divorced you ... 164
66:6 who resist not Allah in that which He commandeth them 81
67:3–4 He Who created the seven heavens one above another ... 54, 56, 64
67:5 And verily We have adorned the nearest heaven with lamps ... 54
67:11 so away with the Companions of the Blaze. 94–5
68:4 Lo! Thou art of a tremendous character. 61
68:42 The Day that the shin shall be laid bare ... 90
69:11 We ... carried you in the floating Ark. 225
69:17 And the angels will be on the sides thereof ... 112
69:32 Further, make him march in a chain ... the length is seventy cubits! 14
71:20 That ye may go about therein, in spacious roads. 14
71:21 They have disobeyed me and ... increase him in naught save ruin. 90
71:25 Because of their sins they were drowned, then made to enter a Fire. 90
71:26 Leave not one of the disbelievers in the land. 86
71:28 O my Lord! Forgive me, my parents, all who enter my house in Faith ... 219, 234
72:1 Say [O Muhammad]: It is revealed unto me ... 54
72:9 And we used to sit on places [high] therein to listen. ... 54
72:17 That We might try them by that [means]. ... 14
72:19 When the servant of Allah stood calling on Him 197
72:20 I ascribe unto Him no partner. 82
73:9 [He is] Lord of the East and the West ... 174
73:11–13 And leave Me those in possession of the good things of life ... 91
73:14 One Day the earth and the mountains ... 44
74:34 And the dawn when it shineth forth 57
74:42 What led you into Hell Fire? 14
75:2 I call to witness the blaming soul. 100, 254
76:13 Reclining on raised thrones they will see there ... 89
79:24 And proclaimed: I, [Pharoah], am your Lord the Highest. 38
80:1–2 He frowned and turned away when the blind man came to him. 72
82:8 Into whatever form He will, He casteth/mounteth thee. 207
84:19 Ye shall surely travel from stage to stage. 142
89:22 And the Lord shall come [with angels, rank on rank]. 50
89:23 He will be led on that day to Gehenna. 90
89:27 O [thou] soul, in [complete] rest and satisfaction! 254
91:8 And inspired it with what is wrong for it and what is right for it. 58, 102
94:5–6 Verily, with every hardship there is ease. 213
97:1–5 We have sent it down in the Night of Power ... 35, 58
98:5 And they have been commanded no more than this: To worship Allah ... 76
99:2 When the earth throws up her burdens. 86
106:2 [For the taming/civilizing/assembly/union of Quraysh] ... 163

INDEX OF HADITH

Adam denied so his children denied; Adam forgot, so his offspring forgot; Adam made mistakes so his offspring made mistakes. 73

Caution does not save from predestination. 123

Do what you wish. I have already forgiven you. 211, 287–8

Every child is born in accordance with *fitra*; then his parents make him into a Jew, a Christian, or a Zoroastrian. 229

God has seventy – or seventy thousand – veils of light and darkness; were they to be removed, the Glories of His Face would burn away everything perceived by the sight of His creatures. 115

God has taught me courtesy. How beautiful is my courtesy! 60

God have mercy on my brother Lot, who sought refuge in a strong support. 96

God the Most High never caused any misfortune to reach me but that I saw three favours in it: the first was that it did not involve my religion; the second was that it had not been greater; and the third was the recompense and the reduction of sin that it contained for me. 72–3

God was and nothing was with Him. 182

He among them who performs works will receive the wage of fifty men who perform works like your works. 48

He loved good omens and he disliked evil omens. 72

He who devotes himself exclusively to God for forty mornings, the founts of wisdom will spring from his heart and upon his tongue. 107

His character was the Qur'an. 61, 188

His mercy precedes His wrath. 269

I am with those whose hearts are broken for My sake. 200

I ask You with every Name by which You have named Yourself, that You have taught to any one of Your creatures, that You have revealed in Your Book, or that You have kept to Yourself in the knowledge of Your Unseen ... 51

I count not Your praises before You. You are as You have praised Yourself. 51, 52

I saw Him as light. How should I see light? 205

I seek refuge in Thy satisfaction from Thy anger, in Thy mercy from Thy punishment, in Thee from Thee. 118, 280, 281

I was a Treasure but was not known, so I loved to be known; I created the creatures and made Myself known to them, so they came to know Me. 182

I was sent with the totality of words. 39

I was sick and you did not come to visit Me; I was hungry and you did not feed Me; I was thirsty and you did not give Me to drink. 156, 194

If My servant approaches Me by a hand's breadth, I will approach him by an arm's length; and if he approaches Me by an arm's length, I will approach him by a cubit; and if he comes to Me walking, I will come to him running. 154, 281

Inability to perceive perception is itself perception. 51

Is there anyone who turns in repentance so that I can turn towards him? Is there anyone seeking forgiveness so that I can forgive him? Is there anyone who is praying so I can answer him? 183

Moses was preaching among the Children of Israel. Someone asked him: Who is the wisest of men? He answered: I am. God took him to task because he had not referred his knowledge back to Him. He revealed to him: I have a servant where the two rivers meet who is wiser than you. 38

My servant has hastened to Me by his own doing; I have forbidden him Paradise. 262

None among the people of the Garden says to a thing 'Be' but that it is. 75
Our Lord descends every night to the nearest heaven in the last third of the night and says: Who will invoke Me so I can answer Him; who will ask Me so I may give to him, who will ask for My pardon so that I may forgive him? 42
Over every truth there is a reality and above every valid issue there is light. Whatever agrees with the holy Qur'an you must follow and whatever does not agree disregard it. 61
Paradise is surrounded by hardships and the Hell-fire is surrounded by temptations. 70
The best of you are those who, when they are seen, God is remembered. 203
The Hour will not arise until man's thigh speaks to him of what his wife and the lash of his whip have done. 48
The last hour would not come unless the Muslims will fight against the Jews ... 180
The people of the Qur'an are the people of God and His elite. 116
The *siyāḥa* of this nation is fasting. 165
The tree will say: O Muslim! There is a Jew behind me. Kill him. 48, 180
There is no *ṭīra*, and the best omen is the *fa'l*. 72
There is nothing that I hesitate doing as much as I hesitate in seizing the soul of the believer who hates death, and I hate to harm him. But he must meet Me. 50
There shall come out of Hell-fire he who has said: 'There is no god but Allah' and who has in his heart goodness weighing a barley-corn; then there shall come out of Hell-fire he who has said: 'There is no god but Allah' and who has in his heart goodness weighing a grain of wheat; then there shall come out of Hell-fire he who has said: 'There is no god but Allah' and who has in his heart goodness weighing an atom. 46
They recite the Qur'an [but] it does not pass beyond their throats. They penetrate the religion as the arrow penetrates the game in which you do not see a trace of the blood of the game. 21
We have more reason to doubt than Abraham when he said, 'My Lord! Show me how You give life to the dead. [Allah] said, 'Have you not believed?' He said, 'Yes, but [I ask] only that my heart may be satisfied. 97
Were it not for this verse I would have whipped whoever travels by sea. 41
Where was our Lord before He created the creatures? He was in a Cloud above and below which was no air. 35, 50, 182
Whoever has learned the Qur'an by heart, prophecy has entered between his two sides. 190
Whoever knows himself knows his Lord. 109, 223, 244
You are the Companion in the voyage and the vicegerent in the family. 143
You have kept to Yourself in the knowledge of Your Unseen. 51

INDEX OF QUOTATIONS FROM THE *FUTŪḤĀT*

(From the 4-volume Beirut edition)

Volume One

I.4 (*Khuṭba*) 61, 182
I.9 (*Khuṭba*) 3
I.36 (*Muqaddima*) 148
I.41 (*Muqaddima*) 144, 183
I.50ff. (Chap. 1) 151
I.54 (Chap. 2) 153
I.55 (Chap. 2) 259
I.57 (Chap. 2) 259
I.80 (Chap. 2) 263
I.81 (Chap. 2) 258
I.83 (Chap. 2) 60, 188
I.84 (Chap. 2) 260
I.101 (Chap. 5) 186
I.104 (Chap. 5) 202
I.106 (Chap. 5) 258
I.111 (Chap. 5) 182
I.112 (Chap. 5) 213, 265
I.123 (Chap. 7) 155
I.123–4 (Chap. 7) 259
I.124–5 (Chap. 7) 153
I.125 (Chap. 7) 153
I.130 (Chap. 8) 121
I.137 (Chap. 10) 259
I.144ff. (Chap. 12) 47, 179, 259
I.147–8 (Chap. 13) 271
I.148 (Chap. 13) 183, 271
I.149 (Chap. 13) 183
I.152 (Chap. 15) 217
I.153 (Chap. 15) 217
I.155 (Chap. 15) 215
I.157 (Chap. 15) 218
I.157 (Chap. 16) 154
I.170–1 (Chap. 21) 137
I.173ff. (Chap. 22) 16
I.192–3 (Chap. 27) 146, 155, 156, 243
I.196 (Chap. 29) 116, 165
I.198 (Chap. 29) 276
I.199 (Chap. 30) 195
I.202 (Chap. 31) 196
I.203 (Chap. 31) 38
I.206 (Chap. 31) 248
I.212 (Chap. 33) 170
I.213 (Chap, 34) 259, 275
I.218 (Chap. 35) 275
I.223 (Chap. 36) 184
I.226 (Chap. 36) 195
I.227 (Chap. 37) 189
I.233 (Chap. 39) 211
I.235 (Chap. 40) 278
I.237 (Chap. 40) 271
I.237 (Chap. 41) 16
I.242 (Chap. 42) 74
I.250ff. (Chap. 45) 52
I.256 (Chap. 47) 79
I.259 (Chap. 47) 123, 288
I.278 (Chap. 54) 169
I.279 (Chap. 54) 20, 277
I.287 (Chap. 57) 59
I.290 (Chap. 58) 52, 90
I.297 (Chap. 61) 90
I.299 (Chap. 61) 46, 75
I.300 (Chap. 61) 90
I.314 (Chap. 64) 46
I.320 (Chap. 65) 44
I.324 (Chap. 66) 81
I.326 (Chap. 67) 215
I.327 (Chap. 67) 80
I.347 (Chap. 68) 283
I.354 (Chap. 68) 285
I.394ff. (Chap. 69) 199
I.395 (Chap. 69) 198
I.396 (Chap. 69) 136
I.421 (Chap. 69) 67
I.468 (Chap. 69) 169, 264, 265
I.481 (Chap. 69) 156
I.493 (Chap. 69) 86, 89, 231
I.515 (Chap. 69) 287
I.534–5 (Chap. 69) 262
I.536 (Chap. 69) 253
I.551 (Chap. 70) 251
I.562 (Chap. 70) 146
I.587 (Chap. 70) 285
I.596 (Chap. 70) 92
I.607 (Chap. 71) 59
I.608 (Chap. 71) 89
I.609 (Chap. 71) 272
I.628 (Chap. 71) 161
I.629 (Chap. 71) 190
I.645 (Chap. 71) 258
I.653ff. (Chap. 71) 265
I.658 (Chap. 71) 35
I.661 (Chap. 71) 211
I.666 (Chap. 72) 151
I.675 (Chap. 72) 94, 236
I.700–1 (Chap. 72) 135
I.710 (Chap. 72) 152
I.744 (Chap. 72) 66
I.745 (Chap. 72) 71
I.746 (Chap. 72) 73
I.747 (Chap. 72) 217

Volume Two

II.9 (Chap. 73) 64
II.10 (Chap. 73) 234, 241, 267
II.12 (Chap. 73) 121
II.20 (Chap. 73) 59
II.21 (Chap. 73) 117
II.22 (Chap. 73) 278
II.23 (Chap. 73) 211, 288
II.32 (Chap. 73) 211

II.43 (Chap. 73) 260
II.44 (Chap. 73) 234
II.48–9 (Chap. 73) 154
II.49 (Chap. 73) 144, 159, 165
II.64 (Chap. 73) 109
II.88 (Chap. 73) 70
II.110 (Chap. 73) 115
II.128 (Chap. 73) 68, 70, 204
II.129 (Chap. 73) 61
II.131 (Chap. 73) 182
II.134 (Chap. 73) 160
II.143 (Chap. 74) 137
II.149 (Chap. 77) 72, 200
II.150–1 (Chap. 78) 206
II.152 (Chap. 78) 267
II.153 (Chap. 80) 67, 197
II.155 (Chap. 82) 25, 138, 277, 279, 280, 281
II.159 (Chap. 85) 289
II.166 (Chap. 88) 67
II.170 (Chap. 90) 216
II.179 (Chap. 95) 233
II.180 (Chap. 95) 239
II.184 (Chap. 100) 119, 120, 278, 281
II.185 (Chap. 101) 282
II.186 (Chap. 103) 119
II.189 (Chap. 108) 77, 240, 289, 290
II.190 (Chap. 108) 254
II.192–3 (Chap. 109) 77
II.193 (Chap. 110) 119
II.194 (Chap. 110) 59, 190
II.205 (Chap. 122) 249
II.205 (Chap. 123) 249
II.207 (Chap. 124) 90, 199
II.212 (Chap. 128) 108
II.213 (Chap. 129) 108
II.213ff. (Chap. 130) 70
II.214 (Chap. 130) 70, 196, 197
II.217 (Chap. 132) 153
II.244 (Chap. 150) 199
II.259 (Chap. 160) 136
II.262 (Chap. 161) 146
II.264 (Chap. 162) 274
II.270ff. (Chap. 167) 291
II.277 (Chap. 167) 113, 272
II.278 (Chap. 167) 91
II.280 (Chap. 167) 14
II.281 (Chap. 167) 291
II.293 (Chap. 174) 116, 135, 286
II.294 (Chap. 175) 174, 262
II.296 (Chap. 176) 56
II.301 (Chap. 177) 203
II.310 (Chap. 177) 35
II.337 (Chap. 178) 252
II.338 (Chap. 178) 256
II.340 (Chap. 178) 103
II.355 (Chap. 178) 62
II.367 (Chap. 182) 199
II.370 (Chap. 185) 211
II.371ff. (Chap. 186) 126
II.380 (Chap. 189) 166
II.381 (Chap. 189) 166, 167
II.382 (Chap. 189) 167
II.382 (Chap. 190) 139, 160
II.383 (Chap. 190) 138, 162
II.384 (Chap. 191) 144
II.384 (Chap. 192) 243
II.385 (Chap. 192) 244
II.386 (Chap. 194) 185, 216, 244
II.391 (Chap 198) 162
II.395 (Chap. 198) 203
II.431ff. (Chap. 198) 259
II.433 (Chap. 198) 259
II.435 (Chap. 198) 36, 219
II.437 (Chap. 198) 79
II.453 (Chap. 198) 89
II.457 (Chap. 198) 172
II.464ff. (Chap. 198) 153
II.469 (Chap. 198) 259
II.485 (Chap. 206) 199
II.488 (Chap. 206) 94, 242
II.493 (Chap. 208) 258
II.512ff. (Chap. 220) 211, 212
II.530 (Chap. 231) 26, 214
II.538 (Chap. 238) 235
II.539 (Chap. 238) 109, 246
II.543 (Chap. 244) 62
II.543 (Chap. 245) 62
II.544 (Chap. 246) 62
II.546 (Chap. 247) 62
II.552 (Chap. 252) 62
II.553 (Chap. 253) 62
II.554ff. (Chap. 255) 95
II.563 (Chap. 264) 42
II.571 (Chap. 269) 248
II.571 (Chap. 270) 37, 175
II.577–8 (Chap. 271) 15
II.580 (Chap. 272) 193
II.594ff. (Chap. 276) 94
II.609 (Chap. 279) 227
II.615 (Chap. 281) 242
II.617 (Chap. 281) 222
II.622ff. (Chap. 283) 168
II.640 (Chap. 288) 86, 190
II.644 (Chap. 289) 190
II.672 (Chap. 294) 63, 192, 193
II.692 (Chap. 299) 35

Volume Three

III.6 (Chap. 301) 49
III.7 (Chap. 301) 208
III.15 (Chap. 303) 73
III.19 (Chap. 304) 145
III.26 (Chap. 306) 90
III.32 (Chap. 308) 197
III.35–6 (Chap. 309) 109
III.37 (Chap. 309) 25
III.49 (Chap. 313) 12
III.50 (Chap. 313) 209, 221
III.51 (Chap. 313) 221
III.57 (Chap. 315) 233
III.67 (Chap. 317) 181
III.90 (Chap. 324) 290
III.93 (Chap. 325) 61, 189
III.94 (Chap. 325) 59
III.97 (Chap. 326) 107
III.100 (Chap. 327) 213
III.110 (Chap. 330) 95
III.111 (Chap. 330) 151
III.114 (Chap. 330) 87
III.116 (Chap. 330) 226
III.116 (Chap. 331) 38, 204, 261
III.117 (Chap. 331) 16
III.119 (Chap. 332) 149, 274
III.120 (Chap. 332) 359
III.127 (Chap. 334) 21
III.128 (Chap. 334) 20, 21, 23

III.141 (Chap. 337) 139, 143, 172, 260
III.142 (Chap. 337) 259
III.143–4 (Chap. 337) 210
III.146 (Chap. 337) 138
III.148 (Chap. 338) 193
III.155 (Chap. 340) 26
III.162 (Chap. 341) 224
III.188 (Chap. 346) 178
III.195 (Chap. 347) 203
III.211 (Chap. 350) 58
III.215 (Chap. 350) 273
III.216 (Chap. 351) 219
III.230 (Chap. 351) 259
III.239 (Chap. 353) 58
III.258 (Chap. 357) 180
III.261 (Chap. 357) 78
III.263 (Chap. 358) 181
III.264 (Chap. 358) 279
III.296 (Chap. 361) 206
III.301 (Chap. 361) 110
III.302 (Chap. 362) 201
III.323 (Chap. 365) 2
III.335 (Chap. 367) 263
III.336 (Chap. 367) 275
III.340 (Chap. 367) 144, 170, 205, 248
III.342 (Chap. 367) 192
III.343 (Chap. 367) 229, 263
III.345–6 (Chap. 367) 229
III.347 (Chap. 367) 252
III.350 (Chap. 367) 3, 163, 260
III.371 (Chap. 369) 63
III.414 (Chap. 370) 20, 59
III.416 (Chap. 371) 158
III.417 (Chap. 371) 83
III.420 (Chap. 371) 149, 184
III.429 (Chap. 371) 50, 182
III.430 (Chap. 371) 184
III.438ff. (Chap. 371) 43
III.439 (Chap. 371) 94, 242
III.440 (Chap. 371) 90
III.442 (Chap. 371) 44
III.459 (Chap. 373) 81
III.461 (Chap. 373) 94
III.481 (Chap. 376) 200
III.489 (Chap. 378) 78
III.514 (Chap. 382) 203
III.531 (Chap. 386) 91

Volume Four

IV.7 (Chap. 405) 201
IV.9 (Chap. 407) 195
IV.28 (Chap. 420) 207
IV.49–50 (Chap. 437) 212
IV.50 (Chap. 438) 282
IV.54 (Chap. 440) 248
IV.60 (Chap. 446) 61
IV.76 (Chap. 462) 118
IV.77 (Chap. 463) 267
IV.78 (Chap. 463) 59
IV.92 (Chap. 465) 192
IV.92ff. (Chap. 466) 192
IV.156 (Chap. 515) 256
IV.163 (Chap. 521) 76, 145, 160, 163
IV.164 (Chap. 521) 147
IV.181 (Chap. 537) 252
IV.183ff. (Chap. 539) 279, 280
IV.196–7 (Chap. 558) 183
IV.197 (Chap. 558) 20
IV.205–6 (Chap. 558) 63
IV.209 (Chap. 558) 67
IV.267 (Chap. 558) 160
IV.214–15 (Chap. 558) 78
IV.315 (Chap. 558) 185
IV.366 (Chap. 559) 164
IV.367 (Chap. 559) 24
IV.431 (Chap. 559) 281
IV.435 (Chap. 559) 109
IV.448–9 (Chap. 560) 276
IV.455 (Chap. 560) 242
IV.460–1 (Chap. 560) 73
IV.472 (Chap. 560) 261
IV.473 (Chap. 560) 264
IV.482 (Chap. 560) 20

GENERAL INDEX

Aaron (Harūn) 3, 17, 107, 111–13, 267, 270–1
'abara (to cross, traverse, interpret) 20, 97, 160, 169, 241, 250–1
'Abd Allāh al-Mawrūrī 118
'Abd al-Qādir 159
Abraham (Ibrāhīm) 3, 37, 38, 91–7, 139, 140, 141, 145, 169, 211, 219, 221, 222, 235–51, 257, 267, 271, 272
Abū al-'Abbās al-Khashshāb 117, 276
Abū al-'Abbās al-'Uraybī 1, 2, 59
Abū al-Su'ūd b. al-Shibl 159
Abū 'Alī al-Daqqāq 8, 9, 246
Abū 'Amr b. Mahīb 102
Abū Bakr al-Ṣiddiq 47, 51, 201
Abū Ismā'īl 'Abd Allāh al-Ansārī al-Harawī 14
Abū Madyan 2, 117, 118
Abū Musā al-Dabīlī 59
Abū 'Uthmān al-Ḥīrī 9
Abū Yazīd al-Bisṭāmī 9, 22, 47, 59, 184, 188, 271, 276, 288
Adam (Ādam) 3, 8, 17, 36, 40, 64, 71–80, 113, 120, 139, 140, 141, 142, 150, 151, 152, 201, 206, 208–10, 213, 214, 221, 231, 242, 257, 258, 267, 278
Aḥmad b. Ḥanbal 165
'Ā'isha 61, 165, 188
Alchemy 10, 36, 91, 216–17, 225–8, 230, 260
Alexander the Great (Dhū al-Qarnayn) 39, 139, 140
'Alī b. 'Abī Ṭālib 47, 89, 196, 230
[K.] *al-Anwār* 17
Aristotle 227, 289
Ark 37, 38, 85–8, 141, 150, 163, 173, 219, 220, 224–7, 229, 233
Astrology 10, 54, 85, 94, 215, 217, 232
Avicenna (Ibn Sīnā) 56, 289

barzakh (Barzakh) 43, 48, 91, 176
Battle of Badr 210, 211, 212
Breath of the All-Merciful 163, 184
Bridge (*ṣirāṭ*) 43
Buber, Martin 21
Burāq 15, 16, 40, 139, 193, 194, 195, 207, 225, 291

Canopy (*surādiq*) 50–2
Cloud (*'amā'*) 35, 50–2, 144, 149, 182–4, 226

David (Dā'ūd) 39, 267
Dhū al-Kifl 214
al-Durrat al-fākhira 2
Dune of Vision 44

Edinger, Edward F. 12
Elias/Elijah (Ilyās) 215, 216, 266
Enoch (Idrīs) 3, 8, 17, 36, 55, 81–5, 94, 139, 140, 141, 142, 214–17, 221, 224, 235, 238, 257, 267
Eve (Ḥawwā') 40, 71, 74, 75, 209, 210

[K.] *al-Fanā' fī al-mushāhada* 186, 246, 262
Farqad al-Sabakhī 47
al-Farrā', Abū Zakariyya 116
Footstool (*kursī*) 164, 213
Frye, Northrop 220
furqān (criterion. discriminator, dispersing) 13, 59, 61, 95, 188, 190
Fuṣūṣ al-ḥikam 4, 5, 12, 19, 24, 25, 37, 57, 80, 84, 92, 93, 111, 123, 137, 148, 153, 185, 206, 216, 218, 220, 221, 222, 229, 230, 235, 236, 237, 238, 244, 247, 248, 252, 253, 258, 270, 271, 272, 277, 279, 287, 290

Gabriel (the Trustworthy Spirit) 39, 56, 58, 60, 84, 111, 113, 139, 140, 188, 193, 217, 267, 271
Garden (Paradise) (*janna*) 36, 43, 44, 70, 73, 75, 76, 79, 81, 89, 153, 178, 208
Gathering (*ḥashr*) 43, 177
gharqad (thorn bush) 179–80, 284
Gog and Magog 39
Goliath 39

al-Ḥasan al-Baṣrī 47
Ḥaydar Āmulī 27
Hell-fire (*nār*) 43, 44, 46, 50, 67, 70, 81, 90, 91, 92, 178
Hermes 80, 216

Ibn ʿAbbās 54, 58, 112, 186, 187, 196, 231
Ibn al-Anbārī 283
Ibn al-ʿArīf 65
Ibn Baṭṭūṭa 164
Ibn Farghānī (Wāsiṭī) 192
Ibn Jinnī 136, 239
Ibn Jubayr 163–4
Ibn Kathīr, ʿImād al-Dīn 24, 209, 264, 270
Ibn Taymiyya 221
Ibrāhīm b. Adham 9
Imru al-Qays 65, 121, 283
Isaac (Isḥāq) 12, 92, 94, 95, 235–6, 238–9, 242, 244, 247, 262
Ishmael (Ismāʾīl) 38, 92, 214, 235–6, 239, 240, 242–3, 262
[*K.*] *al-Isrāʾ* 17
Israfil 267
iʿtibār (inner consideration / crossing over) 42, 62, 160, 165, 251
[*K.*] *al-Ittiḥād al-kawnī* 17

Jābir b. Ḥayyān 228
Jacob (Yaʿqūb) 98, 99, 101, 139, 141, 222, 252, 255–6, 257
Jesus (ʿĪsa) 1, 3, 17, 38, 48, 139, 140, 141, 165, 204, 215, 266, 271
jinn 54, 147, 196, 200, 201, 258 288
Job (Ayyūb) 99
John the Baptist (Yahya) 3
Jonah (Yūnus) 39, 139, 140, 141, 266, 278
Joseph (Yūsuf) 3, 8, 17, 37, 38, 87, 98, 99, 101–4, 110, 139–40, 163, 222, 235, 240, 250, 252–7, 267
Jūdī, Mount 86, 87, 88, 226, 233
al-Junayd, Abū Qāsim 9, 47, 192, 246
Jung, C. G. 12, 229

Kaʿba 3, 135, 151
kasb (acquisition) 75, 236, 239
al-Kashānī, ʿAbd al-Razzāq 14, 18
Kaykāʾūs 4
al-Khiḍr 38, 84, 140, 141, 196, 210, 215, 217, 224, 258, 271
Kierkegaard, Soren 272
al-Kisāʾī, Muḥammad b. ʿAbd Allāh 24

Laylā al-Akhiliyya 186
Lot (Lūṭ) 8, 12, 18, 37, 57, 96–7, 139, 140, 141, 168, 247–50, 257, 278
Lote Tree of the Limit 3, 52, 70, 205

al-Mahdawī 2
Mālik (angel) 81
Mary 38, 220
Masjid al-Aqṣā (Farthest Place of Prostration) 4, 17, 36, 62, 66, 70, 71, 191, 201
Masjid al-Ḥarām (Inviolable Place of Prostration) 36, 62, 66, 70, 191, 201
Merton, Thomas 21
Michael (Archangel) 267
[*K.*] *al-Mīm wa al-wāw wa al-nūn* 266
al-Mīraghī, Ḥamū b. Ibrāhīm b. Abī Bakr 102

miʿrāj (heavenly ascent) 3, 8, 15, 17, 40, 52, 57, 66, 69, 168, 170, 172, 192, 199, 201, 214, 259, 262, 263, 291, 292
Moses (Mūsā) 1, 3, 8, 12, 17–8, 26, 37, 38, 41, 50, 57, 90, 103–123, 138, 140, 141, 149, 155, 156, 159, 160, 164, 168, 171, 179. 196, 200, 210, 219, 224, 227, 233, 234, 240, 245, 247, 254, 257–90
Muḥammad (The Prophet / The Messenger of God) 1, 2, 3, 4, 5, 8, 15, 17, 18, 20, 21, 22, 35, 36, 39, 40, 47, 48, 50, 51, 52, 54, 57, 58, 60, 61, 63, 65, 68, 69, 70, 71, 72, 76, 80, 82, 92, 93, 96, 97, 106, 107, 109, 114, 116, 119, 122, 139, 140, 141, 142, 150, 156, 158, 159, 168, 169, 170, 173, 176, 177, 178, 180, 181, 182, 184, 186, 187, 188, 189, 190, 191, 192, 194, 195, 196, 199, 200, 205, 207, 208, 221, 231, 238, 248, 258, 259, 260, 261, 262, 264, 269, 273, 275, 277, 278, 279, 280, 281, 288
Mulla Ṣadrā 27–8
munāzala (mutual waystation) 15, 191

Najm al-Dīn al-Rāzī 14
naqala (to move) 170
Night Journey (*isrā*) 8, 17–18, 41, 63–7, 122, 139, 168–9, 172, 192, 194–5, 198–9,

201, 205, 225, 258, 262, 285, 290
Night of Power (*Laylat al-Qadr*) 35, 36, 58, 199, 207
Noah (Nūḥ) 8, 12, 37, 85–91, 114, 139, 140, 141, 145, 163, 198, 214, 216, 219–35, 257, 259, 266
al-Nūrī 192

People of Blame (*malāmiyya*) 2
People of the Book (*ahl al-kitāb*) 23, 180–1, 242
People of the House (*ahl al-bayt*) 40, 116, 210, 275
Perfect Human Being (*al-insān al-kāmil*) 144, 151, 186, 205, 206, 209, 210, 224, 227, 233
Pharaoh 38, 118, 123, 138, 141, 225, 254, 277, 279, 280, 285, 288, 290
Pole (*Quṭb*) 37, 84, 118, 153, 175, 192, 215, 217, 279
Potiphar 252

qiṣaṣ al-anbiyā' (tales of the prophets) 7, 23–4, 210
Qur'ān 3, 7, 8, 10, 11, 13, 14, 16–24, 35, 36, 49, 58–61, 63, 64, 107, 110, 116, 135, 137, 139, 145, 147, 150, 154, 155, 158, 163, 164, 165, 168, 173, 174, 177, 185, 186–92, 196, 199, 201, 205, 207, 210, 220, 224, 225, 232, 235, 242, 243, 245, 250–1, 252, 256, 262, 264, 270, 276, 277, 280, 283, 286, 291
al-Qushayrī, Abū al-Qāsim 8, 14, 78, 135, 240, 245, 246

Rābi'a al-'Adawiyya 159
Riḍwān (angel) 81
riḥla (travelling) 76, 159, 163–4
Rūḥ al-quds 2

safar (voyaging) 40, 42, 135, 138, 146, 159–64, 277, 286, 290
Salmān the Persian 276–7
al-Sāmirī 110–13, 241, 247, 269–71
al-Sarrāj, Abū Naṣr 14, 78, 135
Satan (Iblīs) 40, 45, 59, 71, 74, 75, 87, 89, 92, 120, 154, 175, 209, 210, 223, 229, 259
Saul (Tālūt) 39, 139, 140
sayr (going, travel) 144, 154, 158–9
Seth (Shīth) 221
al-Shiblī, Abū Bakr 9
siyāḥa (roaming, wandering) 159, 164–5
siwāk 106, 264–5
subḥāna (glorified be) 65–6, 192–3, 194, 222
sukūn (keeping still, silent) 173
al-Sulamī 192, 200
sulūk (wayfaring) 7, 14–16, 146, 159, 161, 164, 166, 243

al-Ṭabarī, Abū Ja'far 18, 64, 86, 193
tafsīr (interpretation) 18–23, 24, 136, 187
tannūr (furnace) 12, 85–9, 114, 218, 226–7, 230–2, 259, 284
Tawba b. Humayr 57, 186
ta'wīl (interpretation) 19–20, 74, 78, 118, 147, 208
al-Tha'labī, Abū Isḥāq 24
Thoth 80
Throne (*al-'arsh*) 21, 29, 35, 41, 50–3, 70, 111–14, 144, 154, 174, 182–4, 195, 198, 213, 224, 269, 272, 283
al-Tirmidhī 158
al-Tustarī, Sahl b. 'Abdallāh 9, 47, 77, 188, 201

'Umar b. al-Khaṭṭāb 41, 47, 72
Umm Hānī 180
Universal Human Being 61, 186, 191; *see also* Perfect Human Being
Universal Soul 100, 102, 253, 255

wahb (bestowal) 236, 239

[*K.*] *al-Yaqīn* 26, 96, 249, 250
Yaqīn 12, 26, 96–7, 248–50

Zamharīr 89–90
Zulaykha 252, 255